The extended critical interview is especially flexible as a form, by turns tenacious and glancing, elliptical or sustained, combining argument and counter-argument, reflection, history and memoir with a freedom normally denied to its subjects in conventional writing formats. *Lives on the Left* brings together sixteen such interviews from *New Left Review* in a group portrait of intellectual engagement in the twentieth century and since. Four generations of intellectuals discuss their political histories and present perspectives, and the specialized work for which they are, often, best known. Their recollections span the century from the Great War and the October Revolution to the present, ranging across Europe, the Americas, Africa and Asia. Psychoanalysis, philosophy, the gendering of private and public life, capital and class formation, the novel, geography, and language are among the topics of theoretical discussion. At the heart of the collection, in all its diversity of testimony and judgement, is critical experience of communism and the tradition of Marx, relayed now for a new generation of readers.

New Left Review was founded in 1960 in London, which has remained its base ever since. In fifty years of publication, it has won an international reputation as an independent journal of socialist politics and ideas, attracting readers and contributors from every part of the world. A Spanish-language edition is published bimonthly from Madrid.

Georg Lukács

Hedda Korsch

Jiři Pelikan

K. Damodaran

Ernest Mandel

Dorothy Thompson

Lucio Colletti

Luciana Castellina

Adolfo Gilly

Jean-Paul Sartre

Noam Chomsky

David Harvey

João Pedro Stédile

Asada Akira

Wang Hui

Giovanni Arrighi

Lives on the Left

Lives on the Left
A Group Portrait

Edited by

FRANCIS MULHERN

VERSO
London • New York

First published by Verso 2011
All interviews in this book printed by kind permission of *New Left Review*
© *New Left Review* 2011
Introduction © Francis Mulhern 2011

1 3 5 7 9 10 8 6 4 2

Verso
UK: 6 Meard Street, London W1F 0EG
US: 20 Jay Street, Suite 1010, Brooklyn, NY 11201
www.versobooks.com

Verso is the imprint of New Left Books

ISBN-13: 978-1-84467-699-6

British Library Cataloguing in Publication Data
A catalogue record for this book is available from the British Library

Library of Congress Cataloging-in-Publication Data
A catalog record for this book is available from the Library of Congress

Typeset in Galliard by MJ Gavan, Truro, Cornwall
Printed in the UK by Bell & Bain Ltd., Glasgow

Contents

Chronology

Not Yet, No Longer, Not Yet: An Introduction

Francis Mulhern

In the late 1960s, *New Left Review* began to develop the interview form as an integral element of its publishing repertoire. The first in the sequence was with Georg Lukács, in the last months of 1968—though not the first published, as it happened, given the delicacy of his situation in Hungary at that time. The first interviews to appear were with Noam Chomsky and Jean-Paul Sartre, pre-eminent figures in their respective fields of linguistics and philosophy, and exemplars, in their contrasting styles, of independent intellectual engagement on the Left.[1] Over the next three years, another five interviews appeared, including those with Jiři Pelikan and Hedda Korsch, and, after the unavoidable delay, the record of the conversation with Lukács. This concentrated burst of activity established the interview form as an important one for NLR, and indeed for its subjects. Sartre republished his interview in a volume of his *Situations*,[2] that with Lucio Colletti proved a landmark in the growth of interest in his work; another NLR interview project, expanding by magnitudes, eventually appeared as a full-length book, Raymond Williams's *Politics and Letters*.[3] Today, a decade past the millennium year, the *Review* has published nearly one hundred interviews, many of them commissioned and carried out by members of the editorial board, and it is from among these latter that the contents of this collection have mostly been taken.[4]

---

[1] There had been earlier interviews, of course, though not of the kind to which this book is devoted. Isaac Deutscher's historic-political analysis of Israel's Six-Day War was a masterly exploitation of the interview form (NLR I/44, July–August 1967, pp. 30–45). It is worth mentioning that the inaugural issue of the *Review* included a conversation between Raymond Williams and Richard Hoggart, 'Working-class Attitudes' (NLR I/1, January–February 1960, pp. 26–30).

[2] Republished in English in *Between Existentialism and Marxism*, London 1974, pp. 33–64.

[3] *Politics and Letters: Interviews with New Left Review*, London 1979.

[4] Another selection was made for the volume *A Movements of Movements: Is Another World Really Possible?*, Tom Mertes, ed., London 2004, in which the interview with João Pedro Stédile, reprinted here, also appeared.

The great advantages of the interview are its manoeuvrability and range. Beginning, usually, in a conversation and resulting in a printed represen- tation of that, its production process is more complex than this suggests, combining the greater spontaneity and pace of speech with the greater scope and control available to both parties in written revision and supplementa- tion, where in fact much of the work of composition may occur. A singular form only in the minimal sense in which the novel can be said to be one, the interview accommodates a whole array of spoken and written varieties at both poles of the exchange (exposition and narrative, and elicitation, but also argumentative rallies, interjections, anecdotes, asides) and licenses elliptical transitions from one topic to another—jump-cutting—in relative freedom from the constraints of the standard article form. At other times, it may serve the purposes of what might have been an article, creating a monologic argument or narrative with a facilitating second voice, in effect. Some of the interviews reprinted here move at this end of the range, offering extended and methodical historical treatments of their material. But even in those cases, the differences are palpable. For the interview as conceived of here is among other things a kind of portraiture, or rather self-portraiture—and a mode in which, then, however discreetly, thought becomes thinking, some- thing of its character as a process is reanimated, as concepts find their forms and effects in the grain of biographical sequences and historical construc- tion is re-inflected in the lived interpretations of memoir. Even at its most austerely conceptual or political, and in so far as it goes beyond the merest formal simulation of spoken exchange, the interview takes on the distinc- tive colorations of autobiography and memoir. The temporal complexity of these interviews brings a further enrichment of meaning. Each, read alone, is straightforward enough: a specific mix of recollection, statement and expectation framed at a point in time. Read as a confluence of voices, in the order suggested here, their suggestions multiply, often movingly and not least ironically. Shared chronological time is criss-crossed by individual histories, one account varying from other accounts of the same thing, the anticipations of earlier generations sometimes coexisting awkwardly with the retrospects of the younger—and both now exposed, after a greater or lesser lapse of years, to readers who, for now, have the privilege of final retrospect. Impersonal cruces in politics and theory are not rendered less objective or less demanding in this process; the fact of 'complexity' is not an exemption from judgement, and the personal is not a solvent of public contradiction. But they are heard differently, echoing as moments in a collective historical experience.

The sixteen individuals who speak in these interviews do so from dis- tinct generations of the Left, and out of distinct lineages of thought and practice. Lukács and Karl and Hedda Korsch grew up in the Europe of the *belle époque,* and were among the founding generation in their respective Communist Parties, in Hungary and Germany. They participated in the revolutionary upheavals at the end of the First World War, both Karl Korsch and Lukács holding office in Communist governments, and all three fell foul of Comintern orthodoxy in the following years. For a much younger group, the Second World War, its preludes and outcomes, were the critical common reference point. Jiři Pelikan (Czechoslovakia), Dorothy Thompson (Britain), Luciana Castellina and Lucio Colletti (both Italy) joined their respective Communist parties between 1939 and 1950, in the years of Stalin's dominion over the official Communist movement; Ernest Mandel (Belgium) and Adolfo Gilly (Argentina) entered the Trotskyist Fourth International, one just before the war, the other not long after. Pelikan and Mandel were both Resistance fighters; Thompson volunteered for labour service in Yugloslavia after Liberation. K. Damodaran (India) shares features of both groups, and by age stands halfway between them, twenty years younger or older than the others when he co-founded the Communist Party in Kerala in the later 1930s.

Noam Chomsky (United States), by contrast, belongs by age but not politico-intellectual formation: his lineage, as he says himself, is Marxist-anarchist, and he also belongs to the tradition of the *franc tireur*, the intellectual who intervenes on his own recognizance, without benefit or constraint of party, in the struggles of the time. In this, his peers are Sartre (France)—who, along with Damodaran, a near contemporary in years, is a generational anomaly here—and David Harvey (Britain), who like Giovanni Arrighi (Italy), an intercontinental *franc tireur* in a different style, was born significantly later, in the middle 1930s. For this transgenerational group, the medium of association with the Left is Marxism rather than communism. Then, after a gap of twenty years, there follows another generational cluster, this one born in the 1950s and shaped in the later decades of the twentieth century. João Pedro Stédile (Brazil), Asada Akira (Japan) and Wang Hui (China) have operated in dramatically contrasting situations and equally distinct roles. The denominators they share today are in one sense or another negative: capital everywhere unbound, in a time when the historic Communist alternative has either spent itself or metamorphosed into its programmatic antithesis, as the herald of a new era of capitalism.

The interwoven circumstances of these sixteen lives make a compelling group portrait. It is a gathering of intellectuals of different kinds, a majority with significant experience of academic work. Most of them are trained specialists, though in fields that readily lend themselves to discourse of the most general significance (language, literature, philosophy, social theory); some are generalists in their parties or movements, as organizers, leaders and writers. The varying relationship between intellectual and political commitments as it appears here will not gratify received prejudices concerning either professorial socialism or the spiritual costs of partisanship. Academic commitments are not always as secure or as much prized as might be expected; episodes of clandestinity, imprisonment, deportation and exile occur more

Introduction

often than many readers will have guessed, and sometimes with compensating intellectual and political gains, also perhaps unexpected. In classic Gramscian terms, they occupy the whole range from 'traditional' intellectuals—that is, intellectuals speaking from their distinctive place in the given social relations of culture, responding to an internalized ethical demand with no pre-given political mediation of the ordinary kind—and 'organic' intellectuals, that is those who in some sense speak not only *for* but also *from* the classes and groups they seek to represent.[5]

Sartre was the pre-eminent exponent of the first, prophetic mode in his time, and it is telling that his political writings of the 1960s should have included a programmatic *plaidoyer* for intellectuals as such.[6] Just a few years later, in the context of the war in Vietnam, Chomsky published his book on 'the responsibility of intellectuals'.[7] Arrighi and his co-thinkers, at the turn of the seventies, thought to serve militant workers directly, putting specialist knowledge at their disposal in the forum of the Gruppo Gramsci, and for Harvey today, the transmission of critical knowledge from the classroom to the fronts of struggle is direct, an unmediated Marxist theoretical practice in politics. Asada and Wang are similarly engaged, as academics and journalists, in the politics of intellectual life in their respective countries.[8]

The proper range of the second, 'organic' mode remains a matter for debate, but even the strictest accounting will include intellectuals such as Stédile, from a poor farming background and now a key leader of the landless workers' movement in Brazil. An alternative reading of Gramsci, reopening the conduit from Lenin's thought, would associate the organic with the idea of the party as collective intellectual, transcending the given cultural division of labour in a continuing effort of political synthesis as the necessary ground of strategy. This is the ideal space of the intellectual as organized militant, the sphere of activity of more than half of the sixteen, in one form or another, and historical experience of it does not favour simple conclusions. The passage from militant/intellectual via 'leadership' to bureaucrat is a well-worn narrative topic, and it is then the more worthwhile to pause over the instances of the reverse development, as a career functionary recovers his powers of independent thought and action under the pressure of social crisis, or a intellectual devotee of Stalin makes a calm, critical retrospect, in later life, of the youthful fideist he had been. Reflections such as

---

[5] Antonio Gramsci, 'Intellectuals and the Organization of Culture', *Selections From Prison Notebooks*, ed. and trans. Quintin Hoare and Geoffrey Nowell-Smith, London 1971, pp. 5–14.

[6] 'A Plea for Intellectuals', *Between Existentialism and Marxism*, Tokyo and Kyoto 1965, pp. 228–85.

[7] *American Power and the New Mandarins*, New York 1969.

[8] For Wang, see now Zhang Yongle, 'The Future of the Past: On Wang Hui's *Rise of Modern Chinese Thought*', NLR 62, March–April 2010, pp. 47–83; and for a contextualization of his work within contemporary Chinese intellectual production, see Chaohua Wang, ed., *One China, Many Paths*, London 2003.

Damodaran's on Indian traditions of intellectual leadership, or Asada's on the charismatic force of suffering in the discourse of Japanese Communism, must complicate all thinking about the formation of authority relations in political organizations. And then there are those cases where the necessarily complex role of party intellectual has been fulfilled without particular drama from beginning to end.

One variety of the crisis of historical communism in the later twentieth century consisted in renunciation of the party-form as such, as a political mediation of social struggles. For Arrighi, the Italian Communist Party and its allied trade unions were not simply to be opposed on their own plane of constitution and practice, but to be superseded by a new kind of proletarian political subject, the self-mediating, 'autonomous' worker. In this sense, his intervention as an independent intellectual aimed at a certain realization of the Gramscian idea of the organic intellectual. For Asada and still more for Wang, a post-Communist condition, however defined, is not so much a controversial option as a historical given, whose meaning remains to be resolved. So situated, they complete a historical arc. These sixteen testimonies, ranging across one hundred years, twenty and more countries and five continents, make up a continuous record of Marxist socialism and, above all, of Communism—the International and the informal movement that outlived it, and also the organized revolutionary opposition to its Left—from its emergence in the early twentieth century to its dissolution in the 1990s. Lukács speaks as a party member of more than a half-century's standing; the Korsches are early casualties of the tightening bonds of intellectual life in the Comintern; Pelikan and Damodaran reconstruct the histories of their respective parties from the eve of the Second World War to the seventies, as Asada will later do for the history and culture of Communism and the New Left in post-war Japan; Colletti and Castellina review forty years of post-war Italian experience; Sartre and Chomsky speak as independents in struggles of the 1960s, at the waning of the old Communist ascendancy over the radical Left; Wang explores the potentials and conundrums of oppositional politics after the historic metamorphosis in China. Cumulatively, they bear critical witness to the history of a movement and thus, in monographic form, to the general history it did so much to define: the mutual ruin of the old empires in the Great War, the Versailles settlements, the Russian Revolution and the rise of fascism; a Second World War, leading to a dramatic extension of the Communist bloc in Eastern Europe and Asia, a new upsurge of anti-colonial revolution beginning with Indian independence and continuing into the 1970s, and the emergence of the United States as hegemon of the capitalist world; the long post-war boom of Western capitalism and its radically ambiguous cultural legacy, the great desublimation that fuelled both the liberationist movements of the 1970s and the neo-liberalism that swept across the planet in the closing decades of the twentieth century; the remaking of the capitalist order, in conditions of globalization and financial crisis.

For the Marxist Left and labour movement, the sequence encompasses the disintegration of the Second International in 1914–18 and the foundation of a third, Communist, International amidst a revolutionary wave in Central Europe; the struggle against fascism, coinciding in the Soviet Union with the consolidation of party dictatorship under Stalin, Trotsky's expulsion and the eventual formation of the Fourth International; the Second World War, Hitler's invasion of the Soviet Union, the Red Army's decisive role in the Nazi defeat and the creation of Communist regimes from the Baltic to the Adriatic, with autonomous revolutions in Yugoslavia, China, Vietnam and Korea; Indian independence and the progressive dismantling of the European colonial empires; the crisis of Stalinism, with workers' revolts throughout the Eastern bloc, Khrushchev's post-mortem denunciation of Stalin's rule, then the Red Army's invasion of Hungary; the haemorrhage from the Western Communist parties after 1956 and the emergence of New Left currents in the West; revolution in Cuba; the Sino–Soviet split, polarizing much of the Communist world; the Prague Spring and the Warsaw Pact military intervention; the great opening of '1968', with the USA on the defensive in South-East Asia and under siege from anti-war movements at home, in Europe and Japan; working-class insurgency in France, Italy and elsewhere in Europe; the rise of the new social movements, above all women's liberation; the collapse of the Southern European dictatorships and revolution in Portugal; the military coup in Chile and the spread of reactionary dictatorships throughout South America; the rise and early deflation of Eurocommunism; perestroika in Russia and the movement towards the revolutions of 1989; the dissolution of the Soviet Union, the Eastern bloc and the Communist movement; the continuing pulse of resistance to capital, its social crises and its wars, and the tantalizing prospects for 'a movement of movements' as capitalism attains its farthest reach across the earth.

Lukács grew to adulthood in a world without communist parties or early expectations of socialist revolutions—a world, as he would later say, held in the space of the No Longer and the Not Yet. The world of recent times is in important ways not so dissimilar, but with the weighty difference of an intervening century of experience including both the parties and the revolutions, and the myriad struggles in and around, for and against them. It is as if Lukács's temporal figure had been reversed and the overarching story of the Left in the past hundred years were one of a journey from Not Yet to No Longer. But that would be premature as a last word. Today, struggles against capital continue in every part of the world, sustained not least by the demonic energy of capital itself, as it pursues self-increase, and by the violence by which its geopolitical conditions of existence are defended. These struggles are multiform, and the debates they foster—over agencies and means, conditions and goals—have few precedents on the Left in their freedom from inhibition. In this too, we are perhaps closer to 1910 than to 1948 or 1974.

Among the participants in these debates are the inheritors of the various traditions of Marxism and communism in the past century, and it would be as rash to discount the bodies of thought and practical experience they bring as it would be obtuse to expect historical privilege for them. Lukács, after years of circumspection, reasserts the classic revolutionary theme of workers democracy. Gilly, a Trotskyist with a long history of work with popular movements in Latin America, ponders the springs of desire in popular struggles and the customary genealogies that channel them; while Stédile, reflecting on the experience of the landless workers movement in Brazil, calls for the renewal of classical emphases on education, 'a theoretical training for activism'. Wang asks whether the designation 'New Left' is appropriate for the positions he defends in what is a categorically new historical situation for anti-capitalist politics; while Arrighi, after a magisterial *da capo* of capitalist eras and forms of proletarianization ranging over centuries and continents, wonders whether it is not time to find a new designation for the achievable good society beyond capitalism. These are not the signs of exhaustion. What time is it?[9] No Longer, yes, and still Not Yet.

---

[9] *Que Horas São?* is the title of a book by Roberto Schwarz, partly translated in an English-language selection of his work, *Misplaced Ideas: Essays on Brazilian Culture*, London 1992.

1
Georg Lukács
Hedda Korsch

Georg Lukács was born in 1885 in Budapest, into a wealthy Jewish banking family. He studied at universities in Budapest, Berlin and Heidelberg (where he was befriended by Max Weber), and in 1916 published his first major work in the literary field from which his name was to become inseparable, The Theory of the Novel.

Won to Marxism through the inspiration of the October Revolution, Lukács joined the new Hungarian Communist Party in 1918 and in the following year became Commissar for Education and Culture in the short-lived Hungarian Soviet Republic. In exile in Vienna, then Berlin, in the years that followed, he wrote History and Class Consciousness, *the single most influential work in what came to be known as the Western Marxist tradition. There followed the short study* Lenin *and then the so-called* Blum Theses, *in which Lukács tried unavailingly to wean his party from its ingrained leftism. After that defeat, he withdrew from direct politics into philosophical and critical activity, from 1933 onwards in Moscow, where he wrote, among other works,* The Historical Novel. *He remained there until his return to Hungary in the last months of the Second World War.*

Lukács now resumed an active role in the Communist Party, leaving a record that has remained controversial ever since. In the defining crisis of 1956, however, he sided with the popular movement against the flailing Stalinist regime, and accepted office in Imry Nagy's coalition government. After the Soviet invasion at the end of that year, Lukács was deported to Romania and held under house arrest. Spared execution and allowed back to Budapest the next year, he continued to write and publish for the rest of his active life.

The interview published here was given in Budapest in late 1968, soon after the Warsaw Pact invasion of Czechoslovakia, to which the closing exchange tacitly refers. It was first published after Lukács's death in 1971.

Georg Lukács

Life and Work

How do you judge your philosophical writings of the twenties today? What is their relationship to your present work?

In the twenties, Korsch, Gramsci and I tried in our different ways to come to grips with the problem of social necessity and the mechanistic interpretation of it that was the heritage of the Second International. We inherited this problem, but none of us—not even Gramsci, who was perhaps the best of us—solved it. We all went wrong, and today it would be quite mistaken to try and revive the works of those times as if they were valid now. In the West, there is a tendency to erect them into 'classics of heresy', but we have no need for that today. The twenties are a past epoch; it is the philosophical problems of the present that should concern us. I am now working on an *Ontology of Social Being* which I hope will solve the problems that were posed quite falsely in my earlier work, particularly *History and Class Consciousness*.[1] My new work centres on the question of the relationship between necessity and freedom, or as I express it, teleology and causality. Traditionally, philosophers have always built systems founded on one or the other of these two poles; they have either denied necessity or denied human freedom. My aim is to show the ontological interrelation of the two, and to reject the 'either-or' standpoints with which philosophy has traditionally presented man. The concept of *labour* is the hinge of my analysis. For labour is not biologically determined. If a lion attacks an antelope, its behaviour is determined by biological need and by that alone. But if primitive man is confronted with a heap of stones, he must choose between them, by judging which will be most adaptable to his use as a tool; he selects between *alternatives*. The notion of alternatives is basic to the meaning of human labour, which is thus always *teleological*—it sets an aim, which is the result

---

[1] *History and Class Consciousness* (1923), trans. Rodney Livingstone, London 1971. The *Ontology* appeared in English in three volumes, trans. David Fernbach, London 1978–79.

of a choice. It thus expresses human freedom. But this freedom only exists by setting in motion objective physical forces, which obey the causal laws of the material universe. The teleology of labour is thus always coordinated with physical causality, and indeed the result of any individual's labour is a moment of physical causality for the teleological orientation (*Setzung*) of any other individual. The belief in a teleology of nature was theology, and the belief in an immanent teleology of history was unfounded. But there is teleology in all human labour, inextricably inserted into the causality of the physical world. This position, which is the nucleus from which I am developing my present work, overcomes the classical antinomy of necessity and freedom. But I should emphasize that I am not trying to build an all-inclusive system. The title of my work—which is completed, but I am now revising the first chapters—is *Zur Ontologie des Gesellschaftlichen Seins*, not *Ontologie des Gesellschaftlichen Seins*. You will appreciate the difference. The task I am engaged on will need the collective work of many thinkers for its proper development. But I hope it will show the ontological bases for that socialism of everyday life of which I spoke.

England is the only major European country without a native Marxist philosophical tradition. You have written extensively on one moment of its cultural history—the work of Walter Scott; but how do you view the broader development of British political and intellectual history, and its relations to European culture since the Enlightenment?

British history has been the victim of what Marx called the law of uneven development. The very radicalism of Cromwell's Revolution and then the Revolution of 1688, and their success in assuring capitalist relations in town and countryside, became the cause of England's later backwardness. I think your review has been quite right to emphasize the historical importance of capitalist agriculture in England, and its paradoxical consequences for later English development. This can be seen very clearly in English cultural development. The dominance of empiricism as an ideology of the bourgeoisie dates only from after 1688, but it achieved tremendous power from then on, and completely distorted the whole previous history of English philosophy and art. Take Bacon, for example. He was a very great thinker, far greater than Locke, of whom the bourgeoisie made so much later on. But his significance was entirely concealed by English empiricism, and today if you want to study what Bacon made of empiricism, you must first understand what empiricism made of Bacon—which is something quite different. Marx was a great admirer of Bacon, you know. The same thing happened to another major English thinker, Mandeville. He was a great successor of Hobbes, but the English bourgeoisie forgot him altogether. You will find Marx quoting him in the *Theories of Surplus Value*, however. This radical English culture of the past was concealed and ignored. In its place, Eliot and others gave a quite exaggerated importance to the metaphysical poets—Donne and so on—who are much less significant in the whole developing history of human culture. Another revealing episode is the fate of Scott. I have written about Scott's importance in my book on the *Historical Novel*—you see he was the first novelist who saw that men are changed by history.[2] This was a tremendous discovery, and it was immediately perceived as such by great European writers like Pushkin in Russia, Manzoni in Italy and Balzac in France. They all saw the importance of Scott and learnt from him. The curious thing, however, is that in England itself Scott had no successors. He too was misunderstood and forgotten. There was thus a break in the whole development of English culture, which is very visible in later radical writers like Shaw. Shaw had no roots in the English cultural past, because nineteenth-century English culture was by then cut off from its radical pre-history. This is a deep weakness of Shaw, obviously.

Today, English intellectuals should not merely import Marxism from outside, they must reconstruct a new history of their own culture: this is an indispensable task for them, which only they can accomplish. I have written on Scott, and Agnes Heller on Shakespeare, but it is the English essentially who must rediscover England. We in Hungary too had many mystifications about our 'national character' such as you have in England. A true history of your culture will destroy these mystifications. In that perhaps you are helped by the depth of the English economic and political crisis, that product of the law of uneven development of which I spoke. Wilson is doubtless one of the most astute and opportunist bourgeois politicians anywhere today—yet his government has been the most utter and disastrous fiasco. That too is a sign of the depth and intractability of the English crisis.

How do you view now your early literary-critical work, particularly The Theory of the Novel? *What was its historical meaning?*

The Theory of the Novel was an expression of my despair during the First World War.[3] When the war started, I said Germany and Austro-Hungary will probably defeat Russia and destroy Tsarism: that is good. France and England will probably defeat Germany and Austro-Hungary and destroy the Hohenzollerns and Habsburgs: that is good. But who will then defend us from English and French culture? My despair at this question found no answer, and that is the background to *The Theory of the Novel*. Of course, October gave the answer. The Russian Revolution was the world-historical solution to my dilemma: it prevented the triumph of the English and French bourgeoisie which I had dreaded. But I should say that *The Theory of the Novel*, with all its mistakes, did call for the overthrow of the

---

[2] Trans. Hannah and Stanley Mitchell, London 1962.
[3] *The Theory of the Novel* (1920), trans. Anna Bostock, London 1971.

world that produced the culture it analysed. It understood the need for a revolutionary change.

At that time, you were a friend of Max Weber. How do you judge him now? His colleague Sombart eventually became a Nazi—do you think that Weber, had he lived, might have become reconciled to National Socialism?

No, never. You must understand that Weber was an absolutely honest person. He had a great contempt for the Emperor, for example. He used to say to us in private that the great German misfortune was that, unlike the Stuarts or the Bourbons, no Hohenzollern had ever been decapitated. You can imagine that it was no ordinary German professor who could say such a thing in 1912. Weber was quite unlike Sombart—he never made any concessions to anti-Semitism, for instance. Let me tell you a story that is characteristic of him. He was asked by a German university to send his recommendations for a chair at that university—they were going to make a new appointment. Weber wrote back to them, giving them three names, in order of merit. He then added, any three of these would be an absolutely suitable choice—they are all excellent: but you will not choose any one of them, because they are all Jews. So I am adding a list of three other names, not one of whom is as worthy as the three whom I have recommended, and you will undoubtedly accept one of them, because they are not Jews. Yet with all this, you must remember that Weber was a deeply convinced imperialist, whose liberalism was merely a matter of his belief that an efficient imperialism was necessary, and only liberalism could guarantee that efficiency. He was a sworn enemy of the October and November Revolutions. He was both an extraordinary scholar and deeply reactionary. The irrationalism which began with the late Schelling and Schopenhauer finds one of its most important expressions in him.

How did he react to your conversion to the October Revolution?

He is reported to have said that with Lukács the change must have been a profound transformation of convictions and ideas, whereas with Toller it was merely a confusion of sentiments. But I had no relations with him from that time on.

After the war, you participated in the Hungarian Commune, as Commissar for Education. What assessment of the experience of the Commune is possible now, fifty years later?

The essential cause of the Commune was the Vyx Note and the policy of the Entente towards Hungary. In this respect, the Hungarian Commune is comparable to the Russian Revolution, where the question of ending the war played a fundamental part in bringing the October Revolution into existence. Once the Vyx Note was delivered, its consequence was the Commune. Social democrats later attacked us for creating the Commune, but at that time after the war, there was no possibility of staying within the limits of the bourgeois political framework; it was necessary to explode it.

After the defeat of the Commune, you were a delegate at the Third Congress of the Comintern in Moscow. Did you encounter the Bolshevik leaders there? What were your impressions of them?

Look, you must remember that I was a small member of a small delegation—I was not an important figure in any way at the time, and so I naturally did not have long conversations with the leaders of the Russian party. I was introduced to Lenin, however, by Lunacharsky. He charmed me completely. I was able to watch him at work in the Commissions of the Congress as well, of course. The other Bolshevik leaders I must say I found antipathetic. Trotsky I disliked immediately: I thought him a poseur. There is a passage in Gorky's memories of Lenin, you know, where Lenin after the Revolution, while acknowledging Trotsky's organizational achievements during the Civil War, says that he had something of Lassalle about him. Zinoviev, whose role in the Comintern I later got to know well, was a mere political manipulator. My assessment of Bukharin is to be found in my article on him in 1925, criticizing his Marxism—that was at a time when he was the Russian authority on theoretical questions, after Stalin. Stalin himself I cannot remember at the Congress at all—like so many other foreign Communists, I had no awareness whatever of his importance in the Russian party. I did speak to Radek at some length. He told me that he thought my articles on the March action in Germany were the best things that had been written on it, and that he approved them completely. Later, of course, he changed his opinion when the party condemned the March affair, and he then publicly attacked it. By contrast with all these, Lenin made an enormous impression on me.

What was your reaction when Lenin attacked your article on the question of parliamentarianism?

My article was completely misguided, and I abandoned its theses without hesitation.[4] But I should add that I had read Lenin's *Left-Wing Communism: An Infantile Disorder* before his critique of my own article, and I had already been wholly convinced by his arguments on the question of parliamentary participation there: so his criticism of my article did not change anything very much for me. I already knew it was wrong. You remember what Lenin

---

[4] *Political Writings 1919–1929: The Question of Parliamentarianism and Other Essays,* ed. Rodney Livingstone and trans. Michael McColgan, London 1972.

said in *Left-Wing Communism*—that bourgeois parliaments were completely superseded in a world-historical sense, with the birth of the revolutionary organs of proletarian power, the Soviets, but that this absolutely did not mean that they were superseded in an immediate political sense—in particular that the masses in the West did not believe in them. Therefore Communists had to work in them, as well as outside them.

In 1928–29 you advanced the concept of the democratic dictatorship of the workers and peasants as the strategic goal for the Hungarian Communist Party at that date, in the famous Blum Theses for the Third Congress of the HCP. The Theses were rejected as opportunist and you were expelled from the Central Committee for them. How do you judge them today?

The Blum Theses were my rearguard action against the sectarianism of the Third Period, which insisted that social democracy and fascism were twins.[5] This disastrous line was accompanied, as you know, by the slogan of class against class and the call for immediate installation of the dictatorship of the proletariat. By reviving and adapting Lenin's slogan of 1905—the democratic dictatorship of the workers and peasants—I tried to find a loophole in the line of the Sixth Comintern Congress, through which I could win the Hungarian party to a more realistic policy. I had no success. The Blum Theses were condemned by the party and Béla Kun and his faction expelled me from the Central Committee. I was completely alone inside the party at that date; you must understand that I did not succeed in convincing even those who had up till then shared my views in the struggle against Kun's sectarianism inside the party. So I made a self-criticism of the theses. This was absolutely cynical: it was imposed on me by the circumstances of the time. I did not in fact change my opinions, and the truth is that I am convinced that I was absolutely right then. In fact, the course of later history vindicated the Blum Theses completely. For the period of 1945–48 in Hungary was the concrete realization of the democratic dictatorship of the workers and peasants for which I argued in 1929. After 1948, of course, Stalinism created something quite different—but that is another story.

What were your relations with Brecht in the thirties, and then after the war? How do you assess his stature?

Brecht was a very great poet, and his later plays—*Mother Courage, The Good Woman of Szechuan* and others—are excellent. Of course, his dramatic and aesthetic theories were quite confused and wrong. I have explained this in *The Meaning of Contemporary Realism*. But they do not change the quality of his later work. In 1931–33 I was in Berlin, working with

---

[5] Ibid.

the Writers' Union. About that time—in mid 1930, to be precise—Brecht wrote an article against me, defending expressionism. But later, when I was in Moscow, Brecht came to see me on his journey from Scandinavia to the USA—he went through the Soviet Union on that trip—and he said to me: There are some people who are trying to influence me against you, and there are some people trying to influence you against me. Let us make an agreement not be provoked by either into quarrelling. Thus we always had good relations, and after the war whenever I came to Berlin—which was very often—I always used to go and see Brecht, and we had long discussions together. Our positions were very close at the end. You know, I was invited by his wife to be one of those to speak at his funeral. One thing I do regret is that I never wrote an essay on Brecht in the forties: this was an error, caused by my preoccupation with other work at the time. I had great respect for Brecht, always. He was very clever and had a great sense of reality. In this he was quite unlike Korsch, whom he knew well, of course. When Korsch left the German party, he cut himself off from socialism. I know this, because it was impossible for him to collaborate in the work of the Writers' Union in the anti-fascist struggle in Berlin at the time—the party would not permit it. Brecht was quite different. He knew that nothing could be done against the Soviet Union, to which he remained loyal all his life.

Did you know Walter Benjamin? Do you think he would have evolved towards a firm revolutionary commitment to Marxism, had he lived?

No, for some reason I never met Benjamin, although I saw Adorno in Frankfurt in 1930 when I passed through before going to the Soviet Union. Benjamin was extraordinarily gifted, and saw deeply into many quite new problems. He explored these problems in different ways, but he never found a way out of them. I think that his development, had he lived, would have been quite uncertain, despite his friendship with Brecht. You must remember how difficult the times were—the purges in the thirties, then the Cold War. Adorno became the exponent of a kind of 'non-conformist conformity' in this climate.

After the victory of fascism in Germany, you worked in the Marx-Engels-Lenin Institute in Russia with Ryazanov. What did you do there?

When I was in Moscow in 1930, Ryazanov showed me the manuscripts which Marx had written in Paris in 1844.[6] You can imagine my excitement:

---

[6] David Ryazanov (1870–1938), lifelong revolutionary and an outstanding scholar, founded the Marx–Engels Institute in Moscow in 1920. (Lenin's name was added a decade later.) His greatest achievement there was his work to create a complete edition of the writings of Marx and Engels. Banished to a labour camp in 1930, eight years later Ryazanov was executed on Stalin's orders.

reading these manuscripts changed my whole relation to Marxism and transformed my philosophical outlook. A German scholar from the Soviet Union
was working on the manuscripts, preparing them for publication. The mice
had got at them, and there were many places in the manuscripts where the
words had letters missing, or a word missing. Because of my philosophical
knowledge, I worked with him, determining what the letters or the words
that had disappeared were: one often had words beginning with, say, 'g' and
ending with, say, 's' and one had to guess what came between. I think that
the edition that eventually came out was a very good one—I know because
of collaborating in the editing of it. Ryazanov was responsible for this work,
and he was very great philologist: not a theorist, but a great philologist.
After his removal, the work at the Institute declined completely. I remember
he told me there were ten volumes of Marx's manuscripts for *Capital* which
had never been published—Engels of course, in his introduction to Volumes
Two and Three, says they are only a selection from the manuscripts Marx
was working on for *Capital*. Ryazanov planned to publish all this material.
But to this day it has never appeared.[7]

In the early thirties, there were of course philosophical debates in the
USSR, but I did not participate in them. There was then a debate in which
Deborin's work was criticized. Personally, I thought much of the criticism justified, but its aim was only to establish Stalin's pre-eminence as a
philosopher.

*But you did participate in the literary debates in the Soviet Union in the
thirties?*

I collaborated with the journal *Literarny Kritik* for six or seven years, and
we conducted a very consistent policy against the dogmatism of those years.
Fadeyev and others had fought RAPP and defeated it in Russia, but only
because Averbach and others in RAPP were Trotskyist.[8] After their victory,
they then proceeded to develop their own form of RAPPism. *Literarny Kritik*
always resisted these tendencies. I wrote many articles in it, all of which
had some three quotations from Stalin in them—that was an insurmountable necessity in Russia at the time—and all of which were directed against
Stalinist conceptions of literature. Their content was always aimed against
Stalin's dogmatism.

---

[7] See now Karl Marx and Friedrich Engels, *Collected Works* (Economic Manuscripts
1961–63), vols 30–34, London 1988–94.

[8] RAPP, the Russian Association of Proletarian Writers, was created in 1922 as the
All-Union Association of Proletarian Writers (VAPP), changing its name in 1928, as it
entered the phase of its greatest influence. Insisting on a militant and vigilant 'proletarian' orientation in literature and the arts and holding out the promise of a mass cadre of
worker-writers, RAPP flourished in the febrile atmosphere of Stalin's rise to power. Four
years later it was officially dissolved for its excessive ambition and general insubordination.
It was succeeded at length by the more inclusive and compliant Union of Soviet Writers.

You were politically active for ten years of your life, from 1919 to 1929, then you had to abandon immediate political activity altogether. This was a very big change for any convinced Marxist. Did you feel limited (or perhaps on the contrary liberated?) by the abrupt change in your career in 1930? How did this phase of your life relate to your boyhood and youth? What were your influences then?

I had no regrets whatever about the ending of my political career. You see, I was convinced I was utterly right in the inner-party disputes in 1928 and 1929—nothing ever led me to change my mind on this; yet I completely failed to convince the party of my views. So I thought: if I was so right, and yet so wholly defeated, this could only mean that I had no political abilities as such. So I gave up practical political work without any difficulty—I decided I had no gift for it. My expulsion from the Central Committee of the Hungarian party in no way altered my belief that even with the disastrously sectarian policies of the Third Period, one could only fight effectively against fascism within the ranks of the Communist movement. I have not changed in this. I have always thought that the worst form of socialism was better to live in than the best form of capitalism.

Later, my participation in the Nagy government in 1956 was not a contradiction of my renunciation of political activity. I did not share the general political approach of Nagy, and when young people tried to bring the two of us together in the days before October, I always replied: 'The step from myself to Nagy Imre is no greater to take than the step from Nagy Imre to myself.' When I was asked to be Minister of Culture in October 1956, this was a moral question for me, not a political one, and I could not refuse. When we were arrested and interned in Romania, Romanian and Hungarian party comrades came to me and asked me for my views of Nagy's policies, knowing my disagreements with them. I told them: 'When I am a free man in the streets of Budapest and he is a free man, I will be happy to state my judgement of him openly and at length. But as long as he is imprisoned, my only relationship to him is one of solidarity.'

You ask me what my personal feelings were when I gave up my political career. I must say that I am perhaps not a very contemporary man. I can say that I have never felt frustration or any kind of complex in my life. I know what these mean, of course, from the literature of the twentieth century, and from having read Freud. But I have not experienced them myself. When I have seen mistakes or false directions in my life, I have always been willing to admit them—it has cost me nothing to do so—and then turn to something else. When I was fifteen to sixteen, I wrote modern plays, in the manner of Ibsen and Hauptmann. When I was eighteen, I reread them, and found them irretrievably bad. I decided there and then that I would never become a writer, and I burnt these plays. I had no regrets. That very early experience was useful to me later, because as a critic whenever I found I could say of a text I would have written that myself, I always knew this was infallible evidence that it was bad: it was a very reliable criterion. This was my first literary experience. My earliest political influences were reading Marx as a schoolboy, and then—most important of all—reading the great Hungarian poet Ady. I was very isolated as a boy, among my contemporaries, and Ady made a great impact on me. He was a revolutionary who had a great enthusiasm for Hegel, although he never accepted that aspect of Hegel which I always, from the start, myself rejected: his *Versöhnung mit der Wirklichkeit*— his reconciliation with established reality. It is a great weakness of English culture that there is no acquaintance with Hegel in it. To this day, I have not lost my admiration for him, and I think that the work Marx began—the materialization of Hegel's philosophy—must be pursued even beyond Marx. I have tried to do this in some passages of my forthcoming *Ontology*. When all is said and done, there are only three truly great thinkers in the West, incomparable with all others: Aristotle, Hegel and Marx.

Recent events in Europe have posed once again the problem of the relation of socialism to democracy. What are the fundamental differences for you between bourgeois democracy and revolutionary, socialist democracy?

Bourgeois democracy dates from the French Constitution of 1793, which was its highest and most radical expression. Its defining principle is the division of man into the *citoyen* of public life and the *bourgeois* of private life—the one endowed with universal political rights, the other the expression of particular and unequal economic interests. This division is fundamental to bourgeois democracy as a historically determinate phenomenon. Its philosophical reflection is to be found in de Sade. It is interesting that writers like Adorno are so preoccupied with de Sade, because he is the philosophical equivalent of the Constitution of 1793.

The ruling idea of both was that man is an object for man—rational egoism is the essence of human society. Now it is obvious that any attempt to recreate this historically past form of democracy under socialism is a regression and an anachronism. But this does not mean that the aspirations towards socialist democracy should ever be dealt with by administrative methods. The problem of socialist democracy is a very real one, and it has not yet been solved. For it must be a materialist democracy, not an idealist one. Let me give an example of what I mean. A man like Guevara was a heroic representative of the Jacobin ideal—his ideas were transported into his life and completely shaped it. He was not the first in the revolutionary movement to do this. Leviné in Germany and Otto Korvin here in Hungary were the same. One must have a deep human reverence for the nobility of this type. But their idealism is not that of the socialism of everyday life, which can only have a *material* basis, built on the construction of a new economy. But I must add immediately that economic development by itself never produces socialism. Khrushchev's doctrine that socialism would triumph on a world scale when the standard of living of the USSR overtook that of the USA was absolutely wrong. The problem must be posed in a quite different way. One can formulate it like this: Socialism is the first economic formation in history which does not spontaneously produce the 'economic man' to fit it. This is because it is a transitional formation, of course—an interlude in the passage from capitalism to communism. Now because the socialist economy does not spontaneously produce and reproduce the men appropriate for it, as classical capitalist society naturally generated its *homo œconomicus*, the divided *citoyen/bourgeois* of 1793 and de Sade, the function of social- ist democracy is precisely the *education* of its members towards socialism. This function is quite unprecedented, and has no analogy with anything in bourgeois democracy. It is clear that what is needed today is a renais- sance of Soviets—the system of working-class democracy which arose every time there was a proletarian revolution, in the Paris Commune of 1871, the Russian Revolution of 1905 and the October Revolution itself. But this will not occur overnight. The problem is that the workers are indifferent here: they will not believe in anything initially.

One problem in this respect concerns the historical presentation of necessary changes. In recent philosophical debates here, there has been considerable argument over the question of continuity versus discontinu- ity in history. I have come down firmly for discontinuity. You will know the classical conservative theses of de Tocqueville and Taine that the French Revolution was not a fundamental change in French history at all, because it merely continued the centralizing tradition of the French state, which was very strong under the *Ancien Régime* with Louis XIV, and was taken even further by Napoleon and then the Second Empire afterwards. This outlook was decisively rejected by Lenin, within the revolutionary movement. He never presented basic changes and new departures as merely continuations and improvements of previous trends. For example, when he announced the New Economic Policy, he never for one moment said that this was a 'devel- opment' or 'completion' of War Communism. He stated quite frankly that War Communism had been a mistake, understandable in the circumstances, and that the NEP was a correction of that mistake and a total change of course. This Leninist method was abandoned by Stalinism, which always tried to present policy changes—even enormous ones—as logical consequences and improvements of the previous line. Stalinism presented all socialist history as a continuous and correct development; it would never admit discontinuity. Now today, this question is more vital than ever, precisely in the problem of dealing with the *survival* of Stalinism. Should continuity with the past be emphasized within a perspective of improvements, or on the contrary should the way forward be a sharp rupture with Stalinism? I believe that a complete rupture is necessary. That is why the question of discontinuity in history has such importance for us.

Karl Korsch (1886–1961) came up through the protean socialist culture of pre-First World War Germany and Europe, and was then decisively formed politically as a dissident soldier at the front, active as a delegate in the soldiers' councils in 1918 and participating in the creation of the German Communist Party (KPD) in 1920. He was minister for Justice in the Communist–Social Democrat government of Thuringia, in central Germany, in 1923, and later a Reichstag deputy in Berlin.

A teacher at the University of Jena in the early 1920s, Korsch published his key work, Marxism and Philosophy, in 1923—in the same year as Lukács's History and Class Consciousness and with the same fate, official censure in the Communist International. Uneasy from the start about the strict, Moscow-focused centralism of the Comintern, Korsch now passed into open opposition and was expelled from the German party in 1926, in this respect differing from Lukács, for whom continuing party membership was never negotiable. Korsch left Germany after the Nazi seizure of power, eventually settling in the United States.

Hedda Gagliardi (1890–1982) was born into a bourgeois family with strong intellectual and artistic associations. (Her grandmother was the feminist writer and actor Hedwig Dohm.) She married Korsch in 1913 and, like him, rallied to the KPD in 1920. From 1916 onwards, she worked in experimental schools and in the Soviet Trade Mission in Berlin, until the KPD leaders had her dismissed because of her relationship with Korsch. She later taught at the Karl-Marx-Schule in Berlin and left Germany in 1933. Hedda Korsch gave this interview in 1972.

Hedda Korsch

Memories of Karl Korsch

Karl Korsch was born in 1886 in Todstedt near Hamburg. What was his family background?

Korsch came from a medium middle-class background. His father had been through secondary school, had taken the *Abitur*, and possessed great intellectual ambition. He was very interested in philosophy and wrote an enormous unpublished volume on the development of Leibnitz's theories of monads. He tried to put the whole of the cosmos into this philosophical system. It was his life's work and purely theoretical. The family came from East Prussia, from a farming background. But he wanted something more urban and intellectual. Soon after he married Teresa Raikovsky, Korsch's mother, they moved west to Tostedt. The father wanted to be closer to Western culture, and he disliked the agricultural *Junker* environment in which they lived. Because although the Korsch family themselves had only a modest-sized farm, the big estates were all around them and his father had no interest in agriculture. His mother was totally unconcerned with intellectual matters and never read a thing. She was pretty and extremely temperamental: she cooked well when she was in a good humour, burnt everything when she was angry. She was terribly untidy and if there is one reason why Karl was so tidy it was because of his mother. For example, during his last years at school he had a shed at the bottom of the garden where he worked. It was like a monk's cell with no rug on the floor, just a table and a few hard chairs, and he told me that was the style of life he liked. All his pencils lay absolutely straight along the desk. This taste of his for complete order and clarity was greatly furthered by his mother's lack of it.

The first eleven years in that small town on the Lüneburg Heath had a very strong influence on Karl. He could speak the dialect of North Germany and until the First World War he pronounced certain syllables such as the 's' at the beginning of *sprechen* and *stehen* in a North German way. He got rid of these during the war because all the people in his regiment were from

Meiningen and they could not understand what he was saying; in order to be understood by ordinary people—the soldiers—he changed his accent.[1] But he was always full of stories, proverbs and expressions from that part of the world.

When he was eleven the family moved because there was no gymnasium, no secondary school, and Karl showed such abilities that his parents thought he should have a better school. Meiningen was at that time still a Grand Duchy and I do not know why they chose it. It may have been because it was one of the most liberal and enlightened principalities; in contrast to Prussia which was much more reactionary, Meiningen had carried out a number of reforms. It possessed a Hoftheater which was the first theatre in Germany to play realistically and not recite the classical roles in an oratorical fashion. When they moved there, Korsch's father was employed by a bank; in the end he rose to be vice-president of it in Meiningen. The Korsch family lived in Obermassfeld, a village nearby, and Karl used to walk an hour each way when going to school. Some people have suggested that the Korsches were quite affluent, but although they were not poor there were six children (four daughters, two sons) and life was certainly extremely simple. They lived in this village because rents were cheaper than in town and they led a very parsimonious existence.

Korsch remained at school in Meiningen till he got his *Abitur*; most of his teachers were alcoholics, having acquired the habit of excessive drinking as students. He began to read philosophy by himself, in addition to the pre-scribed texts such as Schiller's theoretical essays which were included in the German literature course. Karl's father was working on his theory of monads and so he too encouraged Korsch to read philosophy. He told me later that it was at school that he shed all the idiocies of the typical German students of the time—endless drinking, corporate ceremonies, more beer and more Sunday excursions to the village pub. He said later that he got these out of his system in his last two years at school and never had the slightest inclination to repeat them again.

He then went to university but studied at a number of different institutions. What kinds of activity did he engage in when a student?

After taking his *Abitur* he first went to the university at Jena, where he completed his studies. He also spent one term in Munich because he thought that he should know something about art and Munich was the place to see paintings and listen to good music. After that he spent some time in Switzerland; there he learnt to speak French fluently. He also got a very strong taste of the international community there among students and

---

[1] The Grand Duchy of Saxe-Meiningen, in central Germany, since the 1920s part of the modern state of Thuringia.

political exiles. He met a lot of Russians who had fled from Tsarism, although no famous ones.

He studied law because his father thought it was the only thing for an intelligent young man to study, and from the start he specialized in international law and jurisprudence. He passed all his exams well. He was also a member of the Freie Studentenschaft, a group of students opposed to the existing student *Bunde*. Korsch played a leading role in this movement and he travelled all over Germany working for it—which is how I first met him. There was no formal membership. Historically, it emerged in opposition to the Burschenschaften and the Studentenkorps which represented reactionary anti-Semitism and militarism, with a lot of rituals with ranks and drinking, and membership lists. The Freie Studenten had no lists; they had open groups—sports groups, philosophy groups, mutual help groups. Anyone who wanted could attend. They came into existence around 1900 and they were in outspoken opposition to traditional German codes of behaviour. I do not think that they had any more specific political content, except that they aspired towards an individualistic freedom. They had a slight tendency towards the left of centre, but they were certainly not socialist.

You mentioned his philosophical interests at school: how did these relate to the political positions he later adopted?

Although his father was a Leibnitzian he considered himself at this time to be a Kantian. He often gave talks on a variety of subjects and you could always see he was a Kantian. He insisted that anyone whom he considered intelligent enough should read not only the *Critique of Pure Reason* but Kant's other works as well, especially the *Metaphysic of Morals*. He was also a convinced socialist by the time of his last year in school. He looked around to see if there were any socialists among his school-mates, but he did not find any. He read a lot: I do not know when he first read Marx but I am inclined to think it was at school, because when he was a student he was an outspoken socialist—by conviction, although not a member of any organization. He never joined the Social Democrats (SPD), although he had friends in the party, especially in Jena. He wanted the Freie Studenten to meet workers and socialists and he arranged discussion evenings through a friend of his, Heidemann, whose father was an SPD member of the local parliament in Mecklenburg. The evenings were arranged like a dinner where men and women sit next to each other—in this case workers and students sat alternately.

Jena was a small town dominated by the University and the Zeiss works. It was a cultural centre. Schiller had lived there. Goethe's Weimar was just around the corner and there was a sense of tradition. The Zeiss concern was run by Zeiss and Abbé who were by their own lights social reformers. Zeiss ran the technical optical side of the operation; Abbé organized the social side. From the beginning they had a highly developed system of profit-sharing and they wanted to turn the whole thing over to the workers—but the workers did not want it. The Zeiss works also paid half the costs of the university, while the state paid the other half: Zeiss built a Volkshaus with meeting and theatre rooms. Half the population of Jena were workers and half were students; and people used to say that every night one half of the population lectured to the other. It was the only town in Germany where an experiment in labour relations of this type existed at that time; and although Korsch was not related to the Zeiss works, he was influenced by the atmosphere and used to go to meetings at the Volkshaus. After the war he became extremely involved and was one of their political leaders.

He was also drawn into the Diederichs circle, in which nationalist unpolitical people formed a youth group. Diederichs had a publishing house in Jena and he produced the magazine *Die Tat.* He collected around him a great number of students with whom he celebrated traditional holidays, like the summer solstice, with bonfires and singing, and dancing in the streets, and men jumping over fires with their girlfriends and so on. Most of the young people wore *Schauben*, medieval German coats without sleeves or collars; they were opposed to the uninteresting and confining male clothes of the nineteenth century. None of them ever has collars or cuffs; they were loose shirts open at the neck and photographs show the large cravat that Korsch used to wear. They dressed in colourful clothes, and Diederichs in a quite imaginative and cheerful way cultivated a mixture of old customs and revolt against bourgeois society. I do not think there was much sexual licence among these young people, but it was freer than the conventional behaviour of young men and women at that time.

After completing his studies at Jena, Korsch went to England, where he stayed from 1912 to 1914. His early writings show he was interested in a variety of aspects of English life—the Fabians, Galsworthy, the suffragettes, the universities. What was he doing in England?

It is not true, as some people have written, that he was studying in England. He had a job that involved his working with Sir Ernest Shuster, a professor of law. Shuster, Stephen Spender's grandfather, had written a book on English civil law and procedure and he wanted someone not only to translate it but to edit it so that it was comprehensible to a German student of law. He himself had studied at Jena and Korsch had been recommended to him by the University. Korsch and Shuster got on so well and spent so much time talking that the book proceeded very slowly and it was near completion only by the spring of 1914. I was with him in England: I had wangled a job from my professor transcribing a Middle English manuscript in the British Museum. We observed many aspects of English life at that time, and joined the Fabian Society—the first organization to which he belonged. We regularly attended meetings of the 'Fabian Nursery' for younger members, and used to give reports, especially on German questions.

By the time Korsch and Shuster had finally finished the manuscript it was the summer of 1914 and Karl was summoned by his regiment in Meiningen. He was called to appear for extraordinary manoeuvres. He said to me that this meant war was imminent, because he had already completed the necessary manoeuvres. We discussed at length whether to return to Germany or not, because he had no desire to fight for the 'fatherland', but we decided to go because he said that he had even less of a desire to be imprisoned somewhere as an enemy alien without contact with any movement. He wanted to be with the masses, and they would be in the army.

How did he react to the experience of the war and to the more general political convulsions in Europe?

Korsch was in the same regiment in which he had been trained, and many of the officers were former school-mates from Meiningen. It was the 32nd Infantry Regiment and most of the men in it were country boys. When they left for the war there was no jubilation. The music and bouquets were officially provided; the bands had to play and ladies threw flowers. But the men were moody, sullen or weeping. Korsch's father and I saw him off at the station—his mother did not want to see it. They were sent into Belgium and Korsch always said that he thought it was a criminal breach of international law to march through a neutral country. He condemned it wholeheartedly and so in the second week of the war he was demoted from lieutenant to sergeant. But he made himself useful in Belgium because he used to exert pressure on the officers and men not to loot and requisition food. He became a kind of unofficial quartermaster, making the soldiers pay for eggs and chickens.

Because he was against the war he never carried a rifle or a sabre. He used to point out that it made no difference, since you were just as safe with or without a weapon: the point was that you were safe neither way. He personally was not going to kill people, but he considered it his mission to bring as many men from his unit home alive as he could. That was his war aim. He used to volunteer for patrols and was decorated several times—not for any particular action, just for surviving under all that fire. What we at home could never understand was why he was not court-martialled, but he later said that there were two probable reasons for this. One was that he was useful—he went on patrols, wrote good reports, and gave the officers ideas about how to advance and retreat. The second reason was that everyone knew him from school; and they thought that Korsch had always been crazy, but was not a bad guy. If he had been in a strange regiment he would have been put before a military tribunal straight away. In 1917 there were strikes and unrest among the soldiers as casualties increased; he was re-promoted and ended up as a captain. They used to call his company 'the red company' because they were all for a revolution and for ending the war by not fighting any more. Later, when soldiers' soviets were established, he was immediately elected; and because the authorities were afraid of them they were not demobbed until after many units, not till January 1919. The demobilization took place near Berlin, but because they were from Meiningen they had no contact with revolutionaries in Berlin and took no part in the Spartacist insurrection at that time. Korsch had been in despair for the last six months of the war.

One grenade had hit his company and the first platoon had been wiped out to the last man. Later he told me that he had fallen into paroxysms of crying and then had got drunk because it was more than he could take. Nearly all the people he had started out with in 1914 were dead and he was desperate because of the massacres. But when the 'November Revolution' came he revived and hoped that a better Germany could be built.

The period from the end of the war until his expulsion from the Communist Party in 1926 was the most politically active phase of his life. What did he do on his return from the war?

When he came back he entered the USPD, which I had joined earlier when I heard that they had sent delegates to Zimmerwald and were for ending the war.[2] He attended the USPD conference in 1920 when the party split and the majority opted for fusion with the Communists. Korsch went with the majority although he had great reservations about the twenty-one points that the Comintern had laid down. But it was the same as when we discussed his going back to Germany from London: he did not want to be a member of a small sect, but thought he should be where the masses were and he believed that the German workers were going Communist. His main reservation about the twenty-one points concerned the centralized discipline from Moscow, the degree of dependence on the Russian party that they implied. In everything—as he had been with the students—he was in favour of decentralization, and he was by now very much convinced by the principle of workers' soviets.

Although he went back to teaching in Jena immediately after the war and we lived in the building that housed the local KPD paper *Die Neue Zeitung*, he was also in Berlin for a time working on the Socialization Commission.[3] The Commission was a bourgeois institution with social-democratic members. It was supposed to draw up practical plans for 'socializing' the

---

[2] USPD: the Independent Social Democratic Party of Germany, founded in March 1917 by the left and centre opponents of the SPD's official pro-war orientation.
[3] KPD: the Germany Communist Party, created in 1919 from the nucleus of the revolutionary opposition in Germany Social Democracy, the Spartacists. The USPD's left majority subsequently fused with the KPD, the Right returning to the SPD.

German economy. The original 1919 government contained SPD and USPD members and they wanted to work out the organizational problems of a socialist economy and of the expected transition. Karl was not nearly as sceptical as so intelligent a person should have been. He was also an enthusiast and his writings on socialization reflected this for nearly a year. The Russian Revolution had a big influence on him and we all thought that it was the beginning of a new epoch.

From 1921 onwards he was working on his major text Marxism and Philosophy.[4] *Did he at that time cooperate with Lukács, whose* History and Class Consciousness *appeared in the same year?*

He did not know about Lukács when he was working on *Marxism and Philosophy*. He heard about him only after the publication of his own volume. He said to me that another book had just come out which in many ways contained ideas similar to his own. Later when Korsch gave courses of lectures in Marxism in the 1920s and right up until February 1933 Lukács used to take part and attended pretty regularly. There were always discussions afterwards in the Cafe Adler on the Alexanderplatz and Lukács was there very often. In 1930 Felix Weill organized a *Sommerakademie*, what today would be called a workshop, when we all spent a week discussing and reading papers in a country pub in Thuringia. The fact that Lukács was in the Communist Party and Korsch had left it did not affect their relationship; they both considered themselves to be critical communists. In the new introduction to *Marxism and Philosophy* written in 1929 Korsch said that the points of agreement between himself and Lukács were fewer than he had originally thought. This referred to their differing positions on Russia. That disagreement, rather than any philosophical issue, was the main source of their divergences. Korsch also thought that Lukács still preserved more of his idealist philosophical background than he himself had done. But despite this they remained friendly until Lukács went to the USSR and then they just had no connection any more.

Korsch was a minister in the United Front KPD–USPD *government in Thuringia in 1923, which was crushed by the intervention of the Reichswehr. What was Korsch's role in this experience?*

From 1920 to 1923 he was teaching law at Jena, work he pursued even when he became a deputy in the Thuringia Landtag, or state parliament. He gave political lectures in many places and was active in KPD politics. In Thuringia, the great majority of the masses were either left Social Democrats or Communists, and in September 1923 a coalition government of these two parties was formed.

---

[4] London 1970.

The KPD backed cadres with a formal education. So he became minister of Justice and remained so for six months. He was sceptical about the possibility of a revolutionary insurrection, which the formation of the coalition government was supposed to prepare regionally, but remained active on the grounds that one should participate as long as there was any chance of success. His realistic view was that the Nazis would try to move into Thuringia after the defeat of Hitler's putsch in Munich and that even if a workers' revolution did not succeed in winning power, it would at least be able to prevent the Nazis from seizing the government by force. Korsch with his military experience was in charge of paramilitary preparations; but there was little they could do. A high-ranking Russian officer advised them; they drilled and went on long marches, and worked out which heights to occupy when the Nazis invaded.

The projected insurrection in Thuringia never took place because the Reichswehr invaded before the plans for it were ready. The federal government in Berlin announced that law and order had broken down in Thuringia, that mobs had taken over; in fact, of course, peaceful, everyday existence had not ceased and the soldiers who arrived were to be disconcerted because they couldn't see any disorder and no one attacked them. The members of the regional government had to go underground and the press, including the foreign papers, reported that they had fled to Holland and Denmark. In fact they went as far as Leipzig, one hour by slow train from Jena. Korsch was forced into clandestinity and I was arrested, but four months later there was an amnesty, after the Thuringian government had been dissolved.

In 1924 new elections took place under emergency regulations and the Berlin regime made sure that no socialist or communist government was formed. Indeed Thuringia later acquired one of the first Nazi governments of any region in Germany, which then banned Karl from lecturing at Jena university. But in 1924 he was re-elected to the Landtag, and was also elected to the Reichstag, so we moved to Berlin.

For a year he was editor of the party's theoretical journal and at the centre of KPD politics. But at the moment of his greatest influence within the party, he was already starting to challenge its dominant line. What was his reaction to the changes in the Comintern at that time?

He was growing increasingly concerned about developments in Russia and especially so after the death of Lenin. He had always had doubts, of course. But in Thuringia the KPD was strong and large, and the local comrades were very good people, willing to sacrifice personal comfort, money, time, jobs, for the class struggle. There were lots of meetings and commissions and all that. Then directives began to come more and more from Moscow, saying what was to be discussed at meetings and what resolutions were to be put to them. Whereas during the early 1920s, the rank and file felt that they themselves forged their actions, the international leadership now began to interfere and direct everything. But Karl still thought that the KPD was the only party that still tried to *fight* in any way. There was no question of the Social Democrats doing that. So he stayed in the party although he realized quite early on that he would be expelled. He went to the Fifth Congress of the Comintern in Moscow in 1924 and there he had a feeling that he was in danger. Some comrades warned him that he might be intercepted because he was under strong suspicion for deviations and seditious talk against the Soviet leadership. He left before he was scheduled to depart and formed no real impressions of the Soviet Union while he was there; he was completely wrapped up in the conference itself.

He had contacts with other opposition groups. He met Amadeo Bordiga, the Italian leader, in Moscow. Then he met Sapronov, of the Russian Workers' Opposition, when the latter came to Berlin on what was probably a clandestine trip some time after 1925. They talked a lot and understood each other very well and agreed to cooperate in opposition work. Sapronov and Korsch thought that by proposing measures and motions for greater decentralization and liberties for various groups they could do something worthwhile. They stupidly agreed on a code in which they would correspond with each other, and this code contributed to Sapronov's destruction when it was later found out in Russia. To get a coded letter from Germany was a dangerous thing—and it was not a difficult correspondence to decode because Karl taught me how to do it. So far as I know he had no contact with Trotsky. He thought Trotsky was right about many things and he was in favour of the idea of permanent revolution; but he thought that Trotsky too would have played a power game with alliances in a nationalist way, of which Korsch disapproved. Trotsky also wrote and said things which clearly show that he had a different way of approaching the class struggle: Trotsky laid less emphasis than Korsch on the need for consciousness among workers and laid more emphasis on the question of party leadership.

In 1925 he was dismissed from the editorship of Die Internationale *and in 1926 was expelled from the KPD: What were his subsequent political activities, prior to the Nazi seizure of power? What was the character of his relationship with Brecht?*

When he was expelled from the KPD he produced the magazine *Kommunistische Politik* for two years, paying for it out of his salary as a Reichstag deputy, while we lived off his salary from Jena and my earnings from teaching. The magazine was in a newspaper format and was nearly self-supporting. In that whole period up to 1933, Korsch developed his understanding of several key subjects and continued to lecture on Marxism. He studied geopolitics, world history, and mathematics. He worked very thoroughly through modern mathematical thought with a professor at Berlin University who

later died at the hands of the Nazis. He was a member of the Gesellschaft
für empirische Philosophie. He also went deeply into the problems of what
today would be called the Third World. He studied the development of the
various colonial countries because he thought that the liberation of the colonies was perhaps imminent and could change world politics completely. In
that period we were closely involved with the whole group around the Malik
Verlag, including Felix Weill, the son of a millionaire who had endowed
the Verlag as well as the Institute for Social Research in Frankfurt. He was
an important friend, who gave us the down payment on our house. One
day in August 1928 he invited us to see the première of *The Threepenny
Opera* and we went together; afterwards we went to see Brecht with some
of these other Leftist artists. George Grosz was also there that night and
we were all very excited: it seemed to us really new and worthwhile. From
then on Korsch and Brecht met quite a bit and when Karl gave a course of
lectures in Berlin, Brecht used to attend. But he and Brecht soon found
this inadequate and began to meet at specially arranged gatherings to
which each of them would bring four or five comrades. They continued
to meet until things were too unsafe for ten or twelve people to assemble
together.

Korsch's lectures were given at the Karl-Marx-Schule, a school at which
I taught. It was a very radical experimental school, which comprised everything from kindergarten through the training of high school teachers to
PhDs. We said that it took students 'from the cradle to the grave'. It was
most exciting. The principal was a Social Democrat and there were a number
of older teachers who tried to sabotage the whole thing. But there were a
lot of Communists among the parents because the school was in Neukölln,
a proletarian suburb of Berlin. There were four streams, and three of them
started at the normal high school age of ten. One was for humanistic studies
and ancient languages; one for mathematics and science; one for humanistic
studies with a stress on philosophy, literature and history. The fourth was for
gifted children. We could not all at once revolutionize the German educational system, but we were able to take children out of the public school at
the age of thirteen or fourteen and take them through to the *Abitur* level.
The school was called the Karl-Marx-Schule not because the teachers or the
schoolchildren had decided so, but because it was a completely KPD municipality. We used to give rooms to outsiders to lecture provided they lectured
in the spirit of Karl Marx, and that is where Karl used to speak.

I remember the last lecture he gave, on the night of 28 February 1933.
We were all in the cafe afterwards when the news came that the Reichstag
was burning. Quite a few of the participants did not go home that night.
Others went home and were arrested. The law on political reliability of civil
servants was passed in April, and Korsch and I were thereby deprived of our
salaries. I was dismissed on 1 May and our bank account was confiscated.
So we were without a penny and I went to Sweden to work. At first he

remained in Berlin, not sleeping at home and trying to organize underground anti-Hitler activities. So many people still thought that it could not
last and in the spring he and a former student of mine organized quite a
large meeting in a forest outside Berlin attended by representatives of very
different groups including Christians, trades unions, Communists, Social
Democrats, and other scattered groups like the Gesellschaft für Aesthetische
Kultur. They held a large conference, one of the largest that was ever organized without detection under Hitler. They tried to evolve ways of fighting
from within Germany, but most of them were soon caught and imprisoned
or killed. Korsch was not caught and he remained until late autumn of 1933
when it became impossible to sleep even in the sheds of workers' allotments.
He was by then a liability to his friends. Brecht had invited him to Denmark,
so he went and stayed with him.

He lived in the USA from 1936 until his death in 1961, although after the war
he visited Europe. His writings appear to take on a more pessimistic tone in this
later period and at times seem to abandon Marxism altogether. What were his
political and theoretical activities in these years?

He went to Denmark first, and then to England where he still had contacts. Shuster was dead, but his wife was still alive; and he knew quite a
few young English people like Spender and Isherwood, who had come to
Germany during the Weimar Republic because it seemed a focus of liberty
and experimentation, and who had visited us in Berlin. Karl tried to find
work in England but it was extremely difficult because the local Communists
kept denouncing him to the Home Office. They said that he was a suspi-
cious character who was probably a Nazi agent because since he was not a
Jew, he had no reason to behave strangely and leave Germany in the way he
had. One positive result of his stay in England was that he was asked to write
his book on Karl Marx, which was commissioned by the London School of
Economics. He did not think of his *Karl Marx* as a development of Marxist
research or as a political action on his part; but he gave his own interpretation of Marx's thought and he wrote it as a textbook and an honest work.[5]

In 1936 he went to America, and when he first arrived he kept an open
mind about possible developments here. But that did not last long because
he soon saw the direction in which things were going. On the other hand
he saw that the forces moving within US capitalism were so different and
so strong that one could not predict their direction with great exactitude.
Upheavals *might* happen here, he thought, but the situation was so bad
that the only way in which things would change would be for them to get
worse. He did not engage in any major political activity in the USA, although
he was occasionally invited to lecture to small political groups and used

---

[5] London 1938.

to speak at military schools during the war. His chief activity in the USA was writing.

In his last years he *was* pessimistic about the fate of the world revolutionary movement and completely so about the Soviet Union. He had no hope, even after the death of Stalin. He did not live long enough in good health (i.e. up to 1957) to form much of an opinion about the Chinese revolution, although he was very interested in what was happening in China and had been an old foe of Chiang Kai-shek long ago in Germany. On his last trip to Europe he visited Yugoslavia and was favourably impressed; but he thought the country was extremely primitive and wondered how far it could go and how it might change in the process. His main hope lay with the colonial nations—he thought they would become more and more important and Europe would become less so.

His 1950 lecture, entitled 'Ten Theses on Marxism', is easy to misunderstand and is not a rejection of Marxism. The 'Theses' were not meant for publication, although I later allowed them to be printed.[6] The centre of his interest to the very end was Marxism. But he tried to adapt Marxism as he understood it to new developments, particularly in two ways. One was, as I have mentioned, by studies of the colonial world: he thought that early Marxism had for good reason been concentrated on Europe, but that one now had to look further and this concern tied into his interest in the world historians. In his 1946 article on the Philippines he saw pretty clearly the nature of nominal colonial independence.[7] His other major concern at this time was the widening of Marxism to cope with the advances of other sciences. He thought that as capitalist society had developed since Marx's time, Marxism too should be developed to understand it. His uncompleted text, the 'Manuscript of Abolitions', is an attempt to develop a Marxist theory of historical development in terms of the future abolition of the divisions that constitute our society—such as the divisions between different classes, between town and country, between mental and physical labour.

---

[6] 'Ten Theses on Marxism Today', *Telos*, 26 (Winter 1975–76).
[7] See in the Paul Partos Papers at the International Institute of Social History in the Netherlands (http://www.iisg.nl).

2

Jiři Pelikan

K. Damodaran

Ernest Mandel

Dorothy Thompson

Lucio Colletti

Luciana Castellina

Adolfo Gilly

Jiří Pelikan (1923–99), a teenage partisan from northern Moravia and a veteran of Gestapo jails, rose rapidly in the Czech Communist Party, becoming head of the national Students' Union in 1948, under the new regime. He went on to serve in the party's Central Committee and parliamentary group. He later declared himself ashamed of his role in the bureaucratic purge of Czech universities in the later forties; by 1963, when he became director general of Czech state television, he had become a reformer, a prominent actor in the movement that culminated in the Prague Spring of 1967–68. ('No press has ever been freer than in Czechoslovakia during the spring of 1968' was Sartre's tribute at the time.) The new growths of that period were quickly cut down by Soviet-led Warsaw Pact forces, and within a year Pelikan had gone into exile in Rome. He gave this interview soon afterwards, in 1971.

In the next phase of his career, Pelikan published the émigré magazine Listy, *and collaborated with Charter 77, which had become the principal focus of internal opposition. Statelessness, a letter-bomb attack and a kidnap attempt were the price of his continuing commitment to socialist reform in Czechoslovakia. In 1979–89, by now an Italian citizen, he sat for the Italian Socialist Party in the European Parliament.*

Jiři Pelikan

The Struggle for Socialism in Czechoslovakia

We would like to begin by asking something about the period in which you first became politically active, just before the Second World War. You joined an anti-fascist organization in 1937, while still at school, and became a member of the Czech Communist Party in 1939. Could you tell us how you experienced the major events of those years, the Nazi occupation of Czechoslovakia in 1938 and 1939, the German–Russian pact in the summer of 1939, the invasion of the Soviet Union in 1941 and the Czechoslovak resistance movement?

My case is typical of many people of my generation who entered the political arena as secondary school students in the late thirties. The Spanish Civil War was in progress and the danger of a German invasion already hung over Czechoslovakia. We were, of course, very excited about the fight of the Spanish people against fascism, and saw the important role of the communists in that struggle—though without any real understanding of the problems involved. Then we saw that the Communists were the most resolute opponents of fascism in Czechoslovakia and internationally, and this brought us into sympathy with the Communist Party. It is most important to understand that Czechoslovakia, unlike the other East European countries subsequently liberated by the Red Army, had always had a legal Communist Party before the war. During the twenty years of bourgeois parliamentary government between 1918 and 1938, there had been real guarantees for democratic freedom. The fact that Czechoslovakia was an industrialized country, and had a working class with long revolutionary and democratic traditions, was the basis for the subsequent success of the Communist Party.

When the invasion of Czechoslovakia proper started in 1939, we saw the Communist Party as the only force which opposed it—although there were, in fact, other patriotic groups which did so too. It was at this time that I joined the Communist Party and became a part of its underground network. I helped to produce and distribute leaflets and newspapers, organize students and so on, until 1940 when I was arrested.

The Nazi–Soviet pact, of course, came as a great shock to us. But right from the moment of the invasion, when the resistance started, Russian policy had dismayed us. For example, I remember clearly a friend's case. He was much older, had been a Communist since his university studies in 1933 and was one of the leading members of the party in our city in Moravia. When he received instructions from the Comintern after the Nazi occupation he was extremely shaken. Even messages signed by Gottwald himself stated that the German soldiers who had invaded Czechoslovakia were, in fact, proletarians in soldiers' uniforms and therefore in no way class enemies![1] The real enemies were the Czech bourgeoisie headed by Beneš, and the American and British plutocrats.[2] This was the Comintern line at the time. I remember my friend refused to transmit these instructions to the members of the party. They would have meant that instead of fighting against the occupiers we would be fighting against our own people. In fact the party throughout the country modified these instructions, saying firstly that the comrades in Moscow were not well informed about the situation and secondly that the instructions were completely out of touch with reality. When the German–Russian pact was signed at the end of August, this was a further shock. We had received a lot of explanations of how the Soviet Union had been obliged to do this, because of the refusal of the Western powers to conclude a military treaty and in order to buy time. Despite our feelings, we could appreciate rationally that the pact probably was necessary. But what we did not understand at all were the positive articles which we started to read in the German newspapers about the Soviet Union and the broadcasts we heard from Radio Moscow at the time: instead of working to build up the Resistance, they began toning down all anti-fascist propaganda and just putting out items about how many pigs there were on some kolkhoz or other and how many tons of such and such a product the Soviet Union had produced. I remember the comrades were very angry when they saw that what was involved was not just a pact of non-aggression with a fascist country, but rather some sort of political agreement. Another thing which dismayed us was Molotov's speech after the collapse of Poland, in which he spoke of Poland as an artificial state from its creation, now destroyed forever by the common action of the German and Soviet armies. But all these hesitations came to an end in June 1941, when the war between the Soviet Union and Germany started. After that, of course, the situation changed completely; the Moscow party leaders now gave full support to the Resistance and cooperation with other anti-fascist forces began.

---

[1] Klement Gottwald (1896–1953): founder member of the Czech Communist Party, in which he held successive leading roles. Prime minister, then president of Czechoslovakia between 1948 and his death.

[2] Edvard Beneš (1884–1948): a founding figure of the Czech Republic and its second president (1935–38), head of the wartime Czechoslovak government in exile, and first post-war president (1946–48).

Yet the Communist Party had not lost its position as the main force of resistance in Czechoslovakia during the period from March 1939 to June 1941?

I would not say that the Communist Party was the main force. In fact we claimed after the war that we were the main force, but it is difficult to assess. There certainly were other groups—though not so well organized as the Communist Party. I think the claim that the Communist Party was the only, or the main, force in the Resistance was a sectarian one.

Could you say something about the development of the party during the war? For example what were the relations between the leadership in Moscow and the new leaders in the Resistance? Were there differences destined to be important later on?

To answer that, one must go back to the history of the Communist Party of Czechoslovakia. I have mentioned that the party was always a legal one, unlike in the other Eastern European countries. It was founded in 1921 as the result of a break with the Social Democratic Party. Again, in contrast to other Central and Eastern European countries, it was from the very beginning a real mass party. The leader at that time, Šmeral, developed some sort of conception of a Czechoslovakian path to socialism, which brought him into conflict with the Comintern and with the twenty-one points laid down by it. The mass base of the Communist Party in Czechoslovakia which was the sign of its real success was very adversely affected by the Fifth Congress in 1929, when Gottwald took over the leadership. This Congress, officially called the Congress of Bolshevization, was in fact a congress of subjugation of the Communist Party of Czechoslovakia to the Soviet leadership. It accepted the crushing of the Soviet opposition and Stalin's conception of building socialism in one country, and acknowledged the Soviet Union as the single monopolistic centre of the international revolutionary movement. The acceptance of this line led to the elimination of many outstanding leaders from the party, which lost about 70 per cent of its membership during this period. Later on it won a lot of them back through its fight against fascism, starting in 1934–35 with the new line of the Comintern—the Popular Front. It was in this period between 1929 and 1939 that a new leading nucleus of the party was developed—Gottwald, Slánský, Kopecký and others.[3] They were educated into complete subordination to the Soviet party and to Stalin. It was, in fact, this leadership which was in the Soviet Union during the war, and which came back unchanged to take power after the liberation.

---

[3] Rudolf Slánský (1901–52): veteran Communist, lieutenant of Gottwald and his successor as general secretary in 1946. Arrested and charged, at Stalin's instigation, with high treason in the service of Western imperialism, he was one of eleven out of fourteen Communists found guilty and executed in 1952. Vaclav Kopecký, minister for information and culture in post-war governments.

The people who were inside the country were never, in fact, integrated into the leading positions of the party and they were always viewed with a certain suspicion. Take, for example, Smrkovský. Smrkovský was one of the leaders of the Prague uprising and a central figure in the underground committee of the party at the end of the war. He became vice-president of the Czech National Council in 1945. But the very fact that he organized the popular uprising was held against him. For Gottwald's aim had been that the country should be liberated by the Soviet Army, not by a popular uprising, whereas the whole strategy of the 'internal' party had been directed towards a popular uprising, towards partisan struggle. Of course during the war the contradictions were not apparent, because even Gottwald appealed for an uprising and for armed struggle. But as we learnt later, the Soviet Union insisted categorically that Czechoslovakia should be liberated by the Soviet Army and this fact was of decisive importance. Consequently, in all ideological work and propaganda the role played by the Resistance Movement at home was played down and sometimes even portrayed as hostile. It was in this context that when the political trials started in 1949, Smrkovský was accused of being an agent of the Gestapo, put in prison and condemned, together with many other leaders of the resistance movement. Since they drew their political strength from the popular movement, they were considered insufficiently disciplined or loyal to the Soviet leadership, and for this reason they were viewed with a certain suspicion.

What was your personal involvement in these events? What happened after you were arrested by the Gestapo in 1940?

My personal role was a very small one because I was a young student. When I was arrested I was seventeen years old; I spent about one year in prison, then I was released on parole because I was under eighteen. I was on the point of being arrested again when the German–Soviet war began, but I escaped from where I had been assigned to stay while on parole. I spent the remaining four years of the war underground, with a false name, in various regions of Czechoslovakia. Since I was being looked for by the Gestapo, my parents were taken as hostages, and my mother was killed by the Germans. My brother had been arrested with me in 1940, but he remained in prison for the whole five years the war lasted. I spent the last two and a half years of the war in a small village called Koronec near Boskovice in Moravia. I was the secretary of the local village administration—under my false name of course—and was able to continue my underground work at the same time. There was a partisan movement in the area; there were a lot of Soviet prisoners of war who had joined us and we were able to help our people.

When did partisan struggle begin, and what was its extent?

It began in 1944 and was, of course, strongest in the mountainous part of the country. It was strongest of all in Slovakia, after that in eastern and central Moravia where I was, and it was weakest in Bohemia, which is much more densely populated and industrialized, lies on a plain and was more tightly controlled by the Germans.

What happened when the Red Army liberated Czechoslovakia? Could you tell us how the new administration was established, and about the workers' councils which sprang up in 1945, especially in Bohemia?

During the last years of the war, there was an attempt to create underground *Národní vybory* or National Committees as popular organs for the future, local society. In the factories there were also to be *Závodní vybory* or factory committees formed by the workers and technicians. There were some factories, I would not say that there were many, where such underground committees actually existed; where they did exist they organized the rising of 5 May 1945—above all in Prague. This insurrection, we know today, was launched against the will of the Soviet leadership. The same was true of the uprising in Slovakia in August 1944. Stalin wanted this uprising to start only when the Red Army had already surrounded the frontiers of Slovakia as far as Katowice.

But the uprising broke out spontaneously and although the Soviet Army tried to give it support, it was suppressed. It was a tragedy like that of the risings in Warsaw and elsewhere. I would not say myself that the Russians did not want to help it, but I would say that they did not view with enthusiasm a popular uprising without clear political control from Moscow.

Was there any resistance to the imposition of the Moscow leadership and Gottwald immediately after the liberation?

No, I don't think there was any real resistance, because the war was a victorious one. Everybody knew after Stalingrad that the Soviet Union had played a decisive role in it, and I think that Gottwald was accepted as the acknowledged leader of the Communist Party, and hence also of the resistance movement as a whole. It was argued, I think in *Rude Pravo*, that the liberation of Prague by the Soviet Army was some sort of confirmation of the correctness of the line of Gottwald.

There were some Czech detachments with the Soviet Army, weren't there?

Yes, there were some Czech soldiers who had first tried to fight with the Polish Army in 1939; General Svoboda, at the time a colonel, was their commander.[4] When Poland was defeated they went to the Soviet Union, where they were at first interned in camps. But when the war started with Germany, they were reorganized as a part of the Free Czechoslovak Army, which had units in England and elsewhere.

Was Svoboda himself interned in that period?

Yes, he was. This was, in fact, rather an interesting period of his life. He later explained to a visitor that while he was in prison in the Soviet Union, it was learnt that he knew the Hungarian Military Attaché in Istanbul, who had been with him in military school. He was sent to Turkey on behalf of the Soviet military intelligence service to contact this Hungarian officer, and succeeded in getting some very important information. However, when he returned to the Soviet Union he was put in prison and condemned to death, and was only saved before the execution by the NKVD.[5]

To return to the Prague rising, when it broke out the Czech detachment in the American Army was already in Pilsen, and it naturally wanted to go to help the uprising in Prague. But since they were part of the Allied Forces, they were stopped by order of General Antonov. The Russians themselves have now published an account of how General Antonov sent a cable to Eisenhower saying that the British and American Armies must stop at the line which was established at Yalta. This line went from Pilsen to Budejovice and meant that the British and Americans were only to liberate a small part of Czechoslovakian territory in the extreme south-west of the country. Thus the Prague workers were obliged to fight for three days before Russian troops could arrive from Berlin. They tried to come as soon as possible, but the American Army would have been there in two hours. Nevertheless, the decision was probably a correct one, although psychologically hard to accept for the Czech Resistance. The interesting thing is how the line of demarcation was respected and, in fact, is still respected.

Yes, just as it was respected, although it prevented the victory of a socialist revolution in Greece. What was the situation of the bourgeoisie in Czechoslovakia at the time of liberation? What was the relationship of class forces between the working class and its allies and the bourgeoisie?

I think that the bourgeoisie was discredited. First of all by the defeat of the First Republic in 1938, secondly by the collaboration of part of it with the

---

[4] Ludvík Svoboda (1895–1979): much decorated veteran of two world wars and deputy prime minister 1950–51. Having survived several purges in the early fifties, he became president in 1968, retaining that role for seven years, which included the climax and repression of Czech reform Communism and the 'normalization' of subsequent years.
[5] NKVD: the People's Commissariat for Internal Affairs, for twenty years from 1934 the key executive organ of Stalin's dictatorship.

Germans—although it must be acknowledged that part of the national bour-geoisie also participated in the resistance movement. At all events, the formula of the 'national and democratic revolution', as it was called at the time, allowed the party the occasion to undermine all the economic and political power of the bourgeoisie in 1945. The four parties which were permitted to exist—the Communist Party, the Social Democratic Party, the National Socialist Party and the Catholic Party (there were other parties in Slovakia)—all agreed to put through the programme of the National Front which had directed the resistance. It was a programme for national and democratic revolution, but it already went beyond the programme of any bourgeois government. It was, in fact, the programme of a 'People's Democracy'. It involved the nation-alization of big industry, the banks, all external trade; agrarian reform; the establishment of national committees as the legislative and executive organs of power; a single union federation, and so on. The bourgeoisie lost any real power and the balance of forces was completely in favour of the working class. The peasants supported the workers because they wanted the agrarian reform. Of course, there were still some remnants of the reactionary forces left, and when they had got over the first shock of defeat, they started to oppose the new course and tried to sabotage the realization of the National Front programme. This is what led to the crisis in February 1948.

What was the character of this crisis? It appeared as an attempt to push the social revolution through a further stage, but it also appeared as an episode in the Cold War. How did this seem to you as a Czech Communist at the time?

I think there were both internal and international aspects of the Czechoslovakian crisis of 1948. Inside Czechoslovakia, tension was growing. Although the other political parties supported the programme of the National Front and collaborated with the Communists, the rightist forces which I mentioned had stabilized certain positions of strength within these parties, and even had some support among the population at large—as a result of dissatisfaction with the country's economic development, the diffi-culties, hardship, shortages and so on. As a counteroffensive, the Communist Party launched proposals to extend nationalization even to small industries, to confiscate all personal fortunes exceeding one million crowns, and to carry out a further distribution of land. From this point of view, the 1948 crisis did represent a sharpening of the class struggle. But at the same time, from an international point of view, it was clear from the time of the Informburo meeting in Poland in 1947 that the Soviet Union saw itself not as a base for the revolutionary movements of the world, but increasingly as a great power essentially concerned with the distribution of zones of influence.[6] Moscow

---

[6] Informburo, or Cominform: the Communist Information Bureau, an international organization created by Stalin in 1947, four years after the dissolution of the Communist International. It was wound up in 1956.

wanted to consolidate its influence and power over Czechoslovakia, since these had not been clearly established at Yalta. At Yalta there had been no discussion about Czechoslovakia as such—at least as far as we know. Nobody knows exactly what was discussed, but from all the evidence and documents published it emerges that there was a lot of discussion about Poland, Yugoslavia and Greece, but the Czechoslovakian problem was never discussed at all. Perhaps this was because it was then the only government recognized by everybody. However, I would say that the 1948 crisis was not just a putsch launched by the Soviet Union or by Stalin; it was an internal clash between the progressive and reactionary forces in which the latter were defeated by the tactics of Gottwald, who emerged as the leader of the country.

You mean that neither the Russians nor Gottwald had been restraining class struggle in 1945–46? You have no impression that the workers perhaps wanted to strike some more decisive blows for socialism than had been achieved?

This problem, of course, existed. I remember, for example, I think it was in about 1946, a meeting of the party activists in Prague to which Gottwald was invited and where he was obliged to defend the strategy of the party against heavy criticism. A lot of the delegates, particularly those from factories, were saying: 'What are we doing and where are we going? It is all very well talking about the national and democratic revolution, but we want socialism and the party does not speak about socialism.' Gottwald was trying to explain that, of course, the final aim of the party was socialism, but at the present stage to propagate socialism too much might create problems amongst certain sections of the population, and the party should not go beyond this stage of the national and democratic revolution. I remember that some people were not very much convinced by this, saying that this sort of practice could, of course, be valid if the party publicly declared that its aim was to build a socialist society, but as it was being carried out it appeared that the aim was to deceive the people and confront them with a *fait accompli*. Then again, I was a student at that time, and I remember there was a lot of critical discussion of party strategy among the students. It was felt that the party had no clear strategy or perspective, but was too much involved in day-to-day political problems. Of course, these criticisms were superseded in 1948 when people thought that the way to socialism was open.

What was your personal experience of the internal life of the party in the period between 1945 and 1948? What sort of things were discussed in party circles?

Discussion was quite free. There were none of the limitations which appeared later on, when the party took over power. The leadership wanted discussion to be concentrated mainly on economic problems and on how the Communists could contribute to the building of a new Czechoslovakian State. Gottwald's slogan was 'the better we work, the more we shall be accepted as a leading force'. This line of course implied avoiding real ideological discussion. But the arguments used by other parties against the Communist Party were inevitably reflected within the latter, especially in intellectual and student bodies. There was also frequent discussion about the Czechoslovak road to socialism—about the aim of the whole development. But there was never any clear explanation from the leadership, from the representatives of the Central Committee, on this question.

Another subject of great discussion in 1947 was Zhdanov's speech on proletarian culture, and the measures taken against Akhmatova, Khachaturian and Shostakovich.[7] An exhibition of Soviet painters was put on in Prague at which the so-called socialist realism made its first appearance. There was a violent clash between the party and the communist intellectuals, because the latter were for the most part people who were Communists before the war, when to be a Communist artist meant to be an *avant garde* artist. Many of them were, for example, surrealists. They recognized in Soviet socialist realism the reactionary realism of the bourgeoisie of the First Republic, and they refused to accept this kind of art as real socialist art. The leadership tried to resolve this conflict by explaining that 'socialist realism' was due to the historical development of the Soviet Union, and that at all events in Czechoslovakia there would not be any such imposition of a single style on the artists. Nevertheless, this was a big topic of discussion.

You spoke of 'the Czechoslovak road to socialism'. What did this phrase mean in 1948?

Gottwald and other party leaders, in fact, had promised since 1945 that after the liberation Czechoslovakia would develop according to its traditions and its specific conditions. The reactionary forces used to say, as the 1948 crisis approached: 'If the Communists come to power they will collectivize the land and set up kolkhozes'; or 'they will expel the non-Communist students from the University' and so on and so forth. They pointed to the example of the Soviet Union. The Czech party leaders always denied this, saying that we would not collectivize or establish kolkhozes, because it was not necessary in Czechoslovakia. I even remember a speech by Gottwald in which he said that when he was in Moscow and his shoes were worn out he had spent three days trying to find somebody to repair them. We said to ourselves why, when

---

[7] Andrei Alexandrovich Zhdanov (1896–1948): head of the Leningrad party from 1934 and leader of the wartime defence of the city, chair of the Supreme Soviet (1938–47) and organizer of the Cominform, assumed responsibility for cultural policy in 1946, unleashing an infamous phase of censorship and harassment of the arts. His targets included the poet Anna Akhmatova (1889–1966), and the composers Aram Khatchaturian (1903–78) and Dmitri Shostakovich (1906–75).

there are so many small enterprises in Czechoslovakia, should we liquidate them? Even after we took power in 1948, Gottwald stated categorically at a meeting of small artisans and merchants that we had no intention of nation-alizing petty enterprises. Just one year later, of course, all small enterprises were nationalized and smashed. But to return to the immediate post-war period, when in 1946 Gottwald explained the party's strategy, he referred to the interview which Stalin gave to British Labour Party representatives in Moscow after the war, in which he declared publicly, for the first time it seems, that there might be other ways to socialism than that followed by the Soviet Union—i.e. not through Soviets, but through 'parliamentary elections' and a 'democratic development'. I think you will find that this interview got quite a lot of publicity. Gottwald said that as a result of the changes after the Second World War—the strength of the Soviet Union, the end of capitalist encirclement of the Soviet Union, the great prestige of the Communists because of their participation in the resistance movement—as a result of all these factors we do not need a real armed revolution or to take power through any violent action. In fact, we could win power through elec-tions and transform the national and democratic revolution into a socialist revolution by steps. Indeed, he claimed at the time that the Czechoslovakian state after the war was already actually in transition to socialism. It was no longer a capitalist state because the bourgeoisie no longer owned the means of production and although it was not yet a socialist state, it was in the first stage of a socialist revolution. There was some opposition to this view at the time, although many people were able to accept that perhaps the armed struggle characteristic of the socialist revolution had, in fact, taken place in the form of the clash between the Soviet Army and the German Army, rep-resenting two class systems.

What about the question of workers' power in Czechoslovakia? Were there people who felt that the workers did not get real state power in Czechoslovakia in 1948?

No, I don't think that this view was expressed at all in 1948. The official line in Czechoslovakia in this respect was typical of all the Eastern European countries. Once the Communist Party takes power, the Communist Party which represents the working class, once it has a leading role in the state, the parliament, and the trade unions, then this leading role of the Communist Party is seen as identical to the leading role and to the power of the workers. The workers themselves have nothing to do except follow the instructions of the party. I think this was the original source of the crisis which appeared later. The working class, which had been rather active before the war, during the war and after the war, was systematically being depoliticized by the party's leadership. Party slogans claimed that since the working class was in power, the role of the workers was to work to increase productivity, to compete in Stakhanovite fashion; this would be the best contribution the working class could make towards the building of socialism. Of course, some of the best working-class cadres were taken from the factory floor and made into directors, or given posts in the diplomatic service. The universities were opened to the children of the working class. This was real progress and was also necessary to ensure the stability of the new regime. But we were to realize later that this was an inadequate conception of workers' power. The workers soon discovered that they were in almost the same situation as in a capitalist country. They had to work, they received a money wage and, what is more, they could not buy what they needed even with this wage because of the shortage of goods. However, I do not think that the problem of workers' power was really posed at this time—except by Kalandra, a Communist poet and writer, a Trotskyist, who was arrested in 1948 and executed. A lot of other people whom we did not even know, people who had criticized the Moscow trials in 1936–38, were the first victims after the victory of the Communist Party. Then, of course, after the Informburo resolution on Yugoslavia, the real clash came on the question of the specificity of roads to socialism. The conflict with Yugoslavia was reflected in Czechoslovakia, Poland and elsewhere. I do not think that this conflict broke out because Yugoslavia was the most liberal of all the East European countries. Czechoslovakia, for example, was probably more so. But Yugoslavia was the only country in the Soviet zone in Eastern Europe which had effectively liberated itself. True, it did so in the overall context of the Soviet Army's defeat of Germany, but nevertheless Yugoslavia had a real partisan army, whereas the other countries' resistance was on an altogether smaller scale. For this reason the Yugoslavs did not want to accept the monopoly role of the Soviet Union. In Czechoslovakia, the Yugoslav issue was used as a pretext to break all potential opponents capable of thinking independently or contesting (I don't say they did any real contesting) the leading role of Moscow. If you take the people who were arrested among the Communists, it was the old Communists, those who had been in the Spanish Civil War, those who had been in the resistance movement abroad, people of Jewish origin who had been in exile in the West, the best economists—in short, all the people who were able to think for themselves. The victims were, in fact, themselves Stalinists at the time, but the blow was directed against potential enemies. I should say that I only realized the full significance of the repression of 1949–54 years later. It was after the events in Poland and Hungary in 1956 and there was a meeting of the Central Committee, in 1957 I think, when they were discussed. Kopecký, who at that time was a member of the politburo, said that the reason such events did not occur in Czechoslovakia was that Kádár and Gomułka had been arrested, but not liquidated physically, while we had liquidated all our political opponents physically.[8] Thus we

---

[8] János Kádár (1912–89): leader of the Hungarian Socialist Workers Party from 1956

were able to overcome this crisis because there was no alternative leadership in Czechoslovakia. At all events, the political trials put an end to all attempts at specific national paths of development and initiated the imposition of the Soviet model of socialism in all the Eastern European countries.

If one reads the proceedings of the official 1968 investigation into the trials, which you edited in English, there is one thing in the report which seems very surprising. The impression is given by the report that the choice of Slánský as the ultimate target was somehow not the result of any decision on the part either of Gottwald or Stalin, but was arrived at in the course of interrogation of various figures. This is scarcely credible?

No, I think the report says that the interrogators did not 'discover' anything about Slánský, rather that they compelled those already under arrest to name him. There was even an attempt on the part of Gottwald to stop this. The only question is who the interrogators were and who was behind them. They were, of course, Soviet 'experts'. Was the decision Stalin's or was it an initiative on the part of the secret police? In any case the choice of Slánský, in my opinion, has another meaning. He was of Jewish origin, though in fact from an anti-Zionist family long established in Czechoslovakia, and his arrest coincided also with the change of Soviet policy in the Middle East. Originally the Soviet Union had supported the creation of Israel. The idea was that through Yugoslavia and through Israel they would be able to penetrate to the Mediterranean region. But first of all they did not succeed through Yugoslavia, and then after the establishment of Israel they realized that the place left empty by the British had been filled by the Americans. It was at this point that the Russians decided to play the card of Arab nationalism. But in order to change the former policy, it was necessary to prove they were sincere and hence to condemn that policy. This was not, of course, done through any self-criticism by the Soviet Union, but by putting the main blame on Czechoslovakia, which had played a special role in relations with Israel—naturally on the initiative and with the permission of the Soviet Union. For example, some officers of the Israeli Army were trained in Czechoslovakia. The latter was the Soviet Union's main intermediary in the Middle East (these days it deals direct). So when the Russians wanted to change their old policy, they wanted to show that not only had they stopped Czechoslovakia sending arms and instructors to Israel and training its officers, but that, in fact, it had never been Russian policy to do so—what was involved was some sort of conspiracy, by people like Slánský. At the

until 1988; chair of the Council of Ministers 1956–58 and 1961–65. Władysław Gomułka (1905–82): first secretary of the Polish Workers Party 1943–48, and an influential member of the provisional governments of 1945–47. He was deposed and imprisoned in the early fifties as a 'rightist' and 'reactionary', but was rehabilitated and became leader of the Polish United Workers Party in 1956, continuing until 1970.

time Slánský was chairman of the State Defence Committee, so it was easy to name him the man responsible; after all, he had signed all the relevant documents. A further advantage of choosing Slánský was that he was a man of the party apparatus, which was by now not very popular; choosing him, it became possible to utilize residual anti-socialism and to put the blame for the party's excesses onto people of Jewish origin. All in all, I think there was clearly a premeditated plan to choose Slánský for this role.

Perhaps we could now turn to a somewhat later period. You, of course, in the 1950s and early 1960s became very prominent in the International Union of Students?

From 1953 I was general secretary and from 1955 the president of the IUS.

What was your experience of working within that organization? Was there any contradiction between its subordination to Russian interests and the presence within it of many student unions which were genuine, militant anti-imperialist organizations?

First of all I must say that personally I was very pleased to be able to leave domestic politics; like many other Communists, I did not feel very happy about the way things were going. In the IUS, I found again the genuinely revolutionary, extremely free atmosphere of the student movement. At that time, of course, I had no doubts about the sincerity of Soviet policy. It seemed to me that this policy was basically correct because it was directed against imperialism. Don't forget, it was still the period of the Korean War. There was even felt to be a danger of world conflict, and it was a period when a great number of African and Asian countries were still colonies. So the IUS at the time played a very positive role in mobilizing students against colonialism, and in that respect there was no basic contradiction with Soviet policy, which supported the anti-colonial revolutions. Later, of course, after the Twentieth Congress and Khrushchev's speech, we had our first doubts. But Khrushchev's policy initially seemed positive—broader contacts, a rejection of sectarianism, which we felt had been a great failing of the IUS in the period of the Cold War. We welcomed the opportunity to extend the common front to organizations which, although not Communist, were generally anti-imperialist and anti-colonialist.

But the policy of peaceful coexistence as it was in fact carried out created the first and real problems inside the IUS. There was on occasion a conflict between its anti-imperialist and anti-colonialist mission and the way in which the Russians applied the policy of peaceful coexistence. For example, we were very much involved in organizing support for the national liberation struggle in Algeria. But when Khrushchev went to France, the Soviet representatives became reluctant to vote for IUS resolutions in favour of

Algeria, because to do so would create problems with the French govern-ment. Other conflicts of interest arose. With regard to the Cuban Revolution and the Latin American movement as a whole, whereas the Communist Parties were unenthusiastic the student organizations were very revolution-ary, very progressive. Differences also emerged on the question of peace. The great discussion in the IUS between 1956 and 1960 was about the con-nection between the fight for peace and that for national independence. On the one hand, the tendency of the Soviet Union was to concentrate solely on the fight for peace. On the other, the majority of students in the colonial or newly independent countries felt that the main problem for them was the fight against colonialism, neo-colonialism and imperialism; they were therefore not in favour of this policy of peaceful coexistence. Further con-tradictions arose on the question of atomic weapons, since the Soviet Union was always trying to impose its tactical policy of the moment on the organi-zation. For example, the IUS urged a campaign for stopping all nuclear tests, and then, just as the Congress of the IUS was taking place in Leningrad—I think it was in 1961 after the Youth Festival—there was a nuclear explosion in the Soviet Union. The Japanese delegation proposed that it should be condemned, in line with IUS policy, and there were very heated discussions on the subject; many delegates were frustrated by the fact that the IUS could condemn US nuclear tests but was not allowed to condemn Soviet ones. We tried to explain to Soviet comrades that this was a mistake, because we were convinced that it was due only to their failure to understand the mentality of students. But, of course, it became increasingly clear that they saw the IUS and similar organizations merely as unofficial instruments of Soviet foreign policy.

A further type of contradiction reflected within the IUS derived from the internal conflicts of the international Communist movement—for example, the Sino–Soviet dispute, which had its first impact on the IUS as early as 1957.

What was your own reaction to the eruption of the dispute between China and the Soviet Union? Were you fully convinced by the Soviet case at that time?

First of all we did not realize that it was a real and deep disagreement. We thought of it as mainly due to the difference in mentality of the two Parties and two peoples; also to a clash of personalities between Khrushchev and Mao Zedong. When Khrushchev visited Mao in Peking in August 1958, I had the opportunity of observing them both, and realized what different personalities they had. I must confess frankly that at that time the major-ity of us sympathized more with the Soviet point of view that war should be avoided through agreements and negotiations, whereas we felt that the Chinese view at the time was rather crude. The slogan which they proposed at the IUS congress was that we should not be afraid of war. This was not very well understood. Although I can see now that the Chinese side was not able at the time to explain its attitude to this conflict, there was another thing which disturbed us. Everybody was quoting Lenin and Marx, but the Chinese made constant references to Stalin too. In Eastern Europe, of course, Stalin was the symbol of all the deformations of socialist society. All in all, we were very distressed by this conflict, but hoped that it would not lead to a real split. But both sides were hiding the real reasons for the dispute, and it was very difficult to realize its true dimensions.

Czechoslovakia was the country in Eastern Europe where an unreconstructed Stalinist system seemed to be strongest and to survive longest—up to 1966–67 in fact. How then was it possible for a movement of change and renewal to emerge in the Czech party in 1966–67, a movement which culminated in the Prague Spring of 1968?

This does appear strange on the face of things, but it can be understood if one looks back at the development of Czechoslovakia before and after the war. It was in Czechoslovakia that there were the most favourable conditions for socialism in the whole of Eastern Europe; because of the industrialization of the country, because of the developed working class, because of the role and prestige of the Communist Party and because of the friendship of the people for the Soviet Union. From this point of view it would seem strange that the greatest purge in any Communist Party was that which took place in Czechoslovakia in 1949–54. I think it was precisely because Czechoslovakia had the most favourable conditions that it seemed likely to be the most independent in seeking its own path of development. This did not at all suit the Soviet leadership. They wanted to monopolize Eastern Europe, and to impose the Soviet model. For this reason they were obliged to strike hardest against the Czechoslovakian Communist Party. Parties like the Polish, Hungarian or Bulgarian were just small groups who had been underground for twenty to thirty years; it was not so difficult for them to accept Soviet hegemony. But in Czechoslovakia, although the party was subjectively willing to accept that hegemony, it was nevertheless seen by the Russians as a potential heretic. Naturally, it appeared paradoxical and shocking to us that the number of the victims of repression should be highest in Czechoslovakia, despite all our democratic traditions. Nothing comparable in scale occurred elsewhere in Eastern Europe. Fourteen people were assassinated in the Slánský trial, several hundred people, as the Piller Report revealed, were condemned to death.[9] In Poland it was possible for Bierut

---

[9] The Piller Report was the outcome of a special commission of the Czech Communist Party convened in April 1968 with Jan Piller as chair and charged with inquiring into the political trials of the early 1950s. Piller, deputy minister for Heavy Engineering, was elected to the Party Praesidium at the same session that saw Alexander Dubček succeed to the position of first secretary.

to save Gomułka's life, even though he had been politically disgraced.[10] The same was true for Kádár in Hungary. In the GDR, Bulgaria and Russia, too, the repression was on a lesser scale. In Czechoslovakia there was both the greatest degree of repression and also the deepest crisis as a result of that repression, precisely because of the contradiction between the former favourable conditions for a democratic road to socialism and the complete destruction of the country's democratic tradition. Furthermore, since this political terror created a kind of moral crisis, the Novotny leadership later tried, as far as possible, to avoid any real rehabilitation and hide the truth about the trials.[11]

This was the reason why Stalin's system was maintained for a long time in Czechoslovakia. I would not agree with you that Czechoslovakia was the most Stalinist country up to 1966–67. That was the general impression given in the Western press. But I would say that the crisis in Czechoslovakia goes back to the Twentieth Congress. It is true that it was halted for a time, as a result of the events in Hungary, but it recommenced in 1963, after the report of the so-called Kolder Commission to the Central Committee, when a great part of the truth about the political trials, though not all of it, was revealed. I think the process of liberation began when Novotny, under pressure from various sides, was obliged to make concessions. Pressure was coming from the youth, a section of which had lost all faith in socialism and was creating a lot of problems. There was also a conflict between the party and the intellectuals—writers, film-makers and so on. This did not begin in 1967, but long before. You can see this by looking at Czechoslovak literature and cinema, which had been among the most progressive in Eastern Europe since 1964–65—the so-called Czechoslovakian New Wave. Then there was the conflict between the Czechs and Slovaks—the unsolved national problem. There were the economic difficulties, which led Novotny to accept Šik's proposals for partial economic reform.[12] All these contradictions were already present from 1963 on, and were steadily growing. From time to time Novotny tried to halt the process by administrative measures, but he no longer had the power to do so.

All these contradictions came to a head in autumn 1967 and January 1968, and culminated in this so-called Prague Spring. But this had been prepared for a long time previously. For example, in the ideological sphere, progressive intellectuals had organized themselves into discussion groups which had been working together for several years before 1967. One was

---

[10] Bolesław Bierut (1892–1956): the iconic figure of Polish Stalinism, head of the Polish Workers Party from its inception in 1943 and prime minister from 1952 until his mysterious death in Moscow, where he had gone to participate in the Twentieth Congress of the CPSU.

[11] Antonín Novotný (1904–75): succeeded Slánský as head of the CPCZ (1951) and Gottwald as president (1957). He was ousted from both positions by reformers in 1968.

[12] Ota Šik economist and Central Committee member in the CPCZ, prime architect of the reforms of 1967–68.

the group around Radovan Richta, which was concerned with the scientific-technical revolution. Another group around Zdenék Mlynář was preparing reforms of the political system. There were several other groups too, working inside the party for specific reforms.

I think the Novotny regime falls into two distinct phases. In the first, prior to 1965, Novotny directed the repressive role of the party. But after the Twenty-Second Congress of the CPSU, when Stalin was once again condemned by Khrushchev, Novotny realized that it was impossible to stop the movement towards liberalization. Because there was a continuing trend towards de-Stalinization in the Soviet Union, he could not rely on Soviet support for a continuation of the old policies. He therefore, instead, decided to take the opportunity to get rid of the people most directly responsible for the trials. New people were brought in, and Novotny tried to present himself as the leader of the liberal tendency. But, of course, he could not succeed, since he could not wipe out his own responsibility for the political trials.

What role did the crisis in the Czechoslovak economy play in this whole development?

Certainly it played a role but I do not think it was a decisive one. Economic difficulties always have political repercussions, particularly in socialist countries. They expose the inability of the bureaucratic-centralist system to develop production and increase the standard of living of the masses, thus creating dissatisfaction both in the leading circles and among the population in general. Since the party leadership wants to score economic successes to maintain its political monopoly, it accepts some proposals for economic reform which it hopes will boost production and improve its competitive position vis-à-vis the capitalist economies. In this way Novotny endorsed the proposals for economic reform, but it was to the credit of Šik and other Czechoslovak economists that they clearly linked political with economic reform.

It is interesting to note that popular dissatisfaction with the economic situation in Czechoslovakia was greater in the more recent period, when living standards were much higher, than in the period immediately after the war when the masses believed that austerity was in the service of revolutionary ideas and socialist construction. By replacing revolutionary ideals with the promises of a consumer society, the bureaucrats only create trouble for themselves. On the other hand, it should be stated that an economic crisis itself is not sufficient to bring about a change in the situation since bureaucratic regimes have reserves with which to prevent an explosion caused by purely economic factors.

Perhaps we could turn now to the Prague Spring itself. What do you think of the criticism that has sometimes been made by Marxist analysts, that the Prague Spring involved liberalization—economic reforms, certain individual rights—rather than democratization, in the sense of real control by the workers over the decisive institutions of the State, genuine workers' power in the factory and in political life as a whole?

Yes, I am aware of this line of criticism, but I do not think that it corresponds exactly to the reality of what took place. I would say that the Czechoslovak 'new course' in the spring of 1968 was, in fact, directed more to democratization than to liberalization. The opposition was united in the fight against Novotny, because all agreed that there should be a division of functions between the first secretary of the party and the president, that Novotny was unable to solve the real problems of the country and should be replaced. But part of this anti-Novotny opposition, of course, merely wanted changes in personnel and improvements in the party's methods of work. This group would include people like Indra, Piller, Bil'ak and so on, and it had a majority in the Central Committee. But there was a minority, which would include Smrkovsky, Kriegel, Šik, Špacek, etcetera, who soon became aware that merely to replace Novotny by somebody else was not enough, and that real structural changes were necessary in order to come back to the sources, to renew socialism as a power of the people, to renew the dialogue between the party and the masses, to change the role of the party from administrative to inspirational hegemony. This group did not have a clear programme, because it was effectively impossible under Novotny for those in opposition to meet or discuss. Thus the whole development of the Prague Spring began almost spontaneously, after the palace revolution which overthrew Novotny, and it soon led to a permanent conflict between these two groups. The working class, initially, was rather passive, as a consequence of the depoliticization which it had undergone since 1948. The same was true of the peasants, who had never had any political representation in the system. The groups which reacted most quickly were the intellectuals, who had been prepared by their conflicts with Novotny in the previous years; the youth, in particular, the students, and to some extent the Slovaks. The working class on the whole adopted a wait-and-see attitude. They were not sure whether what had happened might not be some new trick. Moreover, they were also influenced by some of the older workers who said that the economy would collapse. They would have to work longer hours for the same pay, prices would rise and there might even be some unemployment. However, this initial passivity, or suspicion, on the part of the working class subsequently changed, when the workers had more information. I must stress that the demand for freedom of expression, particularly in Eastern Europe, is not at all just an intellectual's demand as some people, even some people on the Left, suppose—it is the basic condition for the workers and peasants to take part in politics. For example, the Czech workers were told that the factory legislation was for them, but they did not even know the financial balance sheet of their factories. They did not know if their factories were working with a surplus or a deficit, or what was planned for them. They had no information at all, even less than in a capitalist country. The explosion of information which followed the abolition of censorship set the working class in motion. This process accelerated after the adoption of the Action Programme of the party. This laid the basis for the workers' councils, though not very clearly, by initiating discussion on the forms in which the working class can really exercise power. This of course was a new problem for Czechoslovakia. There were only a few people who had studied the Yugoslav, Polish or Hungarian experience (nothing was published about them in Czechoslovakia) or who had read left literature from the West.

At all events, the discussion began and developed during May, June and July, with the creation of 'committees of initiative' which were to establish the workers' councils. The workers, for the first time for many years, found that their own speakers were able to appear on radio and television and write articles for the press. They saw that they were able to ask questions and obtain basic information. It was then possible for them to discuss the forms of the participation both through the workers' councils and through independent trade unions, through representation in the national committees, etcetera. In short, I think that there was a clear tendency towards democratization. I say 'tendency' because the Prague Spring was only the beginning. We can only say a tendency, we cannot say that it was definitely this or that. Do not forget the external pressure which started immediately after February. This was mainly directed not against intellectuals talking here and there, but against all measures which weakened the bureaucracy of the party and the state. The Russians were most upset by any talk about workers' self-management or workers' councils, of replacing state ownership by collective ownership, etcetera. On the latter question they said there was no difference; once the working class held state power, state ownership was the most socialist form of ownership in the means of production.

If there had been no Soviet intervention, I am convinced that it would sooner or later have come to a conflict within the Czechoslovakian 'new course'. For there were those who were for real, all-out democratization, and there were also those who were for certain concessions, certain measures of liberalization, but who wanted to maintain the existing structure. The latter were, of course, very much encouraged by the Soviet pressure. They said: 'we cannot do much more, because otherwise the Soviet Union will occupy us'. That was always the argument of those who were against full democratization. But I think the masses had been mobilized to such an extent, had become so active, that the tendency for a thoroughgoing reorganization would have won.

But what about the possibility that the economic policies would have led to the appearance of unemployment, as in Yugoslavia? Do you think then that a working-class opposition would have emerged within the party and ensured that this unemployment was abolished?

In that case, yes, but this argument about unemployment was, in fact, used a lot by the opponents of decentralization, that is to say by those in the economic apparatus of the party and the state. Of course, it may well be that certain factories or even certain branches of industry would have been closed because they were not economically viable. But I think that it would have been possible, in the framework of the socialist economy, to find alternative jobs for the workers. Of course, it is true that local sentiment is always strong. We had one case, for example, where they were proposing to shut down a small factory and said that the workers would all be given jobs in another one. But the latter was five kilometres away and the workers resisted, saying that they wanted to go on working in their own factory, even though it was a hundred years old and the machines were obsolete. Such minor social conflicts were inevitable. But I think that if the party had been able to draw up a real comprehensive plan for the country's future economic development, a plan altering the whole structure of the economy—which had simply been following the Soviet model, concentrating on heavy industry and neglecting branches such as chemicals, for which there were excellent conditions in Czechoslovakia—then it would have been possible to win over the mass of the workers to the new course. If the party had been able to transform the economy, something which clearly could not be done overnight but would take time, I think the people would have accepted certain temporary sacrifices; that is, if they had been convinced that this would be to their advantage in the long term. I think this was possible.

Perhaps there is a difference here between the Czechoslovakian and Yugoslav working classes. For if you look at the statistics published in 1968 about what the workers expected from the councils, there was no immediate demand for them to concentrate on raising wages. The workers said the councils should act to improve the management of the economy and make it more efficient; they should improve conditions of work, they should select really competent people to direct the factories, and they should also give more thought to planning. Nobody said 'now we can take all the money we have produced, and distribute it among ourselves'. One cannot eliminate that danger completely, but I think that in Czechoslovakia the people would have been able to solve this problem.

How about the tendency of a decentralized system to increase economic inequality? Do you think that would have happened in Czechoslovakia?

Yes, I think it would have happened and it was already happening even before 1968, as a reaction against the egalitarian system introduced in 1955. Under the latter, everybody in Czechoslovakia was within a narrow range of salaries. This means that there were no material rewards for responsible jobs, whether for intellectual work or for important posts in the factories. From the ideological point of view, you may say that this was progress. But in the transitional period of development of a socialist society, I think it is necessary to use both moral and material incentives. Precisely because a socialist society should favour technical and scientific development more than capitalist society does, its technical and scientific personnel should be paid accordingly. Of course, even in this period, inequalities did exist, in the sense that even if people had identical salaries, some of them—party leaders for instance—had many other facilities.

Certainly Czechoslovakia in the early 1960s did not give an impression of great equality—quite the opposite. High party officials had cars, large flats, a very comfortable existence in general at a time when this was not true of the mass of Czech workers. There were even special shops where party officials could buy foreign produce and other goods not generally available. This was not equality, was it?

I was coming to that. I was speaking before about the great majority of the population, and I think there was equality among them. For example, if you walked through Prague on Sunday, it was difficult to perceive who was a university professor, who was an engineer and who was a worker. All were roughly on the same level. But, of course, the exceptions were the party leaders. The party bureaucracy had a lot of special privileges. They had been far more numerous in the fifties; by the early sixties they were already diminishing, but they still certainly existed. For example there was a famous story about what happened in 1968, when the party treasurer was dismissed from the Central Committee and as a sort of defence he sent a letter to the Central Committee meeting (the letter has never been published, I might add) in which he enumerated how much money the various members of the leadership had received over and above their official salaries. The leaders named were obliged to pay into the party coffers all the party contributions which they had neglected to pay over the years on their earnings. In some cases this came to enormous sums of money. Even so, these privileges were far smaller in Czechoslovakia than in the Soviet Union or some other Communist countries.

But I was mainly speaking before about the majority of the population, and I think it is true perhaps that we were tending in 1968 towards a greater differentiation of salaries among workers, and also among the intellectuals and the peasants. This differentiation was tied to the real contribution they made to the national economy, or to the productivity of their work.

In general, it meant greater rewards for the intelligentsia, who had been undervalued and underpaid. I do not think this would lead to any very great contradictions, and I do not think that we could apply the same system in Czechoslovakia as in China, with everybody having basically the same salary. I do not think this could be viable in a modern European socialist society. What do you think?

The equality of 'to each according to his needs' is surely the goal of socialism, isn't it?

Yes, it is the goal.

We could come very close to that goal in advanced industrial economies today.

What do you mean by advanced? In Czechoslovakia, which was the most advanced industrial country in the socialist bloc, in fact there was a terrible shortage of the most basic goods. No poverty, of course, but you still cannot apply the formula 'to each according to his needs' until there is an abundance of goods.

Surely it is not just a question of shortages, it is also a question of a bureaucratic system of administration, which is not responsible to the workers and which must repress their initiative if it is to defend its monopoly of decision-making. Very often, large quantities of things are produced that nobody wants to consume. There is a sort of bureaucratic overproduction of goods that can't be sold.

That is not by chance. This is a necessary result of a centralized planning system which imposes the plan of production from a single centre without taking into consideration the real needs of the country. There I would like to take up another left criticism of the Prague Spring. I am referring to the view that Šik's economic reforms were designed to introduce a market economy in Czechoslovakia. This is a misunderstanding of the real aim of the reform. It was to combine the system of centralized state planning with responsiveness to certain pressures of the market; but market in the sense of socialist market, i.e. what the people really need. The aim is precisely to prevent the production of goods which are not needed and cannot be sold, and to ensure that goods which are needed are on the market.

The goal of revolutionary Marxists in a transitional society must be to rediscover the appropriate contemporary form of workers' power, corresponding to the Soviets in Russia during and after 1917. Do you think that this could have been one possible line of development of the Prague Spring, or was the latter merely an attempt to put a human face on bureaucratic socialism?

I think we have already discussed the question of whether the Prague Spring involved liberalization or democratization, and I said that its momentum was towards democratization. The expression 'socialism with a human face' was coined to make clear that the aim was to build a socialist society different from that which had been constructed in the Soviet Union and the other socialist countries. But it is true that there was a real difficulty in using basic Marxist concepts which had lost their original meaning entirely for most people. For example, 'Soviet power' had no meaning beyond that of the Soviet Union; a great power, symbol of 'order', with a specific economic, social and political system which was considered by some communists as a model.

Soviet power only lasted for a short period after the Revolution. The usual explanation is that this was due to foreign intervention and civil war, and it is true, of course, that these played their roles. But the real tragedy in the Soviet Union was that certain measures which were probably necessary as provisional measures for a certain period were then taken as real socialist ones. I am referring above all to the limitation of opposition inside the party—the ban on factions and discussion, which put the party on a semi-military footing appropriate only to a war situation.

Perhaps we could turn now to the question of foreign policy during the Prague Spring. Many people on the Left were concerned about this and felt that Czech foreign policy was tending towards increased rapprochement with the West and decreased emphasis on the anti-imperialist struggle. But was there at the same time any fundamental discussion on what a socialist foreign policy should be? After all one of the things that clearly began to happen during the Prague Spring was that a whole range of problems connected with the nature of Stalinism began to be examined. Many things were published which had previously been banned. Did this discussion of Stalinism go back to the theory of 'socialism in one country' and was there any discussion of foreign policy in terms of a return to proletarian internationalism?

There are two problems here. First, on the ideological level, that of discovering the deep roots of Stalinism. There was a lot of discussion about this and many articles were written on the subject. Moreover, we were able to read certain texts which had previously been prohibited; for example, *Literary Listy* translated Isaac Deutscher and even some texts by Trotsky and Bukharin were published and some articles about the Moscow trials. But such things were discouraged by the party leadership, on the grounds that they would create problems with the Soviet Union, whereas we should try for the time being to avoid anything which might worsen relations. It should never be forgotten, as left critics sometimes do forget, that the whole development of the Prague Spring took place in the shadow of Russian pressure. Furthermore, Moscow did not merely have the ability to exert economic, military and political pressure, it also had a fifth column inside Czechoslovakia, within the security forces, army and state apparatus. This constant Russian pressure certainly explains why some things happened more slowly than many people would have liked—but it would hardly have been able to prevent them permanently.

The second problem concerns foreign policy. This was, in fact, the field least affected by the new course of 1968. This may seem paradoxical, since the Russians justified the invasion at the time principally by the approaches which Czechoslovakia was supposedly making to West Germany, the United States, and so on. But, in fact, Czechoslovakia in 1968 was in total contrast, for example, to Romania, where internal policy remains basically Stalinist while there is a certain freedom and initiative in international politics. In Czechoslovakia in 1968 it was the contrary. There was innovation in internal politics, but on the international level there were no particularly new developments and Czechoslovakia declared quite sincerely that it basically supported the policies of the Soviet Union.

Of course, what was new was that international policy was no longer a monopoly of the party and the Ministry of Foreign Affairs. It began to be possible for people to express their own views about it, which they had not previously been allowed to do, and it began to be influenced by public opinion. For example, take the question of relations between Czechoslovakia and Israel. In the Arab countries it was sometimes alleged that Czechoslovakia was moving closer to Israel. This was not true. Czechoslovakia continued its support for the Arab countries and it continued to supply them with armaments. What was new was that certain people, particularly among the intelligentsia, asked why we had this one-sided policy in the Middle East. They said that we should re-examine whether this policy was really progressive; whether these Arab countries were really socialist as we were told, or whether they were not, in fact, nationalist countries; whether it was correct to have broken off diplomatic relations with Israel when we had diplomatic relations with the United States who were waging the war in Vietnam. At that time I was the chairman of the Foreign Affairs Commission of Parliament, and I defended party policy at many meetings on this topic. At the same time I realized that these critics were quite logical in asking why we had not broken off diplomatic relations when the United States had started to bomb North Vietnam. For this was a far more blatant case of imperialist aggression than the situation in the Middle East. Moreover, Communists were in prison in several of the Arab countries. As for West Germany, we only asked them to annul the Munich Agreement. Scheel was invited to Prague and I received him in my capacity of chairman of the Foreign Affairs Commission.[13] The Soviet Union attacked his visit, calling him a 'war-

---

[13] Walter Scheel (1919–): West German politician instrumental in the formation of the SPD–Free Democrat coalition (1969), in which he served as deputy chancellor and foreign minister, pursuing a policy of detente towards the Eastern bloc.

monger', but only one year later the 'war-monger' went on a friendly visit to Moscow.

Czechoslovakia continued its foreign policy on issues like Vietnam. True, not much popular enthusiasm was shown in support of Vietnam or Cuba, but this was because any popular initiative was quickly absorbed or neutralized by the State. Furthermore, if you are allowed to protest against the political repression in Greece or Spain, but not against student arrests in Poland or Czechoslovakia, you become easily demoralized. For example, the students once decided to collect money for Vietnam following a suggestion from the IUS, but the party came out against it. It was said that as the government had already given money to Vietnam, the best way the people could help Vietnam was to increase production. Again, during the Bay of Pigs invasion, the foreign students in Prague took the initiative and called for a demonstration at the American Embassy. Many Czech students joined in, but it was stopped by the police in case it created problems with the Americans. In the course of time such expressions of international solidarity lost their attraction. The foreign policy at the popular level was characterized by confusion. For example, during the May Day Parade in 1968, some students were carrying placards saying 'Long Live Al Fatah' while others shouted 'Long Live Israel'. For some people, supporting Israel meant opposing the official party policy and that of the Soviet Union. This confusion had its roots in the fact that real problems were never discussed publicly or with the masses.

To conclude the question of foreign policy, there was no shift in the basic alignment. Some people did feel, however, that it should become more independent, that Czechoslovakia should not only repeat what the Soviet Union said.

Could we move on now to the Soviet military intervention? What, in your view, was the decisive reason for the Russian decision?

I think it was the fear of the Soviet bureaucracy that the Czechoslovakian experiment would overcome its difficulties and succeed in creating a different kind of socialist society. For this would have exerted a powerful force of attraction on the neighbouring countries of East Europe and threatened Soviet hegemony over them.

I don't think the Russians really believed for a moment that Czechoslovakia was threatened by invasion from West Germany. Nor do I think that they really believed there was any danger of counterrevolution. They knew the situation, and they knew that right-wing forces were much too weak to take to the streets in Czechoslovakia. Moreover, there was no intervention when the Czech party was genuinely under pressure in March and April. At this time, the party had lost the initiative. There was great pressure from below, but the party had no programme, until the Action Programme was published at the end of April. The 'Progressive Group' had not yet been formed. There was an explosion of information and almost complete freedom of expression; the Communist Party was under fire and on the defensive. In this situation, the Russians did not intervene to prevent counter-revolution. With the publication of the Action Programme and the adoption of measures showing that it really meant to carry this programme out—I am thinking of the law on rehabilitation, the plan for the establishment of factory councils, the new party statutes, etcetera—the party won back the initiative. Thanks to the external pressure, it even became a real national force supported by the majority of the people. When the decision was taken in June to call a party congress, it was already clear that the congress would consolidate the position of the Dubček leadership.[14] There was no danger of any split in the party itself, because the conservative group was quite small and isolated. It was clear that the congress would give the party even more strength to carry out its policy. I think it was precisely this that the Russians feared. They saw that the new Central Committee, with its new statutes, would be much more difficult to control than the old one—which was after all still unchanged from Novotny's time. I think a definite date for the invasion was decided when the Russians realized that the date of the Congress could not be changed. At the Čierna meeting between the two politburos at the beginning of August, the main pressure from Brezhnev was to postpone the congress, which was already convened for 9 September 1968, and to put through certain changes of personnel before the congress took place. It should be stressed that the Czechoslovak party did not seek to present its new course as a model for other countries. On the contrary. Some intellectuals went on about the eyes of the world being on Czechoslovakia, but the party was concerned to dispel any idea that it was setting itself up as a model. But the Soviet Union was well aware that if the Czech experiment was allowed to succeed, it would inevitably have repercussions in the other socialist countries. It was not accidental that Gomułka, Ulbricht and Shelest, the first secretary of the Ukranian Communist Party—that is, the leaders of three countries bordering on Czechoslovakia—should have been the most enthusiastic proponents of intervention.[15]

Who else was pressing for it in the Soviet Union? Do you think the Army command was enthusiastic about it?

That is difficult to say. I think it was seen more as a political than as a military necessity. But the Army was certainly in favour of the invasion. Soviet

---

[14] Alexander Dubček (1921–92), from 1963 leader of the CPCZ in Slovakia, where the signs of Spring came earlier than in Prague, and first secretary of the Czechoslovakian party in 1968–69. He was expelled from the party in 1970 and returned to private life. He served as chair of the Czecho-Slovak Federal Assembly in 1989–92.

[15] Walter Ulbricht (1893–1973), leader of the East Germany Socialist Unity Party from 1950 to 1971.

officers with whom we talked after the intervention claimed that Stalin's greatest mistake, after his failure to prevent the German attack in 1941, was his failure to incorporate the East European countries as constituent republics of the Soviet Union in 1945.

But quite apart from whatever the Russian military may think, the Soviet leadership certainly sees the presence of the Red Army as the only real guarantee of their political control over the other socialist countries. Czechoslovakia was one of the few countries with no Soviet troops on its territory. Novotny himself has said that he was asked several times to accept Soviet military bases, but that he had always refused. The Prague Spring provided a pretext to put Soviet troops into Czechoslovakia. The party bureaucracy really does consider the army as the best means of controlling the Eastern European countries; and as long as there were no Soviet troops in Czechoslovakia they were uneasy.

Incidentally, it is interesting to learn from the Piller Report that this issue had arisen as early as 1949, when Rákósi and Bierut wrote to Stalin and to Gottwald expressing their concern about developments in Czechoslovakia.[16] They pointed out that the Czechs had so far failed to discover any agents of imperialism in the party and they claimed that Czechoslovakia was the weakest link since there were no units of the Soviet Army on Czech soil.

Could you tell us something about the discussions which were taking place inside the Czech party before the invasion? About the possibility of invasion, about the appropriate response to the invasion threat, and about what could be done to make it less likely?

In fact I think there were very few people in responsible positions in the party who really considered the possibility of Soviet military intervention. First of all I think it was probably a mistake for Dubček to hide the true extent of Soviet pressure from the masses. It meant that nobody was aware of how great the pressure was. Of course, there were rumours, there were reports of articles hostile to the Czech development, but the daily pressure which was exerted by the Soviet leadership on Dubček and the other leaders was not known even to the party activists.

What was your own estimate of Soviet reaction to the developments in Czechoslovakia?

I knew something of the way they were thinking, but only through my personal contacts in the Soviet Union. My case was not typical and the position of the Soviet Union was not discussed within the Central Committee

---

[16] Mátyás Rákósi (1892–1971): Stalinist leader of the Hungarian Communist Party (later the Hungarian Working People's Party) between 1948 and 1956.

in a realistic way. At the Dresden meeting in March 1968 the first strongly critical reaction to the Czechoslovakian development was expressed by the other members of the Warsaw Pact. The Western press published some articles about this. Those responsible for radio, television and the press were convened to meet Dubček on his return from this meeting. He told us that economic relations and plans for development and cooperation were discussed, but he did not mention Soviet pressure. I asked Dubček whether the Western newspaper reports were correct in saying that Czechoslovakia had been criticized at Dresden. He replied that they were not. Later, after the invasion, Dubček was criticized by other members of the Czech delegation at Dresden who said that he had hidden from us the criticism by Ulbricht, Gomułka and the others. Dubček then replied that it was true that he had concealed this from us, but that to do so had been the unanimous agreement of the Czech delegation. Novotny was still in the Praesidium and they did not want to encourage the forces he represented; furthermore it was Dubček's sincere opinion during this whole period that to reveal the extent of Soviet pressure would create anti-Soviet feeling, and this he wished to avoid. He did his best to stop rumours about the Soviet position circulating, for this reason. Even in those party circles which were somewhat more aware of the real situation, there was no thought of a military intervention, but rather of some economic pressure or blockade. Dubček himself, and many other people including myself, were convinced that since Stalin had not dared to occupy Yugoslavia, then Brezhnev would not imagine he could do this to Czechoslovakia. After all Stalin at that time was militarily very strong and enjoyed much greater prestige in the international Communist movement than the present Soviet leaders. We thought that after the Twentieth Party Congress and after what happened in Hungary, a crudely military intervention was no longer possible. Dubček personally was convinced that the Soviet Union would exert all kinds of pressure, but would not go this far.

However, there were people like General Prchlik, who was head of the Department for Defence and Security, who wished to submit to the leadership a paper outlining the alternatives in case of a Soviet invasion. The army and the security forces had discovered that the objective of the Soviet Army manoeuvres in Czechoslovakia in June and July had been to put itself in a position where it could control our communications systems. They had made maps of how this system worked, they had laid cables underground and they had established the location of all telephone and postal facilities, including those only used by state organizations. This was known to the security forces, though since some of the security officers were Soviet agents there were conflicting reports. Moreover, the existence of General Prchlik's suggestion for a contingency plan was passed on to the Soviet Embassy through these people. This led to an immediate Soviet reaction. They asked how it was possible for a man capable of such a provocation to be head of the armed forces and a member of the Central Committee. There was an official diplomatic note from the Soviet Union directed against Prchlik, taking as a pretext the fact that he had called at a press conference for some reforms in the Warsaw Pact—very minor reforms which were later, in 1970, to be adopted. Dubček decided to sacrifice Prchlik and dismissed him from his post. I think this was a decisive moment. From this point on the Soviet Union knew that Czechoslovakia would not attempt to defend itself in the case of a military intervention. Prchlik was sacrified as a symbol of our full confidence in the Soviet Union.

The question will be debated for many years whether any course of action could have been taken to avert the Soviet intervention. Some people in the party argued that it could have been avoided if Czechoslovakia had behaved in a more compliant manner. I do not believe this. The experience of Yugoslavia and Romania shows that the only possibility of deterring the Soviet Union would have been to tell the Soviet leaders clearly that although we were willing to continue any discussions and wished [Czechoslovakia] to remain a loyal member of the Warsaw Pact, yet in the case of any attempt at a military solution, Czechoslovakia would defend herself and would mobilize the people and army. The failure to do this was to some extent an expression of the absence of a clear attitude towards democratization which we have already discussed. Our leaders hesitated to mobilize the masses and to give a clear lead to the country, to distribute arms to the people and declare that we would not be moved by threats. I personally am convinced that if such a line of action had been taken by Dubček, the Soviet Union would not have dared to launch the invasion. They would, of course, have continued to exert other types of pressure, but they would not have gone further than that. Some people said that any talk of resistance would simply goad the Soviet Union to extreme action and that Moscow was ready to destroy Prague. But if the Soviet representatives made threats of this sort, then it was just the application of psychological pressure. After all they did not want to create a Vietnam for themselves—it is not so easy for them to envisage massacring thousands of people in Central Europe. The course of action adopted by the Czechoslovak leaders was incapable of opposing the invasion. It showed a serious lack of revolutionary spirit.

What was the situation when the invasion took place? Presumably as soon as it happened it was necessary to decide how to react? At what level was that decision taken and what forms of resistance were discussed inside the party?

We learnt of the invasion only after it had happened, at 11.20 p.m. on 21 August, while a meeting of the Praesidium was still in progress. We know today that certain members of the Praesidium were aware of what was about to happen—Bil'ak, Indra and some others.[17] It seems that there may have

---

[17] Vasil Bil'ak (1917–): a lifelong party functionary sidelined for just a year in 1968–69,

been some misunderstanding between them and the Soviet Union. The pro-Soviet elements in the leadership had hoped to impose a resolution on the Praesidium declaring that there was a danger of counterrevolution and that the party congress, which was imminent and would have consolidated the Dubček leadership, would have to be postponed. However, this resolution had not been voted on at the time of the invasion. Some people say that the plan was not properly coordinated because while it was one o'clock in Moscow it was eleven o'clock in Prague. However, whether or not this played a part, the Praesidium, on learning of the invasion, adopted a resolution condemning it and making it clear that no intervention had been invited. The Praesidium asked the army not to resist and made arrangements for convening a meeting of the Central Committee next day.

Was the possibility of armed resistance discussed in the Praesidium?

No, not at all. The discussion turned on whether the invasion should be condemned. In fact the biggest discussion was about an amendment to the effect that the invasion was a violation of international law and of the norms governing the relations between socialist states. I think it is an illustration of the weakness of the leadership that they condemned the invasion, but without making any appeal to the people or letting them know what they should do. I was in the Central Committee building that night. They were saying that all was lost; the airport had been taken, tanks were moving forward everywhere and units from the airport were already beginning to surround the Central Committee building. The possibility of armed resistance had already been lost, though there were some in the army who were thinking that they should fight and some generals were removed from their posts because of this. But nothing could be done. When the president, who was chief of the armed forces, had given the order to put up no resistance, then the officers had to accept it. The time for contemplating armed resistance was earlier.

What was now possible was to confront the occupiers with a political resistance which they could not ignore and to deny them any political solution on their terms. This was the time for the party leadership to mobilize the masses, to convene the party congress and to study other forms of action such as a general strike. Instead the leaders merely declared that they were against the occupation and did nothing but wait in the Central Committee building to be captured by the Soviet Army. Until six or seven o'clock in the morning they had the opportunity to leave the building by a secret exit of which the Soviet units were unaware. We wanted Dubček to leave, to go to

and an active supporter of Soviet invasion plans. With Alois Indra and three others, he signed the letter of 'invitation' to the Soviet authorities. Bil'ak and Indra were to be members of the triumvirate designated to supplant Dubček.

the CKD factory in Prague 9 and to organize political action from there.[18] But Dubček thought that as they were the leaders of the party and the country they should stay at their posts and do their duty like the captain staying on the bridge of a sinking ship. Dubček was a very honest man and he thought he should sacrifice himself for others. But he was thinking legalistically; a revolutionary leader would have acted in a quite different way, he would have gone to the factories and mobilized the workers. This was proved by what happened. On the initiative of the City Committee of the party in Prague the scheduled congress of the party was convened for an extraordinary meeting. All the delegates for this congress had, of course, been elected prior to the invasion. The congress was held on 23 August in a proletarian district of Prague and there was nothing the occupying forces could do about it. The Russians did not want to send armoured cars into that district to shoot the workers. But although the convening of the Congress was to be a great success, there was still no clear decision on the resistance. Over 1,200 delegates attended the Congress, which the occupation forces did not at all expect. At the Congress there was a long discussion as to whether to declare a general strike or only a one-hour strike. It is very interesting that many were afraid of declaring a general strike on the grounds that it was the workers' ultimate weapon and should not be lightly used. In the event the Congress decided to call for a one-hour general strike. It was observed throughout the country and was a full success, but of course it could not have the same effect as a proper general strike. On the other hand, the Soviet Army did find itself in a political vacuum.

Their attempt to create a so-called workers' and peasants' government with a collaborator at its head did not succeed because of the universal opposition of the masses and because the Congress had made clear that the party was overwhelmingly against the invasion. At this point no potential collaborator had the courage to take on his shoulders the odious task of abetting the occupation. When the Soviet authorities realized that they had failed to secure the basis for a collaboration regime, they invited President Svoboda to go to Moscow. When news of this plan came through we were at the congress in Prague 9. We tried to convince Svoboda from the congress not to go to Moscow. He was still in his official residence in Prague Castle, and we spoke to him by phone. It was clear to us that the Soviet plan was in difficulties since they had no one through whom they could control the country politically. By this time Dubček and other top party leaders had been kidnapped and taken by plane to the Ukraine, where they were held at a military airport. If the occupying powers had succeeded in establishing the so-called revolutionary government, then Dubček and the others would have all been shot as counter-revolutionaries. But since they failed, the Soviet leaders were forced to bring them to Moscow after about five days. They needed to

---

[18] A locomotive works on the outskirts of the city.

negotiate with someone and they needed to find some leadership which would accept the occupation. The solidity of the resistance in Czechoslovakia itself meant that they were forced to bargain with these people whom they had intended to destroy. We tried unsuccessfully to persuade Svoboda not to go to Moscow, pointing out to him that it was not us who were in difficulties but rather the occupying forces. The Soviet Union was being condemned by the whole world, especially by various sections of the communist and workers' movement itself. Although they had invaded Czechoslovakia, they had no control over it. The occupying armies were in a mess; they had shortages of essential supplies, including food. The ordinary Soviet soldier was very confused and demoralized. Everywhere our people were asking them why they were invading a brother socialist country and the Russian soldiers did not know what to answer. There were a number of suicides of Soviet soldiers at this time. A very impressive mass response to the occupation had developed. But although party militants were very active in this, it was difficult for us to draw the full political advantage from it. The leaders in whom the masses had confidence were cut off from them and could not be fully aware of what was happening in Czechoslovakia. If Dubček had been with us in the CKD factory at the Congress and if there had been a full general strike, then the situation would have been very different. I don't say that the Soviet forces would have immediately withdrawn, but the relationship of forces would have been very different. Of course all these problems belong to the past, but they are also problems of general revolutionary strategy. The lesson of Czechoslovakia is that nothing can really be achieved without the action of the masses.

There was, of course, an explosion of popular resistance in the days following the invasion. To what extent did the party organize this?

Those who were most active in organizing the resistance were party members but, in fact, we had no instructions to do what we did. For example, we very quickly developed a series of underground radio stations and newspapers. These were able to report the real progress of the occupation and the difficulties the occupying authorities were running into, to report the worldwide reaction to what happened and to give orientation to our people. But this was all organized on their own account by those who worked in radio, television and the other media. For they found they could enlist the support of citizens in every quarter, in the army and in the state organizations. Of course there were some agents of the occupying power, mainly members of the old security forces, but we were quickly able to neutralize their activities. The numbers of the cars they were using were broadcast over the radio and they found it very difficult to operate. Editors were arranging things for themselves and making sure that they could continue to produce their papers. The fact that the party congress came out so clearly against the invasion and accepted responsibility for opposing it gave it great moral strength and popular support. The occupying forces had an enormous concentration of military firepower, but so long as we maintained a solid front against them they had no political presence in the situation. It is true that they could kill a lot of people, but this did not give them the control of the situation they wanted. At the same time I believe that the resistance could have become much better coordinated and the force that existed could have been organized. But instead this phase of popular resistance was brought to an end by the protocol signed in Moscow between our leaders and the Soviet leaders. For the Czechoslovak Communist Party this was the beginning of the end. The people had been ready for resistance, they were ready to oppose the occupation by all forms.

The leaders of the party in Moscow were cut off from this development. But even if they thought we were defeated, it would have been better not to sign this Protocol. It would have been better to remain as symbols of a new *cause*, which could arise again when circumstances permitted, than to sign this political death warrant. From this point Dubček and the others who signed were being used by the Soviet Union to keep people quiet and to help them get control of the situation again. Yes, they were under intolerable pressure, but the course they adopted was to lead to their own destruction just as surely. At that time the Russians needed them because the people still had confidence in them. All those who were suspected of having collaborated with the invasion were completely discredited. The Moscow Protocol gave time for a thoroughly collaborationist element to establish itself under the protection of Dubček and soon to displace him. Initially, Dubček's prestige was so great that nearly everyone was prepared to go along with what had been done. On 31 August, the day after his return from Moscow, a meeting of the Central Committee was called. This was the old Central Committee but enlarged by the presence of eighty of the delegates to the party congress. Under the terms of the Moscow agreement the party congress was held to have been illegal. By enlarging the old Central Committee, Dubček tried to get round this by some compromise. At this meeting only one representative spoke out against the Moscow agreement. Others may have doubted the wisdom of signing the protocol, but they still had confidence in Dubček. After all, he wanted the best for our people and they felt they should not complicate his task. So when this young man from Moravia said we must destroy the Moscow agreement, they did not allow discussion of this. We may conclude that there were three mistakes made in the course of this whole development. The first mistake was that the leadership did not mobilize against the possibility of an invasion before it took place, and make it clear to the Soviet Union that it would not just be a walkover. The second was that they waited in the Central Committee instead of going to the factories and organizing resistance. The third was that they signed the Moscow agreement.

What has happened to the Communist Party now, more than three years later, and what role will it play in the future?

Well, I would say that the whole process of normalization has made it into a quite different party now. Half a million of the most active members have been expelled or have left. There has been a return of the old Stalinist structure and methods of administration. It is not by chance that they are again glorifying Gottwald, who let his own friends be arrested and executed by Stalin. The Czechoslovak party is now really a branch of the Soviet party. Of course there were always remnants of Stalinism in our party. It cannot be said that this current development has just dropped from the heavens. In 1968 there were the elements for a split in the party. But at that time the new majority wanted to introduce a new statute whereby the minority could maintain its position and fight for it. The Stalinists were in a minority, but we didn't want to expel them; we wanted them to fight for their ideas, but with arguments.

What implications do you think this transformation of the party has for the future?

It means, and I think this applies elsewhere as well as in Czechoslovakia, that basic changes will not come from inside the party. Since the defeat of the Prague Spring the development of the party is such that a socialist renewal could not come from inside this new Stalinist party. This does not mean that all who are in it are completely lost, but those who would like things to change are in a minority and they are passive. Of course, we should try to find allies within the party, within the trade unions and other official organizations. An opposition always develops inside the bureaucracy since it is not capable of solving the problems that confront it. Even when it knows how such a problem can be solved, it cannot implement its solution because it does not have the support of the masses on whom all solutions depend. Generally these parties are very isolated from the masses.

What then is your estimate of the significance of liberalizing trends within the governing bureaucracy?

The goal of revolutionary socialists and the goal of the liberalizers are quite different. But that does not mean that the path to an anti-bureaucratic revolution may not lie through some sort of period of liberalization in these countries. Such a liberalization at least allows the workers, the young people and the intellectuals the chance to organize themselves. In such a period they can find themselves; they can work out and express their aims before the confrontation. Otherwise there is a danger that a spontaneous explosion—for example between workers and police—will lead to bloodshed, but not to any political change. In fact such an explosion could even be used by reactionary and counter-revolutionary forces. This is a complicated problem because the political consciousness of the masses has been very much weakened and confused by the bureaucratic regimes. I think the people have first of all to clarify their ideas in a freer climate if they are to carry through a real revolution inside the revolution.

How do you conceive the revolution needed in Czechoslovakia and similar countries?

I think the countries that call themselves socialist are, in fact, some transitional form of society—it is a sort of state socialism dominated by a bureaucracy which is not controlled by the workers. The path of revolution in these countries will be different from its course in a capitalist country. In some ways the position of the ruling stratum is weaker since it is not built into the structure of production; the bourgeoisie has been eliminated and basic industry has already been nationalized. The problem is to defeat the bureaucracy and to destroy the bureaucratic structures. I would call this a revolution inside the revolution.

As to how we will organize for this new revolution, we have been asking ourselves recently whether the future belongs to the system of political parties or not. The result of the analysis made by my friends in Czechoslovakia is that the old conception of the revolutionary party is not appropriate any longer to our situation. Lenin's theory of the party played a certain historical role, but we think that for us a much more suitable form of organization would be the movement. This would have a common ideological platform but not the rigid structure of the party. I am sure that the moving force in the renewal of socialism in our countries will be really democratic mass organizations; trade unions, workers' councils, local soviets and other forms of direct democracy.

Surely there is no contradiction between, on the one hand, workers' councils and soviets, as the form of organization of the revolutionary state, and, on the other, revolutionary parties which act as a force within these institutions? In the West we have had experience of amorphous, decentralized movements and they usually turn out to be both undemocratic and ineffective. In the context of a soviet or workers' council, political parties could ensure the clarification of different policies and platforms: they would mean that such bodies could follow policies rather than personalities. In this sense political parties are surely complementary to institutions of popular power?

Well, I think a movement could develop political platforms in the same way. You know it is only a question of what we understand by the traditional political party. I agree with you that there is no contradiction between democratically organized parties and soviets or workers' councils. But I had in mind first of all the existing socialist countries and the existing Communist Parties which monopolize all politics in a Stalinist fashion. I know that in Czechoslovakia the people will never willingly accept this system. All these parties are organized in more or less the same way and all of them impose themselves as the leading force in all state institutions and mass organizations. A democratically organized party would operate in a quite different way and could not assume that it would automatically be the leading force in society; if it wanted this position it would have to win it by gaining the confidence of the people. You have got to remember that revolutionaries in our countries are not confronted with a capitalist social structure. In our society there are no basic contradictions between social classes. This means that if we have several parties and movements they would not correspond to different class viewpoints; they would all operate within the framework of socialism, but they would have different conceptions of how socialism should be built.

It is a remarkable fact that oppositions do now exist in Eastern Europe in nearly every country. Even in the Soviet Union there are underground journals and a core of open oppositionists for the first time since the twenties. Do you think there are any parallels between the new opposition which is emerging today and the main oppositional currents in the twenties and thirties?

Well, the situation has completely changed so naturally there are many differences. The Soviet Union's position in the world has altered greatly and the whole society is now much more developed. But there are perhaps some underlying similarities all the same. Firstly they were attacking the same system that we are attacking, the Stalinist system—but whereas they opposed it in its infancy we are now opposing it in its old age. This difference is already clear. The bureaucracy is no longer so effective as it was in the old days. It does not have such a clear conception of where it is going, it cannot accomplish the tasks it sets itself, and it has not been able simply to eliminate all its opponents. The second similarity is that our generation has again recovered the feeling that the situation can be changed. The old revolutionaries, the old Bolsheviks, had this feeling because they had made a revolution. This gave them the courage to struggle for what they believed in despite the ruthlessness of the bureaucracy. Today we again feel that there can and must be a change and that we can help to bring it about. But for us the revolution does not lie in the past—it lies in the future.

K. Damodaran (1904–76) came to Marxism after early experience of militancy and imprisonment in the cause of Indian independence. He was one of the founders of the Kerala unit of the Communist Party of India (CPI) in 1937, and went on to serve on the party's National Council and Central Executive, and in the Rajya Sabha, the upper house of the Indian legislature, in the 1960s.

Damodaran travelled widely in his various party capacities, visiting most of the Communist world and later Western Europe. He had an exceptional appetite and facility for languages and was a prolific writer, publishing in his native Malayalam and also English and Hindi. His many works included popularizing manuals, translations, scholarly studies in Indian philosophy, in which he had taken a particular interest from early days, and agitprop dramas.

In 1964, the CPI suffered a major split, significant numbers of its leaders and a greater proportion of its militants leaving to form the CPI (Marxist). Refusing the proffered logic of the secession, Damodaran stayed with the CPI. He gave this interview in 1975, a year before his death.

K. Damodaran

Memoir of an Indian Communist

Why do you think the Communist Party of India took such a long time to establish itself? What was its early activity and what were its relations with the nationalist movement? Could it be that the infamous Third Period of the Comintern also seriously disoriented Indian Communists by isolating them at a critical phase from the mainstream of the nationalist movement?

My personal experience in this period was restricted to Kerala and I will concentrate on that, but of course the line of march throughout the country was essentially the same. I joined the CPI when it was illegal. It had been banned in 1934 after the Bombay Strike wave, which included a general strike of the textile industry. As a result even the distribution of party literature was extremely uneven and the question of organized internal discussion did not arise. But you must also understand that the CPI was an extremely small organization nationally in that period. In fact the CPI as a national political force only began to develop in 1935–36 after the worst excesses of the Third Period. The politics of the Comintern certainly played a not unimportant part in disorienting the Communist groups which existed regionally in the twenties and early thirties. The Comintern leaders completely underestimated the relative *autonomy* of the Indian bourgeoisie and its political instrument, the Indian Congress. They went through a stage of equating the nationalist movement and imperialism. Kuusinen, Stalin's spokesman on colonial questions, and many writers in the *Inprecor* went so far as to say that the Indian National Congress was a counterrevolutionary force in the struggle against imperialism and the Congress Socialists were branded as 'social fascists'. The attacks on nationalist leaders in the late twenties and thirties certainly were couched in an ultra-left rhetoric and were parroted by the different communist groups which existed in India. However it is not sufficient simply to blame the Comintern: after all, the Chinese party also suffered from the wrong advice of the Comintern, but they recovered and finally captured power.

So while not ignoring the importance of the subjective failures we have to look deeper and, when we do, we shall find that there was an objective basis for the existence of a strong and stable bourgeois democratic party like the Indian Congress. This was the development of an Indian bourgeoisie which was *not* a comprador bourgeoisie and which even in the heyday of the Raj enjoyed a certain independence. Its interests clashed on many occasions with those of British imperialism. The Indian capitalists developed at an unusually rapid rate when Britain was tied down by inter-imperialist wars. The existence of this bourgeoisie side by side with a civil service and army that involved many Indians created the basis for the existence of a colonial state apparatus which succeeded in tying down the Congress to its structures and ensuring a smooth transition when the time for Independence came. So Indian communists confronted a unique economic and political structure which they never succeeded in analysing properly.

While the CPI was in fact properly established in 1934–35 its development was uneven. For instance the first communist group in Kerala was organized only in 1937 by five comrades including Namboodiripad, Krishna Pillai and myself.[1] We decided that we should not openly call ourselves the Communist Party but win ourselves a base inside the Congress Socialists. I think that this was correct, but it did not happen nationally. Accordingly we disseminated communist literature inside the Congress Socialist Party, which itself worked inside the Congress, as an organized grouping. Our influence inside the Kerala Congress was not negligible: Namboodiripad, A. K. Gopalan, Krishna Pillai and, later, myself were all recognized leaders of the Kerala Congress and we held office on the leading committees. Utilizing our position in the Congress we organized trade unions, peasants' organizations, students' unions, and associations of progressive and anti-imperialist writers. We organized a regular Communist Party in Kerala only at the end of 1939. It was our mass work coupled with the fact that we were identified with the nationalist aspirations of the people which undoubtedly played a significant role in ensuring that Kerala became one of the important strongholds of post-Independence communism.

When were you first arrested as a Communist?

In 1938. I was at that time a member of the party, but in the eyes of the masses was still regarded as a nationalist agitator. What brought about my arrest on this occasion was a speech I made to a conference of Youth Leaguers in Trivandrum. I had been asked to preside over the meeting and

---

[1] E. M. S. Namboodiripad, known as E.M.S. (1909–98): became Communist chief minister of Kerala—and the first non-Congress chief minister anywhere in India—in 1956. He sided with the CPI(M) in 1964, later becoming the party's general secretary. Krishna Pillai (1906–48), an exceptionally talented organizer and a poet, died accidentally while in hiding in 1948.

in my opening speech I mounted a diatribe against imperialism: I attacked British imperialism, and the Maharajah of Travancore as embodying the oppression which was being meted out by British imperialism. The right-wing leaders of the State Congress had been saying that the Maharajah was a great man and it was only his local satraps who were to blame and were misleading him. I attacked this absurd concept head on and utilized the experiences of the French and Russian revolutions, observing that their method of dealing with the monarchy was rather more effective than that of the Congress leaders! I also explained to the meeting the necessity of involving the peasants and workers in the struggle and concluded with the slogan of 'Inqilab Zindabad' (Long Live Revolution) which was joyfully taken up by the whole meeting. That same day there were anti-imperialist demonstrations and clashes with the police in Trivandrum. The next morning I was naturally arrested, together with the Youth League leaders. We spent two or three months in prison and were then released. From then on prison became a regular part of my existence.

Could you briefly describe the impact of developments which were taking place in the Soviet Union on Indian communism? After all, the period we are discussing was crucial: virtually the entire leadership of the Bolsheviks at the time of the Revolution was physically eliminated by Stalinist terror as the prelude to a bureaucratic dictatorship which established its total monopoly over all spheres of public life. What was the impact of all this on Indian communists?

As far as I am concerned I can speak mainly about Kerala. I was not part of the All-India party apparatus at that time and, as I have already explained, objective conditions—leave alone subjective ones—did not permit horizontal contact with party members in other parts of the country. I joined the party just before the theses of the Seventh Congress of the Comintern, the Dimitrov theses on the Popular Front strategy. It was after the Seventh Congress that Stalin became well known in India in the sense that he became the 'Great Leader'. In fact the theses did coincide—better late than never—with the need for us to have a united front with the Congress against the British. The sectarian ultra-leftism of the 1929–34 period had isolated us and this was seen as an attempt to correct the mistakes. For us it was a step in the right direction. Not so much in Kerala, but in Bombay and Calcutta. After all in Kerala there was no Communist Party in the early thirties. When people ask me why the CPI became so strong in non-industrialized Kerala as compared to Bombay, I reply that the main reason is that there was no CPI in Kerala in the 1930–33 period and so it was possible to start anew. Most of the Communist leaders in Kerala today were totally immersed in the Civil Disobedience movement launched by the Congress in 1930–32. It explains how they won the support of the masses and were able to shatter the Congress monopoly in a later phase.

But to answer your main question: you must understand that the communists in India were not seriously educated in Marxism. To give you one example: Lenin's theses on the colonial question were not known to Indian communists till the end of the fifties. The Seventh Congress line of Anti-Imperialist United Front in India was considered not as a break from the past but a continuation of the Sixth Congress line and was explained as a tactical change necessitated by the changes in the national and international situation. You may consider it strange that the disastrous colonial theses of the Sixth Congress were translated into Malayalam and other Indian languages precisely in this period. But in practice the United Front was a break from the left-sectarian line. The new line implemented by the party under the able leadership of P. C. Joshi helped us to advance rapidly.[2] The CPI for the first time became a political force with considerable influence in the Congress, among the Congress Socialists and in the mass movements. The rival trade unions were united into a single All-India Trade Union Congress (AITUC) in which the CPI became the leading force. The All-India Kisan Sabha, the All-India Students' Federation and the All-India Progressive Writers' Association came into existence. The Communists played an important role in uniting them and leading their struggles. National unity against imperialism, left unity to counter the compromising and anti-struggle policies of the right-wing, socialist unity to strengthen left unity, the CPI as the basis of socialist unity, mass organizations and mass struggles to build and strengthen the united anti-imperialist front—these were the watchwords and positive elements in the new line. This line certainly brought results and helped to build and strengthen an All-India Communist Party. The membership of the party increased from about 150 in 1934 to more than 3,000 in 1939 and its influence multiplied at an even more rapid rate. But these were also the years of Stalinism.

We were told that Stalin was the 'great teacher', the 'guiding star' who was building socialism in the USSR and the leader of world socialism. And being both new to communism and relatively unschooled in Marxism and Leninism I accepted what I was told. There is a tradition in Indian politics of political gurus enlightening the masses and this tradition suited Stalinism completely. Hence we could accept anything and everything that we were told by the party elders who themselves were dependent for their information exclusively on Moscow. This was the atmosphere in which I was brought up as a communist. However, there were some comrades who were extremely perturbed at the information on the massacres which was coming out of Moscow. Philip Spratt, one of the communists sent to help build the CPI from Britain, became so demoralized and disillusioned with Stalinism that he abandoned communism altogether and became a liberal humanist

---

[2] P. C. Joshi (1907–80): first general secretary of the PCI (1935–47), removed after the party's adoption of the Calcutta Thesis and the turn to armed struggle.

and towards the end of his life an anti-communist. He was an excellent comrade who played an invaluable role in helping us at an early stage. The Congress left wing was also extremely critical of the purges taking place in Moscow and some of their leaders were extremely disgusted by the propaganda contained in the CPI front journal *National Front*, which depicted Trotsky as a poisonous cobra and an agent of Fascism. Even Nehru, who was one of the first congressmen who popularized the Russian Revolution and Soviet achievements, expressed his disapproval of the purges in 1938. But for us, communists, in those days Trotskyism and fascism were the same. I must confess to you that I also believed that Bukharin, Zinoviev, Radek and other victims of Stalinist purges were enemies of socialism, wreckers and spies working in the interest of imperialism and fascism. In discussions with independent-minded socialists I defended Stalin vigorously. I think the main reason for this was that we identified ourselves completely with the Soviet Union, which was then under constant attack by British imperialists and by the Congress right wing. Every strike was supposed to have been inspired by Moscow, every street demonstration was supposed to be led by agitators in the pay of Moscow. We defended the Soviet Union against these people, though, of course, completely uncritically. Hence, when the Soviet Union was attacked from the Left we used the same arguments against these critics as well. Looking back on that period I feel that all this was a big tragedy not just for us, but for the whole Communist movement. Can you imagine: Trotsky had vehemently opposed fascism and had warned the German Communists against the trap they were falling into and this same Trotsky was labelled by us and thousands of others as a fascist. We sincerely believed that in defending Stalinism we were defending the Russian Revolution. I remember writing articles defending Stalin in the Malayalam press in Kerala after Trotsky's assassination and utilizing that book *The Great Conspiracy* to get some factual material or what I genuinely believed to be the truth. The official history of the CPSU which was published at the end of the thirties reinforced my faith in Stalin. This book was first translated and published illegally in Malayalam in 1941 and soon became a textbook of Marxism for our cadres. The study classes I conducted in jail for our comrades were very much coloured by Stalinism. In fact we identified Stalinism with Marxism-Leninism.

What was the first reaction of the CPI towards the war and in what circumstances did that change? One of your former comrades, the CPI(M) leader A. K. Gopalan, argues in his book that the CPI became a mass party during the war.[3] Is this correct?

---

[3] A. K. Gopalan (1904–77): veteran of the independence movement and later a long-serving parliamentarian. He went with the CPI(M) in the 1964 split.

The initial response of our party was to oppose the war and even before 1939 we were pressuring the Congress to step up the struggle against British imperialism. It was the Congress which hesitated immediately after the war began. I remember at the Poona session of the All-India Congress Committee in 1940, I moved an amendment to the main resolution moved by Gandhi, and was supported, incidentally, by Jawaharlal Nehru. Opposing Gandhi's line I called for the start of a new mass struggle against the British. This was the line of the CPI at that stage. Soon after that I was arrested and remained in prison till the end of the war. It is necessary to explain why I was kept in prison when most other communists were released to implement the 'People's War' policy. Immediately on the outbreak of war, and in the year that followed, communists had been arrested in large numbers. In prison controversies started over whether or not our line was correct. Then the Soviet Union was invaded by the Nazi armies. Our controversies became ever more heated. Professor K. B. Krishna who was with us in jail wrote a set of theses developing the 'People's War' line and arguing that now everything had changed and that communists should drop their anti-imperialist activities and their opposition to war. I wrote a set of counter-theses arguing that while the existence of the Soviet Union was vital, nonetheless the best way to help the Russian comrades was *not* by ceasing all anti-imperialist activity, but on the contrary by stepping it up. Our enemy remained British imperialism. The majority of communists inside prison supported my line and only a tiny minority was in favour of the 'People's War' theses. Then some months later we heard that the British party had changed its line and that Moscow was in favour of the change. Outside the jail, the party secretary P. C. Joshi, who was initially one of the strongest opponents of the 'People's War' line, had to change his line and start using his oratorical skills to convince party members, and also the masses, of the importance of helping the war effort. After the change of line most of the pro-war communists were released, but some, including myself, were kept in prison. British intelligence knew perfectly well who to release and who to keep inside.

It seems the atmosphere in jail, as far as discussion and debates within the CP were concerned, was considerably more democratic than it was outside. From what you have said it would appear that all CP members, regardless of hierarchy, were involved in these discussions and that on some subjects there were votes taken.

Yes, that is true, but the debate inside prison did have its limits. As long as the discussion did not directly counter the party line it took place. For instance, even on the war issue, when a circular from the party leadership arrived to our Party Jail Committee instructing us to carry out the pro-war line I automatically dropped my positions and was mocked by the others who said, 'You considered yourself one of the party theoreticians, but you were wrong!' This incident typifies how we were trained as communists. I made a self-criticism and admitted I was wrong. I had to do so because the party was always right, but doubts persisted and in later years I was reassured that I had been correct. Today even the leaders of both the CPI and the CPI(M) are forced to admit that 'some mistakes were made'. That phrase is meant to explain everything. However, in spite of the self-criticism the British did not release me from prison. It is possible that their intelligence services decided that my self-criticism was far too shallow. The official charge sheet handed to me in prison gave as one reason for my continued detention the fact that I had opposed the line of the 'People's War'. This was written black on white on my charge sheet! Of course the CP leadership made numerous representations to the British authorities demanding our release, but to no avail. I was not released till October 1945.

So when the Congress launched the Quit India movement in August 1942, you were still in prison. Was there much resentment towards the CPI on the part of the hordes of Congress volunteers and leaders who filled the jails in the wake of that movement?

There is a view developed by some of the apologists for the 'People's War' line which argues that the CPI gained a lot of support as a consequence of 'swimming against the stream'. I do not subscribe to this view. Of course the party took advantage of legality granted to it by British imperialism to gain new members and increase its trade union strength, but the point is that it was swimming against the stream of the mass movement and was to all intents and purposes considered an ally of British imperialism. It became respectable to be a communist. Many young communists joined the British army to go and 'defend the Soviet Union' in Italy and North Africa. Some of them rapidly shed their 'communism' and stayed in the army even after the war—and not to do clandestine work! It is true that the membership of the party increased from about 4,500 in July 1942 to well over 15,500 in May 1943 at the time of the First Party Congress. Membership of the mass organizations also increased. But most of these new members had no experience of any militant mass struggle or police repression but only the peaceful campaigns conducted by the party to 'grow more food', 'increase production', 'release national leaders', 'form a national government' and 'defend the motherland' from the Japanese invasion which never came. Strikes were denounced as sabotage. The party members also conducted social welfare operations to save the victims of the Bengal Famine of 1943. They organized medical aid for the victims of the smallpox and cholera epidemics. Of course, even this social work paid dividends in India, where there is a terrible disregard for loss of life. But we failed in our basic task, namely to explain the roots of all the problems which confronted the masses.

On the other side, the growth of the Congress and its influence after the Quit India struggle of August 1942 was phenomenal. Millions of men and women, especially the youth, were attracted and radicalized by the struggle, which was considered as a revolution against imperialism. True, we campaigned for the release of the arrested Congress leaders and the formation of a provisional national government to conduct the People's War. But at the same time we branded the Congress Socialists, Bose's followers and other radicals who braved arrests and police repression as fifth columnists and saboteurs. We appealed to Gandhi and other Congress leaders to condemn the violence indulged in by these people. After their release not only Nehru but also the apostles of non-violence, instead of condemning them, praised them as real anti-imperialist patriots—Subhas Bose, Jayaprakash Narain, Aruna Asaf Ali and even obscure figures like Colonel Lakshmi emerged as national heroes and heroines.[4]

In reality the CPI was isolated from the mainstream of the nationalist movement for the second time within a decade. In my view the party's policy virtually delivered the entire anti-imperialist movement to the Congress and the Indian bourgeoisie on a platter. At the time, if the CPI had adopted a correct position the possibility existed of winning over a sizeable and influential section of the Congress to communism. In the 1936–42 period Jawaharlal Nehru himself went through his most radical phase and there were numerous leftward-moving currents (such as the Congress Socialists and Subhas Bose's followers) within the Congress. On my release from prison I experienced the wrath of the left-wing nationalists who used to chant 'Down with supporters of British imperialism' at our meetings. So swimming against the stream when the stream was flowing in the right direction resulted in drowning the possibility of genuine independence and a socialist transformation. We were outmanoeuvred and outflanked by the Indian bourgeoisie.

If the party recovered some ground it was due largely to the militant strike wave which developed immediately after the Second World War in the 1946–47 period and into which we threw ourselves, though our political line was still faulty. We supported, for example, the creation of the confessional state of Pakistan. In Bombay it was the CPI which mobilized support for the naval mutineers of 1946 only to find that our political line of supporting Congress–Muslim League unity hampered any real solidarity as the naval mutiny was broken not so much by the British as by the Congress and League leaders. They united temporarily to confront this new threat on

---

[4] Subhas Chandra Bose (1897–1945?): an early advocate of complete independence for India and president of the Indian National Congress until clashes with Gandhi led to his stepping down, founded the Indian National Army to fight the British, with Japanese support. A controversial figure for his willingness to deal with the Axis regimes. Jayaprakash Narain (1902–79): a leader of the independence movement. Aruna Asaf Ali (1909–96): prominent in the Quit India campaign. The not so obscure Colonel Lakshmi Sahgal (1914–) fought in the women's section of the Indian National Army. A gynaecologist by profession, she joined the CPI(M) in 1971, sitting in the upper house of parliament, and in 2002 running for the Indian presidency on a united left platform.

their left flank which was uncomfortably similar to some of the events of the Russian Revolution. A number of us, including myself, were arrested once again for fomenting class struggles and we were released only on 13 August 1947, a bare twenty-four hours before Independence.

What was the logic behind the notorious Ranadive theses which drove the CPI *on an ultra-left trajectory in the period after Independence?*

I think we have to carefully distinguish a number of interrelated factors. There is no doubt that the theses drafted by Ranadive and adopted by the Second Congress in Calcutta in 1948 were ultra-left,[5] but the criticisms made of them in the late fifties and even today by many Communists and leftist Congressmen have a somewhat hollow ring as they are made from within a reformist problematic.

After the transfer of power there was an anticipatory outbreak of struggles in many parts of the country: these struggles had a dual nature. They both celebrated the transfer of power *to the Congress* and also expected the Congress to carry out all its radical promises. Similar struggles had greeted the election of provincial Congress governments in 1937 while the British were still in India. What these struggles tell us is that there is a link between important victories within the arena of bourgeois politics and the extra-parliamentary mass movement. There was also the struggle in Telengana (Hyderabad) which had begun before Independence and which was being waged against the Nizam of Hyderabad, his administration and their sponsored landlords in the countryside around Hyderabad. Even here the intervention of the Indian Army changed the situation as it effectively removed the Nizam and at the same time blocked the development of the Left.

The post-Independence upsurge involved workers, peasants, students and teachers. Many left-wing Congress supporters participated in these struggles for more trade union rights, for the abolition of landlordism and for more freedoms; their character was essentially one of pressuring the Congress to move left. If the CPI had developed a correct strategy based on an analysis of Indian conditions in the preceding years, it would have been able to play a vital role in these struggles, giving them a lead. In that eventuality the Ranadive theses would have been misplaced but would have had a greater resonance. However, given the twists and turns of the CPI, the ultra-leftism of the 1948 Congress proved to be disastrous. The masses were not prepared to overthrow the Nehru government. On the contrary, large sections of them identified with it, and the CPI slogan: 'This Independence is a Fake Independence' merely succeeded in isolating the party. The armed struggle which was launched together with this slogan led to the deaths of many

---

[5] B. T. Ranadive (1904–90): a member of the CPI since 1928 and a leader of AITUC, he displaced Joshi as general secretary of the party in 1948 and was himself deposed some two years later as a 'left adventurist'. From 1964 he was a leader of the CPI(M).

cadres and imprisonment and torture of others throughout the subcontinent. The analysis of the Nehru government as a comprador stooge government of imperialism was another mistake, as it implied that there was no difference between the colonial British administration and the postcolonial Nehru government. As is now commonly accepted by Marxists, the Indian ruling class was never a comprador class in the real sense of the word. It enjoyed a relative autonomy even during the colonial occupation. To argue that it was a comprador class after Independence was not only ultra-left in the sense that it underpinned a wrong strategic line, it also demonstrated the theoretical inadequacy of Indian communism. Many of the themes of that period were taken up again in the late sixties by the Maoist rebels in Naxalbari and other parts of India and we know with what disastrous consequences. Apart from the fact that hundreds of young people were killed, thousands tortured and the movement went from setback to setback, we still have its legacy in the shape of thousands of political prisoners imprisoned by the Indian ruling class. The tragedy here being that the prisoners are virtually bereft of any mass support.

To return to 1948: a whole number of Communists, including myself, were arrested once again and it was in prison that a number of debates on the Ranadive theses were started. There was a great deal of dissatisfaction with the new line. The trade union comrades were becoming increasingly hostile to the party leadership. The party leadership had issued a call for a national railway strike which had completely flopped. It had only succeeded in identifying the communist supporters in the railway union and many of them were arrested. Then the party leaders said that the communists who were the leaders of the union were revisionists and reformists and that is why the railway strike did not take place. But even this debate rapidly evolved in a particular fashion. There was no effort whatsoever to analyse the conditions which existed in India. It became a session of 'Stalin said ...' to which the opponents in the discussion would respond 'But Mao said the opposite ...'. So the debate itself was largely sterile. Accordingly the result of all these disputes was not to be decided by the party congress after a discussion throughout the party and the preparation of a balance sheet of the Ranadive line. In the best traditions of Stalinism, the party leadership decided to send a delegation to Moscow to meet Stalin. Four leaders were selected for this unique honour: Ajoy Ghosh, Rajeshwar Rao, S. A. Dange and Basava Punniah.[6] Ranadive was eclipsed. They returned with a new tactical line and a new draft programme which were adopted by a special conference of the party held in Calcutta in October 1951. The new line formulated under the direct guidance of Stalin, Molotov and Suslov declared

---

[6] Ajoy Ghosh (1909–62), later general secretary of the party, and Shripat Amrit Dange (1899–1991) represented the 'Indian path', a strategy framed within constitutional bounds, while Rajeswara Rao (1915–94), also a future general secretary, and Basava Punniah favoured the 'Chinese path' of armed struggle.

that the Congress government was installed by the consent of the British imperialists, that the colonial set-up still prevailed in India, that imperialists now covered their rule by the mantle of the Congress government which was completely subservient to imperialism, and that therefore the immediate task of the Communist Party was to overthrow the Indian state and to replace it by a people's democratic state. Thus four years after the transfer of power, Stalin and other leaders of the Soviet Union considered India as a colonial country under British imperialism. Not surprisingly the party conference approved the new line, especially because it had the blessings of the 'greatest Marxist-Leninist and the leader of world revolution'. This was the thinking of the majority of our comrades at least until 1956. I, too, subscribed to this absurd view for some time, but soon doubts arose and I began to argue that India was politically free.

In practice, however, there was a new development. Along with the adoption of the new programme in 1951 the party decided to participate in the general election which was fast approaching. While on its own this was correct, the policies adopted by the party after the elections were a more revealing indication of the turn which had been made. From ultra-leftism the party had now embarked on a course which can only be categorized as parliamentary cretinism. The election manifesto as well as the new programme of 1951 stated that socialism was not the immediate aim of the party as India was still a backward colonial country. The immediate task was the replacement of the anti-democratic and anti-popular Nehru government by a government of people's democracy, on the basis of a coalition of all anti-imperialists and anti-feudal parties and forces. The word 'class' was replaced by the word 'party' and the word 'state' was replaced by the word 'government'. They were not merely semantic changes. From 1948–51 the party had stated that its aim was the setting up of a people's democratic *state*, which was the starting point of the dictatorship of the proletariat. Leaving aside the ambiguities and evasions contained in the formula of 'people's democracy', the aim was nonetheless clear. The Third Congress of the party at Madurai stressed that the central task of the party was the struggle to replace the Congress government with a 'people's government of democratic unity'. And here quite clearly 'people's democracy' was not a synonym for dictatorship of the proletariat. It was conceived as an alliance of the CPI and the anti-Congress 'democratic' parties. The aim of the party became to acquire parliamentary majorities, collecting enough allies to form governments. In its different guises this remains the policy of the CPI and the CPI(M).

Could you explain why, despite all its sectarian mistakes, the CPI *did so well in the 1951 general election? It had suffered repression, it was isolated from the anti-imperialist forces, it had made only a last-minute decision, obviously correct, to participate in the elections.*

I think we were all surprised by the election results. We got about twenty-six or twenty-seven seats in parliament, became the largest party after the Congress and the main focus of opposition to the government. In some cases our candidates got more votes than even Nehru and overnight a whole number of comrades who had only recently been underground or in prison became members of parliament or of provincial assemblies. I think the main reason for this success was not that the people who voted for us thought that our sectarian line was correct. The major factor was that the party cadres were embedded in the mass movement. They worked in the trade unions and the peasants' organizations and many of them were respected for their honesty and courage. Thus the vote for the CPI in the 1951 election was a straightforward class vote and it revealed the potentialities which existed. The fact that these were not realized is shown on one level in the representation of the party inside parliament today, which is roughly the same as in 1951.

After the turn towards parliamentarianism was there any discussion within the party on what extra-parliamentary tactics should be adopted? Surely it would be difficult simply to switch off the involvement of party members in the mass struggles.

Yes, there were discussions on party committees. The Soviet Union had, after the Korean War, embarked once again on a policy of peace and collaboration with capitalist powers, which Khrushchev was to later theorize as 'peaceful coexistence'. Both the Soviet Union and the People's Republic of China began to praise the government of India for its 'progressive' policies, especially its foreign policy based on non-alignment. During their visits to India, Khrushchev and Chou En-lai attracted huge crowds. Nehru became one of the architects of the 'Bandung Spirit'. It was against this background that the debate in our party continued. Is India really free or still subservient to British imperialism? Who do we ally ourselves with in the political arena? I remember the debates we had in the Malabar Provincial Committee of the CPI of which I was the secretary, and in the pre-congress discussion in the Malabar Conference of the party. Some wanted a Congress–Communist coalition government, others argued for an anti-Congress front and concentrated their fire on the Indian National Trade Union Congress (INTUC) which was under the leadership of the Congress. Both conceived of the problem as essentially one of winning elections. What these comrades did not realize was that by attempting to unite the class for struggle against its oppressors we would at the same time have weakened the Congress electorally. I, therefore, disagreed with both these lines. My position at that time was for the CPI to have, first of all, a mass line for the struggles ahead. We should conceive of the struggle basically as one between classes and not parties. Accordingly we should attempt united actions between the AITUC and the INTUC and other trade unions against the capitalists with the aim of uniting the working class and other mass organizations which had been disrupted in the immediate post-war period. I argued that on the basis of class unity we should attempt to unite all progressive sections of the people, including Congress supporters, for the implementation of land reforms, for workers' rights, for more democratic liberties, for a firm anti-imperialist foreign policy, and, through these struggles, wean away the masses from bourgeois influence and build the hegemony of the working class. The political resolution moved by me on the above basis was passed by a majority in the Malabar Party Conference.

The Fourth Congress of the party was held in 1956 at Palghat in Kerala. The emphasis of the majority was on an anti-Congress front. This well suited their theory that the Indian bourgeoisie was subservient to British finance capital. P. C. Joshi, Bhawani Sen, myself and a few others actually distributed an alternative resolution to the official one which Joshi moved on our behalf. Our resolution pointed out that the Congress government was not subservient to imperialism although it occasionally made compromises, that it served primarily the sectional interests of the bourgeoisie and not of the common people, that all the acute problems that plagued our people arose because of the bourgeois leadership of the country and that therefore the real remedy lay in establishing proletarian leadership in completing the bourgeois democratic revolution. It called upon the different trade unions like the AITUC, INTUC, the non-party Hind Mazdoor Sabha and the rest to merge themselves into a single, united trade-union centre. It called for the united mass organizations to intervene to mould the Second Five Year Plan in their own and the country's true interests. It stressed the need to build a United National Democratic Front as a powerful mass movement to fuse together the masses both within the Congress and outside through struggles against the remnants of imperialism and feudalism and against the reactionary policies of the right wing. We thought that such a united democratic front was the means to build the hegemony of the proletariat. Our resolution was defeated but one-fourth of the delegates supported us. Some of the amendments moved on our behalf were incorporated into the official resolution with the result that it was later interpreted in different ways.

What was the direct impact of the Twentieth Party Congress of the CPSU at the CPI congress? Was it discussed at all?

Yes, certainly. A resolution was submitted to our congress on the changes in the Soviet Union. It approved the general drift of Khrushchev's speech, but demanded more discussion on the subjects he had raised. There was, however, not a full discussion on this either at the party congress or after. The reason for insisting on further discussion was because most comrades were not convinced of the correctness of the attack on Stalin. I myself began to rethink radically a whole number of questions after 1956. I wanted to

defend Khrushchev for his attack on Stalin even though I had been a staunch
Stalinist up till that time. For two or three nights after the Twentieth Party
Congress I could not sleep. A man we had been taught to worship, the idol of
our world movement, had been attacked, and by his own former comrades.
Even after reading Khrushchev's secret report I remained in a state of shell
shock; I could not believe it for some time, but after rereading and thinking
I came to the conclusion that Khrushchev was correct and I began to defend
him against the supporters of Stalin. It was for Khrushchev's attack on Stalin
that a number of comrades began attacking him as a revisionist, because his
other theses were not too different to Stalin's own practice.

It was at the 1956 party congress that I was elected to the highest body of
the party, its National Council. Before that I had worked exclusively at the
provincial level and concentrated on building the party in Kerala.

Not long after your Fourth Party Congress, the CPI *won a tremendous victory
in the provincial elections in Kerala, emerging as the largest party in the legislature. Its leader E. M. S. Namboodiripad formed the first ever Communist
government in India. The election clearly showed that the party had mass
support in the province and it also struck a blow against the dominant Cold
War ideology of the time. However, what in your view was the real impact of this
victory both on the mass movement and on the future evolution of the* CPI?

Soon after the formation of the Communist government, there was a
heated discussion within the leadership of the Kerala CP on the nature of the
new government. The dominant view, held by the central leaders including Namboodiripad, was that the workers had captured power in Kerala
by peaceful means, by winning a majority in the elections, and that Kerala
would become the best example of the peaceful road to socialism. It was the
first time that this had happened anywhere in the world and it showed the
way to the future for comrades throughout the world. This was the initial
reaction of the leadership.

I did not agree with this view. I argued that the state remained a capitalist
state despite the Communist victory and that it would be wrong to spread
illusions to the contrary. I was supported by a small number of comrades.
Ajoy Ghosh, the party secretary, was sent from Delhi to discuss with the
Kerala leadership to try and solve the dispute. Both views were put to him.
I spoke for the minority and argued that we were exercising governmen-
tal power in a province, but that the state both provincially and nationally
remained capitalist and that the main problem which confronted us was how
to use this situation in order to strengthen the party and the mass movement. In other words the working class had not come to power. E.M.S.
put forward the majority view and after he had finished Ajoy Ghosh waved
his finger at me and asked: 'You mean to say that E. M. S. Namboodiripad
is bourgeois? Is he not a representative of the working class?' and much

else along the same lines. Needless to say that was not what I had meant. The question was whether the state was bourgeois or not. Namboodiripad was only the chief minister of a provincial government. Ghosh backed the majority and that was that. I held my views, but all opposition ceased. It was only after the Kerala government had been dismissed that Namboodiripad wrote an article in *Communist,* which was then the theoretical organ of the Kerala unit of the CPI, in which he argued that the state had not been a workers' state. If this wisdom had dawned on him earlier it is possible that the situation would have been entirely different, as the party would have given primacy to the extra-parliamentary mass struggle which had swept it to power. But Kerala left within the CPI leaders an overwhelming desire to win power and form ministries through electoral means. We can still see it in both the segments of what used to be the CPI. Alliances are made not on the basis of principle, but to get government office.

The impact of the victory on the masses was tremendous. Immediately after the victory the workers and poor peasants, in the main, were jubilant. They felt very deeply that the new government would satisfy their demands. There was a tremendous feeling of pride and strength in the working class. I remember hearing poor, illiterate workers telling policemen on the streets: 'Now you daren't attack us because our government is in power. Namboodiripad is our leader. We are ruling.' This was not an uncommon view. The reserves of goodwill which existed for the government were considerable. Amongst the poor peasants, sections of the students and teachers there was also a feeling of joy, which increased when they saw how discomfiting the victory was for the landlords, the capitalists and for reactionaries in general. In the first weeks after the election the CP ministers made very radical speeches, constantly stressing their support for the struggle of the workers.

But these promises were, in the main, restricted to speeches. Namboodiripad and his ministers discovered fairly quickly that the civil service was a powerful entity and that the chief secretary, the top civil servant in the province, was functioning on orders from the centre and not from the provincial chief minister. The same went for the police and furthermore no laws could be passed without the sanction of the centre. So even as far as inaugurating a number of *reforms* was concerned the CP ministry found itself powerless. As it had no other real perspectives it found itself in a blind alley. Nothing radically new happened and after a while the novelty of having a Communist government began to wear off. In some cases jubilation turned to passivity and in others to open and bitter disillusionment.

An important test for the new government arose a few months after they had been elected. Workers in a factory near Quilon, a town close to the capital city of Trivandrum, went on strike. The union in that factory was under the leadership of the RSP (Revolutionary Socialist Party). The strike was not against the government, but against the employer in that particular factory. It was a typical trade union struggle. I remember vividly how the situation developed. We were sitting at a meeting of the State Council of the CPI (which consisted of about sixty comrades) when news was brought to us that three workers on strike had been shot dead by the police. We were stunned. Workers had been shot dead by the police while the Communists were in office. The immediate response of *all* the comrades present was to condemn the firing, institute an immediate enquiry, give compensation to the bereaved families, publicly apologize to the workers on strike and give a public assurance that such a thing would never happen again while we were in government. This was our instinctive class response. But a discussion started which lasted for two hours and at the end of it the decisions taken were completely different to our initial response. In my view the whole business was unjustifiable, but it is necessary to understand the context of the time.

The reactionary groups and parties had started a campaign against us under the demagogic slogan of 'Join the Liberation Struggle Against Communist Rule'. They had begun to exploit our weaknesses. The movement was spearheaded by the Roman Catholic priests (as you know Kerala has a significant Catholic population) and the Nair Communalists. But all those opposed to the CPI joined them, including the right and left social democrats (the Socialist Party and the RSP) and the movement was beginning to gather mass support. It was in this context that the police firing took place. The logic of the comrades who advocated changing the initial position on the firing went something like this: if we attack the police, there will be a serious decline in their morale; if there is a serious decline in their morale the anticommunist movement will be strengthened; if the anti-communist movement is strengthened our government will be overthrown; if our government is overthrown it will be a tremendous blow against the communist movement. The final resolution passed by the party defended the police action. It was then decided that someone must go to the spot to explain our point of view, attack the RSP and defend the police action. I was supposed to be one of the party's effective Malayalam orators and I was asked to go and speak on behalf of the Kerala CP. My response was to refuse and maintain that I had been unable to digest the decision taken by the Council and therefore I could not defend it. I was then formally instructed by the party leadership to go and defend the party. I went. I spoke for about an hour and a half and it was pure demagogy. I blamed the deaths of the three workers on the irresponsibility of the RSP and asked them to explain publicly why they had led these workers to be shot. I made vicious attacks on the strike leaders. That night when I returned home I really felt sick inside. I could not sleep. I kept thinking that I should have refused to defend the party and I felt that I was going mad. I shouted at my wife. Instead of having shouted and hurled abuse at the party leaders, who had put me in such a situation, I took it out on my wife. The next day I was asked to speak at three different places and make the same speech. This time I refused point blank and my refusal was accepted.

While the firing obviously had a traumatic effect on a number of party members such as yourself, did it also have a lasting effect on the working class?

Obviously it weakened the government and dented its mass support, but a significant section of our supporters remained solid despite the Quilon incidents. Of course the reactionaries increased their support, but, even at that stage, if the CPI leaders had understood the dialectical interrelationship between parliamentary and mass work and understood that the former must always be subordinated to the needs of the struggle we would have maintained our strength and probably increased it tenfold. In the process we would have been dismissed from office, as we were in any case, but we would have been in an immeasurably stronger situation and we could have educated the masses in the limitations of bourgeois democracy. Real revolutionary consciousness could have been developed. None of this was done and at the same time Namboodiripad made speeches predicting a civil war, which flowed logically from his view that the working class had taken the power. These speeches were then used by the Congress leadership to further attack and weaken the government. It soon became obvious from press reports and statements by Congress leaders that the centre was considering the imposition of President's Rule and the dissolution of the government. The growth of the reactionary-led mass movement within Kerala was also reaching its peak. It soon became difficult for CP leaders to go anywhere without being stoned and this included myself. It was at this time that Nehru decided to visit Kerala and see the situation for himself. He was besieged by petitioners demanding the immediate dismissal of the government. Of course he also met us. He had a number of separate meetings with the government ministers and a delegation of the state committee of the CP. I was one of the members of this delegation. I remember in his discussions with us the first question he asked us was: 'How did you manage to so wonderfully isolate yourself from the people in such a short space of time?' He then suggested that the Communist government could continue on the condition that there would be new elections in order to let the electorate decide. The state committee convened a special session to discuss Nehru's proposal and on Namboodiripad's insistence decided to reject the proposal. We were prepared to accept new elections only in the event that they were held in all the other provinces! I felt even then that it was a wrong decision. We should have accepted Nehru's proposal, won ourselves a breathing space and then entered into battle with the opposition, which in any case was a motley collection of reactionaries, bandwagon opportunists and social democrats. Secondly the elections would have been held with the Communist government in office, which would have neutralized if not completely impeded the intervention against us by the state apparatus: the use of civil servants and the police. In any case we refused and in 1959 the government was dismissed. But in the next election, held a year and a half later, we increased our share of the popular vote though we got fewer seats. So while we were defeated electorally it was not a real defeat in the eyes of the masses. And this despite all our errors and mistakes.

The electoral victory in Kerala undoubtedly made the CPI into a national force; its prestige increased tenfold and communist enthusiasts answering the stale headlines of the bourgeois commentators replied: 'After Nehru, Namboodiripad!' The importance of Kerala in that sense was the feeling that Congress could be defeated and that an alternative existed, namely the Communist Party of India. This was not an unimportant factor given the international situation. Of course even within the CPI there were criticisms of the way in which the E.M.S. ministry had condoned the killing of workers. The state committee of the West Bengal CPI wrote a letter criticizing the Kerala party. But despite all this Namboodiripad drew larger crowds than any other CPI leader and had become a national figure in his own right as the leader of the successful Kerala CPI. The CP congress in Amritsar in 1958 also treated him as a hero and announced that power could be taken electorally, a view which was facilitated by the positions being developed by the Soviet party. There were some amendments to the main resolution and a few comrades expressed doubts, but by and large there was a consensus. The Amritsar line was to be applied nationally.

Was there never a real discussion within the leadership, even after 1959, of the problems posed on a strategic level by electoral victories won by parties pledged to some form of socialist transformation? Surely one of the key weaknesses of the CPI in Kerala, the CPI(M) in West Bengal and, later, the Popular Unity in Chile was that there was no understanding of the necessity of helping to stimulate and create organs of popular power of a Soviet type which could organize the masses independently of the bourgeois state and could be utilized to challenge the state when the need arose. This whole dimension has been absent from the strategy of the Communist parties for many decades.

These problems you mention are very important and vital ones, but I am sorry to say that they did not enter into the discussions which took place. One of the results of Stalinism has been precisely that the key importance of organizing the masses through their own organs of power, such as soviets, has disappeared. The party has been seen as the sole representative of the masses.

As for my own political development, I continued to develop doubts after 1956. The question of Stalin was resolved for me by Khrushchev's speech, but on international issues I was to remain totally confused. For instance on Hungary my position was completely orthodox. I even wrote a pamphlet called 'What Happened in Hungary' to answer the widespread attacks on the Soviet Union in every bourgeois newspaper. So, in spite of 1956, the change in my thinking was gradual. I felt fairly regularly the need to read more, but then the material available to one at that time in India was also very limited. I thought in 1956 that I had broken with Stalinism, but looking back it is obvious that this was not the case. The Amritsar line, the Kerala government, all strengthened my doubts, but that is the level on which matters remained: personal doubts, many of which were not expressed even internally within the party. I am convinced that this must have been the case with many a Communist militant in those days. But there was no revolutionary alternative to the line of the CPI.

A further change took place in 1958 when I had the opportunity to visit the Soviet Union. I visited Tashkent in 1958 as a member of the Indian Writers' Delegation to attend an Afro-Asian writers' conference. The Chinese delegates were also present and were quite open about explaining their difference with the Soviet Union. But I also had an opportunity to see the Soviet Union and, while the tremendous advances made cannot be denied, there was another side which made me uneasy. In Moscow there was a special reception for the Indian delegates which was attended by Khrushchev. During this there was a cultural show and to my surprise I discovered that the empty chair next to me had been taken by Khrushchev. So I used this opportunity to discuss with him and attempt to clear my doubts. At that time you may recall the Pasternak case had excited a great deal of attention. So I asked Khrushchev how he justified the treatment of Pasternak. How was it possible that, fifty years after the revolution, the Soviet government still felt threatened by a novel written by Pasternak? I explained that as a writer I could not justify the treatment meted out to him even though, as a Marxist, I disagreed with his political line. I explained to him that in a country like India where many anti-imperialists had been sentenced to prison for their writings, including poems and short stories, it was impossible to justify and genuinely defend the Soviet party on the Pasternak issue. Khrushchev denied all responsibility for the episode and claimed that it was done by the Writers' Union and suggested that I discuss the matter with them. It was obvious that he was not anxious to discuss the issue. We then discussed the problem of drinking in the Soviet Union and I asked if he had considered prohibition. He replied that they had, but if there was prohibition then immediately illegal distilleries would begin to spring up and it would create graver problems. I responded by suggesting that similarly if they continued to ban books illegal distilleries of books would spring up and could also create problems. Extremely irritated by now he suggested that we concentrate on the ballet! I began to understand the limits of 'de-Stalinization'. Attempts to discuss Yugoslavia and China were also unsuccessful. Discussions with the officials of the Writers' Union were more vigorous, but equally disappointing. As a result my disillusionment began to deepen.

Did you visit any other countries apart from the Soviet Union? Did you, for instance, have an opportunity to visit the People's Republic of China, where the revolution was more recent and in one sense more relevant to the problems confronting India?

After my trip to the Soviet Union I got more opportunities to travel outside and discuss with foreign comrades. This was very vital for my political evolution. For example, in 1960 I attended the Third Congress of the Vietnamese Workers Party in Hanoi. Harekrishan Konar and myself were the fraternal delegates from the Indian party.[7] I gave the fraternal greetings from Indian Communists to the congress and afterwards discussed the situation with numerous comrades from different countries. It was a very exciting period. The National Liberation Front was about to be formed in the South and the Sino–Soviet split was beginning to dominate Communist gatherings. The Soviet delegation invited us to dinner to explain their views, with which we were in any case familiar. The discussion was continued the next day as both Konar and I subjected the Russians to some extremely critical questioning. The positive features of the early period of the Sino–Soviet dispute was that it allowed the possibility of debate and discussion on fundamentals inside the Communist movement for the first time since the twenties.

The Chinese delegation invited us to go to Peking for a lengthy discussion. We were flown to Canton and from there in a special plane to Peking. We spent a total of four days in the Chinese capital including a five-and-a-half-hour session with Chou En-lai and other party leaders. The main item of discussion was the Sino–Indian border dispute. An hour was spent with the most intricate details relating to old maps, border treaties and the like to establish China's claim to the border lands. I stated my views quite openly. I said to the Chinese comrades: legally, geographically, historically you may be correct. The question which concerns me is what political purpose does this dispute over uninhabited territory serve? You have come to an agreement with Pakistan and you have given up some land. Why not do the same with India? It will prevent the reactionaries from whipping up anti-Chinese chauvinism and it will strengthen the left movement in India. We will be able to demonstrate the superiority of the method by which socialist states settle border disputes. We could utilize this to strengthen the bond between the Chinese revolution and the Indian masses. I explained that this had been Lenin's attitude when dealing with bourgeois governments such as Finland or even pre-capitalist monarchies such as Afghanistan. By doing so Lenin strengthened the Russian Revolution and its appeal to the broad masses. Immediately Chou said, 'Lenin did the correct thing.' But he explained it in terms of the Soviet state's isolation and the non-existence of a 'socialist camp'. I responded by arguing that while I did not have the texts on me

---

[7] Hare Krishna Konar was the architect of land reform in West Bengal in the 1960s.

there was considerable evidence to show that Lenin's motives were in reality to develop friendly relations with the peoples of these countries and not to allow the ruling classes to paint the Soviet Union as a big power gobbling up their countries. Finally Chou said that he could not agree and that we should agree to disagree on this point. I had an extremely soft spot for the Chinese comrades and their revolution so I didn't want to leave matters there. I asked Chou: 'Is there any danger of the US imperialists attacking you through these disputed border territories?' He replied in the negative and said the threat was from the Nehru government and not from the Americans in this instance. The next point of discussion was the Sino–Soviet dispute.

Here Chou stressed the betrayal they had felt when the Soviet Union, because of political disagreements, had withdrawn their technicians from China overnight. He was extremely bitter about this and complained that they had even taken the blueprints away! I felt that the Russians had been completely wrong, but I did not speak my mind as I did not want to take sides between the two giants. I returned from the discussion fairly depressed with what the Soviet Union had done, but I was not satisfied with Chou's answers on the border question. I couldn't help feeling there was a trace of chauvinism in his attitudes. Konar was much more sympathetic to the Chinese and on his return to India he organized a number of study circles to explain their views.

What was the attitude of the Vietnamese comrades in those days?

The position of the Vietnamese then was what it remains today. They saw in the dispute then the seeds of further and growing discord which they felt could only aid imperialism. On that level they were not so wrong and the attitude of both China and the Soviet Union towards the Vietnamese struggle was not as it should have been. Before I left for Peking we had a lengthy discussion with Ho Chi Minh in the course of which we discussed Vietnam, India and the Sino–Soviet dispute. On the last question he told us that he agreed neither with China nor the Soviet Union and felt that their quarrels were reaching a stage where they could harm the working-class movement internationally. He was extremely anxious and apprehensive and he suggested that nothing should be done to exacerbate the conflict. I asked why the Vietnamese did not publish their positions in their press as it could be a useful way of keeping the movement united, but he replied that they had decided not to interfere in the dispute at all. He made a few jokes about the Third World War theses and said that Vietnam was a small country and even if a few people survived in China after the war there would be no one left in Vietnam, so from pure self-interest they could not support the theses. But all this was said in a semi-ironic vein. I must confess that I found him the most cultured and charming of all the Communist leaders I have met. He impressed me a great deal by speaking in six languages to welcome the delegations to Vietnam: Chinese, Russian, Vietnamese, French, English and Spanish.

He gave a characteristic reply when I asked him how in his view the Vietnamese party, which in the thirties was not much bigger than the Indian party, had succeeded whereas we had failed. He replied: 'There you had Mahatma Gandhi, here I am the Mahatma Gandhi.' He then went on to explain how they had utilized the anti-imperialist struggle to build their hegemony over the masses. They had become the leading force in the anti-imperialist struggle and moved on to socialism. The clear implication was that in India it was Gandhi and the Congress who had kept control and that the CPI was at fault. He also explained as did other Vietnamese leaders the endemic weaknesses of the Vietnamese bourgeoisie, which of course contrasted very vividly with the strength of the Indian bourgeoisie.

It was trips abroad which undoubtedly opened my mind, even though in the beginning these trips were mainly to the Soviet Union and other non-capitalist countries. I remember visiting the Soviet Union again in 1962 for health reasons. While in prison during 1940–45 I had managed to learn a bit of Russian, enough to read *Pravda*, albeit at a snail's pace. The period I was in Moscow coincided with some anniversary commemorating Napoleon's failure to take Moscow and his subsequent retreat. The very fact that a Tsarist victory was being celebrated was odd enough in itself, but what compounded the error in my view was the lengthy diatribe against Napoleon in the pages of *Pravda*. The nationalist fervour of the article was horrifying to me. Of course Napoleon was a counter-revolutionary in the context of the French revolution, but in a war with Tsarist absolutism if one had to retrospectively take sides, it would be with Napoleon not the Tsar. After all he was carrying the bourgeois-democratic revolution, even in a distorted and impure form, to the territories being conquered. The whole of reactionary Europe was arraigned against him. If anything, there is an analogy with the Red Army's sweep into Eastern Europe at the conclusion of the Second World War and the abolition of the capitalist mode of production. I was lying in the hospital reading this article, and I did not have much else to do, so I decided to write a letter to the editor of *Pravda* expressing my shock and dismay at the reactionary nature of this article. After that I used to grab eagerly a copy of *Pravda* every day to see whether or not it had been printed and every day I was disappointed. After a week I was visited by a member of the Central Committee of the CPSU who ostensibly came to inquire about my health. And then he informed me that he had read my letter to *Pravda*. I asked how he had read it, if it had been addressed to the *Pravda* editor. He preferred to ignore this question and proceeded to defend the *Pravda* assessment of Napoleon. I cut the discussion short by saying I would be happy to discuss with him or any other comrade in the columns of *Pravda*, but I would rather be spared a heavy-handed lecture in my hospital room.

Of course all these things are symptomatic of a more serious disease, but this was the way in which my eyes were opened.

This evolution continued in the years which followed and I visited Western Europe twice in the period 1967–69. In Italy I discussed not only with some of the Communist Party leaders, but also with comrades of Il Manifesto, in France with dissident Communists such as Garaudy and some comrades of the New Left.[8] I also personally experienced the after-effects of May 1968 and then I visited Britain. It was coincidental that I happened to visit Western Europe at a time when it was experiencing new upheavals and a mass radicalization, but nonetheless once there my political evolution continued. I wanted to study developments taking place with an open mind and so I met all the representatives of different currents which existed and discussed with them. I witnessed for myself in France the differences on the streets between the extreme Left and the PCF and I must confess I was inclined to sympathize with the courage and conviction of the far Left demonstrators, even though I could not completely agree with them.

What was the basis for the split in Indian Communism which led to the existence of two major parties—CPI and CPI(M)? Was it a partial reflection of the Sino–Soviet split? Given the fact that the CPI lost Kerala and Bengal, its two main strongholds, to the CPI(M), what was the impact of the split within the CPI?

Many people have written that the CPI/CPI(M) split was a pure reflection of the Sino–Soviet dispute. This is not correct. A more substantial factor was the attitude towards the Sino–Indian conflict. As I have already told you, I was not at all convinced by Chou En-lai's explanation of the Chinese position on the border dispute. I still think that the CPI was correct in opposing the Chinese line. However, there is a big difference between not supporting the Chinese position and supporting your own bourgeoisie. I'm afraid that the statements of some of the CPI leaders were totally chauvinist and merely parroted the speeches made by the Congress leaders. There were even racist slurs of the 'yellow peril' variety directed against the Chinese leaders, and some of the articles written by Dange attacking China and defending the Indian bourgeoisie were outrageous, even for a Communist leader steeped in Stalinist traditions. Many of the comrades who left with the CPI(M) were disgusted by this and correctly so, but even this was not the main reason for the split, which took place in 1964, some years after the Sino–Indian border clashes.

In my view the major reason for the split was internal differences related to the question of electoral alliances. Ever since the fall of the Kerala

---

[8] Roger Garaudy (1913–): at the time a dissident member of the French Communist Party, expelled in 1970 for his denunciation of the Soviet invasion of Czechoslovakia.

ministry a discussion of sorts had been taking place and it reached a head in 1964. If you study the party documents from 1960 to 1964 you can trace the real causes of the split. There is a consistent theme running through all these documents: parliamentary cretinism. On this there are no major differences between the two sides. There is agreement on the need to win more elections in the states and more seats in the Lok Sabha. That is the road to communism in India. There is a supplementary slogan embodied in the formula: 'Break the Congress monopoly'. It is around this that differences develop. Some party leaders state that the key is to break the Congress monopoly, even if this means having the Jan Sangh or the Muslim League as a partner. Others state that the best way to break the monopoly is by aligning with the progressive sections of the Congress against its right wing. Thus the debate which led to a split in Indian Communism was not on differences around how best to overthrow the existing state and its structures, but on how to win more seats. In my view it was tactical differences which led to a split.

Other differences were there: on the Sino–Indian question, on an assessment of the Soviet Union's policies, but the main reason was differences on the implementation of electoral tactics. The immediate reason for the walkout by the comrades who became the CPI(M) leadership was the affair of the Dange letter. This was a letter supposedly written by Dange in 1924 to the British authorities offering his services to them and a copy of this letter appeared in the national archives. The CPI National Council set up a commission to investigate the whole business. The majority of this commission absolved Dange by stating that the letter was a forgery, but a minority stated that there was no proof to indicate that Dange had not written the letter. One-third of the thirty-two members of the Council left the meeting. They were not to return. Of course it was clear that the Dange letter was merely the pretext, but it was also clear that there were no fundamental differences. I think the evolution of the two parties since that time has confirmed this fact. While on the National Council the CPI had an overwhelming majority, the situation in the state councils of the party was different. In West Bengal the CPI(M) had the majority and in Kerala the CPI had a very narrow majority. But even this could be misleading. I'll explain why. If you went below the state council to the district committees the CPI(M) had a majority in some, but if you went even lower down the scale of branches and cells you would see that the CPI was virtually wiped out. A large section of the base went with the CPI(M) in Kerala. In Andhra Pradesh the situation was roughly similar. In those areas where the Party represented a mass current, the CPI(M) gained the upper hand. The reason for this is that many of the CPI(M) leaders after the split and the bulk of their middle cadres, including those who would in the following years break with the CPI(M) and align themselves with Peking, explained the split in terms of the CPI being the 'right Communists' who struggled for reforms via electoral victories whereas the CPI(M) struggled for revolution. Many of the CPI(M)'s middle cadres obviously believed this, but their leadership was engaged not in revolution, but in trying to win elections. Their behaviour after the election victory of 1967 in West Bengal showed this very clearly. But the bulk of those who joined the CPI(M) after the split did so because they genuinely believed that the latter was going to lead them towards the revolution. In addition many of those who were opposed to the line of the CPI and the CPI(M) nonetheless went with the CPI(M) because they believed that the latter had greater potential in the sense that it had taken with it the best and most revolutionary sections of the base. So in all those areas where there was a communist tradition the ranks went largely with the CPI(M).

Why did you personally decide to stay with the CPI?

Because I was opposed to a split. I did not see that there were any fundamental differences between the two groupings and I feared that a split would further divide the trade union movement, which is what happened. Some time after the CPI(M) split, the AITUC was also split, the peasant organizations were split and the student organizations were split. This weakened the Left considerably and enabled the Congress and the parties on its right to strengthen their hold on the masses. It is of course scandalous that the workers' movement has to be permanently divided in this fashion. Leaving aside the broader questions of trade union unity, at least the two communist parties could have maintained a common trade union structure in the interests of the class they claim to serve. The main reason they did not cannot simply be ascribed to sectarianism. The reason is that given the weight they attach to electoralism and the fact that they subordinate the extra-parliamentary struggles to parliament, they need their own trade unions to gain electoral support. Thus both parties utilize their respective trade union, student and peasant organizations mainly for electoral work. The basic concept of unity against the class enemy on every front is lacking from their politics. In any case I saw no reason to split from the CPI and join the CPI(M) and today I am still a member of the CPI. I still maintain that my decision was correct.

There were rumblings in the CPI leadership over the invasion of Czechoslovakia. I know that the CPI(M) defended the invasion without raising any doubts, but within the CPI we heard that there was opposition and that this was not a result of the desire not to offend 'democratic allies' in India?

The National Council unanimously passed a resolution in 1968 approving the measures being carried out by Dubček and pledging its support to 'socialism with a human face'. Then came the military intervention of the Soviet Union. Immediately a discussion began and a number of us visited the Czech Embassy in New Delhi to collect all the materials of the CPCZ. There was an even split on the National Council. I think that those who supported the Soviet Union had thirty-five votes and we had thirty-four (it was not a well-attended meeting of the Council in any case) with two initial abstentions. There was further discussion and both the comrades who had abstained came over to our side so that we now had a majority to oppose the Soviet intervention. Once the party leaders realized that they were going to be defeated, they became very conciliatory and suggested that we should not take an immediate vote, but should open a three-month discussion period throughout the party and circulate all the relevant documents. I agreed because I thought that it would be a good thing if all the literature on this question was discussed throughout the party. It could do us nothing but good to have a real debate. But this promise was never kept.

The next council meeting took place four months later. In that time we had been deluged by visitors from the Soviet Union. Some of them discussed with me as well, but I was not convinced one bit. In fact I pseudonymously edited a book entitled *Whither Czechoslovakia?*, in which all the contributors were pro-CPI, but opposed to the Soviet line. I made sure that not a single contributor could be attacked as an 'enemy of the CPI'. I do not know all the pressures that were applied. In any case at the Council meeting the party apparatus had mobilized all its forces and obtained a majority at that meeting. Immediately afterwards I was questioned about the book and I admitted that I was responsible for it. I was rebuked and an instruction was sent out that this book was neither to be distributed nor read by any CPI members. A public censure of me was proposed in the party press. A party leader suggested that before the censure was published in *New Age* I should be given fifteen days to rethink and recant. I said that it was they who should have time to rethink. They nonetheless gave me fifteen days respite and meanwhile some people came to see me and pressure me to apologize. They said that they didn't want to censure me openly because I was a leader of the party and well respected. I refused point blank. So the censure was published in a small corner of *New Age*. But the very next day it was reported in great detail in all the bourgeois newspapers that I had been censured for writing a book criticizing the Soviet invasion and probably more copies of the book were sold than would have been if the leaders of my party had ignored the whole business. Despite all this, however, it is worth pointing out that a discussion of sorts did take place inside the CPI, in contrast to the CPI(M) which defended the invasion wholeheartedly.

Can you tell me what are your views on Trotsky and Trotskyism?

I am not a Trotskyist. Stalin was my idol. That idol is broken to pieces. I don't want to replace a broken idol with a new idol even if it is not a broken one, because I don't now believe in idolatry. I think Trotsky, Bukharin,

Luxemburg, Gramsci, Lukács and other Marxists should seriously be studied and critically evaluated by all communists. Marxism will be poorer if we eliminate them from the history of the world Communist movement. I don't believe in the Stalinist falsification of history in which Trotsky was depicted as an imperialist spy and a fascist agent. It appears that even Soviet historians have now abandoned such views. In a new history of the CPSU published in the late sixties Trotsky was criticized not for being a fascist spy but for his 'incorrect views'. Even this change is not enough. As Lukács said, one will not understand the history of the Russian Revolution if one does not understand the role of Trotsky in it. I am therefore glad that John Reed's *Ten Days That Shook the World*, which gives an excellent picture of the turbulent days of the Russian Revolution and Trotsky's role in it, has recently been published in the Soviet Union itself along with Lenin's introduction to it. I think some of the important contributions by Trotsky like his essay on bureaucratization published in the *Inprecor* in 1923, *In Defence of Marxism, On Literature and Art, History of the Russian Revolution* and other works are valuable and some of his ideas are still relevant. This does not mean that I agree with everything Trotsky said or wrote. The development of Marxism needs a critical eye.

You've been involved in the Communist movement for well over forty years. You've been on its leading bodies; you've represented it in parliament and at congresses of fraternal parties, you've participated in its debates, not to mention your pioneering role in helping to lay its foundations in Kerala, one of the two regions where it has been most successful. Do you think that the traditional Indian Communist movement—by which I would include the CPI, CPI(M) and the splintered M-L groups which despite differences have a common political and ideological basis—has a future in India. In other words can these groups and parties be reformed or is there a need for a communist party of a new type?

I would reject the view that the entire past of Indian Communism must be negated. Despite all the deformations and mistakes there have been hundreds and thousands of communists in India who have struggled and suffered all sorts of privations for socialism and revolution. A whole number of peasant struggles, struggles for trade unionism and against imperialism were conducted by the finest sort of communist militants. The tragedy was that the leadership, for the reasons we have discussed, was incapable of harnessing their talents and energies in a revolutionary direction. So I would stress that the whole experience must not be written off. There are chapters of it which have to be reappropriated by any new communist movement. At the base of the CPI, the CPI(M) and the M-L groups you have thousands of dedicated activists who want a socialist revolution. They cannot be ignored. Furthermore many of them possess experience of mass struggles. Many young militants who did not experience Stalinism in the traditional parties are also coming forward as Marxists and communists. I firmly believe that the unification of all communist forces in the country on the basis of Marxism-Leninism is essential for the development of the Communist movement. How this will be brought about, whether by a merger or unification of all these forces under a new name through a conference, or by the emergence of a new Communist Party, etcetera, may be left to the future. But unification cannot be brought about by breaking each others' heads, but only by principled discussions and comradely debates and through united actions for a commonly agreed programme. This will succeed only if the ranks of the different Communist parties raise their own theoretical level and enable themselves to intervene in this great debate effectively. I am an optimist and am sure that even if the leaders of the old and ageing generation fail in this task, the revolutionaries of the new young generation will rise to the occasion.

Ernest Mandel (1923–95) was internationally recognized as one of the outstanding Marxist economists of his time. Whether in the scholarly mode of Marxist Economic Theory *or the didactic register of the companion* Introduction, *his authoritative and lucid expositions won many thousands to his understanding of their world. His masterwork,* Late Capitalism, *proposed a striking new account of the dynamics of the capitalist economy, in a study whose predictive power was quickly corroborated in the generalized recessionary wave that set in at the turn of the 1970s. In recognition of this achievement, Mandel was invited to give the Marshall lectures in the Economics Faculty of the University of Cambridge—a large acknowledgement on the part of Keynes's institutional heirs.*

Far fewer of Mandel's readers in, say, the USA, *France, West Germany, Switzerland and Australia would have been aware that he was at one time or another officially barred from their countries, as a threat to national security. This was in his political role as one of the foremost leaders of the Fourth (Trotskyist) International, which he had joined in his home city of Antwerp shortly after its inception in 1938. In his five decades at the heart of the* FI, *Mandel combined the roles of thinker, teacher and polemicist, organizer and leader with unusual distinction. (He appears from time to time in these capacities in Adolfo Gilly's recollections elsewhere in this volume.) No less gifted as a public speaker than as a writer, he was fluent in half a dozen languages, and ready to travel to any country that would admit him. In later life he also held academic positions in the Free University of Brussels.*

Ernest Mandel

The Luck of a Crazy Youth

*You were ten years old when Hitler seized power in Germany and sixteen when
the Second World War broke out. It was surely an awful time to be young,
especially for someone like you, from a Jewish background. What are your first
memories of that period?*

Well, strangely enough—but this is probably part of a special mentality, not
very close to the average—I have no bad memories at all of that period. On
the contrary, I have rather a memory of tension, yes, excitement, yes, nervousness, but not at all of despair. Absolutely not. This has something to do
with the fact that we were a highly politicized family.

Your father was an activist?

At that time my father was not an activist. He had been an activist at the
time of the German Revolution. He had fled from Belgium to Holland in
the First World War because he didn't want to do his military service. He
was already a very left-wing socialist and he had met Willem Pieck—who was
later president of the German Democratic Republic—in Holland. When the
German Revolution broke out they went to Berlin together. He worked for
some months in the first press agency of Soviet Russia in Berlin. He knew
Radek personally and met a lot of other people. And so I found on our book-
shelves a fantastic collection of old publications—books by Marx, books by
Lenin, books by Trotsky, the International Correspondence (*Inprecor*) of
that time, Russian literature and so on. He dropped out of politics around
1923. His life was very much attuned to the general ups and downs of
world revolution. When Hitler came to power he got a shock. He was very
conscious of what that would mean for the world. I remember—it's perhaps
my first political memory, I was nine years old in 1932—at the time of the
so-called Papen putsch when the Social Democratic government of Prussia

was eliminated, and Severing, the Minister of the Interior, together with the chief of the police, made this famous or infamous statement, *Ich weiche vor dem Gewalt*—'I yield before violence'. A lieutenant and two soldiers had entered his office and he dropped all the power they had accumulated in the fourteen years since 1918. He dropped it in just five minutes. This news appeared in the social-democratic daily paper of Antwerp, our home town. My father made very sharp comments. He said it will end very badly: this is the beginning of the end. I remember that very well. And then when Hitler came to power we had some of the first refugees come to our home, also some members of our family and some friends. The years 1933 to 1935 were terrible years in Belgium; it was the depth of the crisis and people were very hungry. Of course it was much worse than today, much worse. The Belgian queen became popular simply because she distributed bread and margarine to the unemployed. One of the refugees who came to our home told us, as if it was normal, that they had sold their bed in order to buy bread in Berlin. They were sleeping on the ground because they had to buy bread. These were terrible times. My father also went through some bad periods, but we never were so badly off as that. We never went hungry but we saw our standard of living drop dramatically in that period. These years 1933, 1934, 1935 were a bit less political.

Your political engagement began when the war broke out?

Much earlier than that, 1936 was a turning point for me, and for my father. Two things came together, the Spanish Civil War and the Moscow trials. These events had a major impact on us. The working-class movement in Antwerp and in Belgium played an important role. The Spanish Civil War evoked a tremendous wave of solidarity. I remember well the demonstration of May Day 1937. There were perhaps a hundred thousand people in the streets, and the people coming back from the International Brigades in Spain and people collecting money. They were received by an ovation which I will never forget. Prior to the Vietnam Solidarity Campaign, it was the biggest international event we had ever had in Belgium. Then there were the Moscow trials, which were a tremendous shock for my father. He had personally known several of the defendants of the first trial who were functionaries of the Comintern. Radek was one of the main defendants of the second trial. My father got angry beyond description—beyond description —and on the spot he organized a committee of solidarity with the Moscow trial defendants. He got in contact with a small Trotskyist group in Antwerp. They met at our place and I became, at the age of thirteen, a Trotsky sympathizer—not a member because the organization was not so stupid that it would let a child of thirteen into its ranks. But I was present at meetings, listening, and was considered a bright youngster so they didn't oppose my listening. I was fifteen years old when I was formally admitted. And it was an interesting moment because this was a little after the founding conference of the Fourth International.[1]

When was that?

In 1938. The Young People's Socialist League of the United States, the youth organization of the Socialist Workers Party, sent a man called Nattie Gould to speak to us about the founding conference.[2] I still see him before my eyes. He toured several Western European countries to give a report on the founding conference and explain the work of the SWP. He came to Antwerp and to our place where the Antwerp cell of the organization met. I think that it was after that meeting that I was formally admitted as a candidate member. Then there was a certain vacuum, the most difficult period probably in our country. In 1939 everybody was sure the war would break out. We were very isolated. We distributed a leaflet on the main streets of Antwerp—it was not such an intelligent way to act, because of the climate.

What did the leaflet say?

It was against the war. It said the war is coming, but this is not our war and so on and so forth. It was not received very well and was written in a very abstract and propagandist way. I didn't write it and don't take any responsibility for it!

But did you distribute it?

I distributed it, obviously.

You were fifteen when you distributed your first leaflet?

I was nearer to sixteen. That was a very difficult time, probably the most difficult time we have had. Our organization comprised two sectors in Belgium. One was a little mass base we had in one of the coal-mining districts where there were around six hundred members who had come to us from social democracy. We had the absolute majority in one mining town and the response of the employers was to immediately close down the pit in that town and it never opened subsequently. All those miners who voted for the extreme Left were victimized for their political engagement. Before the war, during the war, after the war, they were never employed again. Comrade Arthur Scargill will recognize this. There's nothing new under the sun.

---

[1] The conference took place near Paris in September 1938.
[2] The US section of the Fourth International.

When did you join the resistance?

Well, the group that I have been talking about dropped out as soon as the organization had to go underground. Their leader was killed by the Stalinists with the slanderous accusation of collaboration with the Nazis. This was just a lie. After the war these comrades—I have to call them that, though they were not Trotskyists any more, but oppositional socialists, left socialists—they ran for the municipality and again got the absolute majority. So that is an indication that they were not collaborators with the Nazis: this was a ridiculous slander. With the loss of these people we reached a low point of the organization. We had perhaps a dozen or two dozen members in the winter of 1939–40, just before the German invasion. The organization was underground. The atmosphere in the country was terrible. The German army invaded on the tenth of May, and military operations were concluded with the capitulation on the twenty-eighth of May. The country was occupied and the first weeks produced total disorientation. Henri de Man, the leader of the Socialist Party, remained as assistant prime minister. He capitulated before the Nazis. He made a public appeal to collaborate with the occupation. Part of the trade-union apparatus supported him. As for the Communist Party, it published a legal newspaper. Because of the Stalin–Hitler pact they were prepared to submit to the Nazi censorship. All these events were a shock to us. We were very weak and very small. Then we heard of the murder of the Old Man, the murder of Trotsky. The Belgian papers published the information around the twenty-first of August. Immediately one of the legendary figures of Belgian Communism, a comrade Polk who had been a founding member of the party, a member of the central committee in the twenties and who had become a Trotskyist, a left oppositionist, came to my father's house. He was crying. He had known the Old Man personally. Others came too. There were seven or eight people who all said the same thing. The only way to answer this assassination was immediately to restart the organization, to show this dirty murderer that he just can't suppress ideas and he can't suppress a current of resistance. We decided to rebuild the organization and sent people to other parts of the country.

Was this done clandestinely?

It was totally clandestine. We found out that the comrades in Brussels were thinking along exactly the same lines. Within a couple of weeks we set up the skeleton of an organization. We started to publish our first illegal newspaper before the end of the year, 1940. We set up a little illegal print shop, and all that started to function, I must say, rather well under the circumstances. There was a small illegal organization and we had a good response in some workers' quarters because, in a certain sense, we had a monopoly.

The Communist Party was not at all identified with resistance. The Social Democrats were identified, rather, with collaboration. I must add immediately that resistance was not so popular. Most people still thought the Germans would win the war. They were in the best of cases abstentionist and passive. In the worst of cases they wanted to get on the side of the victors.

You were still isolated?

After the winter things changed. The defeat of the Germans in the Battle of Britain had something to do with that. The experience of the winter was very bitter, very hard. Food rations were very low, so there was much discontent among the workers. The first strikes broke out in March. Then the Communist Party started to change. It's not true that they waited until the attack on the Soviet Union. As soon as they saw some movement, movement of a mass character, they acted cautiously in order not to be cut off completely from events. They did not wish to give us and other new resistance groups a monopoly, because that would have been the price for doing nothing. And of course when the attack on the Soviet Union took place, then they were bolder. Then it became more difficult for us but at the same time the general scope of the mass resistance enlarged. I must say that I never doubted for a single day that the Nazis would lose. I can say that with a certain self-satisfaction when I look back. I was a young man, not very mature—very foolish from many points of view—but I must say that I never doubted that one day the Nazis would be defeated. Of that I was absolutely convinced. This led me into some crazy actions.

You distributed leaflets to German soldiers?

Yes, but that was not the most crazy thing to do. That was rather correct. When I was arrested for the first time, I managed to escape prison. I was caught a second time, and escaped from the camp. The third time I was caught I was brought to Germany. I was very happy. I didn't understand at all that there was a ninety-nine-point-nine per cent chance that I would be killed.

Because you were both a Marxist and a Jew?

A Jew, a Marxist, a Communist and a Trotskyist. There were four reasons to be killed by different groups of people, if you can put it like that. I was happy to be deported to Germany because I would be in the centre of the German Revolution. I was just saying, 'Wonderful, I'm just where I want to be.' It was completely irresponsible of course.

And you did try to escape again?

Well, this also is a story of folly. The fact that I am still alive is really the exception to the rule. In a certain sense, again, I can say with satisfaction that my outlook helped—I shouldn't exaggerate because there was just luck in it too. But through political behaviour and I think a correct approach to a certain number of basic problems, I could immediately establish good relations with some of the guards. I did not behave like most of the Belgian and the French prisoners who were very anti-German. I deliberately looked for politically sympathetic warders. That was the intelligent thing to do even from the point of view of self-preservation. So I looked for Germans who were friendly, who gave evidence of some political judgement. I immediately found some former Social Democrats, even a few old Communists.

Amongst the guards in the concentration camp?

Amongst the guards, yes. It was not a concentration camp, it was a prison camp. I was sentenced, so this was already an advantage. In a concentration camp you had the SS, the worst people. In these prison camps you had functionaries of the prison system, like in a British prison. So you had some people who had been there since the twenties or thirties; I thought some of them would be Social Democrats because Social Democrats had been ministers of the interior for so long. And that was exactly the case, as I found out. Also amongst the prisoners I tried to find some young Germans—many of them, more than you might think—who were Leftists and were anti-war. I found them and made friends. My first friend there was a very fine person who had been condemned to life imprisonment because he had spoken against the war. He was the son of a socialist railway worker in Cologne. After seeing that he could have confidence in me, he gave me his father's address and the address of friends of his father, saying 'If ever you escape go to their place, they will help you, they will put you on a train, you can go back to your country.' So I developed a plan. But the whole thing was crazy anyway, you understand. We worked in an unforgettable place—one of the largest plants in Germany, perhaps it was even the largest.

What did you produce?

Gasoline, synthetic gasoline for the war machine, for the airplanes and the tanks. That was like a microcosm of Europe. You had the Russian prisoners of war, Western prisoners of war, political prisoners, and inmates of concentration camps, civilian forced labour, and civilian free labour, some German workers. There were sixty thousand people working there. It was like a microcosm of European society under the Nazis. And there was a group of Belgian workers, even some from Antwerp, from my home town. I befriended them and I asked them to give me clothes so that I could change out of my prison uniform. I looked at the electric security fences around the camp and found that they were turned off for specific reasons in the morning when they had to change the watch in the towers. I saw that and I just climbed over the wall, over that wire. I had gloves, but I was absolutely crazy, absolutely crazy.

The sort of crazy act that saved your life.

In a certain sense. It was a terrible risk that I would be caught and shot immediately. In fact unfortunately I was caught. I had three days of freedom, which were very exhilarating, very intoxicating. I obtained some fresh fruit for the first time since I had been in prison. A German woman gave me apples and pears, and that made me very happy. I knew the way to the border near Aachen. But I was caught in the woods on the third night. I was again very lucky. I started to talk to the *garde du chasse*, who had arrested me. I said to him, 'Listen, have you seen the newspapers? The Allies are already in Brussels, they will be in Aachen soon. If you kill me now you'll get into big trouble very soon. Better put me in prison without too much trouble.' He understood and was rather sympathetic. He even gave me a big loaf of bread. I don't want to boast; what I did was elementary. Of course, I gave a false name. I didn't give the exact name of the camp from which I had escaped, so they took me to another prison. But they eventually found out, and after two weeks I was held in very bad conditions, in irons and so on, because they knew I was an escaped prisoner. But I was much safer there despite the conditions. The commander of the camp from which I had escaped came to see me in the prison—a terrible, dark cell—and he said to me, 'You are a rare bird. Do you know that if you had been brought back you could have been immediately hanged?' I said yes. So he just looked at me in total amazement. But of course in this new prison he couldn't hang me. I was already under sentence so they kept me there in Eich from October 1944 until the beginning of March 1945. Then I was transferred to another camp for three weeks and liberated at the end of the month.

*Dorothy Thompson was born Dorothy Towers in London in 1923. After grad-
uating in History from the University of Cambridge, she worked in adult
education in the North of England and remained active in the Communist
Party, which she had joined at the end of the 1930s. She resigned from the party
after the Soviet invasion of Hungary. From 1968 to 1988 she taught in the
School of History in the University of Birmingham, where she wrote a series of
highly regarded books about Chartism and other topics in nineteenth-century
British history—among them,* Early Chartists *(1971),* Chartism in Wales and
Ireland *(1987),* Outsiders: Class, Gender and Nation *(1993) and* Queen
Victoria: Gender and Power *(2001). Her edited volume* Over Our Dead
Bodies: Women Against the Bomb *(1983) testified to her engagement with
post-war peace movements. She was married to the historian Edward Thompson
(1923–93). This interview was given to Sheila Rowbotham in 1993.*

Dorothy Thompson

The Personal and the Political

Your book Outsiders *suggests a general feature of your work—an awareness of class as a general feature of society but also of the cultural nuances which bind or separate people into or between classes.[1] Was there something in your family background which encouraged this approach?*

I suppose anyone growing up in England starts asking questions about class almost as soon as they can speak and I suppose the milieu that I grew up in—a South London theatrical and craft background—cut across traditional working-class areas. Nobody in my family ever worked for anyone else, except in the short term, but on the other hand nobody ever employed more than a few people. We were the artisanal layer, I suppose, and we had a very strong tradition of independence and self-education. My paternal grandfather, a shoemaker by trade, worked part time on the music halls. Two of my uncles were full-time dance band musicians. Others were tumblers and that kind of thing. My father and mother were both professional musicians, although my father set up a business running music shops and my mother mostly spent her life teaching, but also did some performing.

You lived in south London for most of your childhood?

Yes, I'm quite proud of being a third-generation Londoner. We are rather a rare species; people usually move out of London by the time they earn enough money to be able to afford it. I had a lot of relatives in places like Forest Gate, Woolwich and Greenwich. I was born in Greenwich and so I knew a lot of London families, mainly connected with the river or with the theatre—at the lower levels, not the top theatre people. And there was also a branch of the family who were descended from Huguenot weavers in Bethnal Green. They still had their own memories of the weaving community.

---

[1] *Outsiders: Class, Gender and Nation*, London 1993.

What is your first memory of a political event?

It's difficult to date this kind of thing but I do remember the General Strike in 1926. I remember my father bringing some people home—he had a little motorcar—and these people were stranded because of the strike, we were told. My brother sent the contents of his money box to the miners. I remember an item in the newspaper, the *Daily Herald*, which said that Tommy Towers had sent the contents of his money box to the miners. So I can date that clearly in 1926. I don't know how far it influenced me but certainly it's an early memory.

Can you say what influenced you politically?

My earliest childhood memories are of a time when we'd moved out of central London to Keston, in northern Kent, and we lived in a village mainly occupied by labourers' families. I remember the little girl who was our daily maid telling me very indignantly that the people next door had taken a lift from my father to the polling station and he was only offering to take Labour voters. But she knew they were Tories because they took the *Daily Mail*. So I was aware of the difference between the *Daily Mail* and *Daily Herald* by the time I was about five. That's not really politics but it's certainly the rhetoric of politics.

You got involved in politics when you were quite young?

Yes. The family always supported Labour and I decided I was a communist quite early on. I joined something called the Labour Monthly Discussion Group when I was about fourteen, then the Young Communist League and then the Communist Party. There was very much a political atmosphere in my family although no one ever belonged to anything. I was the first one I think to do that. But they had always read radical journals and newspapers.

When did your interest in history begin?

I had to make my choices about subjects at university just at the beginning of the war and my first choice would have been languages, linguistics or European languages, but that was obviously out because of the war—one couldn't travel, I couldn't go and study abroad. We had a very good teacher at school who got us very excited by history. It was when I was about sixteen or seventeen that I realized that history was a problem-solving discipline and not just an information-absorbing one. I got interested in history because it linked up with my interest in politics, and with family memories. For instance I was always enormously puzzled that one branch of the family had actually left their native country, left a comfortable living to come and live in the East End of London, simply because their version of Christianity was different from the dominant one. This seemed to be a major historical problem of considerable interest, because in my generation nobody in England seemed to feel that strongly about religion. To have given up everything for a sectarian difference seemed remarkable. This led on to political questions—why one group of people differ so profoundly when in fact they're on the same side in a sense. The question of political theory, political thought, political analysis was something that I got very interested in as a teenager.

When did you go to university?

In 1942. Edward had been there for a year by the time I went and had already gone off into the army. [2] I didn't meet him till we both came back in 1945. By 1942 the political situation was very tense: the invasion of the Soviet Union, the need to open a second front. The campaign to persuade the British authorities to invade Europe occupied an enormous amount of people's time on the Left. There were huge demonstrations in Trafalgar Square. I remember nothing of that size until the CND demonstrations. I went up to Cambridge and the second front came during my first year as a student so that the war and the politics of the war, the question of the Soviet alliance, all these things came together in the student politics of that time. We had a huge socialist club of a thousand members. Even in Bromley, in Kent, where I lived at this time, we had a YCL of nearly a hundred. I shouldn't think they'd ever had more than about four or five before—or since. This was a time when—with the Soviet Alliance—there was a tremendous interest in left-wing and Communist politics.

Did any of your tutors at Cambridge have any effect on you?

Yes. The person who interviewed me for Girton College, subsequently my personal tutor, was Helen Cam, who was a great medievalist but also a very staunch Labour Party supporter. She couldn't understand why the Labour Party wouldn't accept me as an officer of their club—she wanted me to be the secretary of the University Labour Party. I pointed out that I was a member of the Communist Party and she didn't see why that should be any objection. She was naive perhaps but very strongly socialist in her outlook. She was also a wonderful historian. She was a marvellous person to work with. She did have a lot of influence on me although in fact I didn't study medieval history, I moved into the modern period. There was another tutor, Jean McCloughlan, who later became headmistress of a school in Scotland, who was very lively and interested in European revolutionary politics. I

---

[2] Edward Thompson, the historian.

think the atmosphere at that time at Cambridge made it easy to be a radical and a historian.

This emphasis on the importance of mass political involvement is something that's been important in your life. Do you think this is because when you first became interested in politics it was a time when there was a genuine connection of left-wingers to society on a wide scale?

I think this question of involvement in politics is a very interesting one. I always believed, until really quite recently, probably till about twenty years ago, that in an ideal society everybody would take part in politics, that it was natural for people to wish to have some control over their lives and that the best way of achieving this was by political structures and political activity in the broadest sense—through tenants' committees, students' committees, workers' committees and so forth. It always seemed to me that this was what most people, if they had the time and the freedom and the education, would want to do. Only fairly recently did I discover that most people want a quiet life and that the dedicated committee person is the exception rather than the rule. I think this is one of the things I learnt by being involved in politics. As long as you are involved you think it is really the most important human activity, you think you really are changing the world and affecting history. But you have to be able to stand back a bit and realize that most people don't see it in that way. One of the biggest shocks I ever had in Cambridge was when I discovered that people in the college lumped me together with the Conservative secretary, because we were both interested in politics. I thought we were at the absolute opposite ends of world experience, but in fact to the rest of the students the politicos, left and right, were much of a muchness.

Even during the Second World War?

Even during the war, yes. Obviously we took up different positions but nevertheless the fact that we both went to Union debates and attended political meetings put us in a minority. I see this now but in those days I was staggered when I found that people saw us as alike.

Do you think that even in periods of heightened mass involvement in politics it can only be at best a large minority that takes part?

It depends what you mean by involvement. In terms of actually going out on the streets, attending demonstrations, signing petitions, yes. But there have been periods when I've been absolutely amazed at the way totally non-political people have responded. In the early days of the peace movement, for example, my mother was a teacher in a rather posh private school. The headmistress asked her what she thought of those people who had broken in and sat down in a defence establishment, the first Committee of 100 action.[3] My mother said she thought what they were doing was very necessary and that it was about time something like this was done. The headmistress replied, 'So do I, so do I.' My mother discovered that many of her non-political friends were supportive. I think that there are times when one can underestimate the amount of quiet and passive support for specific political campaigns. But as far as participation goes, it will always be a minority, I think.

Even in the days before we had universal suffrage, would you say that this was the case? For example in the periods about which you have written. Didn't the big Chartist movements at least reflect a widespread mood and aspiration, even amongst those who never went on a demonstration?

Some historians would disagree with that. It's a question that is almost impossible to measure. But if perhaps 80 per cent of the population vote in parliamentary elections, I think you can say that 80 per cent of the population would have taken one view or another about the vote, the men anyway. So many contemporaries say that this was the general opinion among working men, that the Charter was something they wanted, that I think it is so. But when you get a situation where half the population don't vote, then it does suggest widespread alienation from politics.

When you and Edward came to Yorkshire, what was the effect of the people that you met in labour politics, women and men, on how you saw socialism?

One of the things about being in the Communist Party, and it was probably true at certain times about the Labour Party as well, is that it supplied a ready-made network of contacts and friends. I think the present generation of young people is unfortunate because such opportunities have declined. I don't mean that they ought to join the Communist Party or whatever, but wherever you moved in those days you moved into a ready-made social set, so to speak: you went to a strange place, you got in touch with the Communist Party, and you had a circle of comrades. If you went abroad in the army to India, or American soldiers came over to Britain, to Cambridge, the Communists got in touch with each other. You were accepted, you were invited into their homes. This was certainly true when we went to Yorkshire. We soon got to know a group of very lively, very intelligent, very interesting people, through the Communist Party, as well as through our work with the adult education movement, which also had a structure there ready for us. By this time we were earning our livings, we were of an age when we were no

---

[3] Committee of 100: an offshoot of the Campaign for Nuclear Disarmament, founded in 1961 and committed to the tactics of non-violent civil disobedience.

longer students, we were no longer junior members of middle-class households, we were setting up our own household, having our own children. We met people on equal terms and one of the things that we discovered, I suppose everyone discovers, is how very ordinary students are; that a lot of the people we met who were engineers or nurses or factory workers knew a lot more than we did. This is perhaps brought home particularly when you go into adult education. You're teaching but in many more ways you're learning all the time. In Yorkshire we met people much more politically experienced and politically sophisticated than we were; certainly people with whom an exchange of views and experience was enormously enriching and valuable.

You once said that Simone de Beauvoir's vision of emancipation missed out the really important thing, which was how you both have children and maintain your independence. That period in Yorkshire, both because of the women that you met and the fact that you were having your own children, must have affected how you saw the position of women.

Yes, it did. I was brought up by feminists—in my own family the women were certainly as talented and as influential as the men. Women taught me at school, an all-girls school and I went to an all-women college. These were brilliant women, scholars who could take their place in the world of scholarship with any men around. They very much wanted us, whom they saw as able girls, to go ahead and make our names in the profession. But because of prevailing social arrangements none of them had children. Most didn't have husbands, and our generation of young female scholars, young female graduates, realized we had to make a choice—that we couldn't, as we saw it, have a husband and family and home, if we wished to have a career. In those days, for instance, it would be very difficult to envisage a situation in which a husband and wife each had a job and he got the chance of promotion or a better job and they would not automatically go to where his better job was. Even the most enlightened and liberated women would think like this. Certainly by the time you started to have children there was no question of your having a totally independent career, because looking after the children was too demanding. So that many of my generation, the girls I was at school with particularly, didn't go on to further education; they chose a husband and family and home-making and all that goes with it. It wasn't all just drudgery, it was also having a home where friends and family could meet, and entertaining and amateur dramatics, and taking part in church and political activities. All these things went with having only one wage-earner in the family, and there were very few families that had two wage-earners to begin with, while the children were small. I carried on with my independent research and part-time work more than most people of my generation, but even so I wouldn't have considered a full-time job until Edward gave up full-time work or until the children were old enough not to need support at home. So that the Beauvoir situation of two independent intellectuals having independent households and unlimited affairs was just not open to anyone who chose the option of children and home and family.

There's a very strong awareness in your historical writing of the understandings that come from women's activities in the home. While you are clear that these should not be imposed as a destiny, you also emphasize the positive potential of domestic experience, something that needs to be affirmed and brought into society.

A lot of the women in Yorkshire, in fact most of the married women I knew, did work. They went to work in factories and they hated it. They wanted the right not to have to work when their children were little. They didn't see it as very liberating, that they had to make everyone's breakfast, park the children with Granny and rush off and work eight hours in a factory where they'd get their heels trodden on and their bottoms smacked. Of course, there were things they liked. If they gave up working when their children were small, when they were bigger they often went back on the evening shift—for which they earned very little, but they missed the company in the factories. There are a whole number of tensions and contradictions: you may hate the work, but you like the company, you like the regularity, you like a bit of money of your own even if it's not a big wage. The two-wage family was the norm in the Yorkshire textile districts when we were there, and you didn't see this as an enormously liberating thing, although you did see these women as having a certain independence and strength and liveliness that the women in the South who were just coffee-morning and afternoon-tea sort of people didn't have.

Your writing on women and Chartism shows that women cannot be conceived of as one group, as if all women share essentially the same experiences. Do you see this as still politically significant?

Yes. Some feminist writers—I'm sorry, I mustn't knock feminism—but some women writers declare that women want this, women want that, women say this, women say that, as though they speak for all women. This is particularly true of some American academic ladies who are amongst the most privileged people in the whole world, and in the whole history of the world, and who think they speak for all women. In fact there are as many differences amongst women as there are amongst men. There are old women and young women, fit women and weak women, rich and poor. There are women who really get enormous satisfaction out of looking after their parents and their children, and those who do not. Perhaps all would like more space, and I don't think anyone likes being totally confined to housework. But there are many women who would make a good life seeing the home and their children as the main focus through a large part of their life. There are others who simply don't find any satisfaction in that at all. It's rather like saying that all men ought to be gardeners, they'd all actually prefer to be digging gardens. I also think that parenting and relations between the generations are very important to men and women alike and that men, particularly working-class men who rarely saw their children when they were small, missed something very important. They were out at work before the children were up and back at work when they were in bed. I think they missed a whole dimension of human experience.

After the war, and after the defeat of fascism, there was a real feeling of hope that a new world was being constructed. You went to Yugoslavia to help to build a railway there. What do you feel today as Yugoslavia breaks apart and its peoples opt for nationalism? The railroad that you worked on was in Bosnia, a country that you now see being destroyed.

Everyone must be appalled by what's happening there now. I think both as academics and in our own lives most radicals and communists and socialists of my generation thought that the basic conflicts were class conflicts between the exploited and the exploiters, or between the conquered, the victims of imperialism, and the conquerors. We saw these as the major conflicts. Nationalist and other ethnic conflicts were seen as epiphenomenal, encouraged by the exploiters in order to divide the workforce. I think we probably were very wrong on this, and in our analysis of what in fact impels human action, particularly the kind of absolutely destructive and self-sacrificing activity of the volunteer soldier—as Tolstoy said, war demands not only the ability to die for your country but to kill for it. And what people will kill for actually turns out not to be class issues, or gender issues, but very often these very difficult racial, national, ethnic, religious divisions which seemed to people of our generation very superficial, quite unimportant. If you walk through Bosnia you would not know a Croat, a Serb or a Muslim if they were all drinking together. There would be no way you could tell, except at Ramadan when the children might wear traditional clothes. But the women don't wear the veil, or they didn't when I was there. There was no way you could differentiate these people and they all seemed to think, having defeated the Germans, that they were building a country in which these differences were recognized but were not essential. I think there was always a very deep Serb–Croat division; after all, the Ustashe had murdered horrifying numbers of Serbs. You could feel that in the air, but in the main even that was something that they were putting behind them. Well, obviously we were wrong if we thought this was what was happening, because things could not have erupted in the way they have now if those ethnic and ʾgious and linguistic divisions had been as superficial as we thought. But I am still shocked and horrified at the persistence of ethnic hatreds. I suppose it is the same thing on the Indian subcontinent. That India had got its freedom was one of the great triumphs in our lifetime, and yet these antagonisms have led to thousands of people being killed today and yesterday.

What was the feeling amongst the group you were with from Britain?

There were Fabians, there were Communists. We saw people as good workers or bad workers. My electrician who has a black assistant says we electricians see people as good electricians or bad electricians, we don't notice their colour. We didn't really look at people's politics very much if they were good workers. (I don't wish to gossip but there were one or two very well-known persons out there then on the Left who were extremely unpopular.) It was a job of work, we were building a railway. We met groups of people from all over the world—but significantly no Soviet people. There were meant to be no Americans either, though a few adventurous ones, typically, managed to squeeze in by bicycling and pretending they were doing something else. Mostly the youth workers were from different parts of Europe and they all worked together, they had campfires together, they sang songs, shouted, went to meetings, or slept through meetings, together. The Romanians and the British always snored deeply when slogans were being shouted out, but there was a great sense of international cooperation and of course an enormous sense of hope.

What was your working day like?

We got up at half past five, washed in cold water, then went off to work at the rock face at six o'clock. We had a break at half past eight, when we had a sandwich of black bread and apple jam and some acorn coffee, and then we worked on till about midday. At midday we went back and had the main meal of the day which was eaten on the campsite—big dishes of tea and vegetables and things. In the afternoon everyone could do what they liked. Some of us went walking, some of us had classes with other groups, some people slept. In the evenings we had camp fires and political speeches and singing and dancing. You did about six hours solid manual work, digging rocks, loading up trucks, pushing them along and tipping them over the embankment, and the rest of the time socialized with the other groups.

And was this where you first met Edward Thompson?

No, we went together, or rather we got there by different routes but we decided to go together. We had already known each other for two years at Cambridge since he'd come back from the army and I'd come back from the drawing office where I was an industrial draughtsperson. I was then married to someone else but it was a very short wartime marriage and broke up without a great deal of difficulty as far as I remember. Edward and I were both interested in history, both members of the Communist Party, I fancied him, he fancied me. I suppose that's all one can say.

What about getting married?

Well I was married to someone else, as I say, and Edward and I lived together—in those days you couldn't get a divorce until you'd been married for three years so that I couldn't just get a divorce from my first husband until the three years were up. By that time I was pregnant with our first son. In fact we got married a week before Ben was born, which puts me in the wrong with the modern generation but also with the last generation. I was too soon for the present lot and too late for the older lot, but that was why we got married. In those days you did feel that if you were having children you should be married because all kinds of legal, property and identity things were overcome if you were married—the child had a name and if there was any property in the family, it would inherit. Nobody really thought twice about getting married once they were pregnant. I don't think any of my friends had babies before they were actually married, but most of them married pretty close to giving birth.

In an essay on C. Wright Mills, Edward wrote approvingly that his biography had been very distinctly changed by history, in other words he wasn't just an academic but his life responded to events in the world. Could one say that this applies to Edward and yourself and in fact to a whole generation of historians, philosophers? To what extent do you regret any of that, the fact that your biographies have been moulded by history?

This may not exactly answer your question but the idea of becoming an academic aged twenty-four and staying there till you're sixty-five seems to me the ultimate hell—well perhaps not the ultimate hell, there are worse jobs to be stuck in. But the idea of staying in one job and just slogging away at it without a change of scene and a change of emphasis and a change of atmosphere would seem to me absolutely frightful. I know some people do it but for intellectuals the rigid career structure is only a fairly recent development really, except for people like clerical dons. Most people in the past moved in and out of political activity or writing or academic work. For our generation this was still possible. When I first went to Birmingham Charles Madge was professor of sociology. As far as I know he didn't have a degree but he had worked in Mass Observation and other work and he brought his experience into academe and taught sociology from it. I think that I would not have felt I could write about working-class history and popular movements if I hadn't spent quite a lot of time taking part in them, not just because it gives you the experience but because it takes you out of the purely academic approach to things. You don't necessarily write about the things you've done but it does help. I think our generation has been very fortunate in that we've had a much more varied experience. People were in the army or industry and then moved to academic jobs or political jobs. It's becoming more difficult for people to do this kind of thing, and I suppose those who do move in and out of different spheres of work feel that they're more exposed to what's happening in the world at large than people who just progress from being lecturer to senior lecturer to professor and if they move, move from Oxford to York.

Is there any sense in which you feel that the years before 1956 when you were in the Communist Party were wasted ones?

When people give interviews they often spend their time pointing out that whatever they did was the perfect path and that's why they've ended up as such perfect persons. I certainly wouldn't claim that. On the other hand I did enjoy a lot of my time in the Communist Party. I met some wonderful people and got to know people of quite different backgrounds and of different nationalities whom I wouldn't have met otherwise. So in that sense I don't regret it. I just cannot know what sort of a mind and intellectual development I should have had if things had come out otherwise. I've absolutely no way of telling so I can't say whether I might have ended up as a brilliant scientist or a brilliant historian if I hadn't been tied down by Communist experience. But I would say I don't regret it in the sense that I have many very good memories. As a historian I try not to theorize too much about what would have happened. All you can do is understand what you think did happen.

Could you explain how you have tried to explore this relationship between the public and the private in your work?

During the nineteenth century the articulation of the ideology of 'separate spheres' and the separation between the public (male) and the private (female/familial) was usually put forward as an argument against the granting of citizen's rights to women. The rhetoric has to be treated with some care, but I think it is still of some value to recognize areas of public and private concern. I found myself thinking of this when I wrote about Queen Victoria. One reason why she is so fascinating is that she is the first person in history, as far as I know, to undertake both public and private roles simultaneously and in the same office. She is a mother and wife, but she is also the Queen and never steps down from that role. She talks about ruling by example rather than by fiat, although she does in fact take a close personal interest in the politics of government. In spite of the presence of a woman in the highest office of state, however, the mainstream political rhetoric of her reign is concerned with keeping women out of the expanding public areas— the areas of the press, of the constantly expanding constituency of parliament and the electorate, of the increasingly masculinized professions and of the burgeoning local public structures of town halls, local councils and social agencies. Women preachers are forced out of most dissenting churches, and even those with a traditionally strong female presence, like the Society of Friends, see an increasing division, spatial and organizational, between male and female sections of their work. In literature and politics these public/ private divisions are constantly emphasized, but the ideal domestic realm over which woman rules does not exist for the working people. While laws are passed restricting factory women's labour to prevent them from working at hours in which they should be caring for husbands and children, the far greater number of women domestic servants have no such protection and no opportunity of participating in a private sphere except as menials in the family life of their employers. For the poor there was little private life of any kind, and little chance to make choices about moral questions in a family life in which all access to the agencies of choice—legal, medical or social—depended upon money. So if upper-class women, especially the unmarried or talented among them, were restricted by the public/private rhetoric, working-class women might often have welcomed a greater oppor- tunity to do their work and care for their children with more privacy and less interference from outside than they were given. I do think that there is a need for a public/private boundary, though not a gender-based one. There should be areas in which the state has no right to intervene. I don't think this applies only to sexual and familial questions. I think there ought to be areas of thought and behaviour which are not the responsibility of the state and which the education system has no right to intervene in. I don't think children ought to be educated in a particular religion. But I also don't think they ought to be educated to believe that all religions are the same, which is just as bad as teaching them that one is better than the others. You know, I think real secular education is something that we have hardly begun to envisage yet. And it probably should be accompanied by an expansion of facilities for small groups to develop programmes of additional educa- tion, which are controlled by the family and not by the state. But this raises enormous questions, enormous problems. If you go too far along the road of minority education then you may disadvantage people who belong to minority groups. If they're only ever exposed to the social values of a very small and narrow sect, they may be less employable and have less access to the major areas of public life. So I think this, again, is one of the tensions that's constantly present in every social decision, and one of which we have to be constantly aware.

You have a very critical attitude to any idea that there is continuous progress in history. It is a modern version of the Greek view of history that everything's tending towards some improvement.

That again is a huge subject. I certainly don't think anyone living today could see human history as a history of progress. But you can see—the word progress is a very dangerous, very nineteenth-century one. And the various teleologies of which Marxism was certainly one saw history as progressing inevitably and in stages, towards some final state, whether it's the Kingdom of God, or the classless society or a realized Utopia. Either you get there or the whole thing blows apart. It's a very dangerous view and it also leads to a kind of fanaticism and self-sacrifice in the interest of an unknown future, which often means the sacrifice of a present generation. So no, I wouldn't accept an idea of progress, or a linear or teleological development, in history. But I wouldn't go to the other extreme and say that all virtue lies in static societies. Especially for women. I should think of the women peasants, probably 50 per cent might have been happier staying as peasants, and the other 50 per cent would have given anything to get out of the narrow, prurient and morally deterministic society in which they grew up. There are always these tensions around traditional values, which may benefit many people, but which often isolate and marginalize the creative or the different or the inventive person.

Do you think there are insights in the movement before the emergence of modern socialism in the late nineteenth century which would be relevant to thinking about the problem which you said you thought now faced people—that of how to create a society which people really want to live in?

When you introduce the word create, that's fine if you're God, but if you're anyone else 'creating' is problematic. I think one of the most interesting arguments about the practicalities of a desirable social community is that between Edward Bellamy and William Morris which took place in the late nineteenth century. Bellamy saw the future as an urban society in which work is limited. Everyone does three hours' work a day, in a conscript army that does all the work, and then the rest of the time is spent in leisure activities and people entertaining and amusing each other. They use science to limit the amount of work that needs to be done. Morris responded in fury to this 'Cockney Utopia' and wrote *News from Nowhere*—describing a rural and small-town society in which everybody has fulfilling and pleasant work. Everyone changes their work often enough so nobody gets stuck as a bricklayer all their life, they do other jobs. On the one hand there is the idea that work is an evil that has to be done and has to be got round and, therefore, should be organized in such a way that we all benefit from it, but don't have to do too much of it. And the other view is that we only exist—we are working animals and are only happy—if we're working. I think, again, this is one of the tensions within human consciousness. The very rich people in the eighteenth or nineteenth century, who didn't need to work, nevertheless set up most elaborate structures of seasonal behaviour, from fox-hunting to court attendance for themselves; they had to be in action at a certain time or place—because just doing nothing, or being generally cultured, was not satisfying. So perhaps one fundamental question is how to organize work so that it is rewarding and to a degree satisfying, and perhaps fulfils what may be a basic human need for a certain regularity and a certain challenge in daily life but, at the same time, not to end up with a society in which all the nasty work is done by a section who get no fulfilment and no pleasure. This is, again, one of the tensions, one of the motivating ideas behind socialism, to which different socialist programmes offered totally different answers. I don't think we have answers but we do constantly have to pose the questions. We have all the time to weigh factors against each other. Structure and routine against freedom, but how much freedom? What sort of freedom do people want? Shorter hours and greater leisure meant more fulfilling and agreeable work for most people. They have for some. But modern work patterns haven't necessarily meant shorter hours. Some of the people who do the most useful work, or the most necessary work, are still working just as long hours as before, while millions are without work. We haven't really sorted out the problem of work—maybe it's not a sortable problem but it points to tensions and contradictions that left-wing and socialist people have to look at.

You have said that the Chartists did not differentiate between economics and politics. They thought bold political changes would be tantamount to social transformation.

I think Chartism came at a time when, as George Eliot says in one of her novels, everybody believed that politics was the route to change, that everything could be achieved by political action. You could regulate factory hours, you could emancipate women, you could introduce freedom—everyone felt that political change would work wonders. And then you have a great swing against that after 1848, in the fifties, sixties and seventies, towards organized self-help—trade unions and cooperative societies. And partly under the influence of Marxist and Owenite teaching, the idea grew that the decisive area of transformation was the economic sphere. This approach was very general. Thus the liberal free traders believe that free trade will solve all the problems, and you don't need the state, except just to hold the ring and to sustain a military force to stop your ships getting sunk. But free trade, the free play of the market, was going to be the real answer. Everyone could be encouraged to 'build a better mousetrap'. Amongst the socialists it was the expropriation of the economic forces that was going to transform society. And politics really did take a back seat for the labour movement until after the First World War, and even then the political programme was always tentative. The Labour Party never really saw it as possible to bring about political change because socialism was always in the way. Labour politicians tended to believe that you had to have socialism before you could really make political change. In the twenties and thirties, socialism was never really on the agenda and they could not proceed without the expropriation of the expropriators. They tinkered around with social and economic policy, but without really making any attempt at fundamental change. It's not till 1945 that you begin to get an attempt, through politics, to alter social structures and change social attitudes. By the time you get to the forties, you're swinging back one hundred years because, in those days, the Chartists didn't see the industrial and political as being two discrete entities. They thought you could limit the rapacity of capitalists by limiting the hours of work, by legislating about wages, by regulating women's labour, by introducing compulsory education. All these kinds of things they saw as political moves, which would improve their social situation; post-1945 we came back to this approach, with an interaction between political and social and economic factors. The Thatcher period has seen drastic political action coming from the Right to reshape society and the economy. I think you've never had a period in human history—well in British history anyway—when there was so much ideological politics exerted on the economy as there has been in the last fifteen years. The economy has been totally sacrificed to political dogma, and I think this again is one of the tensions that has to be resolved. The whole of socialist history is about achieving some sort of balance and coordination between social mobilization, political action and economic transformation.

Lucio Colletti (1924–2001) was born in Rome and took his degree in literature and philosophy at Rome University, where he later became professor of Theoretical Philosophy. In 1950 he joined the Italian Communist Party (PCI), and in 1957 was appointed to the editorial board of its principal cultural journal, Società. *The PCI leadership closed the journal in 1962 and two years later Colletti resigned from the party, as a left critic of its political and ideological orthodoxy. He sustained this role for more than a decade, defending the political and philosophical positions he set out in this interview, which took place in 1974.*

The end of the seventies marked a second, more drastic watershed in Colletti's thinking. The compilation Tra marxismo e no *(1979) signalled a crisis in his relations with Marxist tradition, and by the early eighties he had transferred his political hopes to the Socialist Party. His final political move took him unambiguously to the right, into the camp of Silvio Berlusconi, whose Forza Italia he served as a parliamentary deputy from 1996 until his death.*

Lucio Colletti

A Political and Philosophical Interview

Can you give us a brief sketch of your intellectual origins, and entry into political life?

My intellectual origins were similar to those of virtually all Italian intellectuals of my generation. Their starting point during the last years of fascism was the neo-idealist philosophy of Benedetto Croce and Giovanni Gentile. I wrote my thesis in 1949 on Croce's logic, although I was already by then critical of Croceanism. Then between 1949 and 1950 my decision to join the Italian Communist Party gradually matured. I should add that this decision was in many ways a very difficult one, and that—although this will perhaps seem incredible today—study of Gramsci's writings was not a major influence on it. On the contrary, it was my reading of certain of Lenin's texts that was determinant for my adhesion to the PCI: in particular, and despite all the reservations which it may inspire and which I share towards it today, his *Materialism and Empirio-Criticism*. At the same time, my entry into the Communist Party was precipitated by the outbreak of the Korean War, although this was accompanied by the firm conviction that it was North Korea which had launched an attack against the South. I say this, not in order to furnish myself with an *a posteriori* political virginity, but because it is the truth. My attitudes even then were of profound aversion towards Stalinism: but at that moment the world was rent into two, and it was necessary to choose one side or the other. So, although it meant doing violence to myself, I opted for membership of the PCI—with all the deep resistances of formation and culture that a petty-bourgeois intellectual of that epoch in Italy could feel towards Stalinism. You must remember that we had lived through the experience of fascism, so that all the paraphernalia of orchestrated unanimity, rhythmical applause and charismatic leadership of the international workers' movement were spontaneously repugnant to anyone of my background. Nevertheless, in spite of this, because of the Korean conflict and the scission of the world into two blocs, I opted for entry into the PCI. The left wing of the Socialist Party did not provide any meaningful alternative, because at that time it was essentially a subordinate form of Communist militancy, organically linked to the policies of the PCI. It is important to emphasize the relative lateness of my entry into the party—I was about twenty-five or twenty-six—and my lack of the more traditional illusions about it. For the death of Stalin in 1953 had a diametrically opposite effect on me to that which it had on most Communist or pro-Communist intellectuals. They felt it as a disaster, the disappearance of a kind of divinity, while for me it was an emancipation. This also explains my attitude towards the Twentieth Congress of the CPSU in 1956, and in particular towards Khrushchev's Secret Speech. While most of my contemporaries reacted to the crisis of Stalinism as a personal catastrophe, the collapse of their own convictions and certitudes, I experienced Khrushchev's denunciation of Stalin as an authentic liberation. It seemed to me that at last Communism could become what I had always believed it should become—a historical movement whose acceptance involved no sacrifice of one's own reason.

What was your personal experience, as a young militant and philosopher, within the PCI from 1950 to 1956?

My membership of the party was an extremely important and positive experience for me. I can say that if I were to relive my life again, I would repeat the experience of both my entry and my exit. I regret neither the decision to join nor the decision to leave the party. Both were critical for my development. The first importance of militancy in the PCI lay essentially in this: the party was the site in which a man like myself, of completely intellectual background, made real contact for the first time with people from other social groups, whom I would otherwise never have encountered except in trams or buses. Secondly, political activity in the party allowed me to overcome certain forms of intellectualism and thereby also to understand somewhat better the problems of the relationship between theory and practice in a political movement. My own role was that of a simple rank-and-file militant. From 1955 onwards, however, I became involved in the internal struggles over cultural policy in the PCI. At that time, the official orientation of the party was centred on an interpretation of Marxism as an 'absolute historicism', a formula which had a very precise meaning—it signified a way of treating Marxism as if it were a continuation and development of the historicism of Benedetto Croce himself. It was in this light that the party also sought to present the work of Gramsci. Togliatti's version of Gramsci's thought was, of course, not an accurate one.[1] But the fact is that Gramsci's writings were utilized to present Marxism as the fulfilment and conclusion of the tradition

---

[1] Palmiro Togliatti (1893–1964): succeeded Gramsci as leader of the PCI in 1927, and retained that role for the rest of his life.

of Italian Hegelian idealism, in particular that of Croce. The objective of the internal struggles in which I became engaged was by contrast to give priority to the knowledge and study of the work of Marx himself. It was in this context that my relationship to Galvano Della Volpe, who at that time was effectively ostracized within the PCI, became very important for me.[2] One outcome of the theoretical struggle between these two tendencies was the entry of Della Volpe, Giulio Pietranera and myself into the editorial committee of *Società*, which was then the main cultural journal of the party, in 1957–58.

To what extent was the change in the composition of the editorial committee of Società *at that time a consequence of the Twentieth Party Congress in the USSR and of the Hungarian Revolt?*

It was a consequence of Hungary, for a very simple reason. After the rising in Budapest, the majority of Italian communist professors abandoned the party, which was left virtually without university luminaries. One of the few professors who remained in the party was Della Volpe. The new situation induced Mario Alicata—who was then in overall charge of the party's cultural policy, and who, it must be said, was a highly intelligent man—to change his attitude towards Della Volpe, who had hitherto been intellectually proscribed within the party. The result was that Della Volpe was finally accepted on to the editorial board of *Società*, and with him a good part of the Della Volpean tendency, including Pietranera (who died today) and myself. This lasted until 1962. In that year, the party then decided to dissolve *Società*, for reasons which were not only ideological but political. The suppression of the journal was basically motivated by the fact that after the composition of the editorial committee had changed, the review became steadily radicalized, if only on an ideological level: Marxist and Leninist articles were becoming predominant, and this theoretical turn to the Left disquieted the party leadership for a very good reason. The PCI had for many years previously ceased to recruit young people. But from 1959–60 onwards, it started to register gains amongst youth once more—especially after the popular demonstrations which overthrew the Tambroni government in 1960. There now started to emerge a new levy of young Communist intellectuals—some of whom occupy comparatively important positions in the PCI today, while others have left it—influenced by Della Volpean positions. Alarmed by the leftward shift of these younger intellectuals, who soon dominated the Youth Federation of the party, the PCI leadership decided to suppress *Società* as the source of their theoretical inspiration.

---

[2] For an introduction to the work of Della Volpe, see NLR 59, January–February 1970, pp. 97–100.

Yet within the editorial committee of Società *there were other currents—represented for example by Mario Spinella or Cesare Luporini, who joined the journal at more or less the same time as Della Volpe and yourself. Wasn't there a plurality of contending influences on* Società, *consequently?*

No, there were no real debates as such in the pages of the review. Spinella was in principle the chief editor; but after the entry of Della Volpe onto the editorial board, some of its members—while remaining formally on the masthead—simply ceased to collaborate with the journal. So in practice there was no public confrontation of views in *Società*. Moreover, you must remember that the journal was a publication produced by the party, which meant that the preparation of its issues was tightly controlled from above, in particular by Alicata. In practice, most of the contributions came from the so-called Della Volpean group, but more for reasons of inertia and boycott by its antagonists on the journal. Thus, without a true political debate, *Società* eventually came to reflect—within its own ideological-cultural limits—a new commitment to themes proper to Marxism and Leninism.

Surely towards the end of this period there were some quite important debates on political questions in the review: for instance, the polemic between yourself and Valentino Gerratana on the nature of the representative state?

It would be misleading to call this episode a debate within the review. It occurred within the party. For some years back, I had been attacking the notion of the 'constitutional State' (*Stato di diritto*), to some extent also in the journals of the Left of the PSI like *Mondo Nuovo*. The theme of my polemics was that it was strange to call for the advent of a 'constitutional State', since in my view this already substantially existed in Italy—it was none other than the liberal-bourgeois state. I failed to understand how the status quo could become a future objective of the party. To organize a reply to such criticisms, the party convoked a conference on the 'concept of the constitutional State', at which Gerratana delivered a report rebutting positions expressed in an article of mine. The two texts were published in *Società*, but the debate did not derive from within the journal.[3]

You left the party two years after the closure of Società *in 1964. What were the reasons for your departure? Was it mainly inspired by a persistent Stalinism, or by a growing reformism, in the* PCI?

---

[3] See L. Colletti, 'Stato di Diritto e Sovranità Popolare', *Società*, November–December 1960; and V. Gerratana, 'Democrazia e Stato di Diritto', *Società*, November–December 1961—the last issue of the journal. For Gerratana's work, see his important essay 'Marx and Darwin', NLR I/82, November–December 1973.

My decision to leave was the result of the overall evolution of the party. In one sense, the process of renovation for which I had hoped after the Twentieth Party Congress had failed to occur—but in another sense it had occurred, in a patently rightward direction. I slowly came to realize in the period from 1956 to 1964 that both the Soviet regime itself, and the Western Communist parties, were incapable of accomplishing the profound transformation necessary for a return to revolutionary Marxism and Leninism. It had become structurally impossible for either the CPSU or the Western Parties to undergo a real democratization—in other words, not in the sense of a liberal or bourgeois democracy, but in the sense of revolutionary socialist democracy, of workers' councils. This conviction gradually matured within me during the experience of these years. I found myself ever more marginalized within the party, where I was permitted to pay my dues, but little else. Thus when I finally came to the conclusion that there was no chance even of a slow transformation of either the Soviet regime or the Western Communist parties towards a renewed socialist democracy, membership of the PCI lost any meaning for me, and I left the party silently. There was no dramatic scandal or rupture in my departure. I left in 1964, the year of Khrushchev's fall. There should be no misunderstanding about my attitude towards this. I was naturally aware of all the criticisms to be made of Khrushchev, whom I never idealized. Nevertheless, Khrushchev did represent a crucial point of no return in post-war history. For his Secret Speech was a formal denunciation of the sacred character with which all Communist leadership had surrounded itself for four decades. This desacralization of Communist bureaucratic leadership remains an achievement that cannot be cancelled. Thus Khrushchev's importance for me was that he did symbolize an attempt—however inadequate and debatable—to unleash a process of transformation of Soviet society, by a radical and violent indictment of Stalin. If this process had succeeded, it would have transformed the Western parties too. In the event, as we know, it failed.

So far as Italian communism is concerned, the PCI does possess certain traits that are distinct from those of other parties of classical Stalinist formation, and which are in some ways more rightist and revisionist. However, in essence—in its mechanisms of policy-making, its selection of leadership, the whole way in which the political will of the organization is formed—the PCI has remained a fundamentally Stalinist party. The expulsion of the *Manifesto* group in 1970 shows how limited the real margins for political debate and struggle in fact are within the party. Naturally, this does not mean that there is no political conflict within the PCI. There is: but it is masked and hidden from the base of the party, which remains ignorant even of the terms of the stealthy struggles at the summit. The rank and file consequently remains confined to a perpetually subaltern and atomized condition. The ordinary communist militant is converted from a vanguard to a rearguard element, whose function is simply to execute political directives determined over his head. My rejection of this type of party can be summed up in a single formula. The real mechanisms of power in contemporary Communist parties are these: it is not the Congress that nominates the Central Committee, but the Central Committee that nominates the Congress, it is not the Central Committee that nominates the Executive Committee, but the Executive Committee that nominates the Central Committee, it is not the Executive Committee that nominates the Political Bureau, but the Political Bureau that nominates the Executive Committee.

The major early influence on your philosophical work was Galvano Della Volpe, with his concern for the nature of scientific laws, his notion of the role of specific-determinate abstractions in cognition, and his stress on philological precision in the study of Marx. What is your assessment of Della Volpe today?

The essential lesson I learnt from contact with the writings of Della Volpe was the need for an absolutely serious relationship to the work of Marx—based on direct knowledge and real study of his original texts. This may sound paradoxical, but it is important to remember that the penetration of Marxism in Italy in the first post-war decade, from 1945 to 1955, was intellectually and theoretically very superficial and exiguous. Let me explain. The official Marxism of that epoch, as it remains today, was Soviet-style dialectical materialism. Now, Togliatti was cultivated and intelligent enough to be aware that this Stalinist compendium was too blatantly crude and dogmatic to have much attraction for the Italian intellectuals whose adhesion to the PCI he was anxious to obtain. Consequently, there were few orthodox dialectical materialists in Italy: compatriot charity forbids me to mention names. What Togliatti sought to substitute for Soviet orthodoxy in his cultural policy was an interpretation of Marxism as the national heir to the Italian historicism of Vico and Croce—in other words, a version of Marxism that did not demand any real break of these intellectuals from their former positions. Most of them were Crocean by formation. The party simply asked them to take one small step more, to adopt a historicism that integrated the basic elements of Croce's philosophy, repudiating only the most patently idealist propositions of Croceanism. The result was that up to 1955–56 Marx's work itself, above all *Capital*, had a minimal diffusion in the cultural ambience of the Italian Left. It was in these conditions that Della Volpe came to symbolize a commitment to study Marxism rigorously, where it is actually to be found, namely in Marx's writings themselves. For Della Volpe, Marx's early *Critique of Hegel's Philosophy of Right* was a central starting point. But this naturally represented only the beginning of a direct knowledge of the work of Marx, which necessarily had as its conclusion an intense study and analysis of *Capital* itself.

*Would it be true to say that in the period after 1958, Della Volpeanism as a theo-
retical current within the* PCI—*by its emphasis on the paradigmatic importance
of* Capital, *and the necessity of determinate abstractions for the formulation of
scientific laws—implied a covert political opposition to the very moderate goals
officially pursued by the* PCI, *the 'democratic' objectives which were justified by
the party on the grounds of the relative backwardness of Italian society? Some of
your 'historicist' adversaries at the time argued that the real meaning of Della
Volpeanism was a denial of the hybrid and retarded character of the Italian
social formation, which dictated democratic rather than socialist demands, for
a fixation with the general laws of pure capitalist development as such, to justify
inappropriately 'advanced' objectives for the working class in Italy. How valid
was the interpretation?*

It is certainly true that the diffusion of Della Volpean positions—a phenomenon whose dimensions should not be exaggerated, incidentally—was
combated in the party, with the accusation that they were pregnant with
political sectarianism and ultra-leftism. For it was evident that while the historicist tradition tended to give priority to the peculiarities of Italian society,
playing down the fact that despite all its particularities it was still a capitalist
society, the systematic study of Marx that was central to Della Volpeanism
gave priority precisely to the concept of the capitalist socio-economic formation and the laws of motion of capitalism as such. In the latter perspective,
Italy was analysed essentially as a capitalist country. Naturally, there was no
question of denying that Italian capitalism had idiosyncratic characteristics of its own, but merely of affirming that despite these peculiarities, the
predominant characteristic of Italian society was that it was capitalist. The
opposing theoretical trends of the time thus could well lead to divergent
political conclusions.

*If this was so, how is the subsequent political role of some of the leading members
of the Della Volpean school to be explained? Della Volpe himself was always
unquestioningly loyal to the official line of the party, even exalting the Stalin
Constitution of 1936 in the* USSR *as a model of radical democracy. Pietranera
went on to theorize and justify 'market socialism' in Yugoslavia and Eastern
Europe generally. What explains the apparent combination of methodological
rigour and political weakness or complaisance?*

Firstly, Della Volpe himself was an intellectual of the old style, who always
worked on the assumption that there should be a division of labour between
theory and politics. Politics could be left to professional politicians. Secondly,
it is important to stress that the Della Volpean school proper was a very circumscribed phenomenon; it involved a few collaborators, among whom, as
events were rapidly to show, there was no basic identity of political views at
all. Della Volpeanism was a phenomenon limited in both space and time, of

very short duration, after which the members of this so-called 'school' went their separate ways. Most of them have remained in the PCI to this day.

Turning to your own later philosophical writings, you have expressed an increasingly marked respect and admiration for Kant in them—a preference unusual among contemporary Marxists. Your basic claim for Kant is that he asserted with the greatest force the primacy and irreducibility of reality to conceptual thought, and the absolute division between what he called 'real oppositions' and 'logical oppositions'. You argue from these theses that Kant was much closer to materialism than Hegel, whose basic philosophical goal you interpret as the absorption of the real by the conceptual, and therewith the annihilation of the finite and of matter itself. Your revaluation of Kant is thus complemented by your devaluation of Hegel, whom you criticize implacably as an essentially Christian and religious philosopher—contrary to later Marxist misconceptions of his thought. The obvious question that arises here is why you accord such a privilege to Kant? After all, if the criterion of proximity to materialism is acknowledgment of the irreducibility of reality to thought, most of the French philosophers of the Enlightenment, La Mettrie or Holbach for example, or even earlier Locke in England, were much more unambiguously 'materialist' than Kant. At the same time, you denounce the religious implications of Hegel—but Kant also was a profoundly religious philosopher (not to speak of Rousseau, whom you admire in another context), yet you appear to pass over his religiosity in polite silence. How do you justify your exceptional esteem for Kant?

The criticisms you have just made have been levelled at me many times in Italy. The first point to establish is the difference between the Kant of the *Critique of Pure Reason* and the Kant of the *Critique of Practical Reason*.

Isn't that the same sort of distinction that is commonly made between Hegel at Jena, and Hegel after Jena—which you reject?

No, because the difference between knowledge and morality is a central one for Kant himself. He explicitly theorizes the difference between the ethical sphere and the cognitive-scientific sphere. I cannot say whether Kant is important for Marxism. But there is no doubt whatever of his importance for any epistemology of science. You have remarked that La Mettrie, Holbach or Helvetius were materialists, while Kant fundamentally was not. That is perfectly true. But from a strictly epistemological point of view, there is only one great modern thinker who can be of assistance to us in constructing a materialist theory of knowledge—Immanuel Kant. Of course, I am perfectly aware that Kant was a pious Christian. But whereas in Hegel's philosophy there is no separation between the domain of ethics and politics and the domain of logic, because the two are integrally united in a single system, in Kant there is a radical distinction between the domain of knowledge and the domain of morality, which Kant himself emphasised. Thus we can leave Kantian morality aside here. What is important to see is that the *Critique of Pure Reason* is an attempt by Kant to arrive at a philosophical comprehension and justification of Newton's physics: the work is essentially an inquiry into the conditions that render possible true knowledge—which for Kant was represented by Newtonian science. Naturally, there are many shades and contradictions in Kant's epistemological work, with which I am perfectly familiar: I have used only certain aspects of it. But there is one basic point that must always be remembered, nevertheless. While Hegel died at Berlin delivering a course of lectures on the proofs of the existence of God, and reaffirming the validity of the ontological argument (which a century later was still being upheld by Croce), Kant—despite all his contradictions—from his text of 1763 on the *Beweisgrund*[4] to the *Critique of Pure Reason* never ceased to criticize the ontological argument. His rejection of it was founded on the qualitative (or as Kant says, 'transcendental') gulf between the conditions of being and the conditions of thought—*ratio essendi* and *ratio cognoscendi*. It is this position that provides a fundamental starting point for any materialist gnoseology, and defence of science against metaphysics. The problem of an overall interpretation of Kant is a very complex one, which we cannot resolve in an interview. I have singled out and stressed one particular aspect of his work—the Kant who was the critic of Leibniz, and the scourge of the ontological proof. In this respect, although Kant was not a materialist, his contribution to the theory of knowledge cannot be compared to that of La Mettrie or Helvetius.

Thus my interest in Kant has nothing in common with that of the German revisionists of the Second International, Eduard Bernstein or Conrad Schmidt, who were attracted to Kant's ethics. I have tried, on the contrary, to revalue Kant's contribution to epistemology, as against the legacy of Hegel. In fact, my own interpretation of Kant is precisely that of Hegel himself— except that whereas Hegel rejected Kant's position, I have defended it. For Hegel, Kant was essentially an empiricist. In his introduction to the *Encyclopaedia*, Hegel classifies Kant together with Hume as examples of the 'second relation of thought to objectivity'. There is no need to remind you of the stature of David Hume in the history of the philosophy of science. One could say, indeed, that there are two main traditions in Western philosophy in this respect: one that descends from Spinoza and Hegel, and the other from Hume and Kant. These two lines of development are profoundly divergent. For any theory that takes science as the sole form of real knowledge—that is falsifiable, as Popper would say—there can be no question that the tradition of Hume–Kant must be given priority and preference over that of Spinoza–Hegel.

---

[4] Colletti's reference is to Kant's work *The Only Possible Ground for a Proof of the Existence of God*.

Finally, I believe that my attempt to separate the Kant of the *Critique of Pure Reason* from the Kant of the *Critique of Practical Reason* has a real basis in history. For bourgeois thought and civilization succeeded in founding the sciences of nature; whereas bourgeois culture has been incapable of generating scientific knowledge of society and morality. Of course, the natural sciences have been conditioned by the bourgeois historical context in which they have developed—a process which raises many intricate problems of its own. But unless we are to accept dialectical materialism and its fantasies of a 'proletarian' biology or physics, we must nevertheless acknowledge the validity of the sciences of nature produced by bourgeois civilization since the Renaissance. But bourgeois discourses in the social sciences command no such validity: we obviously reject them. It is this discrepancy between the two fields that is objectively reflected in the division within Kant's philosophy between his epistemology and his ethics, his critique of pure and of practical reason.

But is there such a complete separation between the two? Marxists have traditionally seen the Kantian notion of the thing-in-itself—Ding-an-sich—as the sign of a religious infiltration directly into his epistemological theory, surely?

There is a religious overtone to the notion of the thing-in-itself, but this is its most superficial dimension. In reality, the concept has a meaning in Kant's work that Marxists have never wanted to see, but which Cassirer—with whose general interpretation of Kant, based on careful textual studies, I am in considerable sympathy—has rightly emphasized. When Kant declares that the thing-in-itself is unknowable, one (if not the only) sense of his argument is that the thing-in-itself is not a true object of cognition at all, but a fictitious object; that is, nothing more than a substantification or hypostasization of logical functions, transformed into real essences. In other words, the thing-in-itself is unknowable because it represents the false knowledge of the old metaphysics. This is not the only meaning of the concept in Kant's work, but it is one of its principal senses, and it is precisely this that has never been noticed by the utterly absurd reading of Kant that has prevailed among Marxists, who have always reduced the notion of the thing-in-itself to a mere agnosticism. But when Kant states that it is an object that cannot be known, he means that it is the false 'absolute' object of the old rationalist metaphysics of Descartes, Spinoza and Leibniz; and when Hegel announces that the thing-in-itself can be known, what he is in fact doing is to restore the old pre-Kantian metaphysics.

Your work often appears to define materialism essentially as acknowledgement of the real existence of the external world, independent of the knowing subject. But has materialism not traditionally meant something more than this, both for Marxism and for classical philosophy as well—a specific conception of the subject of knowledge itself? In Italy, for example, you have been reproached by Sebastiano Timpanaro with ignoring the 'physicality' of the knowing subject and its concepts: he has accused you, in effect, of reducing materialism to realism by your silence on the latter score.[5] Would you accept this criticism?

No, in my view Timpanaro's argument is completely mistaken. For a number of reasons. First of all, my own concern has been above all with materialism just in *gnoseology*. Now, on the one hand, it is not true that a gnoseological materialism can be reduced merely to acknowledgement of the reality and independence of the external world. This is, of course, a fundamental thesis, but it in turn provides the basis for the construction of an experimental logic, and the explanation of scientific knowledge. Scientific experiments signify that ideas are only hypotheses. Such hypotheses must be checked, verified or falsified, by confronting them with data of observation, which are different in nature from any logical notion. If this diversity of the material contents of knowledge is denied, hypotheses become hypostases or ideal essences, and sensible and empirical data become purely negative residues once again, as in Leibniz or Hegel. On the other hand, Timpanaro's writings reveal a type of naturalism that remains somewhat ingenuous, with its single-minded insistence on the sheer physicality of man as the main basis for a philosophical materialism. Of course, once one acknowledges the existence of the natural world, there can be no disagreement that man too is a natural entity. Man as a physico-natural being is an animal. But this particular natural species is distinguished from all others by its creation of social relationships. To use Aristotle's formula: man is a *zoon politikon*, a political animal. Men live in society and have a history, and it is this level of their existence that is essential for historical materialism. The specificity of man as a natural being is to refer to nature in so far as he refers to other men, and to refer to other men in so far as he refers to nature. This dual relationship is precisely what is grasped in Marx's concept of 'social relations of production'. For Marx, there can be no production—that is, relationships of men to nature—outside or apart from social relationships, that is relationships to other men; and there can be no relationships between men that are not a function of relationships of men to nature, in production. The peculiarity of the 'nature' in man is to find its expression in 'society'. Otherwise, any discourse on man could equally be applied to ants or bees. The distinguishing characteristic of man as a natural-physical species is its generation of social relations of production, rather than honeycombs or cobwebs. It is in the nature of man to be a social-historical subject.

---

[5] Timpanaro's criticisms of Colletti have been developed in an essay entitled 'Engels, Materialism, "Free Will"', included in his volume *On Materialism*, London 1975. For Timpanaro's general philosophical positions, see his essay 'Considerations on Materialism', NLR I/85, May–June 1974.

Within historical materialism it was, of course, Engels who classically insisted most on the physical structure of man, and on the relationships between man and nature, in his later writings. You have tended to counterpose Marx against Engels in an extremely radical way in your work. For example, you attribute the entire responsibility for the notion of 'dialectical materialism' to Engels. Elsewhere, you suggest that it was Engels who introduced the first deleterious elements of political fatalism into Marxism, in the Second International. By contrast, you absolve Marx of any errors in either of these directions. Indeed, in one passage you have gone so far as to speak of 'the gulf between the rigour and complexity which characterize every page of Marx, and the popular vulgarization and at times dilettantism of the works of Engels'.[6] Would you really maintain such a formulation today? Marx, after all, not only read and approved, but collaborated on the Anti-Dühring; *and in his introductions to* Capital, *there are surely statements implying a fatalism and mechanism at least as equivocal as anything in the later Engels? Above all, does not any over-dramatic polarization of this type between Marx and Engels contain the grave danger not merely of at times unjustly criticizing Engels, but also of creating by contrast a kind of sacred zone about Marx, who conversely becomes above criticism?*

I absolutely agree with your last comment about the creation of a sacred zone about Marx. You musn't forget that the passage you quote was written seventeen years ago. My view of the relationship between Marx and Engels is now much less rigid and more nuanced, in the sense that I have become aware that in Marx too there are critical areas of uncertainty and confusion about the dialectic. I am currently preparing a study that will deal with this question. Thus I fully accept your objection: it is shameful to confer a sacred aura on any thinker, including Marx. I now utterly reject such an attitude, although I admit that I may have encouraged it in the past. This is a self-criticism. Having said this, however, I continue to maintain that the traditional image of the theoretical twins who presided over the birth of the labour movement is infantile and absurd. The facts, after all, speak for themselves. Everyone knows that Marx spent a large part of his life studying in the British Museum, while Engels was working in a cotton business in Manchester. Twin souls are miracles that do not exist in the real world; no two minds think exactly alike. The intellectual differences between Marx and Engels are evident, and have been discussed by many authors besides myself: Alfred Schmidt, George Lichtheim, or Sidney Hook when he was

---

[6] This passage occurs in the long introduction which Colletti wrote to an edition of Lenin's *Philosophical Notebooks* in 1958. The introduction was then reprinted a decade later as the first part of the Italian volume *Il Marxismo e Hegel*, Bari 1969. The English edition of *Marxism and Hegel* (London 1973) is a translation of the second part of the Italian volume, which was written as a book in itself by Colletti in 1969. The passage above is to be found in *Il Marxismo e Hegel*, p. 97.

still a Marxist, among others. Then, too, there is no historical malice in recalling the letters which Marx wrote against Engels in his lifetime, and which were destroyed by his family after his death. So far as the dialectics of nature are concerned, while I concede certain exaggerations in my writings, I would still insist that in the end all Marx's work is essentially an analysis of modern capitalist society. His basic writings are the *Theories of Surplus Value*, the *Grundrisse* and *Capital*: all the rest is secondary. While in the case of Engels, one of his major writings is indubitably the *Dialectics of Nature*—a work 90 per cent of which is hopelessly compromised by an ingenuous and romantic *Naturphilosophie*, contaminated by crudely positivist and evolutionist themes.

But what about the supposed political contrast between the two men—an allegedly proto-reformist Engels set off against an unswervingly radical Marx? Engels, after all, never committed such involuntary blunders as Marx's prediction that the mere introduction of universal suffrage—bourgeois democracy—would ensure the advent of socialism in England, a far more parliamentarist statement than anything to be found in Engels?

I concede this point. I would merely say that in the space of this interview I cannot develop all my present critical reflections on the question.

You have accorded an exceptional importance to Rousseau, as the central precursor of Marxism in the field of political theory. You have argued, in particular, that it was Rousseau who first developed a fundamental critique of the capitalist representative State, of the separation of the citizen from the bourgeois, and a counter-theory of popular sovereignty, direct democracy and revocable mandates—all themes directly inherited by Marx and Lenin. You sum up your emphasis on these ideas in a formulation which recurs in your writings, and appears to be a very shocking one: 'So far as "political" theory in the strict sense is concerned, Marx and Lenin have added nothing to Rousseau—except for the analysis (which is of course rather important) of the "economic bases" of the withering away of the State'.[7] It is the reduction of Marxist political theory solely to a critique of the bourgeois representative state and a model of direct popular democracy beyond it, that appears very strange or outré in this judgement. For it seems to ignore entirely the strategic side of Marxist political thought, above all as developed by Lenin: his theory of the construction of the party, of the alliance between proletariat and peasantry, of the self-determination of nations, of the rules of insurrection, and so on—in other words, the whole theory of how to make the socialist revolution itself. Moreover, even confining political theory in the 'strict sense' to analysis of the capitalist state, this century has seen important types of bourgeois state never dreamt of by Rousseau—above all the fascist

---

[7] *From Rousseau to Lenin*, London 1972, p. 185.

states, which were classically analysed by Trotsky. How can you exclude all this from Marxist political theory?

Let me reply in this way. Firstly, the formulation you have quoted obviously refers only to political philosophy proper, in the sense of the most general questions of principle in the theory of Marx and Lenin, which are derived from Rousseau—those you have mentioned: critique of the representative state and of the separation of civil society from political society, non-identification of government and sovereignty, rejection of parliamentary representation, notion of revocable delegates of the people, and so on. In this connection, we must realize that Marx's own discourse on the State never developed very far. His basic texts on the question are the *Critique of Hegel's Philosophy of Right* of 1843 and the *Jewish Question* of 1844; then much later the pages on the Paris Commune in the *Civil War in France* of 1871. These writings all reiterate themes to be found in Rousseau. Naturally, my statement has no validity in the field of revolutionary strategy—party-building, class alliances or fascism. It was more limited in scope. At the same time, however, I should make it clear that it contained an element of deliberate provocation. It was intended to draw attention to a particular fact—the *weakness* and sparse development of political theory in Marxism. In other words, you can also read it as a way of saying that Marxism lacks a true political theory. All the elements of Lenin's work to which you have pointed—his writings on the party, the peasantry, the national question and so on—are of great importance: but they are always tied so closely to particular historical events that we can never extrapolate them to a level of generalization where they are simply transferable to a historical environment profoundly different from that in which Lenin thought and acted. Thus the real meaning of my statement was a polemical one. The development of political theory has been extraordinarily weak in Marxism. There are doubtless many reasons for this debility. But a crucial one is certainly the fact that both Marx and Lenin envisaged the transition to socialism and the realization of communism on a world scale as an extremely swift and proximate process. The result was that the sphere of political structures remained little examined or explored. One could formulate this paradoxically by saying that the political movement inspired by Marxism has been virtually innocent of political theory. The absurdity and danger of this situation are manifest, now that it has become clear that the so-called phase of transition to socialism is actually an extremely protracted, secular process whose length was never foreseen by Marx or Lenin, during which Communist leaderships today exercise power in the name of Marxism, in the absence of any real theory of this power—let alone any control by the masses over whom they rule.

What is your judgement of Louis Althusser and his pupils? The Della Volpean school in Italy was the first radically anti-Hegelian current in Western Marxism since the First World War. It developed a whole complex of themes whose aim was to demonstrate Marx's rupture with Hegel by the constitution of a new science of society, which was then compromised by the reintroduction of Hegelian motifs into historical materialism after Marx. A decade or so later, many ideas very close to these were developed by Althusser in France, where they have gained a wide intellectual influence. How do you view Althusser's work today?

It is not easy to reply to this question. I knew Althusser personally, and for some years corresponded with him. Then I would fail to reply to him, or he to me, and gradually the letters between us ceased. When we first met in Italy, Althusser showed me some of the articles he later collected in *For Marx*. My initial impression on reading them was that there was a considerable convergence of positions between ourselves and Althusser. My main reservation about this convergence was that Althusser did not appear to have mastered the canons of philosophical tradition adequately. Della Volpe's discourse on Hegel was always based on a very close knowledge and analytical examination of his texts, not to speak of those of Kant, Aristotle or Plato. This dimension was much less visible in Althusser. On the contrary, it was substituted by the intromission of simplifications of a political type. For example, in these essays there would be a series of references to Mao, which appeared to be an intrusion of another sort of discourse into the philosophical text itself. Politically, it should be added, none of the Della Volpeans had any weakness towards Maoism. At any rate, with these reservations, the articles which later made up *For Marx* otherwise seemed to show a pronounced convergence with the classical theses of the Della Volpean current in Italian Marxism. Then Althusser sent me *Reading Capital*. I started to read it, and found—I say this without any irony—that I could not understand the presuppositions and purpose of the work. What perhaps struck me most was something that Hobsbawm later remarked, in an otherwise very laudatory review of Althusser in the *Times Literary Supplement*: that *Reading Capital* did not actually help anyone to read *Capital*. I had the impression of a lengthy theoretical construction erected, so to speak, behind the back of *Capital*. I did not find it particularly interesting as such, and did not pursue it any further.

Subsequently, the essays in *Lenin and Philosophy* appeared, including 'Lenin Before Hegel', and it became increasingly obvious that Althusser was intent on salvaging 'dialectical materialism', at least in name. Now, so far as I am concerned, dialectical materialism is a scholastic metaphysic whose survival merely indicates the deep inadequacy hitherto of the attempts by the working-class movement to come to terms with the great problems of modern science. It is an evening-class philosophical pastiche. Although Althusser interpreted it somewhat idiosyncratically, I could never understand why he still clung to the notion of dialectical materialism. More recently, however, I think I have grasped the real function it fulfils in Althusser's work, and which situates the latter more readily within the prior history of Marxism. There is a passage in a polemic of Godelier with Lucien Sève which is very revealing in this connection. Godelier cites a letter from Engels to Lafargue of 1884,[8] which anticipates a thesis that was later developed by Hilferding in his preface to *Finance Capital*. This is the idea that there is a fundamental difference between Marxism and socialism, and that you can accept the one while rejecting the other: for Marxism is value-free science, without any ideological orientation or political finalism. In Althusser, the same theme takes the form of his recent discovery that Marx did, after all, directly inherit a central notion from Hegel—the idea of a 'process without a subject'. Philologically, of course, this claim is absurd: it could only be made by someone who had read Hegel a very long time ago, retaining the dimmest memory of him. For the Hegelian process emphatically does have a subject. The subject is not human, it is the Logos. Reason is the subject of history in Hegel, as his famous expression *Der List der Vernunft*—'the cunning of reason'—makes clear. But apart from questions of scholarship, what does it mean to say that for Marx history is a process without a subject? It means that history is not the site of any human emancipation. But for the real Marx, of course, the revolution was precisely this—a process of collective self-emancipation.

In his latest work, the *Reply to John Lewis*, Althusser once again restates at length his thesis of the process without a subject. But for the first time, he is also forced to admit that the theme of alienation is present in *Capital*. In fact, the truth is that the themes of alienation and fetishism are present not only in *Capital*, but in the whole of the later Marx—not only in the *Grundrisse*, but in the *Theories of Surplus Value* as well, for hundreds of pages on end. The *Grundrisse* and *Theories of Surplus Value* merely declare in a more explicit terminology what the language of *Capital* states more obliquely, because Marx was resorting to a greater extent to the scientistic vocabulary of English political economy itself. But the problems of alienated labour and commodity fetishism are central to the whole architecture of Marx's later work. Althusser's admission, however reluctant, of their presence in *Capital*, in fact undermines his whole previous formulation of the 'break' between the young and the old Marx; it also disqualifies the notion of history as a process without a subject. But it is this component of Marxism that Althusser essentially rejects. I think that this is what explains his organic sympathy with Stalinism. In his *Reply to John Lewis*, of course, Althusser tries to establish a certain distance from Stalin. But the level of this brochure makes one throw up one's arms, as we say in Rome, with its mixture of virulence and banality. Nothing is more striking than the poverty of the categories with which Althusser tries to explain Stalinism, simply reducing it to

---

[8] See the polemic, published in Italian, between Maurice Godelier and Lucien Sève, entitled *Marxismo e Strutturalismo*, Turin 1970, pp. 126–7.

an 'economism' that is an epiphenomenon of the Second International—as it were, a mere ideological deviation, and a long-familiar one at that. Naturally, Stalinism was an infinitely more complex phenomenon than these exiguous categories suggest. Althusser is certainly a highly intelligent person, and I have a great human sympathy for him. But it is impossible to escape the impression that his thought has become increasingly impoverished and arid with the passage of time.

In your introduction to Lenin's Philosophical Notebooks, *written in 1958, you end by saying that the young Lenin of 1894 had not read Hegel when he wrote* Who Are the Friends of the People?, *but nevertheless managed to understand him better than the older Lenin of the* Notebooks, *who did study him in 1916, but misunderstood him. Then, in a cryptic conclusion, you add that this paradox indicates 'two divergent "vocations" which still today contend within the soul of Marxism itself. To explain how and why these two "vocations" became historically conjoined and superimposed would be a formidable task: but it must nevertheless be confronted.'[9] What did you mean by this?*

You must remember that I was young and enthusiastic when I wrote those lines. I was given to exaggeration. It is true that Lenin did not know Hegel at first hand when he wrote *Who Are the Friends of the People?*. But this text is marked by the positivist culture of the time: the esoteric meanings I sought to attribute to it I would firmly repudiate today. The occasionally positivist overtones of my 1958 introduction are, I think, corrected and overcome in my 1969 study on *Marxism and Hegel*. However, through these successive divagations and oscillations, I was groping towards a real and serious problem, which has now preoccupied me directly for a number of years. There are two possible lines of development in Marx's own discourse, expressed respectively in the title and subtitle of *Capital*. The first is that which Marx himself advances in his Preface to the first edition, and Postscript to the second edition, in which he presents himself simply as a scientist. Marx, according to his own account here, is performing in the field of the historical and social sciences a task that had already been performed in the natural sciences. This too was Lenin's interpretation of Marx in *Who are the Friends of the People?*, and my own introduction of 1958 went in the same direction. The title of *Capital* itself spells this direction out. It promises that political economy, which started with the works of Smith and Ricardo but remained incomplete and contradictory in them, will now become a true science in the full sense of the term. The subtitle of the book, however, suggests another direction: a '*critique* of political economy'. This notion found little echo in the Second or Third Internationals. Lenin would certainly have rejected the idea that Marxism was a critique of

---

[9] *Il Marxismo e Hegel*, pp. 169–70.

political economy: for him it was a critique of *bourgeois* political economy only, which finally transformed political economy itself into a real science. But the subtitle of *Capital* indicates something more than this—it suggests that political economy as such is bourgeois and must be criticized *tout court*. This second dimension of Marx's work is precisely that which culminates in his theory of alienation and fetishism. The great problem for us is to know whether and how these two divergent directions of Marx's work can be held together in a single system. Can a purely scientific theory contain within itself a discourse on alienation? The problem has not yet been resolved.

The original Della Volpean school interpreted Marx's work as something like a strict analogue of that of Galileo. There are obvious difficulties, however, in transferring the experimental procedures of the natural sciences into the social sciences. History is notoriously not a laboratory in which phenomena can be artificially isolated and repeated, as they can in physics. Lenin would often say: 'This moment is unique: it can pass, and the chance it represents may never return ...'—just the opposite of repeatability. There is a striking passage in your introduction to the Philosophical Notebooks, *however, in which you say: 'Logic and sociology are constituted simultaneously, in the same relationship of unity-distinction as obtains between the consciousness they represent and social being: thus logic falls within the science of history, but the science of history falls in its turn within history. That is, sociology informs the techniques of politics, and becomes a struggle for the transformation of the world. Practice is functional to the production of theory; but theory is in turn a function of practice. Science is verified in and as society, but associated life in its turn is an experiment under way in the laboratory of the world. History is thus a science of* historia rerum gestarum, *practice-theory; but it is also a science as* res gestae *themselves, theory-practice; or in the words of a great maxim of Engels, "history is experiment and industry". We can thereby understand the deep nexus between the "prophet" or politician, and the scientist, in the structure of the work of Marx himself.'[10] Do you still find this solution satisfactory?*

You have selected the best page of that text—the one in which I strove most to square the circle! I no longer agree with it, because what then seemed to me a solution I now realize is still an unanswered problem. I am currently in a phase of radical rethinking of many of these questions—whose outcome I cannot yet wholly foresee. I will probably publish a short work soon on the theory of capitalist contradictions in Marx. In this, I will take a still further distance from Della Volpe's work, and try to show through a study of Kant's *Attempt to Introduce the Notion of Negative Quantities into Philosophy* in 1763, that Marx's concept of a capitalist contradiction is not the same as Kant's notion of a 'real opposition'. I am confident of this point, but it

---

[10] *Il Marxismo e Hegel*, pp. 126–7.

remains a limited one, of whose implications I am still uncertain. However, in reply to your question, my answer would be that the sense of my argument in this forthcoming study is that Marx cannot simply be equated with Galileo; he would only be so if capitalist contradictions were real oppositions in Kant's meaning of the term.

One of your most central themes in Marxism and Hegel *is that contradictions exist between propositions, but not between things. Confusion between the two is for you the hallmark of dialectical materialism, which defines it as a pseudo-science. Yet in the last essay of your* From Rousseau to Lenin, *written a year later, you repeatedly speak of capitalist reality itself as 'upside-down', a system that 'stands on its head'.[11] Isn't this simply a metaphorical way of reintroducing the notion of a 'contradiction between things'—by a literary image rather than a conceptual axiom? How can the idea of an 'upside-down reality' be reconciled with the principle of non-contradiction, which you insist is central to any science?*

That is the very problem on which I am working: you are absolutely correct to point out the difficulty. For I stand firmly by the fundamental thesis that materialism presupposes non-contradiction—that reality is non-contradictory. In this respect, I agree with Ajdukiewicz and Linke, and I fully reiterate my critique of dialectical materialism. At the same time, rereading Marx, I have become aware that for him capitalist contradictions undeniably are dialectical contradictions. Della Volpe tried to save the day by interpreting the opposition between capital and wage-labour as a real opposition—*Realrepugnanz*—in Kant's sense: that is, an opposition without contradiction, *ohne Widerspruch*. If the relationship between capital and labour were a real opposition of the Kantian type, it would be non-dialectical and the basic principle of materialism would be safe. But the problem is actually much more complex. I continue to believe that materialism excludes the notion of a contradictory reality: yet there is no doubt that for Marx the capital–wage-labour relationship is a dialectical contradiction. Capitalism is a contradictory reality for Marx, not because being a reality it must therefore be contradictory—as dialectical materialism would have it—but because it is a capsized, inverted, upside-down reality. I am perfectly conscious that the notion of an upside-down reality appears to jar with the precepts of any science. Marx was convinced of the validity of this notion. I do not say that he was necessarily right. I cannot yet state whether the idea of an inverted reality is compatible with a social science.

But I would like to comment on the problem of the relationship between the social and natural sciences, which you raised earlier. I no longer uphold the optimistic position of my introduction of 1958, which was too facile

---

[11] See *From Rousseau to Lenin*, pp. 232–5.

in its assumption of a basic homogeneity between the sciences of nature and the sciences of society. On the other hand, I can see that of the two broad positions that are generally adopted on this problem, both raise acute difficulties. The first position is that which I took up in my introduction, and which derived from Della Volpe: it effectively identified the social and natural sciences—Marx was 'the Galileo of the moral world' for us then. Today, this formula strikes me as highly debatable: apart from anything else, it presupposed that the capital–labour relationship in Marx was a non-contradictory opposition, which is not the case. On the other hand, there is a second position which insists on the heterogeneity of the social and natural sciences. The danger of this alternative is that the social sciences then tend to become a qualitatively distinct form of knowledge from the natural sciences, and to occupy the same relationship towards them as philosophy used to occupy towards science as such. It is no accident that this was the solution of the German historicists—Dilthey, Windelband and Rickert. It was then inherited by Croce, Bergson, Lukács and the Frankfurt School. The invariable conclusion of this tradition is that true knowledge is social science, which because it cannot be assimilated to natural science is not science at all but philosophy. Thus either there is a single form of knowledge, which is science (the position I would still like to defend)—but then it should be possible to construct the social sciences on bases analogous to the natural sciences; or the social sciences really are different from the natural sciences, and there are two sorts of knowledge—but since two forms of knowledge are not possible, the natural sciences become a pseudo-knowledge. The latter is the ideologically dominant alternative. Continental European philosophy in this century has been virtually united in its attack on the natural sciences—from Husserl to Heidegger, Croce to Gentile, Bergson to Sartre. Against the dangers of this spiritualist idealism, I personally would prefer to incur the opposite risks of neo-positivism. But I am divided on the issue, and have no ready solution to the problem.

Turning to Capital *itself, as an exemplar of scientific method, you once wrote that 'the conclusive verification of* Capital*, which we can call external, has been provided by the ulterior development of history itself: a verification to which Lenin referred when he wrote that "it is the criterion of practice—that is, the evolution of all the capitalist countries in the last decades—that demonstrates the objective truth of all the economic and social theory of Marx in general". Let it be noted—all the theory: which means that it is not just this or that part, but the entire work of Marx, that constitutes an ensemble of verified hypotheses, and thus of laws to be continuously controlled and adjusted in the light of real historical experience.'[12] What is your attitude to these claims today?*

Youthful errors, pure and simple.

---

[12] *Il Marxismo e Hegel*, p. 160.

In a recent text, you seem to accept that there is a theory of 'collapse' in Capital, although your analysis is a prudent one which suggests the presence of counter-elements in Marx's work. You identify the main strand of 'collapse' theory as the postulate of the falling rate of profit in Capital.[13] Do you regard this as a scientific law that has been 'conclusively verified by the ulterior development of history itself'?

Absolutely not. Indeed I believe there is something much graver to be said about the predictions contained in *Capital*. Not only has the falling rate of profit not been empirically verified, but the central test of *Capital* itself has not yet come to pass: a socialist revolution in the advanced West. The result is that Marxism is in crisis today, and it can only surmount this crisis by acknowledging it. But precisely this acknowledgment is consciously avoided by virtually every Marxist, great or small. This is perfectly comprehensible in the case of the numerous apolitical and apologetic intellectuals in the Western Communist parties, whose function is merely to furbish a Marxist gloss for the absolutely unmarxist political practice of these parties. What is much more serious is the example set by intellectuals of truly major stature, who systematically hide the crisis of Marxism in their work, and thereby contribute to prolonging its paralysis as a social science. Let me cite two instances, to make myself clear. Baran and Sweezy, in their introduction to *Monopoly Capital*, inform their readers in a brief note that they are not going to utilize the concept of surplus value, but that of surplus, nor that of wage-labour, but that of dependent labour. What does this actually mean? It means that Baran and Sweezy decided that they were unable to use the theory of value and of surplus value, in their analysis of post-war US capitalism. They had every right to do so; they may even have been correct to do so—we need not enter into that question here. But what is significant is their way of doing so. They effectively blow up the keystone of Marx's construction: without the theory of value and surplus value, *Capital* crumbles. But they merely mention their elimination of it in a note, and then proceed nonchalantly as if nothing had happened—as if, once this minor correction were made, Marx's work remained safer and sounder then ever.

Let us take another case, of a great intellectual and scholar for whom I have the highest respect, Maurice Dobb. Presenting an Italian edition of *Capital* a century later, Dobb has written a preface in which he gives out that everything in it is in order, except for a very small blemish, a tiny flaw in the original. This little error, says Dobb, is the way in which Marx operates the transformation of values into prices in Volume III of *Capital*: fortunately, however, the mistake has been rectified by Piero Sraffa, and all is now well again. Dobb may well be right not to content himself with Marx's

---

[13] See Colletti's introduction to L. Colletti and C. Napoleoni, *Il Futuro del Capitalismo: Crollo o Sviluppo?*, Bari 1970, pp. c-cv ff.

solution of the transformation problem, just as it is possible that Sweezy has good grounds for rejecting the theory of value. For the moment, we can suspend judgement on these issues. But where they are certainly wrong is in believing or pretending to believe that the central pillars on which Marx's theoretical edifice rests can be removed, and the whole construction still remain standing. This type of behaviour is not merely one of illusion. By refusing to admit that what it rejects in Marx's work is not secondary but essential, it occludes and thereby aggravates the crisis of Marxism as a whole. Intellectual evasion of this sort merely deepens the stagnation of socialist thought evident everywhere in the West today. The same is true of the young Marxist economists in Italy who have adopted most of Sraffa's ideas. I do not say that Sraffa is wrong; I am willing to admit as a hypothesis that he may be right. But what is absolutely absurd is to accept Sraffa, whose work implies the demolition of the entire foundations of Marx's analysis, and at the same time pretend that this is the best way of shoring up Marx.

Pivotal questions for contemporary Marxism do not, of course, concern only its economic theory. They are also political. In two recent texts, you have made a distinction between the notion of a 'parliamentary road' and a 'peaceful road' to socialism. Thus in the penultimate essay of From Rousseau to Lenin *you argue that* State and Revolution *was not directed by Lenin merely against reformism as such, and is not centred on any assertion of the necessity for physical violence to smash the bourgeois state—but is rather concerned with a much more profound theme, namely the need to substitute one historical type of power for another: the parliamentary representative state for direct proletarian democracy, in workers' councils, that are already no longer in full sense a state at all.[14] In a more recent article on Chile, you have repeated that violence is essentially secondary for a socialist revolution—something which may or may not occur, but never defines it as such.[15] You cite Lenin's article of September 1917 in which he said that a peaceful accession to socialism was possible in Russia, in both of these essays, to support your argument. But surely this use of a passage from Lenin is very superficial? By September 1917, there had already occurred the colossal historical violence of the First World War, which had cost millions of Russian lives and essentially broken the whole army as a repressive apparatus of the Tsarist state. Moreover, the February Revolution had overthrown Tsarism itself by violent riots: a popular explosion that was in no sense a peaceful process. It was only in this context, after the liquefaction of the Tsarist military machine and the nationwide establishment of soviets, that Lenin said that for a brief moment a transition to socialism without further violence was possible, if the Provisional Government transferred its power to the soviets. In practice, of course, the October Revolution proved necessary all the same—an*

---

[14] From *Rousseau to Lenin*, pp. 219–27.
[15] Colletti's article on the lessons of Chile was published in *L'Espresso*, 23 September 1973.

organized insurrection for the seizure of power. The whole of Lenin's work is surely saturated with insistence on the necessity and inevitability of social violence to break the army and police apparatus of the ruling class. In general, you seem to pass too casually over this fundamental theme of Lenin's revolutionary theory. Has the need which you have obviously felt to resist the whole tradition of Stalinist nihilism towards proletarian democracy, and its massive utilization of police violence against the working class itself, not perhaps led you involuntarily to minimize the proletarian violence inherent in any mass revolutionary rising against capital?

You may be right in saying that I have tended to underestimate this dimension of any revolution. But what was my basic aim in writing my essay on *State and Revolution*? You have indicated it yourself. It was to confront and attack a conception that Stalinism had entrenched in the workers' movement, that simply identified revolution with violence. For this tradition, it was only violence that was the real hallmark of a revolution: everything else—the transformation of the nature of power, the establishment of socialist democracy—was of no importance. The difference between Communists and Social Democrats was simply that the former were for a violent revolution, while the latter were against a revolution because they were pacifists. If Communists created a bureaucratic political dictatorship after the revolution anywhere, or even a personal tyranny like that of Stalin, it was of minor significance: the regime was still socialism. It was against this long tradition that I sought to demonstrate that revolution and violence are by no means interchangeable concepts, and that at the limit there could even be a non-violent revolution. This is not just an isolated phrase in Lenin; there is a whole chapter of *State and Revolution* entitled 'The Peaceful Development of the Revolution'.

The only important passages where Lenin affirms the possibility of a peaceful revolution as such are those in which he envisages a phase of history in which the ruling class has already been expropriated by violent revolutions in the major industrialized countries of the world, and the capitalists of the remaining smaller countries capitulate without serious resistance to their working classes, because the global balance of forces is so hopelessly against them. This is not a very relevant scenario yet.

I don't think we disagree on the substance of the issue. The really important question is the political nature of the power that emerges after any revolution, whatever the coercive force of the struggles that precede it. My main preoccupation has been to combat the heritage of Stalinist contempt for socialist democracy.

This concern remains very understandable. Still, the Communist parties of the West themselves have now long since ceased to speak of violence in any form, let alone exalt it: on the contrary, they speak only of peaceful progress towards

*an 'advanced democracy', within the constitutional framework of the exist-
ing bourgeois state today. At most, they will say that if the bourgeoisie does not
respect the constitutional rules of the game after the election of a government
of the Left and attacks it illegally, then the working class has a right to defend
itself physically. Whereas in Engels, Lenin or Trotsky, proletarian insurrection
is envisaged essentially as an aggressive weapon of revolutionary strategy, in
which the essential rule is to take and keep the initiative—Danton's watchword of 'audacity'. You do seem to play down this central heritage of Marxist
thought. Surely polemical confrontation with the Italian Communist Party
today cannot avoid it?*

It is true that, as you say, the Western Communist parties no longer mention
violence today. But unfortunately small groups have arisen on the far Left in
the same period, which reproduce Stalinist fixations on violence, and whose
influence, especially on youth, cannot be ignored; it is often greater on the
younger generation of Marxists than that of the Communist parties themselves. You have cited my article on Chile. In it, I wrote that there can be
no socialism without the freedom to strike, freedom of the press, and free
elections. These were widely regarded here as outrageously parliamentarist
statements. Why? Because in the deformed Stalinist mentality of most of
these groups, freedom of the press or the right to strike are simply equated
with parliament: since a socialist revolution will abolish parliament, it must
also suppress all free elections, newspapers and strikes. In other words,
install a police regime, not a proletarian democracy. Against this disastrous
confusion, it is necessary to remind socialists again and again that civic liberties—of election, expression and right to withhold labour—are not the same
thing as parliament, and that the mere exercise of violence is not the same
thing as the revolutionary transformation of social relationships, and does
not guarantee it.

*True. But this was not the problem in Chile. No one on the Left there was
threatening to suppress the right to strike. The central problem, on the contrary,
was just the opposite: trusting confidence in the neutrality of the repressive apparatus of bourgeois state. It was that which led to disaster in Chile. Moreover, it
was not just the groups on the far Left who spoke of the Chilean situation. The
Communist parties were also vocal in their commentaries. Wasn't it necessary
to say something about them too?*

You are right. What happened was that I had to write a very short article
quickly, in a very brief space of time. I now realize that I exposed my flank
towards the Communists. I admit this.

*But isn't it possible that there are theoretical—not just conjunctural—reasons
for your underestimation of the importance of the coercive apparatus of the*

capitalist state? For all your interest in the bourgeois state has been essentially concentrated on what the whole Marxist tradition since Marx has largely neglected (Lenin included)—that is, the reality of parliamentary democracy, as an objective historical structure of bourgeois society, and not as a mere subjective trick or illusion created by the ruling class. The political and ideological efficacy of the bourgeois-democratic state in containing and controlling the working class in the West has been enormous, especially in the absence of any proletarian democracy in the East. Nevertheless, the duty to take the whole system of parliamentary-representative state with the utmost seriousness, and to analyse it in its own right as the foreground of bourgeois political power in the West, should not lead one ever to forget the background of the permanent military and police apparatuses arrayed behind it. In any real social crisis, in which class directly confronts class, the bourgeoisie always fall back on its coercive rather than its representative machinery. The Chilean tragedy is there to prove the consequences of forgetting it.

I accept the justice of these criticisms. You are right to make them.

In this connection, it is the particular merit of Gramsci to have started to try to think through some of the specific strategic problems posed by the social and political structures of the advanced capitalist countries, with their combination of representative and repressive institutions. You have never referred much to Gramsci in your major writings. Presumably in your Della Volpean phase you regarded him as a dangerously idealist influence in Italian culture, viewing him essentially in a philosophical context, rather than as a political thinker. Is this still your attitude?

No, I have changed my opinion of Gramsci completely. Your assessment of my earlier attitudes is accurate. It was difficult for us, in our situation as a minority with an extremely weak position inside the PCI, to be able to separate Gramsci from the way in which the party leadership presented Gramsci. This is completely true. However, since then, I have reflected on Gramsci a great deal, and I now understand his importance much better. We should be quite clear about this, keeping a sense of proportion and avoiding any fashionable cult. I continue to believe that it is folly to present Gramsci as an equal or superior to Marx or Lenin as a thinker. His work does not contain a golden theoretical key that could unlock the solution to our present difficulties. But at the same time there is an abyss between Gramsci and a thinker like Lukács, or even Korsch—let alone Althusser. Lukács was a professor, Gramsci was a revolutionary. I have not yet written on Gramsci, in part because I am waiting for the critical edition of his *Prison Notebooks* to appear;[16] I think it is important to have fully accurate texts before one

---

[16] *Quaderni del carcere*, 4 vols, ed. Valentino Gerratana, Turin 1975; and see *Prison Notebooks*, 3 vols, ed. Joseph A. Buttigieg, New York 1991–2007.

when writing on an author. In this case, I doubt whether there will be any major surprises in the definitive edition. However, the way in which the *Prison Notebooks* have been published hitherto in Italy has been completely aberrant. For example, the first volume was entitled 'Historical Materialism and the Philosophy of Benedetto Croce', as if Gramsci intended to construct a philosophy. Actually the *Prison Notebooks* are really concerned with a 'sociological' study of Italian society. This was precisely the whole difference between Gramsci and Togliatti. For Gramsci, cognitive analysis was essential to political action. For Togliatti, culture was separated and juxtaposed to politics. Togliatti exhibited a traditional culture of a rhetorical type, and conducted a politics without any organic relationship to it. Gramsci genuinely fused and synthesized the two. His research on Italian society was a real preparation for transforming it. This was the measure of his seriousness as a politician.

In fact, I believe that we can appreciate Gramsci's stature better today than it was possible to do twenty years ago, because Marxism is now in a crisis which imposes on us a profound self-examination and self-criticism—and Gramsci's position in the *Prison Notebooks* is precisely that of a politician and theorist reflecting on a historical defeat and the reasons for it. Gramsci sought to understand the reasons for this defeat. He believed that the 'generals' of the proletariat had not known the real nature of the whole social terrain on which they were operating, and that the precondition for any renewed offensive by the working class was to explore this terrain fully beforehand. In other words, he undertook an analysis of the peculiar characteristics of Italian society in his time. The great fascination and force of his work in this respect lies for me, paradoxically, in his very limitations. What were Gramsci's limitations? Basically, that he had an extremely partial and defective knowledge of Marx's work, and a relatively partial one even of Lenin's writings. The result was that he did not attempt any economic analysis of Italian or European capitalism. But this weakness actually produced a strength. Just because Gramsci had not really mastered Marxist economic theory, he could develop a novel exploration of Italian history that unfolded quite outside the conventional schematism of base and superstructure—a couplet of concepts that is very rare in Marx himself, and has nearly always led to retrograde simplifications. Gramsci was thus liberated to give a quite new importance to the political and moral components of Italian history and society. We have become so accustomed as Marxists to looking at reality through certain spectacles, that it is very important that someone should now and again take these spectacles off: probably he will see the world somewhat confusedly, but he will also probably perceive things that those who wear spectacles never notice at all. The very deficiency of Gramsci's economic formation allowed him to be a more original and important Marxist than he might otherwise have been, if he had possessed a more orthodox training. Of course, his research remained incomplete and fragmentary. But

Gramsci's achievement and example are nevertheless absolutely remarkable, for all these limitations.

You have singled out Gramsci from his contemporaries in Western Europe after the First World War, as on a level apart. How would you summarize your judgement of Trotsky?

My attitude to Trotsky is such that I am generally considered as a 'Trotskyist' in Italy, although I have never actually been one. If you go into the university here in Rome, you will see signs painted by students—Maoists and neo-Stalinists—which demand: 'Hang Colletti'. Anti-Trotskyism is an epidemic among Italian youth: and so I am commonly considered a Trotskyist. What is the fundamental truth expressed by Trotsky—the central idea for whose acceptance I am quite willing to be called a Trotskyist? You could condense it very laconically by saying that in any genuinely Marxist perspective, the United States of America should be the maturest society in the world for a socialist transformation, and that Trotsky is the theorist who most courageously and unremittingly reminds us of that. In other words, Trotsky always insisted that the determinant force in any real socialist revolution would be the industrial working class, and that no peasantry could perform this function for it, let alone a mere Communist Party leadership. The clearest and most unequivocal development of this fundamental thesis is to be found in the work of Trotsky. Without it, Marxism becomes purely honorific—once deprived of this element, anyone can call themselves a Marxist. At the same time, so far as the Soviet Union is concerned, I consider Trotsky's analyses of the USSR in *The Revolution Betrayed* to be exemplary, as a model of seriousness and balance. It is often forgotten how extraordinarily measured and careful *The Revolution Betrayed* is in its evaluation of Russia under Stalin. Nearly forty years have passed since Trotsky wrote the book in 1936, and the situation in the USSR has deteriorated since then, in the sense that the bureaucratic caste in power has become stabilized and consolidated. But I continue to believe that Trotsky's fundamental judgement that the Soviet State was not a capitalist regime remains valid to this day. Naturally, this does not mean that socialism exists in the USSR—a species of society that has still not been properly catalogued by zoologists. But I am in basic agreement with Trotsky's position that Russia is not a capitalist country. Where I diverge from his analysis is on the question of whether the USSR can be described as a degenerated Workers' State: this is a concept that has always left me perplexed. Beyond this doubt, however, I cannot propose any more precise definition. But what above all I respect in Trotsky's position is the sober caution of his dissection of Stalinism. This caution remains especially salutary today, against the facile chorus of those on the Left who have suddenly discovered 'capitalism' or 'fascism' in the USSR.

How do you now view your personal development as a philosopher to date: and what do you see as the central problems for the general future of Marxism?

We have discussed the Della Volpean school in Italy, in which I received my early formation. What I would finally like to emphasize is something much deeper than any of the criticisms I have made of it hitherto. The phenomenon of Della Volpeanism—like that of Althusserianism today—was always linked to problems of *interpretation* of Marxism: it was born and remained confined within a purely theoretical space. The type of contact which it established with Marxism was always marked by a basic dissociation and division of theory from political activity. This separation has characterized Marxism throughout the world ever since the early twenties. Set against this background, the Della Volpean school in Italy is necessarily reduced to very modest dimensions: we should not have any illusions about this, or exaggerate the political differences between the Della Volpeans and the historicists at the time. The real, fundamental fact was the separation between theoretical Marxism and the actual working class movement. If you look at works like Kautsky's *Agrarian Question*, Luxemburg's *Accumulation of Capital*, or Lenin's *Development of Capitalism in Russia*—three of the great works of the period which immediately succeeded that of Marx and Engels—you immediately register that their theoretical analysis contains at the same time the elements of a political strategy. They are works which both have a true cognitive value, and an operative strategic purpose. Such works, whatever their limits, maintained the essential of Marxism. For Marxism is not a phenomenon comparable to existentialism, phenomenology or neo-positivism. Once it becomes so, it is finished. But after the October Revolution, from the early 1920s onwards, what happened? In the West, where the revolution failed and the proletariat was defeated, Marxism lived on merely as an academic current in the universities, producing works of purely theoretical scope or cultural reflection. The career of Lukács is the clearest demonstration of this process. *History and Class Consciousness,* for all its defects, set out to be a book of political theory, geared to an actual practice. After it, Lukács came to write works of a totally different nature. *The Young Hegel* or *The Destruction of Reason* are typical products of a university professor. Culturally, they may have a very positive value: but they no longer have any connection with the life of the workers' movement. They represent attempts to achieve a cognitive advance on the plane of theory, that at the same time are completely devoid of any strategic or political implications. This was the fate of the West. Meanwhile, what happened in the East? There revolutions did occur, but in countries whose level of capitalist development was so backward that there was no chance of them building a socialist society. In these lands, the classical categories of Marxism had no objective system of correspondences in reality. There was revolutionary political practice, which sometimes generated very important and creative mass experiences, but these occurred in a historical theatre which was alien to the central categories of Marx's own theory. This practice thus never succeeded in achieving translation into a theoretical advance within Marxism itself: the most obvious case is the work of Mao. Thus, simplifying greatly, we can say that in the West, Marxism has become a purely cultural and academic phenomenon; while in the East, revolutionary processes developed in an ambience too retarded to permit a realization of socialism, and hence inevitably found expression in non-Marxist ideas and traditions.

This separation between West and East has plunged Marxism into a long crisis. Unfortunately, acknowledgement of this crisis is systematically obstructed and repressed among Marxists themselves; even the best of them, as we have seen in the cases of Sweezy and Dobb. My own view, by contrast, is that the sole chance for Marxism to survive and surmount its ordeal is to pit itself against these very problems. Naturally what any individual, even with a few colleagues, can do towards this by himself is very little. But this at any rate is the direction in which I am now trying to work: and it is in this perspective that I must express the most profound dissatisfaction with what I have done hitherto. I feel immensely distant from the things that I have written, because in the best of cases they seem to me no more than an appeal to principles against facts. But from a Marxist point of view, history can never be wrong—in other words, mere a priori axioms can never be opposed to the evidence of its actual development. The real task is to study why history took a different course from that foreseen by *Capital*. It is probable that any honest study of this will have to question certain of the central tenets of Marx's own thought itself. Thus I now completely renounce the dogmatic triumphalism with which I once endorsed every line in Marx—the tone of the passages of my introduction of 1958, which you have quoted. Let me put this even more strongly. If Marxists continue to remain arrested in epistemology and gnoseology, Marxism has effectively perished. The only way in which Marxism can be revived is if no more books like *Marxism and Hegel* are published, and instead books like Hilferding's *Finance Capital* and Luxemburg's *Accumulation of Capital*—or even Lenin's *Imperialism*, which was a popular brochure—are once again written. In short, either Marxism has the capacity—I certainly do not—to produce at that level, or it will survive merely as the foible of a few university professors. But in that case, it will be well and truly dead, and the professors might as well invent a new name for their clerisy.

Luciana Castellina was born in Rome in 1929. She joined the Italian Communist Party (PCI) in 1947 and went on to become a leading figure in the life of the Italian Left from the 1960s onwards. Excluded from the PCI for her part in the oppositional journal il manifesto, *in 1974 she co-founded the Partito di Unità Proletaria per il communismo (PdUP), and in the late seventies led the party's parliamentary fraction as part of the united list of Democrazia Proletaria. In 1984 the PdUP decided to migrate to the PCI—the critical juncture at which Castellina gave this interview.*

Just a few years later, the PCI voted to remake itself as a party of the 'democratic left' (PDS). The former PdUP refused to follow, and joined with other recusant Communists and elements of the New Left to create Rifondazione Comunista. Then, in 1995, Rifondazione split over the issue of parliamentary support for the centrist government of Lamberto Dini. At this point, Castellina and her co-thinkers, who favoured support for Dini, launched the Movimento dei Comunisti Unitari, remaining until a majority decided to dissolve themselves into a new centre-Left, Democratici di Sinistra. Once again, she declined the invitation to overwrite her Communist identity.

From 1979 to 1999, Castellina was a member of the European parliament. She has been at different times editor of the Communist youth magazine Nuovo Generazione, *the daily* manifesto *and the weekly* Liberazione. *Her books include* Eurollywood: il difficile ingresso della cultura nella construzione dell'Europa *(2008).*

Luciana Castellina

Il Manifesto and Italian Communism

Can you clarify in broad terms the differences on international and domestic affairs and on internal party organization which led to the emergence of the Manifesto group and its expulsion from the Communist Party in November 1969?

It is not quite right to say that we were expelled, which would suggest our being kicked out and not allowed in principle to rejoin. We were subject to a much milder measure such that we were no longer party members but 'without prejudice'. This came at the end of a lengthy debate between Left and Right in the party—with Ingrao symbolizing one side and Amendola the other—which had begun in the early sixties and become more open after Togliatti's death in 1964.[1] Moreover, by 1969 many of the issues at stake in the internal debate had entered into the culture and practice of the mass movement that had grown up in the previous year or so outside the party. Putting things very schematically, I would say that there were three broad areas in the debate: international policy, the party's attitude to the mass movement, and its internal life. On the first of these, the Soviet invasion of Czechoslovakia was of course a major turning point. We felt that although the PCI leadership had taken a firm position against the invasion, it had not drawn the necessary conclusions about the Soviet experience as a whole—the kind of conclusions that Berlinguer was to draw in December 1981 when he said that the Russian Revolution had lost its role as the historical driving force of the movement. At the same time, we were influenced by the Chinese positions in the sense that our approach to the Soviet Union involved a left-wing critique of its interpretation of peaceful coexistence and its behaviour as a world power.

---

[1] Pietro Ingrao (1915–) and Giorgio Amendola (1907–80): parliamentarians and writers, and historic leaders of the PCI's left and right wings respectively.

Did you concern yourselves with the problem of characterizing the Soviet Union as a social formation?

Not so much. Most of our discussion centred on its role in world politics: on its relationship to the national liberation movements in the Third World, and its fear of anything that might destabilize the two spheres of influence. However, we never became dogmatically Maoist as other New Left currents did after 1968. At a time when leaders of parties with fifteen members were being received in Peking as if they were heads of state, we had no official relations with the Chinese. Our position was perhaps more akin to that of *Monthly Review* in the United States.

With regard to the second focus of debate, it should be borne in mind that the situation in Italy was rather different from that in France, for example, since the new mass movement was fundamentally a working-class phenomenon rooted in the factories rather than a university-based revolt of student youth. At any event, whereas the PCI remained tied to an analysis of backward capitalism, these new movements launched a critique of advanced capitalist societies, and of the new contradictions that had typically emerged within them, indicating a clear awareness that a deep systemic crisis was under way. Among the points raised in this qualitative critique were a series of egalitarian demands, and attacks on hierarchical structures and work organization on the shop floor.

The third issue at stake was the internal party regime, in which no scope was given for the expression of dissentient positions. Still, after we decided to bring out a magazine of our own, there were several months of discussion with the leadership before our party membership was annulled. In the French Communist Party we would not have lasted more than a couple of days.

How did your relations with the leadership develop during this period?

Well, the two editors of the magazine were Rossana Rossanda and Lucio Magri.[2] Rossana, who had been responsible for cultural policy until the supporters of Ingrao's theses were marginalized after the 1966 Congress, was still a member of the Central Committee, as were Luigi Pintor, Massimo Caprara and Aldo Natoli.[3] We also had five MPs, including Milani who joined us a little later. The leadership tried to persuade us not to publish the

---

[2] For Rossana Rossanda (1924–) and Lucio Magri (1932–), see, for some relevant background, Rossanda, 'The Comrade From Milan', NLR 49, January–February 2008, pp. 76–100; Magri, 'Parting Words', NLR 31, January–February 2005, pp. 93–105 and 'The Tailor of Ulm', NLR 51, May–June 2008, pp. 47–62.

[3] Luig Pintor (1925–2003), editor-in-chief of *il manifesto* after its mutation from monthly to daily in 1971. Massimo Caprara (1922–2009), for many years secretary to Togliatti, the PCI leader, rediscovered Catholicism as the pole star of his intellectual life. Aldo Natoli (1913–), was a prominent figure in the PCI's Rome organizations.

magazine, and when we refused, Alessandro Natta, who was then chairman of the Control Commission, wrote a critique of the Manifesto positions and had it circulated for discussion in party branches. However, an unexpectedly large number of people expressed their agreement with us, and the discussion was cut down to a much shorter period than it should have been. When the question then came back to the Central Committee, it was decided with only two votes against and three abstentions that we should be removed from membership of the party.

In the political atmosphere of that time, not only in Italy, with its hot autumn of 1969, but in Europe and the world as a whole, it must have seemed that you now had the opportunity to develop a quite new type of socialist politics.

Recently many people have asked us whether we thought in 1969 that we would ever rejoin the PCI, and we have all confessed that we did. We were never really a group of the New Left and remained part of the PCI in the sense that we thought a new revolutionary party would grow out of its crises and betrayals. The problem was to establish and keep open the channels of communication between the traditional culture of the historical Left and the new movements which were emerging. Originally we had seen the magazine as the way of keeping discussion alive on these questions, and it was only as a result of subsequent developments that we began to think of ourselves as an independent political group. We never called on PCI members to leave together with us: indeed, the majority of those who joined Il Manifesto were 'sixty-eighters' who had never been in the PCI. They just gathered around the magazine in various towns and, over the next few years, started writing to us that they had 'constituted themselves' as Manifesto groups. This forced us to get in touch with them, and in the process we became an organized movement for the first time.

When was the party actually founded?

Il Manifesto itself always regarded the term 'party' as rather excessive, and it was only adopted after our fusion with a number of other groups in 1974 to form the new Partito di Unità Proletaria (PdUP). The most important of these was a section of the Partito Socialista di Unità Proletaria (PSIUP)—an early sixties left-wing breakaway from the Socialist Party which, although it had won a million or so votes in the 1972 elections, had failed to cross the threshold for parliamentary representation'. Following this setback, the great majority decided to fuse with the PCI and two Central Committee members went back to the Socialist Party. The other minority, which formed the original PdUP and fused with us in 1974, included a number of prominent trade unionists like Elio Giovannini and Antonio Lettieri who were in the national secretariat of the CGIL, and metalworkers' leaders like Vittorio Foa and Pino

Tagliazucchi.[4] This background in the historical institutions of the Italian Left made them a quite different group from Il Manifesto, which did not have any trade unionists except at grass-roots level.

What would have been the rough size of your group in 1974?

We were a very militant, very active organization and we never had a proper membership census. Apart from those of us who had come out of the Communist Party, everyone had a New Left origin and was very young. In fact, at the last Manifesto congress before the fusion, we were so ashamed to admit our average age that we pushed it up for the public announcement. The PCI people were naturally much older. As to the size of the membership, there must have been between fifteen and twenty thousand of us at that time.

Did you have a proper party structure with offices in the main towns?

Il Manifesto already had local sections in the main towns—we called them *collettivi* because we were always something between a movement and an organization.

In 1970 New Left Review *published a critical article by Lucio Magri on Leninism.[5] He did not reject it totally but argued for a different form of party structure in advanced countries, stressing in particular the need for links with the mass movements. Could you give us some idea of your mode of functioning? Did you have democratic centralism, for example? Presumably you would take votes, with majorities and minorities?*

We did. But we always thought that the real problem of democracy was not so much to have the right of tendency within the party as to establish a new relationship with the mass movements, so that the party could take in and give representation to their experiences. The traditional Leninist position was that the party alone had general ideas, while the mass movements came forward with sectoral or economic demands. But the new movements that developed in the sixties and seventies already had their own general way of considering problems and interpreting the world. In our view, then, they had a right to be seen as political in the full sense of the word.

Nevertheless, unlike some of the spontaneist tendencies, you did have regular congresses at which leading members presented theses that were then freely discussed and voted upon.

---

[4] CGIL: the Italian General Confederation of Labour, founded 1944 and after 1950 predominantly Communist in orientation.

[5] Magri, 'Problems of the Marxist Theory of the Revolutionary Party', NLR I/60, March–April 1970, pp. 97–128.

That is quite true, and it was not only leading members who submitted these. As to the spontaneist movements—and Lotta Continua in particular was very strong at one time—they believed that their function was to express the immediate needs arising from struggles and that they did not need to have a synthesis, a programme or a project. We firmly criticized this approach and insisted that the immediate demands of various movements and struggles had to be synthesized in some kind of general programme. This was never understood in the New Left, and when we put forward the theses of Il Manifesto in 1970 they all regarded us with a good deal of suspicion. We seemed to them to be part of the old Communist culture because we wanted to draw things together and develop a rational analysis. In fact, there was more discussion of our theses within the official structures of the Communist Party than among the New Left.

But Livio Maitan, for example, wrote a pamphlet replying to your theses.

Yes, but the Trotskyists were as old as us and from the same culture. Besides, they are very small and have little influence in Italy. The most typical and interesting movement of the New Left was Lotta Continua, which largely originated in the populist radicalization of people coming from Catholic organizations.

When you look back at that period do you have a sense of missed opportunities? Could things have happened differently if Il Manifesto or other left groups had developed a superior politics? Or were there essentially objective reasons why such a powerful movement arose and then declined again?

I think that we did miss great opportunities, as a result of our own mistakes and those of the Communist Party. The famous channel of communication that we wanted to open was never really established. On the one hand, the Communist Party refused to take up and discuss the new experiences of the movement; and on the other hand the *operaio massa* or assembly-line worker—whom we thought of as the key protagonist in the new era—never abandoned its historical organizations. Even in places like Fiat where a significant shift did take place, this only affected a minority of the workforce. The rank-and-file cadres used the pressure of the New Left to open a dialectic within the unions, and this led to the creation of the workers' councils. But although there was considerable interaction on the fringe of the two sectors of the Left, they never overcame their separation. The Communist Party leadership paid some attention to new developments, but it remained essentially closed and incapable of seizing the opportunity to renew its strategic thinking. For our part, we tended in practice to oversimplify our policy orientations, to fall into extremist errors, and to underestimate the question of alliances. In our critique of delegate democracy we did not attach due weight to problems of consensus and intermediate objectives. At the same time, I think we had the merit of being the first in Italy to discuss openly the dimensions and qualitative novelty of the growing crisis of the system, and to fight within this context for a critical re-evaluation of the entire ideological basis of reformist perspectives.

Nonetheless, in the early and mid-seventies the Italian social movements did have a number of big successes, or at least inflicted serious defeats on the ruling class and the Christian Democrat government. The referendum on the legalization of divorce, which the Communist Party was eventually pulled into supporting, won a surprising popular majority that represented a major setback for the clericalist Christian Democrat Party. Secondly there were powerful class mobilizations to secure the indexation of wages to retail prices—the famous scala mobile which in Trotsky's Transitional Programme, *for example, is regarded as a transitional demand, as an intermediate objective for the revolutionary struggle against capitalism. This undoubtedly unbalanced the ruling class in Italy. Finally, a great deal of pressure was placed on the state to democratize access to the media:* il manifesto *itself was distributed by law at every newsvendor's, and radios were later established by shop stewards' movements and so forth. All these things seem quite extraordinary in comparison with other West European countries.*

It is true that the period after 1968 was very different in Italy and, say, France. Whereas the extremely strong French movement ran out of steam soon after the reverse of the June 1968 elections, there was a tremendous impact at mass level in Italy: in the minds of ordinary men and women, shop stewards, rank-and-file workers, technicians, intellectuals, professional workers, and also of the middle classes. Their culture changed in a quite dramatic way, and the trade unions were forced to respond to this. If the unions proved far more open than the Communist Party, it was largely because the newly established workers' councils achieved a high degree of working-class autonomy while never cutting their links with the unions. The CGIL operated in a very astute manner, trying to incorporate the workers' councils instead of simply opposing them. Yet it was a dialectical process, and these very attempts helped the councils to spread from their initial strongholds at Fiat or Pirelli to the rest of the country. At the wages level, the achievement was not so much an indexation to retail prices—which had already existed since the 1950s—as a levelling of index-linked rises for high and low earners. This reduced differentials enormously and, in conjunction with attacks on narrow skill definitions, set up an egalitarian dynamic at the workplace. Workers acquired real political power inside the factories: the right to have open political assemblies at which everything from shop-floor conditions to the Vietnam War could be discussed. The bosses were really threatened.

Even workers who were laid off had the right to a very large proportion of their old wage.

Yes. These were the years of the *statuto dei lavoratori,* which gave enormous rights to workers. You had to kill the boss before you could be fired. This naturally cushioned workers against unemployment, which became a phenomenon affecting above all young people.

Did this not tend to open a divide between workers with legal job security and those who were not covered by the new legislation? The latter would seem to have been the main base for the autonomisti.

There was certainly a very big difference between workers with and without these legal guarantees. At the same time, the trade union movement was greatly strengthened by the close collaboration—one could almost say unity—of the three federations at this time: the CISL, CGIL and UIL.[6] The Catholic unions moved so far and so fast that sections of them were sometimes to the left of the Communist and Socialist unions.

You have mentioned these obviously crucial developments in the workers' movement. But is it not true that the really major political defeat for the established order was the outcome of the divorce referendum?

One can see this as both a positive and a negative thing. The powerful social movements I have been talking about retained their momentum until 1973–74, but then the economic crisis ensued in 1975–76. (As a matter of fact, we were the first on the Italian Left to realize the nature of the crisis, and it was over this question that we had our first serious dispute with the leaders of the original PdUP, who saw it all as an invention of the bosses to drive back the workers' movement.) Anyway the trade unions suddenly found themselves facing new problems of economic policy and development, and the struggle for higher wages and shop-floor control began to fade in importance. As the unions grew increasingly paralysed, all the radical pressure shifted from the anti-capitalist perspectives of the previous movements to the new ground of divorce, abortion and civil liberties represented by essentially democratic movements. Their struggles proved to be highly effective, but they no longer had that cutting edge which had been eroding capitalist power at a much more fundamental level.

---

[6] CISL and UIL: the Confederation of Italian Labour Unions and the Italian Labour Union, respectively Christian Democrat and Socialist splits from the CGIL in 1950.

*On the other hand, when Christian Democracy, the established bourgeois party,
was defeated on the divorce referendum, it lost its majority on a very important
issue.*

It paid very heavily in electoral terms and entered into its long period of
crisis. But it should be remembered that the beneficiary was the Communist
party, not the PdUP or any other New Left group, nor even the Radicals. We
too made a certain advance in 1975 and 1976, but we still received only 2
per cent in the 1976 parliamentary elections. Even in Milan, where we had a
joint slate with Avanguardia Operaia, we only won 3 per cent—less than the
PdUP total in the 1975 regional elections. Our position in the movements
and struggles of society was never accurately reflected in electoral terms.
People would say: We would like to support you, but we are going to vote
for the PCI.

*The initiative on democratic issues, especially the divorce referendum but also
the prison system or the media, often seems to have come not from the Socialist or
Communist Party, nor even from the PdUP, but from the middle-class Radicals.
Is this because you did not consider these issues to be very important?*

No, that's not correct. Take the feminist movement, for example, in which
the first groups actually developed within Il Manifesto. We also played a
significant role on the question of divorce, which we regarded not just as
an isolated bourgeois right but as something to be related to a new way of
thinking about the family. In this respect, too, we were quite distinct from
Lotta Continua or Avanguardia Operaia, who considered our concern with
feminist or ecological issues to be bourgeois; and even in our own party we
had an open quarrel with Foa about divorce. But our starting point was
not simply that Italy should bring itself into line with Britain or the United
States, but that the whole issue should be taken up in its much broader
cultural dimensions.

   After divorce legislation was passed in parliament, with the Left and the
secular bourgeois parties voting against Christian Democracy, the Right
took the initiative of calling a referendum. The Communist Party wanted
to downplay the issue, fearing that a popular majority could not be won
and that it would suffer a serious defeat, but this only proved how out of
touch it was with real trends in society. As to abortion, the question was
even more complicated. There was a parliamentary debate in 1975 and the
Christian Democrats split when a vote was taken the next year. A general
election was then held, and the new Parliament passed a very advanced piece
of legislation. When the Right then demanded a referendum, the Radicals
also opposed the act on the grounds that it was not sufficiently progressive.
We ourselves had some detailed criticisms of the legislation, but it compared
quite favourably with that prevailing in many other European countries. The

real problem was and is that there is a serious shortage of hospital beds in Italy.

Would it be right to say that the divorce referendum and the new interpretation of the scala mobile *happened independently of and before the historic compromise?*

Berlinguer started talking about the historic compromise after the Chilean coup in autumn 1973, but for some time it remained a theoretical discussion about the need to avoid a dangerous Left–Right confrontation and to achieve a broader consensus for change that would include the Catholic world. That was, of course, a very ambiguous formulation: at one level one could hardly disagree, but for Berlinguer the Catholic world tended to become reduced to the Christian Democratic Party, which is a very different matter.

From what you were saying earlier, Lotta Continua could be seen as in a sense part of the Catholic world.

Yes. Even in the PdUP there were a lot of Catholics: indeed, one of the in-jokes among Christian Democrats was that the PdUP was the second Catholic party in the country.

Are there members of a Marxist party who actually go to confession?

Oh, yes. The same is true of the Communist Party. But the most militant Catholics were in the New Left, and even in the Red Brigades. The first terrorist group came from the Catholic stronghold of Trento. After all, it is understandable that once Catholics started moving left they kept the same kind of fundamentalism and sought to draw the most far-reaching conclusions. If there is evil loose in society, then it has to be fought with all one's strength, including weapons.

What was the PdUP's reaction to the strategy of the historic compromise?

We tried not to oversimplify our judgement or to interpret it as just a matter of betrayal. What we criticized was the way in which it was implemented: the point was not to reach an agreement with the Christian Democrats but to deepen the crisis within their party. For the PCI, on the other hand, it was the old question of going furthest in the development of bourgeois democracy—which now meant an agreement with Christian Democracy to democratize and modernize Italian society.

There would presumably be a difference between yourselves and the PCI on the question of the state ...

Yes: on whether the state can be democratized or whether it has to be transformed; on the concept of continuity against that of a radical break. In reality, however, it was only after 1975 that the discussion of the historic compromise developed in PCI thinking into the concretized or banalized notion of a national unity agreement with the Christian Democrats. The period of 1976–79 was one of the worst in Italian history, from which all the tragedies have stemmed. At that time 95 per cent of political forces were lined up behind the government: the only opposition was from the far Left on one side and the far Right on the other. Can you imagine what society was like in those conditions?

You yourself were a member of parliament at that time?

Yes. In the Democrazia Proletaria list PdUP had three deputies, Avanguardia Operaia two and Lotta Continua one. It was an incredible parliament in which everything was decided through compromise. We had a Christian Democrat government, with a majority that included Communists, Socialists, Republicans, Social Democrats and Liberals. The Communist Party thought that it would be able to influence government decisions and introduce some changes, but the actual result was complete paralysis at official level. The social forces represented by these parties were so much in contradiction with one another that the government lacked any resolve. The bills passed by 95 per cent of parliament were so noxious not because they were reactionary but because they decided nothing. Underneath, the right-wing state machine followed its course quite freely. Thus a parliamentary committee, in which the PCI was represented, was set up to exercise control over the secret services, the army, and so forth. But then, with the help of P-2, the secret services simply organized underground and established links with people who were afraid of the growing role of the Communist Party.

The story took a new turn in 1977 when the tiny terrorist groups expanded into something much larger. The first reaction of the PCI was to say that it was the work of the CIA and the secret services—an attempt to undermine national unity and to keep the Communists out of government. Of course there may well have been some police infiltration, as there always is in such cases, but it is necessary to go back to the original discussions of terrorism at the beginning of the 1970s. The key group then was Potere Operaio, which though very small was probably the most sophisticated politically. Unlike the Marxist-Leninist terrorists, who thought in terms of a strong group taking over the state and then establishing a new society, the Potere Operaio spontaneists believed that capitalism had exhausted all its possibilities and that communism had already matured within existing society. All that was necessary was to lop off the state-capitalist head and communism would be ensured.

In point of fact, it was a small, isolated Marxist-Leninist group with a Catholic background which initiated terrorist activity in the early 1970s: it got together with some old partisans and set itself up as the Gruppi di Azione Partigiana, the name of a wartime resistance organization. In the same years, Potere Operaio started a major debate at a theoretical level which reverberated in many groups. In the event, the New Left chose a completely different strategy, involving mass action, trade union work and participation in elections, and the terrorist perspective was roundly defeated. But when the Communists turned towards National Unity in 1975 and 1976 and the trade unions found themselves paralysed in the face of the growing capitalist crisis, there was a tremendous disillusionment on the Left. It was the old story which repeats itself in every country whenever the political parties linked to the trade unions are in government. For many urban youth left out in the cold—the 'urban Indians', as they were sometimes called—Christian Democrats and Communists, trade unions and employers' associations, bosses and workers with job security all formed part of a single enemy. The terrifying new wave of violence, which really picked up speed in 1977, was quite unlike the creative movement of 1968 and had none of its broader appeal.

Perhaps there was a common emphasis on subjectivity and personal expression, which in a situation of great frustration can lead to religious fanaticism or terrorism.

Well, there was a creative aspect or even wing of the 1977 movement—the people who have been described as 'creative Indians'. But it was the new terrorists who held centre stage: they started by throwing stones at Lama, the trade union leader, in a famous incident at Rome University. Although the majority of armed attacks were directed at judges and members of the state apparatus, it was the PCI and the unions who were regarded as the main *political* enemy, precisely because they were felt to be closer.

The terrorist movement culminated in the kidnapping and killing of the Christian Democrat politician Aldo Moro, who was a symbolic figure of the historic compromise. Would it be right to say that this was destroyed by the Moro affair?

In a way, yes. In the new civil war atmosphere hundreds of people were killed and tens of thousands put in jail. A series of emergency laws, which could plainly be termed fascist, were passed with the approval of the Communist Party, and with only ourselves and the Radicals voting against.

But however strong the terrorists were, we are still only talking of a few thousand people with very primitive weapons, whereas the Italian state is a very power-

ful body. It seems remarkable that you were unable to make any Communist or Christian Democrat unhappy with what you call fascist laws. What kind of opposition did you put up in parliament?

The opposition was very strong, and many deputies in the majority were uneasy about these laws. They told us so, but they still voted for them.

It was the same with the Prevention of Terrorism Act in Britain, which nearly all Labour MPs voted for in the end.

There were demonstrations and other protest actions, but you should not underestimate the extent of terrorism at that time. There were tens of thousands of active participants and an even broader circle of sympathizers who would not denounce them to the police. There was a good film which gives some idea of the dilemmas involved. It is about a university lecturer from the sixty-eight generation who, though not a terrorist himself, has a number of friends who are. One day his thirteen-year-old son finds out that a terrorist who has just been killed was a friend of his father's and he goes straight to the police to report the fact. The father is then taken in and interrogated for hours on end. When he is eventually released, he says to his child: 'For God's sake why did you tell them?' And the son replies: 'Didn't you tell me that terrorism is such a negative thing?' We were all saying that! 'Of course I said it,' the father continues. 'But what does that have to do with going to the police?' 'Well,' the son comes back, 'if you want to defeat them, why not go to the police?' And the father can only retort: 'Because I would never go to the police.' He is unable to give an answer. The film ends when the wife of the terrorist comes and asks the father for money. He gives and thus becomes involved himself. I know that there are many real-life stories along similar lines.

During this period there was an eruption of indiscriminate terrorism from the Right—for example, the explosion at Bologna railway station—which was against ordinary citizens, not against people in authority. What was the logic of that?

Destabilization, and a large, proven element of police or secret service provocation designed to bring about a strengthening of the state machine.

Would it be right to say that the position on terrorism played a major role in the split between yourselves and the other PdUP forces?

Yes. We were against the special laws, but we were also against any agreement with the terrorists for the release of Moro. If such a compromise had been made, it would have been a way of legalizing terrorism and laid the ground for the declaration of a state of emergency. We did not identify ourselves with the state, but in a sense we did defend it at that moment. Democracy, though imperfect and incomplete, seemed to us preferable and worth keeping, when the alternative would have been something much worse. The other position, prevalent among those in the New Left who had rejected terrorism, was that they should remain neutral between the Red Brigades and the state. This difference also implied distinct judgements of the 1977 movement as a whole.

Do you think that anything positive came out of the movement?

Not really. Part of it went into drugs, which started to become a mass phenomenon. And there was a powerful wave of disillusion, fed in part by the influence of the *nouveaux philosophes*. In a sense it was the best elements who went into armed struggle, basing themselves on an analysis that fascism had already triumphed. In our view that was clearly not the case—and perhaps I exaggerated a moment ago when I referred to the special laws as fascist. Nor were the Communists the same as the Christian Democrats, however wrong their policy may have been. That was another issue in the split with the comrades who continue to publish *il manifesto*.

Have the various positions evolved since the split?

Yes. Things have changed a great deal. *il manifesto* is now just a newspaper: it does not believe that the New Left should express itself through political parties.

Do you feel that the situation inside the PCI *is such that you will be able to develop the ideas you have been advocating outside? If you have differences over a major issue like* NATO, *will you be able to raise your ideas freely and present them to the mass of party militants? Since the split with* il manifesto, *you have only had a membership bulletin,* Compagne e Compagni, *which will presumably not be maintained. But what possibilities do you have for publishing in the* PCI *press?*

There is no problem in publishing in *Rinascita* and debating whatever we want. For example, when the PCI Central Committee debated the convergence with PdUP, and some members argued against it on the grounds that we were opposed to NATO, the discussion was printed in the party press. Something like that could not have happened fifteen years ago. The real problem we face is rather different: namely, how to achieve a synthesis in what is after all a rather eclectic body—a party in which there are a number of fragments from different cultural traditions with relatively distinct identities. So we have a fragment of the feminist movement as such, a fragment of the ecological movement as such, and neither they nor the great bulk of the Communist Party have changed much as a result of their recruitment.

It is quite true that there are still many problems to be resolved in terms of rights, internal democracy and debate, and so forth. But we felt that many of the things we stood for had been acquired in the Communist Party: the real issue now was how it could overcome the contradiction between its enormous strength in society and its lack of effective power, how it could put together the different and very eclectic fragments of social experience that exist within and around it. It would have been much easier for us to remain outside, without having to face the problems and responsibilities of a mass party, but we would have been bound to become just a group of intellectuals, possibly effective in introducing new themes but nevertheless deserters from the key political (and theoretical) arena of party activity. Our greater freedom would have been a kind of personal solution.

Could you say something about how the process of unification was prepared in the PdUP?

The congress which took the final decision was preceded by three months of discussion that was open to others on the New Left. It was a very interesting experience, because it proved how much common ground there was in the PCI, the PdUP and a large part of the unorganized New Left. It should also be remembered that in the 1983 and 1984 elections we had stood on a common list with PCI candidates, with quite impressive results. So there was a great deal of interest in the press and elsewhere about the prospect of the PdUP merging with the PCI.

Does this also demonstrate a powerful desire for unity in the working class and the other oppressed social layers?

Yes. Many people who felt psychologically unable to vote for us as independent candidates were overjoyed when we put ourselves forward on a joint list.

Perhaps a process of unification of working-class and progressive forces would have set up a strong popular dynamic in the mid-seventies.

The times were not ripe then, although a different policy would certainly have helped.

Did Communist Party members also take part in discussion meetings?

Yes. They were very intensively involved at a purely informal level, including former members of Il Manifesto and the PdUP who had joined the PCI over the previous fifteen years and often won key positions. Our meetings were rather like feminist consciousness-raising sessions, in the sense that everyone talked about their personal experiences and brought the whole discussion alive. One working-class PCI member, from the small town of Massa Cararra, expressed a typical view when he said: 'I never thought of you as the enemy when you were kicked out. I thought of you as a kind of expeditionary force. Now you have come back and you will bring what you found outside.'

Adolfo Gilly (b. 1928) is most widely known for his classic study La revolución interrumpida *(in English,* The Mexican Revolution*), which has gone through thirty reprints in Spanish since it first appeared in 1971. Gilly has been for many years a professor of History and Politics at the Universidad Nacional Autónoma de México, but as he explains in this interview, the book took shape far from academic settings, in the life of a revolutionary militant whose commitments took him all the way across Latin America and to Europe, into clandestinity, exile and the Mexican jail where his book was conceived and written. Today, Gilly combines university teaching and research with his older vocation of political journalist, writing in solidarity with popular movements in Mexico and elsewhere in Latin America. He gave this interview in 2009–10.*

Adolfo Gilly

'What Exists Cannot Be True'

How would you describe your background and political formation?

I was born in Buenos Aires in 1928. My father was a lawyer, though he had been a lieutenant in the navy before that; my mother was a house-wife. My paternal grandfather was an Italian immigrant, with the surname Malvagni. Gilly was my mother's maiden name, possibly of French origin; I later adopted it as my *nom de plume*, since in Argentina your mother's name doesn't appear on your passport. My first political activity came in 1943, when I joined the local Comité de Gaulle, without really knowing what it was, out of sympathy with the Free French. France always had a large cultural influence on Argentina, and de Gaulle of all the leaders had not sur-rendered to the invaders. The first political demonstration I went to was to celebrate the liberation of Paris in August 1944, at the age of sixteen. The following year, there was a general strike in Buenos Aires, with mass mobi-lizations of workers in October that forced the military government to call elections, which the Junta's Labour minister, Juan Domingo Perón, won in February 1946.

This was a decisive moment in what I would call my 'sentimental edu-cation'. That year I joined the Juventud Socialista, the youth wing of the Socialist Party, and then the Socialist party itself. Together with some other school students, I worked on a party newspaper called *Rebeldía* (Rebellion), but we had only put out four issues before the leadership closed us down. I left the Socialists in 1947, and joined an organization called the Movimiento Obrero Revolucionario. By the time I turned twenty, I had quit my law studies and got a job as a proof corrector at a publishing house. This was a very particular milieu, because the proofreaders always saw themselves as intellectuals, but underprivileged ones. It was around this time, 1948–49, that I began to live the workers' movement. In Argentina, this was a move-ment with a strong socialist and anarchist tradition—largely because of Italian and Spanish immigration into the country, which coincided with the initial wave of worker organization in the 1880s and 1890s. This, by the way, is a feature common to Brazil and Uruguay as well, where anarchists also had a significant presence. These Mediterranean immigrants brought with them a culture that had an anarchist tradition—anarchist and Catholic. Later, I discovered that many features of Peronism, such as the proposal for a general strike in 1945, came from the world of anarchism or anarcho-syndicalism, rather than that of communism or social democracy.

I was increasingly drawn to Trotskyism, and in 1949, two of us in the MOR— Guillermo Almeyra and myself—decided to join the Fourth International. At this point, we had to choose which of three currents within the FI to support. There was one strand which saw Perón as an agent of British imperialism. Braden, the US Ambassador at the time, had made public statements against Perón during the campaign; so posters appeared everywhere saying 'Braden or Perón', posing the election in nationalist terms, as a choice between the two. It seems absurd now, but one current in the FI thought that the British were behind all of this. A second strand argued that Perón's support base was composed of backward masses of newly proletarianized workers. They were like an avalanche that buried the previously existing proletariat, over which the Socialist Party had had an influence in the 1930s. According to this interpretation, these 'backward masses' were now following a leader—as if Perón were some sort of snake charmer with a flute.

The third current, which was led by Homero Cristalli—better known under his pseudonym, Juan Posadas—maintained that Perón was a representative of the Argentine industrial bourgeoisie, engaged in a struggle for political power with the old landowning oligarchy, but that his base was a genuine nationalist mass movement.[1] The rapid growth of industry during the Second World War had brought large numbers of peasants and artisans into the capital from the interior, effectively creating a new proletariat. This was not the traditional peasantry of a colonial country—they were peasant workers, in a countryside where capitalist relations dominated the large meat- and wheat-exporting haciendas, and small producers descended from European immigrants. When they moved to the city and became industrial workers, they created unions with an impressive mass base. Perón's popularity rested on a series of laws on holidays, severance pay, pensions, guaranteed rights of organization, holiday resorts. It's important to have holidays, of course, although it may not seem like a radical change in anyone's life. But for the Argentine working class that developed during the Second World War, fifteen days' holiday a year was a real gain; something comparable happened in France in 1936 under the Popular Front. This third current was saying that the workers may have been following a charismatic leader, but they did so for their own reasons. Peronism was the specific form that the organization of the working class took in our country, and we had to understand it.

---

[1] Juan Posadas (1912–81).

I joined this third current within the Argentine organizations affiliated to the FI—the one led by Posadas. The world of the Fourth International might now seem like another planet. There were always two elements within it, one focused on revolution in Europe, the other on the colonial world. Both dreams were Trotsky's, and they cohabited in the FI, but there was always a tension between them. Ernest Mandel and Michel Pablo represented the two visions.[2] Mandel, who had been formed in the world of manufacturing and mining in Belgium, was convinced the vector of revolution would be the industrial proletariat. Pablo, whose real name was Michalis Raptis, was born in Alexandria and grew up in Greece, a country with a long history of struggle for national independence; in the 1950s and 1960s he saw the huge upsurge of movements for independence in the colonial world. Ernest would become animated when talking about the German Revolution, Rosa Luxemburg and so on, while Pablo would come alive when telling heroic stories of the Algerian revolution or the war of liberation in Greece; in that sense, he was something of a Balkan conspirator. There were many disagreements between them, because they had such different dreams. But they had warm personal relations all the same. In 1995 I was in Greece to do an interview with Pablo, who called me one afternoon to tell me Mandel had died; he then recorded some very emotional recollections of Ernest, with whom he had argued time and again. This kind of warmth is something social-democratic parties lack, because they are in a sense too secular: they lack devotion to the idea of revolutionary Marxism. Though that phrase has always struck me as a pleonasm—for me it was always a given that any Marxism would have to be revolutionary.

What would you say were the main intellectual influences on you early on?

I came of age in a country that was not in the First World, but was not a peasant country either, which gave it a very particular form. My initial commitment to the revolutionary movement came first—books came afterwards. What I read seemed rather to confirm what my experience and intuition had already been telling me. In fact, I think this is generally the case: one is led towards rebellion by sentiments, not by thoughts. At the end of his statement to the Dewey Commission, Trotsky described being drawn to the workers' quarters in Nikolayev at the age of eighteen by his 'faith in reason, in truth, in human solidarity', not by Marxism. But perhaps the most crucial sentiment is that of justice—the realization that you are not in agreement with this world. There is a story that Ernst Bloch was asked by his supervisor, Georg Simmel, to provide a one-page summary of his thesis before Simmel would agree to work on it. A week later, Bloch obliged with one sentence:

---

[2] For Mandel, see pp. 98–105. Michel Pablo (1911–96) left the Fourth International in 1963 and subsequently became a government minister in Algeria.

'What exists cannot be true.' The thesis later became *The Principle of Hope*.[3] It was this kind of ethical moment that was crucial for me—the discovery that there was a necessary connection between justice and truth.

I remember reading Trotsky's *Revolution Betrayed* when I was eighteen, but what really brought me to Trotskyism were two articles of his on Lázaro Cárdenas that analysed the post-Revolutionary Mexican government's continual oscillations between subordination to imperialism and forwarding workers' interests.[4] According to Trotsky, this variation was due to the weakness of the national bourgeoisie, and to the relative power of the proletariat. In his view, *cardenismo* was a *sui generis* form of Bonapartism, attempting to raise itself 'above classes', and making concessions to the workers in order to secure some room for manoeuvre against foreign capital. I was very struck by the force of Trotsky's arguments.

If I had to choose a handful of books that made a particular impression, there would be André Breton's *L'amour fou*, which I read in 1949, and C. L. R. James's *The Black Jacobins*, which I read in French on a train to Bolivia in the late 1950s, as well as his study of Melville, *Mariners, Renegades and Castaways*. Curiously, when reading *Moby Dick* some fifteen years earlier I had been struck by the very same sentence from which James took his title. Melville and James are marked by the same refusal of injustice I mentioned earlier. I also found it in José María Arguedas, a Peruvian who wrote an extraordinary autobiographical novel called *Los ríos profundos*, and in the poetry of another Peruvian, César Vallejo. And of course it's present in Frantz Fanon. I recall buying *Les damnés de la terre* in Rome, in a bookshop on the via Veneto on 4 December 1961—I remember the day exactly because I read the book in one sitting, and it made a big impact on me. I discovered Gramsci around the same time, during a stay in Italy. I also read the work of Raniero Panzieri, Mario Tronti and the group around *Quaderni rossi*, and of course the writings of Rossana Rossanda, Pietro Ingrao and the leftist tendencies inside the Italian Communist Party.[5] I became familiar with Subaltern Studies and the work of Ranajit Guha and Partha Chatterjee in the late 1980s. I only really read Edward Thompson in the 1990s. His *Making of the English Working Class* and *Customs in Common* lay a lot of emphasis on the category of experience, which in my view is extremely important to Marxist thought.

Taken together, all of these works have in common a concern with the preoccupations of the people, based on the impulse to understand their world and what motivates them. The reasons why people rise up in revolution are not incidental, they are substantive. In his *History of the Russian Revolution*,

---

[3] Ernst Bloch (1885–1977), *The Principle of Hope* (1938–47), Cambridge, MA 1986.

[4] Lázaro Cárdenas del Río (1895–1970), President of Mexico, 1934–40. The essays are Leon Trotsky, 'Mexico and British Imperialism' (1938) and 'Trade Unions in the Epoch of Imperialist Decay' (1940).

[5] *Quaderni rossi* (1961–66), one of the formative journals of the Italian New Left.

Trotsky writes that the masses didn't rise up because they were thinking of the future, but because what they were experiencing in the present was intolerable. Walter Benjamin expresses a similar thought in his theses on history. When Guha writes of the 'autonomous domain' of the subaltern, and of ways of conducting politics 'below' official politics, it comes from his experience as a communist militant in India. In a way, when I wrote on the Mexican Revolution I was concerned with the same phenomena of social life as in Guha's work, though mine took a more elemental form. Many look at the support for Perón or Cárdenas and say they were Peronists, or Cardenistas. But the parties in question were just the epiphenomenal form taken by the desires of all these people. Parties often think they are the ones organizing and instructing the people on how to mobilize, but that's not the case—they were the best institutional form for securing particular ends, and the impulse comes from elsewhere, from long years of suffering, from an intolerable reality.

You left Argentina for Bolivia in 1956 at the age of twenty-eight. Could you tell us more about the situation in Bolivia, and the political work you did there?

I went as a member of the FI. I was initially supposed to be there for six months, but ended up staying for four years. I arrived just in time for the April anniversary of the 1952 revolution, and saw the miners' militias parading through La Paz with their rifles. I was deeply affected by this. Of course, the military was busily rearming itself at the time, but still, the very fact that the miners had kept their weapons meant that the monopoly of legitimate violence had been broken. This made a substantial difference to the balance of forces for some time, creating what was effectively a miners' territory in the country.

I went to work with a Bolivian Trotskyist group, the Partido Obrero Revolucionario (POR). It was one of two parties of that name formed by a split in the original Trotskyist core in 1954, over the meaning of mass support for the MNR and its Nationalist union leaders. The division was similar to the Left's debates over Peronism in Argentina. One of the PORs was led by Hugo González Moscoso and put out a paper called *Lucha obrera*; it was strong in the mines, among the peasantry and workers in some sectors in La Paz, and sought to understand why the organization of the masses in Bolivia had taken a nationalist political form. The other POR, led by Guillermo Lora, had its base in the mines at Catavi-Siglo xx, and its paper was called *Masas*. Lora was very critical of the Revolutionary Nationalist Movement (MNR), and concentrated more on attacking the nationalist leadership. There were also some Trotskyists who held that the masses themselves were nationalist in character, and peeled off to join the MNR—among them such figures as Erwin Moller and Lidia Gueiler, who eventually became Interim President of Bolivia for eight months.

During my stay in Bolivia I started writing for the Uruguayan weekly *Marcha*, edited by Carlos Quijano.[6] I was based in La Paz to begin with, and then in the mining town of Oruro. Both of them were very different places from what I had known in Buenos Aires, but I was still living in a world of workers that was familiar to me. Bolivian miners, though, were not industrial workers as in Argentina or the US—they were still tied to the land in many ways, almost a kind of industrial peasantry. In that sense they were like the figure of the worker in Gramsci, in whom north and south Italy combine. The time I spent in Bolivia was marked by constant attempts by the Nationalist government to assert control over the miners and peasants. The MNR openly took the Mexican Institutional Revolutionary Party (PRI) as its model, hoping to replicate its success in setting up a nationalist state out of the revolution. The miners, meanwhile, maintained their militias, and in the mid-fifties began to set up their own radio stations, which helped to coordinate struggles among mines that were large distances apart.

What would you say are the specificities of Bolivia, compared to other Latin American countries?

The weight of the mines in that society is one important difference. Another is that, historically, the dominant class in Bolivia was much poorer and smaller than elsewhere, and its domination was based on a form of colonial racism against the vast indigenous majority, both peasant and urban. There is an excellent historical study of this social and racial domination: *Revolutionary Horizons*, a book by Sinclair Thomson and Forrest Hylton. The present movement in Bolivia is first and foremost an insurrection against it. By contrast, colonial Peru had the pomp of the viceregal court in Lima, and a coastal oligarchy that lived on after independence; Mexico had the court and culture of New Spain. Bolivia was locked away in the *altiplano*, cut off from the sea, and for a long time seemed to be a mining enclave that had to ask its neighbours' permission to get its products to the coast and out into the world's markets. On a personal level, I was struck by a difference in the sense of time. To begin with I put it down to poor timekeeping, or lack of discipline, or the habits of peasant life. But then I realized it was just another way of dealing with time. When I went to Europe in 1960, someone asked me what the difference was between Amsterdam and La Paz, and I replied: 'Here all the public clocks show the same time, whereas over there each shows whatever time it likes.'

---

[6] Founded in 1939, *Marcha* was a leading Latin American political and cultural weekly. Contributors included Che Guevara, Borges, Faulkner, Céline, Cortázar and Vargas Llosa; its first literary editor was the novelist Juan Carlos Onetti. Two of its editors were imprisoned by the Bordaberry dictatorship, which closed it down in 1975.

What were your impressions of the European Left in the early sixties, and of the intellectual scene?

I spent the years from 1960 to 1962 in Europe, working as a Latin American member of the Secretariat of the Fourth International. I met Mandel in Brussels in the spring of 1960, when he was just finishing his *Traité d'économie marxiste*. I went to see him about getting travel documents for some Algerian comrades, and remember being very struck by his old house and his enormous number of Bach records. It was around this time that the break between Mandel and Pablo was unfolding, which I imagine was very painful for both of them. Pablo was at that time in prison in Holland for his activities in support of the Algerian Revolution. Moscow character-ized the Algerian War of Independence as a bourgeois nationalist movement which deserved no backing, while the Socialists were part of the French government that was fighting the Algerians with torture, blood and fire. The Algerians had to organize their own networks and even set up a secret arms factory in Morocco, where some Trotskyist metalworkers—Argentines and Greeks—had gone to work. But the Algerian Revolution brought to the fore the differences between Mandel and Pablo I mentioned earlier. The first focused his hopes on proletarian revolution, the second on national and anti-colonial movements. Though neither of them posed it in that way, these different visions led to different priorities and forms of struggle. When Pablo pressed to put the Fourth International fully behind the Algerian Revolution, Mandel resisted it. The rupture was complex and confused, but from then on Mandel took over from Pablo as leading figure in the organization.

That same year I also spent time in Italy. There I found the Trotskyists to be more focused on political questions—what line should be taken—rather than on the very real changes that had been taking place in the factories. Automation had brought about significant shifts in the labour process, and it seemed to me that there had also been a shift in the mode of domina-tion, which needed to be understood in order to develop different forms of labour organization. When I was there, I witnessed the beginnings of the *autonomia* movement and workers' councils. In my view these were similar to the internal commissions set up in factories in Argentina in the 1940s, and which had been misunderstood by much of the Left. The rebirth of these councils in many ways prepared the way for the hot autumn of 1969. The current that seemed to me closer to these preoccupations was the *Quaderni rossi* group, which developed the form of the 'worker's enquiry'. It struck me that the enquiries were focused on the same question that always inter-ested me—what do these people want?

You then spent time in Cuba. What was your experience of the place, in the wake of the revolution?

I was in Cuba from 1962–63, as a writer and a journalist. The Cuban hierarchy knew I was a Trotskyist, but as long as I didn't openly do any political organizing, my presence was not a problem—that is, until 1963, when I was put on a plane to Italy. I remember the atmosphere during the Missile Crisis, when I was very impressed by the people's readiness to defend the Revolution. There were signs saying 'To Arms!' all over Havana, and members of the popular militias doing their exercises in the rain. There was no sign of alarm or terror, only a refusal to bow before the atomic threat. It was this non-acceptance, which everyone to this day remembers, that saved Cuba and the revolution, and was a real moment of glory. I wrote a long reportage chronicling the October Days of the Missile Crisis, which was published as a special edition of *Monthly Review*, 'Inside the Cuban Revolution', in 1964.

In the mid-sixties you were active in Guatemala, supporting leftist guerrillas there against the Peralta dictatorship. What was distinctive about the Movimiento Revolucionario 13 de Noviembre (MR-13) as a political formation?

The origins of MR-13 lay in a military revolt by young nationalist lieutenants in November 1960. The senior leader, Lieutenant Colonel Augusto Vicente Loarca, was older than the others, at forty-eight; Lieutenants Marco Antonio Yon Sosa and Luis Augusto Turcios Lima, the actual leaders in the field, were in their late twenties or early thirties. They rebelled both on anti-imperialist grounds, against the use of Guatemala as a base for US attacks on Cuba, and for the completion of the agrarian reform that had begun under Jacobo Árbenz, but had been aborted after the CIA-sponsored coup that toppled him in 1954. The MR-13 grouping formed part of a long line of military nationalists in Latin America. In Bolivia, it starts with Germán Busch in 1937–39, and continues with Gualberto Villarroel in 1943–46 and Juan José Torres in 1970. In Mexico there was Lázaro Cárdenas, and in Peru, Juan Velasco Alvarado. You could say Hugo Chávez belongs to this same tradition, as a nationalist soldier confronting imperialism with the support of a mass movement.

In Guatemala the nationalist, anti-imperialist movement begins with Árbenz and continues with the young officers of MR-13. There is a clear continuity—Loarca had even served with Árbenz. But MR-13 marked a distinctive programmatic development. Part of the movement was allied with the local Communist Party, the PGT, which wanted to subordinate the soldiers to its own political line; this hinged on a 'stageist' approach—first the bourgeois democratic revolution, then the struggle for socialism. But many in MR-13 had already experienced the bourgeois revolution, with Árbenz; they had seen a mild agrarian reform but no change in social relations. It seemed logical to them that the revolution had to be socialist. So the MR-13 adopted socialist revolution as its platform—the first Latin American guerrilla movement to do so, making explicit what had been implicit in Cuba. This was an important step, and was immediately seen as such: it was emulated by the MIR in Peru, a section of the FALN in Venezuela, and by groups in Uruguay, Argentina, Brazil.[7] It also prefigured Che Guevara's celebrated statement, 'Either a socialist revolution or a caricature of revolution.'

The Guatemalans arrived at this decision themselves, but there were two important outside influences. Firstly, the example of Vietnam, which was in everyone's minds in the mid-sixties. The guerrillas knew all about the Vietnamese villages that had organized themselves in resistance, they read the reports of Wilfred Burchett. Second, there were the Mexican Trotskyists of the POR, with whom MR-13 had entered into contact, seeking support. The Mexicans debated and discussed with them, but far more importantly they sent militants to help MR-13 and smuggled arms across the border, breaking the Guatemalan Communists' control over the weaponry the movement received. I was in Guatemala for part of 1964 and all of 1965, and travelled with the guerrillas in the central highlands of the Sierra de las Minas. I wrote a report about it, published as a book at the time, which circulated a great deal in Latin America.[8] Régis Debray's *Revolution in the Revolution?*, which came out two years later, is in part a polemic—though Debray does not name it directly—against the current I was describing, and against the platform that was agreed at the MR-13's conference in December 1964. I remember having a theoretical discussion there with Yon Sosa about the programme. He insisted that the movement proclaim an 'agrarian and socialist revolution', while I told him that the second term necessarily included the first. He agreed, but said people would not understand, so it had to remain in the programme. And he was right. The urban and industrial labour force had been the base for proletarian revolutions in Europe and parts of Latin America in the past. But this had left out the immense mass of humanity—the peasantry, the rural population, the indigenous, and the vast colonial world. As I see it now, it is the revolt of the colonial world that gives the twentieth century its meaning.

In 1966, you were arrested in Mexico on your way back to Guatemala, and then spent six years in Lecumberri Prison. What was the prison regime like?

Of course, it was unjust that I was there at all, but the regime was almost like a monastery. It was good to be insulated from all the turbulence of political praxis—which deputy voted how, getting leaflets out, and so on. I had time to read a lot of literature, and read all of *Capital* again. As an

---

[7] MIR: the Movement of the Revolutionary Left, founded in 1962, inspired by the Cuban example. The Venezuelan FALN (Armed Forces of National Liberation) was founded in 1962.

[8] *El movimiento guerrillero en Guatemala*, Buenos Aires 1965; published in English the same year in two parts by *Monthly Review*.

experiment, I read the eleven or twelve volumes of the Marx–Engels correspondence chronologically, from cover to cover, in order to follow the course of the two men's thought as they were writing to each other. I read Hegel, and reread Trotsky's *History of the Russian Revolution*. In a sense, prison also saved my life: one of the Mexican police agents who beat me once or twice told me I should be thankful, since the Guatemalans were 'real sons of bitches'; and it's true that all my comrades there were killed by the Guatemalan security services.

You were in prison in Mexico during the events of 1968. What was their resonance in Lecumberri?

We kept close track of world events on TV and in the newspapers, and each group in prison was in contact with its comrades outside. The number of prisoners swelled by about 250 after the Tlatelolco massacre and the crackdown that followed, but then shrank down to seventy or so. I remember watching the Olympics on TV—the broadcast was accompanied by the Orwellian slogan 'everything is possible in peace'—and seeing the Black Power salutes of the US athletes as well as the Czech gymnast holding her arm across her chest, head bowed, when the Soviet anthem was played. At the time, not many people would have thought we were living through a major historical change, though they might have felt it at some level. But it wasn't so much France that influenced us as Vietnam, which was where 1968 really began, with the resistance to the war in the US itself.

It was in Lecumberri that you wrote La revolución interrumpida, *the first serious history of the Mexican Revolution written from the Left. You trace the arc of the revolution across the decade 1910–20, from the disintegration of the ancien régime of Porfirio Díaz through its successive phases: the triumph of the liberal wing of the bourgeoisie under Francisco Madero in 1911; his two-year presidency, marked by its failure to suppress the peasant insurgency of Emiliano Zapata in the south, and ending in his ouster and assassination by General Huerta in 1913; the defeat of Huerta in 1914 by bourgeois Constitutionalist forces; and, finally, what you describe as a 'long, grim downturn' from 1914 to 1920, as the Constitutionalist armies pushed back the peasant armies of Zapata and Pancho Villa, eventually quelling their resistance. What prompted you to begin this project, and what inspired your interpretation of these events?*

An old Trotskyist teacher, Nicolás Molina Flores, who visited me and brought me books while I was in jail—and himself ended up imprisoned in Lecumberri in 1968, during the great Mexican student movement of that year—said to me one day that I should write a book about the Mexican Revolution. To begin with I dismissed the idea. Of course, I had long been aware of it: until Cuba, the Mexican Revolution was *the* revolution for Latin

Americans, and it had a mythical significance for my generation. For example, the second issue of *Rebeldía*, the student paper I worked on, carried an Orozco painting on its cover, and a reproduction of Rivera's mural from Bellas Artes as its centrefold. But my interest in the idea of writing on the Mexican Revolution grew after reading more of the existing books on it. In Jesús Silva Herzog's official history from 1958, written from the left wing of the PRI, everyone was a good guy, and it was totally unclear why they all ended up killing each other. The Communist Party books on the subject were boring and badly written.

The key, as I saw it, was to find the inner impetus behind the movements of the masses—not who won which battle, but what the hell all these people wanted. The idea for the architecture of the book came from Trotsky's prologue to his *History of the Russian Revolution*, where he describes the curve of the revolution. My idea was to try to establish the equivalent shape for the Mexican Revolution. In my account, the culmination came not with the signing of the Constitution of 1917 in Querétaro, as in official accounts, but with the occupation of Mexico City by Villa's and Zapata's armies in December 1914. Villa's División del Norte had inflicted a crushing defeat on government troops at Zacatecas in the summer of 1914, and at the Aguascalientes Convention that October he and Zapata joined forces to insist on a programme of land redistribution. The country was at boiling point. But after they marched into the capital in December, the two peasant leaders did not know what to do with it. The person who did know what to do was Álvaro Obregón, who was able to exploit the political weakness of Villismo, and eventually break it apart. From that point on, the revolution traces a long, descending curve. In fact, it was only when things had calmed down sufficiently that the Constitution was signed in 1917. In the first version of the book I explained Villa's and Zapata's failure by the lack of a proletarian leadership. This was teleological and silly; I took it out of the English translation, and then adjusted the Spanish editions.[9] When I finished the book, I sent it from prison to several publishers, but none of them took it on. It was thanks to Rafael Galván, the former leader of the electricians' union and a sympathizer of Trotsky's, that it got published. Galván, a Cardenista who later became a PRI senator, rang El Caballito publishers and urged them to do it. The book came out in 1971 and went through four editions in the space of a few months. It has since been through forty successive editions, and is on history reading lists in Mexico's high schools and universities.

---

[9] *The Mexican Revolution*, translated by Patrick Camiller, London 1983; New York 2005.

What happened after your release?

I was released in 1972, and deported to France. I spent the next four years in Europe, mainly in France and Italy. In Paris I joined the local Posadist section of the Fourth International and took part in its meetings. But I found I didn't understand anything; the atmosphere was conspiratorial, sectarian and rigid. I had felt much freer in prison. In any case, a sect of whatever kind is a prison for thought. After a year and a half, I left. This marked my definitive break with what had been the party of Posadas. In hindsight, the break had been in preparation while I was in prison. A Mexican friend who read *La revolución interrumpida* had told me I would be thrown out before long—that the book was written by a person who was clearly on a different path from the party of which he was a member. I returned to Mexico in 1976, and secured a teaching job at UNAM; I've been based there ever since. I've been a Mexican citizen since 1982.

You wrote a great deal on the Central American guerrilla movements of the late 1970s and early 1980s—notably in the books La nueva Nicaragua *(1980) and* Guerra y política en El Salvador *(1981). What connections do you see between these and the earlier Guatemalan experience, and the reasons for their failure?*

I'm not sure one can speak of failure. They were defeated, rather than simply failing. And in each case, the experience remained. As for the relations between them, this is a subject that would require a long discussion. For me, MR-13 represents a continuation of Árbenz's nationalist movement. Other Latin American guerrillas, whether led by communists or Castroists, were something different. In Nicaragua, for example, the Sandinistas came from the revolutionary petty bourgeoisie, and though their struggle was also agrarian, they were linked to Cuba, whereas MR-13 was not. In Guatemala, both types were actually present, and there were disputes between them. The case of Guatemala is particularly terrible because there were two waves: the first was defeated in 1967; the second began in 1972. This second wave was very different from MR-13: it no longer had the socialist programme, for example.

What about the indigenous component of these movements?

This only began to come to the fore, or rather reappear, in Guatemala in the 1970s. Of course, the indigenous themselves were present beforehand—all the peasants are indigenous, and a peasant revolution *is* an indigenous one— but the revolution was defined in other terms: nationalist, socialist, agrarian. In Guatemala's second wave, the indigenous component gained enormous salience. There were massacres of the indigenous, and Rigoberta Menchú became a real symbol in this period. But perhaps the real novelty came with the Zapatistas in Mexico, which on 1 January 1994 seized four towns by force. This was a purely indigenous movement, putting forward indigenous demands, speaking indigenous languages. Its success has strongly influenced indigenous movements in the rest of Latin America, which had never ceased to exist, but now re-emerged. In each place, they acted in accordance with their own genealogies of rebellion: in Bolivia, the Aymaras and Quechuas have traditions of revolt dating back to Túpac Katari's uprising of 1781. The Peruvians and Guatemalans have their own genealogies too.

It's these genealogies that I constantly look for—the continuities between earlier nationalist upsurges and the anti-imperialist rebellions of the 1960s, or those of the indigenous movements. I insist very stubbornly on drawing a distinction between genealogies and politics—not in order to oppose one to the other, but to find genealogies that in many cases explain the political choices. Tactics and strategy can normally be traced to a particular economic situation, the influence of a mass movement or the position of a given state. But the genealogy of the movement which is manifested in that situation is something different. The predecessors of the Bolsheviks were the Russian Populists, the Paris Commune's antecedents lie in the French Revolution and 1848. Each space has a different formation, giving rise to a different genealogy.

In 1994 you published a book on Cárdenas, with the subtitle A Mexican Utopia, *in which the nationalization of Mexico's oil in 1938 serves as the focal point for an exploration of the character and trajectory of Cardenismo as a whole.*[10] *How do you see the relation between this and your earlier work?*

I see Cárdenas as the continuation and conclusion of the Revolution. What had been interrupted—hence the Spanish title of the earlier volume—was finished there. Communists tended to ignore or patronize Cárdenas, and all but two Trotskyist currents considered him a national-bourgeois. The exceptions were Trotsky himself and Posadas's section, which saw Cárdenas as a petty bourgeois soldier supported by the workers' and peasants' movements. He was much more radical than Perón—Cárdenas did all he could for the Spanish Republic, and distributed twenty million hectares of land to the peasants. I am now planning a third volume on the Mexican Revolution, completing a sort of trilogy. It will focus on the División del Norte, led by Pancho Villa and Felipe Ángeles. The destruction of the army of the old regime in formal battle by peasants, miners, railwaymen and cowherds profoundly altered power relations in Mexico.

---

[10] *El cardenismo, una utopía mexicana*, Mexico City 1994.

Apart from your historical work, you've also played an active part in Mexican political struggles.

Yes. For example, I took part in the university strike at UNAM in 1986–88, as one of a minority of professors supporting the students' protests against the introduction of tuition fees. Many things were at stake, but the main point was whether public education remained free—whether it remained a right, rather than a service. It was about defending a certain form of republic. That time we won, but by the time of the next strike, in 1999–2000, an extreme version of neo-liberalism had been pushed through under Salinas and Zedillo; the students were poorer and angrier, and the government was much further to the right. A much smaller minority of professors backed the movement this time around. I was not on the front line, but wrote numerous articles in support of the students. Although police broke up the campus occupation, the campaign was at least successful in once again preventing tuition fees from being introduced.

In 1987, a powerful mass political and electoral movement—democratic, nationalist and anti-imperialist—emerged in Mexico, led by Cuauhtémoc Cárdenas, son of Lázaro Cárdenas. Many social organizations of the Mexican Left converged within it. A group of leaders and militants who came out of the university movement of 1986–88—myself included—were among the first on the Left to support this new Cardenista movement, in the presidential election of 1988. Cárdenas won that election, but his victory was not recognized by the PRI government, which instead installed its own candidate, Carlos Salinas de Gortari. It was from this movement that the Partido de la Revolución Democrática (PRD) emerged. I took part in its foundation in 1989 and in its first leadership; and in 1997 I was part of Cárdenas's government of Mexico City: the first elected government the city had had. Afterwards I distanced myself. As it gained control of local governments and increased its number of parliamentary representatives, the PRD gradually moved towards the centre, becoming an organization solely dedicated to electoral politics and the unprincipled alliances this entails.

I have also been politically active in support of the Zapatista rebellion. As I mentioned, the EZLN is an indigenous movement, joined by some radical elements from the middle class, such as Marcos himself; I respect them tremendously. I met the Zapatistas for the first time in May 1994, in their territory. Later I had an exchange with Marcos about Carlo Ginzburg's celebrated essay on 'Clues', which I had sent him; Marcos wrote me a long letter by way of response, saying he hadn't seen what the point of the essay was, and I replied in comradely fashion, pointing out where Marcos had misread or misunderstood Ginzburg.[11] In 1998 I wrote a study of the Zapatista

---

[11] The Ginzburg text is 'Clues: Roots of an Evidential Paradigm' (1979), in Ginzburg,

movement, 'Chiapas and the Rebellion of the Enchanted World'.[12] We have our differences, and I expressed some of these at the Zapatistas' 'Festival of Dignified Rage' in Chiapas in January 2009. But I continue to support their struggle and their resistance. Since the 2009 Festival they have closed themselves off, and maintained virtual silence. For the moment they are dug in, keeping their people organized in resistance, in a sort of unstable equilibrium. But the government hasn't been able to suppress them.

Viewed from outside, the Mexican Left seems to be in disarray, and yet there are still many signs of a living left culture, not least in a paper like La Jornada.[13] *How do you explain this disparity?*

I think one has to draw a distinction between the established left parties and the broader Left. The PRD, after all, is at best an anti-neo-liberal nationalist party which originated in the PRI, whereas *La Jornada* is fed by a much broader left culture. But at present, in Mexico as elsewhere, the space for a classical revolutionary organization of the Left, along twentieth-century lines, is small or non-existent. This is because of the form that capitalism takes today, rather than being the fault of any particular individuals. The place formerly occupied by unions, workers' and peasants' organizations and their political reflections has shrunk, and politics has become the exclusive domain of capital and its negotiators. Yet the masters of the world are having to pay a price for this: an expansion of the space occupied by rage and fury. In Mexico, the anger has grown as a result of a series of disasters in the past twenty years: the electoral fraud of 1988; the assassinations of hundreds of PRD activists under Salinas; the violation of the San Andrés Accords by the Zedillo government; the new electoral fraud in 2006; the repression in Oaxaca and Atenco; not to mention the stream of deaths in Ciudad Juárez and elsewhere—there are now scores of people being killed every day on the streets, many of them tortured before being killed.

Almost ten years ago, when the government refused to make good on its formal commitments to legalize the indigenous movement and organization, along with indigenous autonomy, Subcomandante Marcos said: 'You are opening the gates of hell.' The turbulent and fragmented Mexico of today shows he was right. There is much more rage now than before. In circumstances like these, rage and anger will be essential components in the organization of any new mass revolutionary movement. But through its genealogy, it will also receive the intangible legacy of the experience

---

Clues, Myths and the Historical Method, Baltimore 1989. The three texts—Ginzburg's, Marcos's letter and Gilly's reply—were published, together with an interview with Marcos, as *Discusión sobre la historia*, Mexico City 1995.

[12] 'Chiapas and the Rebellion of the Enchanted World' in Daniel Nugent, ed., *Rural Revolt in Mexico*, Durham, NC 1998.

[13] Daily newspaper founded in Mexico City in 1984.

accumulated by the oppressed and dispossessed during the tragic twentieth century, a century of wars and revolutions. To articulate the past historically, says Walter Benjamin, means 'to seize hold of a memory as it flashes up at a moment of danger'. The twentieth century was not the century of enlightenment, nor of progress. It was the century of that lightning flash, the memory and experience of which we will need to recover in order to illuminate the present moment of danger.

3
Jean-Paul Sartre
Noam Chomsky
David Harvey

Jean-Paul Sartre (b. 1905, Paris) was the commanding intellectual presence of mid-twentieth-century France, and one of the most important, and controversial, figures of his generation, as a philosopher, novelist, playwright and political writer. At the end of the 1960s, when this interview took place, he was still at the height of his powers. The Critique de la raison dialectique, *in which he sought to re-found Marxism philosophically, had come out in 1960, and a successor volume was in preparation. The work on Flaubert—*L'Idiot de la famille—*had begun to appear. His political interventions continued, with the report of the International War Crimes Tribunal, in which he charged the United States with genocide in Vietnam; a decisive repudiation of the Stalinist order, in the aftermath of the 1968 invasion of Czechoslovakia; and public dialogue with* il manifesto, *where the philosophical categories of the* Critique *were brought into tense communication with the experience of workers' struggles in France and Italy in the late 1960s. Here, speaking to* New Left Review, *he discussed his personal and political itinerary from the days of the wartime Resistance onwards; abiding cruces in his thought—the status and prospects of literature, especially the novel, and the claims of psychoanalysis—the place of the* Critique *in his philosophical career, and the significance of his engagement with Flaubert.*

Sartre sustained his writing projects and public political role into the 1970s, but in the face of deteriorating health. He died in 1980.

Jean-Paul Sartre

Itinerary of a Thought

How do you envisage the relationship between your early philosophical writings, above all L'Etre et le Néant, *and your present theoretical work, from the* Critique de la raison Dialectique *onwards? In the* Critique, *the typical concepts of* L'Etre et le Néant *have disappeared, and a completely new vocabulary has taken their place. Yet when reading the passages of your forthcoming study of Flaubert published in* Les Temps modernes *one is struck by the sudden re-emergence of the characteristic idiom of the early work—thetic consciousness, ego, nihilation, being, nothingness. These notions are now juxtaposed in the text with the distinct set of concepts which derive from the* Critique—*serialization, totalization, practico-inert, collectives.*[1] *What is the precise relationship between the two in your current thought?*

The basic question here, of course, is my relationship to Marxism. I will try to explain autobiographically certain aspects of my early work, which may help to clarify the reasons why my outlook changed so fundamentally after the Second World War. A simple formula would be to say that life taught me *la force des choses*—the power of circumstances. In a way, *L'Etre et le Néant* itself should have been the beginning of a discovery of this power of circumstances, since I had already been made a soldier, when I had not wanted to be one. Thus I had already encountered something that was not my freedom and which steered me from without. Then I was taken prisoner, a fate which I had sought to escape. Hence I started to learn what I have called human reality among things: being-in-the-world.

Then, little by little, I found that the world was more complicated than this, for during the Resistance there appeared to be a possibility of free decision. For my state of mind during those years, I think that the first plays I wrote are very symptomatic: I called them a 'theatre of freedom'. The other

---

[1] *Being and Nothingness* (1943), trans. Hazel Barnes, New York 1956; *Critique of Dialectical Reason*, vols 1 (1960) and 2, London 2002, 2006. *L'Idiot de la famille* appeared in book form in 1971 (vols 1 and 2) and 1972 (vol. 3).

day, I reread a prefatory note of mine to a collection of these plays—*Les Mouches, Huis clos* and others—and was truly scandalized. I had written: 'Whatever the circumstances, and wherever the site, a man is always free to choose to be a traitor or not ...'. When I read this, I said to myself: it's incredible, I actually believed that!

To understand how I could have done so, you must remember that there was a very simple problem during the Resistance—ultimately, only a question of courage. One had to accept the risks involved in what one was doing, that is, of being imprisoned or deported. But beyond this? A Frenchman was either for the Germans or against them, there was no other option. The real political problems, of being 'for, but' or 'against, but', were not posed by this experience. The result was that I concluded that in any circumstances, there is always a possible choice. Which is false. Indeed, it is so false that I later wanted precisely to refute myself by creating a character in *Le Diable et le bon dieu*, Heinrich, who cannot choose. He wants to choose, of course, but he cannot choose either the Church, which has abandoned the poor, or the poor, who have abandoned the Church. He is thus a living contradiction, who will never choose. He is totally conditioned by his situation.

However, I understood all this only much later. What the drama of the war gave me, as it did everyone who participated in it, was the experience of heroism. Not my own, of course—all I did was a few errands. But the militant in the Resistance who was caught and tortured became a myth for us. Such militants existed, of course, but they represented a sort of personal myth as well. Would we be able to hold out against torture too? The problem then was solely that of physical endurance—it was not the ruses of history or the paths of alienation. A man is tortured: what will he do? He either speaks or refuses to speak. This is what I mean by the experience of heroism, which is a false experience.

After the war came the true experience, that of *society*. But I think it was necessary for me to pass via the myth of heroism first. That is to say, the pre-war personage who was more or less Stendhal's egotistical individualist had to be plunged into circumstances against his will, yet where he still had the power to say yes or no, in order to encounter the inextricable entanglements of the post-war years as a man totally conditioned by his social existence and yet sufficiently capable of decision to reassume all this conditioning and to become responsible for it. For the idea which I have never ceased to develop is that in the end one is always responsible for what is made of one. Even if one can do nothing else besides assume this responsibility. For I believe that a man can always make something out of what is made of him. This is the limit I would today accord to freedom: the small movement which makes of a totally conditioned social being someone who does not render back completely what his conditioning has given him. Which makes of Genet a poet when he had been rigorously conditioned to be a thief.

Perhaps the book where I have best explained what I mean by freedom is, in fact, *Saint Genet*.[2] For Genet was made a thief, he said 'I am a thief', and this tiny change was the start of a process whereby he became a poet and then eventually a being no longer even on the margin of society, someone who no longer knows where he is, who falls silent. It cannot be a happy freedom, in a case like this. Freedom is not a triumph. For Genet, it simply marked out certain routes which were not initially given.

L'Etre et le Néant traced an interior experience, without any coordination with the exterior experience of a petty-bourgeois intellectual, which had become historically catastrophic at a certain moment. For I wrote *L'Etre et le Néant* after the defeat of France, after all. But catastrophes have no lessons, unless they are the culmination of a praxis. Then one can say, my action has failed. But the disaster which overwhelmed the country had taught us nothing. Thus, in *L'Etre et le Néant*, what you could call 'subjectivity' is not what it would be for me now, the small margin in an operation whereby an interiorization re-exteriorizes itself in an act. But 'subjectivity' and 'objectivity' seem to me entirely useless notions today, anyway. I might still use the term 'objectivity', I suppose, but only to emphasize that everything is objective. The individual interiorizes his social determinations: he interiorizes the relations of production, the family of his childhood, the historical past, the contemporary institutions, and he then re-exteriorizes these in acts and options which necessarily refer us back to them. None of this existed in *L'Etre et le Néant*.

In L'Etre et le Néant, *you radically rejected the concept of the unconscious, saying that it was a philosophical contradiction. The model of consciousness in your early work effectively excludes any idea of it whatever. Consciousness is always transparent to itself, even if the subject creates a false screen of 'bad faith'. Since then, you have among other things written a film script on Freud—*

—I broke with Huston precisely because Huston did not understand what the unconscious was.[3] That was the whole problem. He wanted to suppress it, to replace it with the preconscious. He did not want the unconscious at any price—

The question one would like to ask is how you conceive the precise theoretical statute of the work of Freud today? Given your class position, it is not perhaps so surprising that you did not discover Marx before the war. But how did you miss Freud? Surely the opaque evidence of the unconscious, its resistances, should have been accessible to you even then? They are not exactly comparable to the class struggle.

---

[2] *Saint Genet: Actor and Martyr* (1952), trans. Bernard Frechtman, New York 1963.
[3] *The Freud Scenario*, trans. Quintin Hoare, London 1985.

The two questions are linked, however. The thought of both Marx and Freud is a theory of conditioning in exteriority. When Marx says: 'It matters little what the bourgeoisie thinks it does, the important thing is what it does,' one could replace 'the bourgeoisie' by 'a hysteric', and the formula would be one of Freud. Having said this, I must try to recount my relationship to Freud's work biographically. I will begin by saying that I undoubtedly had a deep repugnance for psychoanalysis in my youth, which needs to be explained as much as my innocence of the class struggle. The fact that I was a petty-bourgeois was responsible for the latter; one might say that the fact that I was French was responsible for the former. There would certainly be a lot of truth in this. You must never forget the weight of Cartesian rationalism in France. When you have just taken the *bachot* at the age of seventeen, with the 'I think, therefore I am' of Descartes as your set text, and you open *The Psychopathology of Everyday Life*, and you read the famous episode of Signorelli with its substitutions, combinations and displacements, implying that Freud was simultaneously thinking of a patient who had committed suicide and of certain Turkish mores, and so on—when you read all that, your breath is simply taken away.

Such investigations were completely outside my preoccupations at the time, which were at bottom to provide a philosophical foundation for realism. Which in my opinion is possible today, and which I have tried to do all my life. In other words, how to give man both his autonomy and his reality among real objects, avoiding idealism without lapsing into a mechanistic materialism. I posed the problem in this way because I was ignorant of dialectical materialism, although I should add that this later allowed me to assign certain limits to it—to validate the historical dialectic while rejecting a dialectic of nature, in the sense of a natural process which produces and resolves man into an ensemble of physical laws.

To return to Freud, however, I have to say that I was incapable of understanding him because I was a Frenchman with a good Cartesian tradition behind me, imbued with a certain rationalism, and I was therefore deeply shocked by the idea of the unconscious. However, I will not say *only* this because I must add that I remain shocked by what was inevitable in Freud— the biological and physiological language with which he underpinned thoughts which were not translatable without mediation. Right up to the time of Fliess, as you know, he wrote physiological studies designed to provide an equivalent of the cathexes and equilibria he had found in psychoanalysis. The result is that the manner in which he describes the psychoanalytic object suffers from a kind of mechanistic cramp. This is not always true, for there are moments when he transcends this. But in general this language produces a *mythology* of the unconscious which I cannot accept. I am completely in agreement with the *facts* of disguise and repression, as facts. But the *words* 'repression', 'censorship', or 'drive'—words which express one moment a sort of finalism and the next moment a sort of mechanism—these

I reject. Let us take the example of 'condensation', for instance, which is an ambivalent term in Freud. One can interpret it simply as a phenomenon of association, in the same way as your English philosophers and psychologists of the eighteenth and nineteenth centuries. Two images are drawn together externally, they condense and form a third: this is classical psychological atomism. But one can also interpret the term on the contrary as expressive of a finality. Condensation occurs because two images combined answer a desire, a need. This sort of ambiguity occurs again and again in Freud. The result is a strange representation of the unconscious as a set of rigorous mechanistic determinations, in any event a causality, and at the same time as a mysterious finality, such that there are 'ruses' of the unconscious, as there are 'ruses' of history; yet it is impossible to reunite the two in the work of many analysts—at least early analysts. I think that there is always a fundamental ambiguity in them; the unconscious is one moment *another consciousness*, and the next moment *other than consciousness*. What is other than consciousness then becomes simply a mechanism.

Thus I would reproach psychoanalytic theory with being a syncretic and not a dialectical thought. The word 'complex', indeed, indicates this very evidently: interpenetration without contradiction. I agree, of course, that there may exist an enormous number of 'larval' contradictions within individuals, which are often translated in certain situations by interpenetrations and not by confrontations. But this does not mean these contradictions do not exist. The results of syncretism, on the contrary, can be seen in the idea of the Oedipus complex, for instance: the fact is that analysts manage to find everything in it, equally well the fixation on the mother, love of the mother, or hatred of the mother, as Melanie Klein argues. In other words, anything can be derived from it, since it is not *structured*. The consequence is that an analyst can say one thing and then the contrary immediately afterwards, without in any way worrying about lack of logic, since after all 'opposites interpenetrate'. A phenomenon can mean this, while its contrary can also mean the same thing. Psychoanalytic theory is thus a 'soft' thought. It has no dialectical logic to it. Psychoanalysts will tell me that this is because there is no such logic in reality. But this precisely is what I am not sure of: I am convinced that complexes exist, but I am not so certain that they are not structured.

In particular, I believe that if complexes are true structures, 'analytic scepticism' would have to be abandoned. What I call the 'affective scepticism' of psychoanalysts is the belief of so many of them that the relationship which unites two people is only a 'reference' to an original relationship which is an absolute: an allusion to a primal scene, incomparable and unforgettable—yet forgotten—between father and mother. Ultimately, any sentiment experienced by an adult becomes for the analyst a sort of occasion for the rebirth of another. Now, there is a real truth in this: the fixation of a girl on an older man may well come from her father, or the fixation of a young man on a girl may derive from a profusion of original relationships. But what is missing in conventional psychoanalytic accounts is the idea of dialectical irreducibility. In a truly dialectical theory, such as historical materialism, phenomena derive from each other dialectically: there are different configurations of dialectical reality, and each of these configurations is rigorously conditioned by the previous one, while preserving and superseding it at the same time. This supersession is, however, precisely irreducible. While one configuration may preserve another, it can never simply be reduced to its predecessor. It is the idea of this *autonomy* that is lacking in psychoanalytic theory. A sentiment or a passion between two persons is certainly highly conditioned by their relationship to the 'primal object', and one can locate this object within it and explain the new relationship by it; but the relationship itself remains irreducible.

Thus there is an essential difference in my relationship to Marx and my relationship to Freud. When I discovered the class struggle, this was a *true* discovery, in which I now believe totally, in the very form of the descriptions which Marx gave of it. Only the epoch has changed; otherwise it is the same struggle with the same classes and the same road to victory. Whereas I do not believe in the unconscious in the form in which psychoanalysis presents it to us. In my present book on Flaubert, I have replaced my earlier notion of consciousness (although I still use the word a lot), with what I call *le vécu*—lived experience. I will try to describe in a moment what I mean by this term, which is neither the precautions of the preconscious, nor the unconscious, nor consciousness, but the terrain in which the individual is perpetually overflowed by himself and his riches and consciousness plays the trick of determining itself by forgetfulness.

In L'Etre et le Néant, *there is not much room for the phenomenon of dreams. For Freud dreams were a privileged 'space' of the unconscious, the zone where psychoanalysis was discovered. Do you try to situate the space of dreams in your current work? This would be a concrete test of your present relationship to Freud.*

My work on Flaubert deals with dreams. Unfortunately, Flaubert himself reports very few of his dreams. But there are two extremely striking ones—both nightmares—which he recounts in *Mémoires d'un fou*, an autobiography he wrote at the age of seventeen, and which are thus perhaps partly invented. One concerns his father, the other his mother: both reveal his relationship to his parents with an extraordinary evidence. The interesting thing, however, is that otherwise Flaubert virtually never mentions his parents in his writings. In fact, he had very bad relationships with both his father and his mother, for a whole number of reasons which I try to analyse. He says nothing about them. They do not exist in his early works. The only time that he speaks of them, he speaks of them precisely where a psychoanalyst would like him to do, in the narrative of a dream. Yet it is Flaubert himself who spontaneously does so. Thereafter, at the very end of his life, five years before he died, he published a novella called *La Légende de Saint Julien l'Hospitalier*, which he said he had wanted to write for thirty years: it is in effect the story of a man who kills his father and his mother and who becomes a writer by doing so.

Thus Flaubert has two quite different conceptions of himself. One is at the level of banal description, for example when he writes to his mistress Louise: 'What am I? Am I intelligent or am I stupid? Am I sensitive or am I stolid? Am I mean or am I generous? Am I selfish or am I selfless? I have no idea, I suppose I am like everyone else, I waver between all these.' In other words, at this level he is completely lost. Why? Because none of these notions has any meaning in themselves. They only acquire a meaning from intersubjectivity, in other words what I have called in the *Critique* the 'objective spirit' within which each member of a group or society refers to himself and appears to others, establishing relations of interiority between persons which derive from the same information or the same context.

Yet one cannot say that Flaubert did not have, at the very height of his activity, a comprehension of the most obscure origins of his own history. He once wrote a remarkable sentence: 'You are doubtless like myself, you all have the same terrifying and tedious depths'—*les mêmes profondeurs terribles et ennuyeuses*. What could be a better formula for the whole world of psychoanalysis, in which one makes terrifying discoveries, yet which always tediously come to the same thing? His awareness of these depths was not an intellectual one. He later wrote that he often had fulgurating intuitions, akin to a dazzling bolt of lightning in which one simultaneously sees nothing and sees everything. Each time they went out, he tried to retrace the paths revealed to him by this blinding light, stumbling and falling in the subsequent darkness.

For me, these formulations define the relationship which Flaubert had with what is ordinarily called the unconscious, and what I would call a total absence of knowledge, but a real comprehension. I distinguish here between comprehension and intellection: there can be intellection of a practical conduct, but only comprehension of a passion. What I call *le vécu*—lived experience—is precisely the ensemble of the dialectical process of psychic life, in so far as this process is obscure to itself because it is a constant totalization, thus necessarily a totalization which cannot be conscious of what it is. One can be conscious of an external totalization, but one cannot be conscious of a totalization which also totalizes consciousness. 'Lived experience', in this sense, is perpetually susceptible of comprehension, but never of knowledge. Taking it as a point of departure, one can know certain psychic phenomena by concepts, but not this experience itself. The highest form of comprehension of lived experience can forge its own language—which will always be inadequate, and yet which will often have the metaphorical structure of the dream itself. Comprehension of a dream occurs when a man can express it in a language which is itself dreamt. Lacan says that the unconscious is structured like a language. I would say that the language which expresses it has the structure of a dream. In other words, comprehension of the unconscious in most cases never achieves explicit expression. Flaubert constantly speaks of *l'indisable*, which means the 'unsayable', only the word does not exist in French, it should be *l'indicible* (perhaps it was a regional usage in Flaubert's time, but in any case it is not the normal word). The 'unsayable', however, was something very definite for him. When he gave his autobiography to his mistress at the age of twenty-five, he wrote to her: 'You will suspect all the unsayable.' Which did not mean family secrets or anything like that. Of course, he hated his elder brother, but this is not what he was talking about. He meant precisely this kind of comprehension of oneself which cannot be named and which perpetually escapes one.

The conception of 'lived experience' marks my change since *L'Etre et le Néant*. My early work was a rationalist philosophy of consciousness. It was all very well for me to dabble in apparently non-rational processes in the individual, the fact remains that *L'Etre et le Néant* is a monument of rationality. But in the end it becomes an irrationalism, because it cannot account rationally for those processes which are 'below' consciousness and which are also rational, but lived as irrational. Today, the notion of 'lived experience' represents an effort to preserve that presence to itself which seems to me indispensable for the existence of any psychic fact, while at the same time this presence is so opaque and blind before itself that it is also an absence from itself. Lived experience is always simultaneously present to itself and absent from itself. In developing this notion, I have tried to surpass the traditional psychoanalytic ambiguity of psychic facts which are both teleological and mechanical, by showing that every psychic fact involves an intentionality which aims at something, while among them a certain number can only exist if they are comprehended, but neither named nor known. The latter include what I call the 'stress' of a neurosis. A neurosis is in the first instance a specific wound, a defective structure which is a certain way of living a childhood. But this is only the initial wound: it is then patched up and bandaged by a system which covers and soothes the wound, and which then, like antibodies in certain cases, suddenly does something abominable to the organism. The unity of this system is the neurosis. The work of its 'stress' is intentional, but it cannot be seized as such without disappearing. It is precisely for this reason that if it is transferred into the domain of knowledge, by analytic treatment, it can no longer be reproduced in the same manner.

There is an obvious question raised by your work on Flaubert. You have already written a study of Baudelaire—

—A very inadequate, an extremely bad one—

Then the long book on Genet, after that an essay on Tintoretto and then an autobiography, Les Mots.[4] *After this succession of writings, what will be the methodological novelty of the book on Flaubert? Why exactly did you decide to return once again to the project of explaining a life?*

In the *Question de méthode*, I discussed the different mediations and procedures which could permit an advance in our knowledge of men if they were taken together.[5] In fact, everyone knows and everyone admits, for instance, that psychoanalysis and Marxism should be able to find the mediations necessary to allow a combination of the two. Everyone adds, of course, that psychoanalysis is not primary, but that correctly coupled and rationalized with Marxism, it can be useful.

Likewise, everyone says that there are American sociological notions which have a certain validity, and that sociology in general should be used—not, of course, the Russian variety which is no more than an enumeration or nomenclature. Everyone agrees on all this. Everyone in fact *says* it—but who has tried to *do* it?

I myself was in general only repeating these irreproachable maxims in *Question de méthode*. The idea of the book on Flaubert was to abandon these theoretical disquisitions, because they were ultimately getting us nowhere, and to try to give a concrete example of how it might be done. The result can look after itself. Even if it is a failure, it can thereby give others the idea of redoing it, better. For the question the book seeks to answer is: how shall I study a man with all these methods, and how in this study will these methods condition each other and find their respective place?

You feel you did not have these keys when you wrote Saint Genet, *for example?*

No, I did not have them all. It is obvious that the study of the conditioning of Genet at the level of institutions and of history is inadequate—very, very inadequate. The main lines of the interpretation, that Genet was an orphan of Public Assistance, who was sent to a peasant home and who owned nothing, remain true, doubtless. But all the same, this happened in 1925 or so and there was a whole context to this life which is quite absent. The Public Assistance, a foundling—these represent a specific social phenomenon, and anyway Genet is a product of the twentieth century; yet none of this is registered in the book.

Whereas today I would like the reader to feel the presence of Flaubert the whole time; my ideal would be that the reader simultaneously feels,

---

[4] *Baudelaire* (1947), trans. Martin Turnell, New York 1967; 'The Prisoner of Venice' (1957), *Situations,* trans. Benita Eisler, New York 1965, pp. 9–49; *Words,* Harmondsworth 1967.
[5] *The Problem of Method* (1960), trans. Hazel Barnes, London 1964 and published in the United States as *Search for a Method,* New York 1968.

comprehends and knows the personality of Flaubert, totally as an individual and yet totally as an expression of his time. In other words, Flaubert can only be understood by his difference from his neighbours.

Do you see what I mean by this? For example, there were a considerable number of writers who elaborated analogous theories at the time and produced more or less valid works inspired by them, Leconte de Lisle or the Goncourts, for example: it is necessary to try to study how they were all determined to produce this particular vision, and how Flaubert was determined similarly yet otherwise, and saw it in another fashion. My aim is to try to demonstrate the encounter between the development of the person, as psychoanalysis has shown it to us, and the development of history. For at a certain moment, an individual in his very deepest and most intimate conditioning, by the family, can fulfil a historical role. Robespierre could be taken as an example, for instance. But it would be impossible to pursue such a study of him, because there are no materials for doing so. What would be necessary to know is what was the encounter of the revolution which created the Committee of Public Safety, and the son of Monsieur and Madame Robespierre of Arras.

This is the theoretical aim of your present work. But why exactly the choice of Flaubert?

Because he is the imaginary. With him, I am at the border, the barrier of dreams.

There have been writers or politicians who have left a certain work and who could equally well provide the material for such a study—

In theory, yes. There were a number of reasons, however, which led me to select Flaubert. Firstly, to give the strictly circumstantial cause of this selection: Flaubert is one of the very rare historical or literary personages who have left behind so much information about themselves. There are no less than thirteen volumes of correspondence, each of six hundred pages or so. He often wrote letters to several persons the same day, with slight variations between them, which are often very amusing. Apart from this, there are numerous reports and witnesses of him; the Goncourt brothers kept a diary and saw Flaubert very frequently, so that we see him from the outside through the Goncourts and we also have a record of what he said to others about himself, recorded by the Goncourts—not an altogether trustworthy source, of course, since they were rancorous imbeciles in many ways. Nevertheless, there are many facts in their journal. Besides this, of course, there is a complete correspondence with George Sand, letters of George Sand on Flaubert, memoirs of him, and so on. All this is completely circumstantial, but it is of great importance.

Secondly, however, Flaubert represents for me the exact opposite of my own conception of literature: a total disengagement and a certain idea of form, which is not that which I admire. For example, Stendhal is a writer whom I greatly prefer to Flaubert, while Flaubert is probably much more important for the development of the novel than Stendhal. I mean that Stendhal is much finer and stronger. One can give oneself completely to him—his style is acceptable, his heroes are sympathetic, his vision of the world is true and the historical conception behind it is very acute. There is nothing like this in Flaubert. Only, Flaubert is much more significant than Stendhal for the history of the novel. If Stendhal had not existed, it would still have been possible to go straight from Laclos to Balzac. Whereas, let us say, Zola or the *nouveau roman* are inconceivable without Flaubert. Stendhal is greatly loved by the French, but his influence on the novel is minimal. Flaubert's influence by contrast is immense, and for this reason alone it is important to study him. Given that, he began to fascinate me precisely because I saw him in every way as the contrary of myself. I found myself wondering: 'How was he possible?' For I then rediscovered another dimension of Flaubert, which is besides the very source of his talent. I was used to reading Stendhal and company, where one is in complete accord with the hero, whether he is Julien Sorel or Fabrice.

Reading Flaubert one is plunged into persons with whom one is in complete disaccord, who are irksome. Sometimes one feels with them, and then somehow they suddenly reject one's sympathy and one finds oneself once again antagonistic to them. Obviously it was this that fascinated me, because it made me curious. This is precisely Flaubert's art. It is clear that he detested himself, and when he speaks of his principal characters, he has a terrible attitude of sadism and masochism towards them: he tortures them because they are himself, and also to show that other people and the world torture him. He also tortures them because they are not him and he is anyway vicious and sadistic and wants to torture others. His unfortunate characters have very little luck, submitted to all this.

At the same time, Flaubert writes from within his characters and is always speaking of himself in a certain fashion. He thus succeeds in speaking of himself in a way that is unique. This type of discomfited, refused confession, with its self-hatred, its constant reversion to things he comprehends without knowing, wanting to be completely lucid and yet always grating—Flaubert's testimony about himself is something exceptional, which had never been seen before and has not been seen since. This is another motive for studying him.

The third reason for choosing Flaubert is that he represents a sequel to *L'Imaginaire*. You may remember that in this very early book I tried to show that an image is not a sensation reawakened, or reworked by the intellect, or even a former perception altered and attenuated by knowledge, but is something entirely different—an absent reality, focused in its absence

Lives on the Left

through what I called an *analogon*: that is to say, an object which serves as an analogy and is traversed by an intention.[6] For example, when you are going to sleep, the little dots in your eyes—phosphenes—may serve as an analogy for every kind of oneiric or hypnagogic image. Between waking and sleeping, some people see vague shapes pass, which are phosphenes through which they focus on an imagined person or a thing. In *L'Imaginaire*, I tried to prove that imaginary objects—images—are an absence. In my book on Flaubert, I am studying imaginary persons—people who, like Flaubert, act out roles. A man is like a leak of gas, escaping into the imaginary. Flaubert did so perpetually; yet he also had to see reality because he hated it, so there is the whole question of the relationship between the real and the imaginary which I try to study in his life and work.

Finally, via all this, it is possible to ask the question: what was the *imaginary social world* of the dreamy bourgeoisie of 1848? This is an intriguing subject in itself. Between 1830 and 1840 Flaubert was in a *lycée* in Rouen, and all his tests speak of his fellow pupils there as contemptible, mediocre bourgeois. It so happens, however, that there were five years of violent, historic fights in the *lycées* of that time! After the revolution of 1830, there were boys who launched political struggles in the schools, who fought and were defeated. The reading of the romantics, of which Flaubert speaks so often as a challenge to their parents, is only explicable in this perspective: when these youths finally become *blasés*, they have been recuperated as 'ironic' bourgeois, and they have failed. The extraordinary thing is that Flaubert does not say a word about any of this. He simply describes the boys who surround him as if they were future adults—in other words, abject. He writes: 'I saw defects which would become vices, needs which would become manias, follies which would become crimes—in short, children would become men.' The only history of the school for him was the passage from childhood to maturity. The reality is, however, that this history was that of a bourgeoisie seized with shame at itself in its sons, of the defeat of these sons and thereby the suppression of its shame. The end result of this history will be the massacre of 1848.

Before 1830, the bourgeoisie was hiding under its blankets. When it finally emerged, its sons cried 'Bravo! We are going to declare the Republic,' but their fathers found they needed an eiderdown after all. Louis-Philippe became king. The sons persuaded themselves that their fathers had been duped, and continued the struggle. The result was an uproar in the schools: in vain, they were expelled. In 1831, when Louis-Philippe dismisses Lafayette and the road to reaction is open, there were boys of thirteen or fourteen in Flaubert's school who calmly refused to go to confession, having decided that this was an excellent pretext for a confrontation with the authorities, since after all the bourgeoisie was still officially Voltairean. Confession was

---

[6] *The Psychology of Imagination* (1940), New York 1948.

a survival from Louis XVIII and Charles X, and raised awkward questions about compulsory religious instruction, which might eventually get as far as the Chamber of Deputies. I take off my hat to these boys of fourteen who planned this strategy, knowing very well that they would be expelled from the school. The chaplain descended on them—'Confess!' 'No!'—then another functionary—'No, No, No!'—they were taken to the principal and thrown out of the school. Whereupon there was a gigantic uproar in the whole college, which was what they had hoped for. The fourth-year class threw rotten eggs at the vice principal, and two more boys were expelled. Then the day-boys of the class met at dawn and took an oath to avenge their comrades. The next day at six in the morning the boarders opened the doors to them. Together, they seized and occupied the building. Already, in 1831! From their fortress there, they bombarded the Academic Council which was deliberating in another building within reach of their windows.

The principal was meanwhile throwing himself at the feet of the older pupils, imploring them not to solidarize with the occupation—successfully. Eventually, the fourth-year class did not achieve the reinstatement of their comrades, but the authorities had to promise that there would be no sanctions against them for the occupation. Three days later, they found they had been tricked: the college was closed for two months. Exactly like today!

The next year, when they came back, they were naturally raging and there was constant turbulence in the *lycée*, This was the time in which Flaubert lived, and yet he did not experience it like that. He wrote a great deal about his childhood and youth—but there is not a single text which refers to this history. In fact, what happened, of course, was that he lived the same evolution of this generation in his own way. He was unaffected by this violent episode and yet he arrived at the same result by a different route somewhat later. The philosophy teacher in the school fell ill, and a substitute took over for him. The pupils decided the substitute was an incompetent and made life impossible for him. The principal tried to victimize two or three, and the whole class solidarized with them: Flaubert now wrote their collective letter to the principal, denouncing the quality of the course and the threats of punishment. The upshot was that he and two or three others were expelled from the school. The meaning of the protest this time is very clear: Flaubert and his classmates were young bourgeois demanding a proper bourgeois education—'Our fathers are paying enough, after all.' The evolution of a generation and of a class are manifest in this second episode. These different experiences produce a bitter literature on the bourgeoisie and then this generation resigns itself to becoming merely ironic—another way of being bourgeois.

Why have you opted for biography and the theatre in recent years, and abandoned the novel? Is it that you think Marxism and psychoanalysis have rendered the novel as a form impossible, by the weight of their concepts?

I have often asked myself that question. It is, in fact, true that there is no technique that can account for a character in a novel as one can account for a real person, who has existed, by means of a Marxist or psychoanalytic interpretation. But if an author has recourse to these two systems within a novel, without an adequate formal device for doing so, the novel disappears. These devices are lacking, and I do not know if they are possible.

You think that the existence of Marxism and of psychoanalysis prevents any novelist from writing, so to speak, naively today?

By no means. But if he does so, the novel will all the same be classified as 'naive'. In other words, a natural universe of the novel will not exist, only a certain specific type of novel—the 'spontaneous', 'naive' novel. There are excellent examples of the latter, but the author who writes them has to make a conscious decision to ignore these interpretative techniques. Thereby he necessarily becomes less naive. There is another type of novel today in which the work is conceived as a sort of infernal machine—fake novels like those of Gombrowicz for example. Gombrowicz is aware of psychoanalysis, and of Marxism and many other things, but he remains sceptical about them, and hence constructs objects which destroy themselves in their very act of construction—creating a model for what might be a novel with an analytic and materialist foundation.

Why have you personally stopped writing novels?

Because I have felt no urge to do so. Writers have always more or less chosen the imaginary. They have a need for a certain ration of fiction. Writing on Flaubert is enough for me by way of fiction—it might indeed be called a novel. Only I would like people to say that it was a true novel. I try to achieve a certain level of comprehension of Flaubert by means of hypotheses. Thus I use fiction—guided and controlled, but nonetheless fiction—to explore why, let us say, Flaubert wrote one thing on 15 March and the exact opposite on the 21 March, to the same correspondent, without worrying about the contradiction. My hypotheses are in this sense a sort of invention of the personage.

You have reproached a book like The Children of Sanchez *for not being a literary work because the people in it speak a language like that of all of us when we are not writers. You think such works lack invention?*

The Children of Sanchez is not a literary work, but it renders a mass of literary works redundant.[7] Why write a novel on its characters or their milieu? They

---

[7] Oscar Lewis, *The Children of Sanchez* (1961), London, 1964.

tell us much more by themselves, with a much greater self-understanding and eloquence. The book is not literature because there is no quest for a form that is also a meaning in it: for me the two—form and meaning—are always linked. There is no production of an object, a constructed object.

You continue to write plays?

Yes, because plays are something else again. For me the theatre is essentially a myth. Take the example of a petty bourgeois and his wife who quarrel with each other the whole time. If you tape their disputes, you will record not only the two of them, but the petty bourgeoisie and its world, what society has made of it, and so on. Two or three such studies and any possible novel on the life of a petty-bourgeois couple would be outclassed. By contrast, the relationship between man and woman as we see it in Strindberg's *Dance of Death* will never be outclassed. The subject is the same, but taken to the level of myth. The playwright presents to men the *eidos* of their daily existence: their own life in such a way that they see it as if externally. This was the genius of Brecht, indeed. Brecht would have protested violently if anyone said to him that his plays were myths. Yet what else is *Mother Courage*—an anti-myth that despite itself becomes a myth?

You discussed the theatre with Brecht?

I saw Brecht three or four times in a political context, but we never had a chance to discuss the theatre. I admire Brecht's plays very much, but I think that what Brecht said about them is not always true. His theory of *Entfremdung*—distanciation—is one thing: the actual relationship between the public and his characters is another. The blind and deaf girl in *Mother Courage* calls to the people when she falls from the roof, dying. This is a scene of pathos, and yet it is precisely a passage of the play where Brecht most wants to establish a contestation and recoil from the drama. Mother Courage herself is an anti-heroine who—unavoidably, by her very mystification—becomes a heroine. The *Caucasian Chalk Circle* presents the same paradox—scenes such as the flight of the servant or the adjudication of the child, which despite all Brecht's efforts are extremely moving in the most classical tradition of the theatre. Brecht was tremendously astute in his use of theatre, but he could not always control the final result of his writing.

The Critique de la raison dialectique *appears to be constructed on the idea that there is a fundamental homogeneity between the individual and history: the central theme of the book is the reversible relationships—interversions—between the individual, worked matter, the group, the series, the practico-inert, collectives. To adopt its vocabulary, your formal aim is to show how the totalizing acts of every individual are totalized in exteriority by others and become other to their agents, just as groups become other to themselves through serialization. The* Critique *deals in a very systematic way with that aspect of history which presents itself as alienation and degradation of intentional projects, whether by individuals or groups, in their encounter with materiality and alterity, in the world of scarcity. There is, however, another aspect of history which is not accounted for by the* Critique. *Social facts are not simply a totalization in exteriority of the totalizing acts of a multiplicity of individuals and groups, which may during certain privileged moments achieve an apocalyptic sovereignty, but which normally fall into the practico-inert. They have an intrinsic order of their own, which is not deducible from the criss-crossing of innumerable individual totalizations. The most obvious example of this is language—which can in no way be described as a simple totalization of all the speech-acts of linguistic agents. The subject who speaks never totalizes linguistic laws by his words. Language has its own intelligibility as a system which appears heterogeneous to the subject. Can the themes of 'totalization' and the 'practico-inert' ever account for the emergence of ordered social structures, not merely random alienation of subjective projects?*

But there is totalization in language. You cannot say a single sentence which does not refer, by its elements, to opposites. Thereby the whole of language, as a system of differential meanings, is present in its very absence, as linguists themselves admit. Every sentence is a levy on the entire resources of speech, for words only exist by their opposition to each other. There is thus certainly totalization in language.

The question is whether there is only totalization? There are two central examples in the Critique *of a multiplicity of totalizations which fall into the practico-inert and become an alien power denaturing the intentions of their agents. One is that of different Chinese peasants cutting down trees to enlarge their cultivation of land, thus creating erosion, which thereby causes floods which then ruin their lands. The other is of the impact of gold in sixteenth-century Spain— whereby the individual decisions of each single producer to raise prices caused an uncontrollable general inflation which eventually resulted in the collective impoverishment of all of them. These two examples do not have the same type of intelligibility—*

I agree. The deforestation of the Chinese peasants is a product of individuals, each acting on their own, directly on nature, in ignorance of the others. They are not united by any collective object, and it is only gradually that the end result of their acts imposes itself on them. The counter-finality of these peasants is cultural, but it concerns above all the relationship of a multiplicity of individuals with nature. Whereas the impact of gold in Spain presupposes money, which is a social institution. Money has nothing natural about it, it is a conventional system in some ways very similar to language. Thus gold is a pre-eminently social fact. I therefore am perfectly in agreement that there is a specific reality of social facts. This reality implies precisely that every totalization of the individual in relation to this reality either fails, is deviated by it or is a negative totalization. When I speak, I never say completely what I want to say and I often do not know what I say, given that my words are robbed from me and revealed to me as other than what I intended. But the important thing is that these social facts are, in spite of everything, the product of the social activity of collective ensembles. I will be discussing this in the second volume of the *Critique*. Language exists only as a convention.

But where does the order of this convention come from? To ask the same question in a different way: by the end of the Critique *the reader has been taken through all the different reversible relationships of individuals, groups, series and the practico-inert, which constitute for you 'the formal elements of any history'. Yet from this perspective there seems to be no reason why history should not then be an arbitrary chaos of inter-blocking projects, a sort of colossal traffic jam?*

There are a number of reasons. The first is that accumulation exists. There are crucial domains where accumulation occurs: science, capital, goods—which thereby produce a history: change. This is something different from a mere transition. There are periods which are transitions, until something is invented that changes. For example, the whole feudal period of the eleventh, twelfth and thirteenth centuries is a perpetual turmoil: there were events everywhere, yet there was no emergence from the Middle Ages because the elements for doing so did not exist. Then, one day, a certain number of processes coincided, social and economic facts like the indebtedness of the lords, the ruin of the Church, the change in the nature of Catholicism, the peasant revolts, scientific discoveries, and a spiral development of history resulted. Science, of course, in a sense advanced in a straight line through all its conversions, hesitations and errors. These mistakes and confusions might be classified as 'subjective'—they have little importance in the development of science. On the other hand, they whirl about every level of science and deform its discoveries and practices, changing them into other than themselves: a discovery made because of war in time of war will serve in peace, while a discovery in time of peace will serve for war. Simultaneously, there are whole plateaux where the class struggle changes because there is a new mode of production. I have not discussed any of this in the first volume of the *Critique*, both because I believe in the general schema provided by Marx and because I intend to study it at the level of history proper. For it is at the level of history that one should determine to what extent there is or is not progress, to what extent progress exists only where there is accumulation, and whether it produces in its train total modifications which are not necessarily progressive.

What is going to be the architecture of the second volume of the Critique*?*

I will simply try to show the dialectical intelligibility of a movement of historical temporalization.[8]

A movement?

The movement. The difference between the first and second volume is this: the first is an abstract work where I show the possibilities of exchange, degradation, the practico-inert, series, collectives, recurrence and so on. It is concerned only with the theoretical possibilities of their combinations. The object of the second volume is history itself. But I know no other history than our own, so the question 'What is history?' becomes 'What is our history?'—the history in which Mahomed was born and not one in which he never lived. It is irrelevant to wonder whether there are other histories in other galaxies. Perhaps there are, but we know nothing of them, and they consequently have no importance for us. Thus all the notions which will emerge from the second volume will be rigorously applied to our own history; my aim will be to prove that there is a dialectical intelligibility of the singular. For ours is a singular history. It is determined by the forces of production and the relations of production, their correspondences and their conflicts. It is possible that in completely primitive societies there exist the 'global facts' of which Mauss speaks—a kind of undifferentiated social conditioning. But even if this were so, it is not the history that I will be studying. What I will seek to show is the dialectical intelligibility of that which is not universalizable.

It is still very difficult to see how a multiplicity of individual acts can ever give birth to social structures which have their own laws, discontinuous *from the acts which for you formally constitute a historical dialectic? A tribe can speak a language for centuries and then be discovered by an anthropologist who can decipher its phonological laws, which have been forever unknown to the totality of the subjects speaking the language. How can these objective laws be deduced merely from words spoken?*

I believe that all the same language is a totalized and detotalized result of the ensemble of human activities during a certain time. Language is imposed on each of us as a practico-inert.

The connotation of 'practico-inert' is precisely that of a brute, random mass alien to human agents. The problem is, how does this mass happen to have a rigorous structure—the laws of grammar or, more fundamentally, the relations

---

[8] *Critique*, vol. 2.

of production? These structures are never intentional objects—they are hetero-geneous to the historical acts of individuals?

There is a historical problem of the passage from non-language to language in early human communities: it is impossible to reconstruct this passage, but probably it was accomplished within certain early institutions. For language sustains institutions, institutions are a language, and language is itself an institution. From the moment that a limited system of signs exists, which has an institutional character, both invented by the group and already dividing the group, language can change men into collectives. I have tried to explain this in the *Critique*. An institution or collective object is always a product of the activity of the group in *matter*, whether verbal matter or physico-chemical matter, and is thereby sealed and surpassed by an inertia which separates the group and imposes itself on it as the instituted and sacred. The subjective here capsizes into the objective and the objective into the subjec-tive: the result is an instituted object. Thus I am in complete agreement that social facts have their own structures and laws that dominate individuals, but I only see in this the reply of worked matter to the agents who work it.

Why is this 'reply' a coherent discourse?

For me the fact of being worked does not endow matter with a system, but the fact of becoming inert converts work into a system.

Not everything that is inert is a system.

Structures are created by activity, which has no structure, but suffers its results as a structure.

How can individual acts result in ordered structures, and not a tangled labyrinth—unless you believe in a sort of pre-established harmony between them?

You are forgetting the level of power and therefore of generality. If a deci-sion is taken at a certain level of political or religious power, an objective unity is given by the project at that level. What then happens is that others deviate and deform the project, but they simultaneously create something else by their work: other structures with their own internal relations which constitute a queer kind of object, but a potent and significant one. In the last chapter of the *Critique*, entitled 'Towards History', I started to discuss this problem. I tried to argue that an object created by a plurality of dif-ferent or antagonistic groups is nevertheless, in the very moment of their shock against each other, intelligible. In the second volume, I was going to take the elementary example of a battle, which remains intelligible after the

confusion of the two armies engaged in combat in it. From there I planned
to develop a study of the objects constituted by entire collectivities with
their own interests. In particular, I want to analyse the example of Stalin
to see how the objects which constituted Stalinist institutions were created
through the ensemble of relationships between groups and within groups
in Soviet society, and through the relationship of all these to Stalin and of
Stalin to them. Finally, I was going to end by studying the unity of objects in
a society completely rent asunder by class struggle, and considering several
classes and their actions to show how these objects were completely deviated
and always represented a detotalization while at the same time preserving
a determinate intelligibility. Once one has reached this, one has reached
history. Hence I had the embryo of an answer to the question you have been
asking me. There is an institutional order which is necessarily—unless we
are to believe in God the Father or an organicist mythology—the product
of masses of men constituting a social unity and which at the same time is
radically distinct from all of them, becoming an implacable demand and
an ambiguous means of communication and non-communication between
them. Aesop once said that language is both. The same is true of institutions. Indeed, I would like to write a study of work and technology to show
exactly what happens to material in industry, how it becomes an inhuman
image of man, by its demands. For I believe that the existence of different
ethics in different epochs is due to matter: it is because of inert, inanimate
objects that there are demands in us. A demand is fixed and inert: a duty has
no life in it, it is always immobile and imbecile, because whenever anyone
tries to do his so-called duty, he always finds himself in opposition to others.
This contradiction ultimately derives from the demands of materiality in
us. To sum up what I have been saying in a sentence: my aim in the second
volume of the *Critique* was precisely a study of the paradoxical object, which
is an institutional ensemble that is perpetually detotalized.

There is another dimension of the Critique *which must be striking for any new
reader of it today. The book in some respects appears an anticipation of two of
the major historical events of recent ears, the May Revolt in France and the
Cultural Revolution in China. There are long analyses of the dialectical relationship between class, cadres, trade unions and political party during factory
occupations, taking 1936 as a model, which often seem to prefigure the trajectory
of the French proletariat in May 1968. At the same time, there is a passage where
you evoke the official parades in Tiananmen An Minh Square in the Peking
of the early sixties as a sort of pyramidal 'mineralization of man', whereby a
bureaucratic order manipulates dispersed series beneath it to confer on them
a false semblance of groups. Do you then interpret the Cultural Revolution as
an attempt to reverse the deterioration of the Chinese Revolution into a set of
bureaucratically institutionalized groups manipulating passive masses, by a
sort of gigantic 'apocalypse' throughout China which recreates 'fused groups'*

such as once made the Long March and the People's War—to use the language of the Critique*?*

I should say that I regard myself as very inadequately informed about the Cultural Revolution. The specific level of the phenomenon is that of ideology, culture and politics—in other words, superstructures which are the higher instances of any dialectical scale. But what happened at the level of infrastructures in China which led to the initiation of this movement in the superstructures? There must have been determinate contradictions at the base of the Chinese socialist economy which produced the movement for a return to something like a perpetual fused group. It is possible that the origins of the Cultural Revolution are to be found in the conflicts over the Great Leap Forward, and the investment policies undertaken at that time: Japanese Marxists have often maintained this. But I nevertheless must confess that I have not succeeded in understanding the causes of the phenomenon in its totality. The idea of a perpetual apocalypse is naturally very attractive—but I am convinced that it is not exactly this, and that the infrastructural reasons for the Cultural Revolution must be sought.

You do not think that the Sino–Soviet conflict was a crucial determinant? Part of the Chinese leadership appears to have consciously been determined to avoid any reproduction of the present state of the USSR *in China. Is it necessary to assume insurmountable contradictions within the Chinese economy to explain the Cultural Revolution?*

I certainly do not think that the Cultural Revolution is in any way a mechanical reflection of infrastructural contradictions: but I think that to understand its total meaning one should be able to reconstruct the precise moment of the historical process and of the economy at which it exploded. It is perfectly clear, for instance, that Mao was virtually marginalized for a certain time and that he has now reassumed power. This change is undoubtedly linked to internal Chinese conflicts, which go back at least to the Great Leap Forward.

Equally striking are the contradictions within the Cultural Revolution. There is a central discordance between the unleashing of mass initiatives and the cult of the leader. On the one side, there is the perpetual maintenance of the fused group with unlimited personal initiatives within it, with the possibility of writing anything in big-character posters, even 'Chou En-lai to the gallows'—which did, in fact happen in Peking; on the other side, there is the fetishization of the Little Red Book, read aloud in waiting rooms, in airplanes, in railway stations, read before others who repeat it in chorus, read by taxi drivers who stop their cab to read it to passengers—a hallucinating collective catechism which resounds from one end of China to the other.

Your own analysis of the fundamental reason for the degradation of groups into
series in the Critique *is that scarcity ultimately renders inevitable the fall of any*
collective project into the practico-inert. China remains a very poor country,
with a low level of development of productive forces. Your own account of the
reign of scarcity leads to the conclusion that it is impossible to abolish bureauc-
racy in such a country; any attempt to overcome bureaucratic degradation
of the revolution will inevitably be profoundly marked by the objective limits
imposed by scarcity. This line of argument would explain the bureaucratic
safety-rails, whether institutional like the army or ideological like the cult of
personality, which trammel mass initiative in China?

It is evident that completely untrammelled initiatives can lead to a sort of
madness. Because the free and anarchic development of the individual—
not the social individual of the future, but the free practical organism of
today—may not endanger his own reason, but can endanger a society. But
to insist on his total freedom within a fused group and at the same time to
put pebbles in his head, called the Thoughts of Mao, is not to create a whole
man. The two halves of the process are in complete contradiction.

Perhaps the paradox of a cultural revolution is that it is ultimately impossible
in China, where it was invented, but is somewhat more possible in the advanced
countries of the West?

I think that is correct. With one qualification: is a cultural revolution possible
without making *the* revolution? French youth during May wanted a cultural
revolution—what was missing for them to achieve one? The ability to make
a real revolution. In other words, a revolution which is in no way initially
cultural, but is the seizure of power by violent class struggle. Which is not
to say that the idea of cultural revolution in France was merely a mirage: on
the contrary, it expressed a radical contestation of every established value of
the university and society, a way of looking at them as if they had already
perished. It is very important that this contestation be maintained.

What were the main lessons of the May Revolt for you?

I have always been convinced that the origins of May lie in the Vietnamese
Revolution. For the French students who unleashed the process of May, the
Vietnamese war was not merely a question of taking the side of the National
Liberation Front or the people or Vietnam against US imperialism. The fundamental impact of war on European or US militants was its enlargement
of the field of the possible. It had previously seemed impossible that the
Vietnamese could resist successfully such an enormous military machine and
win. Yet that is what they did and by doing so they completely changed the
horizon of French students, among others: they now knew that there were

possibilities that remained unknown. Not that everything was possible, but that one can only know something is impossible once one has tried it and failed. This was a profound discovery, rich in its eventual consequences and revolutionary in the West.

Today, over a year later, it is clear that to a certain extent we have discovered the impossible. In particular, as long as the French Communist Party is the largest conservative party in France, and as long as it has the confidence of the workers, it will be impossible to make the free revolution that was missed in May. Which only means that it is necessary to pursue the struggle, however protracted it may be, with the same persistence as the Vietnamese, who after all are continuing to fight and continuing to win.

May was not a revolution: it did not destroy the bourgeois state. To make the revolution next time, organization will be necessary to coordinate and lead the struggle. What sort of political organization do you judge to be the appropriate instrument today?

It is obvious that anarchism leads nowhere, today as yesterday. The central question is whether in the end the only possible type of political organization is that which we know in the shape of the present Communist parties: hierarchical division between leadership and rank and file, communications and instructions proceeding from above downwards only, isolation of each cell from every other, vertical powers of dissolution and discipline, separation of workers and intellectuals? This pattern developed from a form of organization which was born in clandestinity in the time of the Tsars. What are the objective justifications of its existence in the West today? Its purpose here appears merely to ensure an authoritarian centralism which excludes any democratic practice. Of course, in a civil war situation, a militarized discipline is necessary. But does a proletarian party have to resemble the present-day Communist parties? Is it not possible to conceive of a type of political organization where men are not barred and stifled? Such an organization would contain different currents, and would be capable of closing itself in moments of danger, to reopen thereafter.

It is always true, of course, that to fight something one must change oneself into it; in other words one must become its true opposite and not merely other than it. A revolutionary party must necessarily reproduce—up to a certain limit—the centralization and coercion of the bourgeois state which it is its mission to overthrow. However, the whole problem—the history of our century is there to prove it—is that once a party dialectically undergoes this ordeal, it may become arrested there. The result is then that it has enormous difficulty in ever escaping from the bureaucratic rut which it initially accepted to make the revolution against a bureaucratic-military machine. From that moment on, only a cultural revolution against the new order can prevent a degradation of it. It is not a benevolent reform that is occurring in China today, it is the violent destruction of a whole system of privilege. Yet we know nothing of what the future will be in China. The danger of a bureaucratic deterioration will be powerfully present in any Western country, if we succeed in making the revolution: that is absolutely inevitable, since both external imperialist encirclement and the internal class struggle will continue to exist. The idea of an instant and total liberation is a utopia. We can already foresee some of the limits and constraints of a future revolution. But he who takes these as an excuse not to make the revolution and who fails to struggle for it now, is simply a counter-revolutionary.

Abroad, you are often seen as a classical product of French university culture. The university system in which you were educated and made your early career was the exact target of the first explosion which set off the upheaval of May. What is your judgement of it now?

It is certainly true that I am a product of this system, and I am very aware of it: although I hope I am not only that. When I was a student, only a very small elite got to university, and if one had the additional 'luck' to get into the École Normale, one had every material advantage. In a sense the French university *system* formed me more than its professors, because in my time the latter, with only one or two exceptions, were very mediocre. But the system, above all the École Normale, I accepted as absolutely natural: son and grandson of petty-bourgeois intellectuals, it never occurred to me to question it. The lectures of the *cours magistral* seemed idiotic to us, but only because the teachers who gave it had nothing to tell us. Later, others saw that the lecture course itself was irredeemable. We merely abstained from ever going to the Sorbonne: only once, when law students threatened to invade it, did we go to the lectures there—otherwise never. Most of the École Normale students of my time were very proud if they became *agrégés*, for instance (although there were a few who thought the hierarchy of *agrégés* and *licenciés* was monstrous). Nizan was an exception, of course.[9] He detested the École Normale, for very good reasons—its class function in creating a privileged elite. Although he was academically 'successful', he never, never fitted into the system. By the third year he was in such a state of malaise that he escaped to Aden. Of course, this was related to neurotic problems in his personal history, but the fundamental fact was that he could not breathe within these institutions designed to perpetuate a monopoly of knowledge.

---

[9] Paul Nizan (1905–40): a close friend of Sartre, Nizan joined the French Communist Party in the late 1920s and became one of its most prominent intellectuals. He resigned from the PCF in 1939 in disgust at the Molotov–Ribbentrop Pact, and thereafter endured a classic campaign of vilification in the party press. Called up at the outbreak of war, Nizan was killed in action near Dunkirk in May 1940. His novel *La Conspiration* (1938) is an unsparing group portrait of youthful revolt at the École Normale. (*The Conspiracy*, trans. Quintin Hoare and with an Afterword by Jean-Paul Sartre, London 1988).

What is your view of a correct Marxist practice within the institutions of bourgeois culture—the educational system—after May?

Is a positive revolutionary culture conceivable today? For me, this is the most difficult problem posed by your question. My frank opinion is that everything within bourgeois culture that will be surpassed by a revolutionary culture will nevertheless ultimately also be preserved by it. I do not believe that a revolutionary culture will forget Rimbaud, Baudelaire or Flaubert, merely because they were very bourgeois and not exactly friends of the people. They will have their place in any future socialist culture, but it will be a *new* place determined by new needs and relations. They will not be great principal values, but they will be part of a tradition reassessed by a different praxis and a different culture.

But how can they be reassessed today, when a revolutionary culture does not exist? They have only one place within existing society—the site assigned to them by bourgeois culture. What is the 'correct use' of Rimbaud for a young socialist militant in Vincennes or Nanterre? The question is unanswerable. It is true that a certain number of university intellectuals of an older generation became revolutionaries within a society that dispensed this culture to them. But the situation has changed radically since then. To take only the material conditions of a university education: in my time an orthodox lecture course was trundled out to perhaps fifteen or twenty people. It was less shocking, because it could formally be contested: a student could interrupt and say he disagreed, and the lecturer would tolerate this because it hid the completely authoritarian character of the whole course. Today, there are a hundred or two hundred students where there were once fifteen. There is no longer any chance of this. Where it was once possible to turn bourgeois culture against itself, showing that Liberty, Equality and Fraternity had become their opposites, today the only possibility is to be against bourgeois culture. For the traditional system is collapsing. The baccalauréat in France is something incredible, in its antiquation. In Rouen-Le Havre recently, the subject of the philosophy paper was: 'Epictetus said to a disciple: "Live Hidden". Comment.' Can you imagine—giving a question like that to schoolchildren of sixteen in this day and age! Not only the reference is outrageous, of course, 10 per cent to 20 per cent of the candidates thought that *Vis caché* (Live Hidden) was *Vices cachés* (Hidden Vices), imagining perhaps that this was ancient orthography, and interpreted the quotation to mean: 'Hide your vices'. They then developed at length the idea of Epictetus along the lines 'If you have vices, satisfy them, but secretly.' The funniest, and saddest, thing of all is that they approved the formula of Epictetus! 'For it is like that in society, one can have a vice, but one should practise it in solitude.' Innocent answers, showing what bourgeois morality is in fact like; pitiful answers because these pupils obviously thought, 'Epictetus must be famous, if I criticize him I might get four out of twenty and fail, the only thing to do is to agree with him.' There is no relationship, no contact whatever between these young people and their teachers. Bourgeois culture in France is destroying itself. Thus for the moment, regardless of the eventual future, I believe that a radical negation of the existing culture is the only possible option for young militants—a negation which will often take the form of violent contestation.

Are you going to write a sequel to Les Mots? *What are your future plans?*

No, I do not think that a sequel to *Les Mots* would be of much interest. The reason why I produced *Les Mots* is the reason why I have studied Genet or Flaubert: how does a man become someone who writes, who wants to speak of the imaginary? This is what I sought to answer in my own case, as I sought it in that of others. What could there be to say of my existence since 1939? How I became the writer who produced the particular works I have signed. But the reason I wrote *La Nausée* rather than some other book is of little importance. It is the birth of the decision to write that is of interest. Thereafter, what is equally interesting are the reasons why I was to write exactly the contrary to what I wanted to write. But this is another subject altogether—the relationship of a man to the history of his time. Thus what I will write one day is a political testament. The title is perhaps a bad one, since a testament implies the idea of giving advice; here it will simply be the end of a life. What I would like to show is how a man comes to politics, how he is caught by them, and how he is remade other by them; because you must remember that I was not made for politics, and yet I was remade by politics so that I eventually had to enter them. It is this which is curious. I will recount what I did politically, what mistakes I committed, and what resulted from it. In doing so, I will try to define what constitutes politics today, in our own phase of history.

Noam Chomsky (b. 1928) grew up in New York City, and studied at the University of Pennsylvania, where he majored in Linguistics. By the turn of the 1960s, he was coming to be recognized as a leader in his field, pioneer of a powerful new approach to syntax and an incisive critic of the prevailing behaviourist ethos in cognitive psychology. Not long afterwards he also emerged as one of the boldest opponents of the us *war in Vietnam. His essay 'The Responsibility of Intellectuals', published in the* New York Review of Books *in early 1967, was a J'accuse for its time and place, a meticulous, unflagging indictment of Washington's serviceable policy and technical intelligentsias, their key role in sustaining the war and their personal investments in doing so. The book-length version of the essay came out as* American Power and the New Mandarins *in 1969—the year in which he gave this interview.*

Within twelve months, in May 1970, as the war and the resistance alike grew fiercer, troopers of the Ohio National Guard opened fire on a peaceful campus demonstration at Kent State University. Four students died and nine were injured; the anti-war movement responded with a country-wide strike involving some four million students. The Paris Peace Accords ending direct us *military involvement in Vietnam were signed eighteen months later, in January 1973.*

Chomsky has continued to make major contributions to linguistics, cognitive psychology and the philosophy of mind. American Power and the New Mandarins *was the first of his forty or more works of political advocacy and exposure.*

Noam Chomsky

Linguistics and Politics

It is clear from your writings that you were thinking deeply about politics long before the Vietnam War became a dominant issue in America. Could you tell us something about the background to your present political stand?

I have been involved in politics, intellectually if not always actively, since early childhood. I grew up among the radical Jewish community in New York. This was during the depression and many of my immediate relatives were active in various left-wing and working-class movements. The first 'political' article I remember writing was in a school newspaper, an article about the fall of Barcelona. The Spanish Civil War, of course, was a major experience from childhood which stuck. I was connected loosely with various types of group, searching for something that was within the Marxist or at least revolutionary tradition, but which did not have the elitist aspects which seemed to me then and seem to me today to be disfiguring and destructive. In the 1940s, when I was a teenager, I would hang around left-wing bookshops and the offices of offbeat groups, and periodicals, talking to people—often very perceptive and interesting people who were thinking hard about the problems of social change—and seeing what I could pick up. Then I was much interested in a Jewish organization which was opposed to the Jewish state in Palestine and worked for Arab–Jewish cooperation on a socialist basis. Out of all this, from my relatives and friends, I learned a great deal informally and acquired a certain framework within which my own way of thinking developed. In fact, I more or less got into linguistics this way, through my connections with these political groups. I was very impressed by Zellig Harris, who was the head of the Linguistics Department at the University of Pennsylvania, and I found I had political interests in common with him. He had a kind of semi-anarchist strain to his thought. Then I withdrew during the fifties from political involvements, though of course I retained my intellectual interest. I signed petitions, over the Rosenberg case, for instance, and went on occasional demonstrations, but it did not amount to much.[1] Then, in the sixties, I began to become more active again. Like most people, I had something to do with the civil rights movement. But in retrospect I think I was very slow in getting involved. It was only when the Vietnam War began escalating that I began to take any really active political role. Much too late, I am afraid.

How effective do you think the anti-war movement in America has been? How effective do you think it can be in the future?

I think if the movement was able to consolidate and act it could probably end the war. I think it is a great tragedy that it has more or less collapsed in the last few months. In the past I think it has had a marginal effect. The major factor has been the National Liberation Front and the struggle in Vietnam itself. But I think there is some evidence that political action in America has limited and retarded American aggression. I think the will to prosecute the war has been weakened by the turmoil and dissidence in American society itself. The domestic cost began to become too high. Of course, without the Tet offensive, this would not have weighed so greatly but I think it has been an important factor nonetheless. Pressure for ending the war became really quite substantial. The *Wall Street Journal* opposed the war, for instance. I think that if, after Nixon was elected, there had been sufficient disruption and turmoil and demonstrations, then it might have hastened the end of the war considerably. But, for various reasons, this did not take place.

Do you think that the chain of insurrections on the campuses is a form of solidarity with the Vietnamese, apart from the anti-war movement as such?

I am of two minds about that. These insurrections are not specifically directed against the war so it is not so obvious that they are part of the cost of the war. There was a shift in student politics between the Pentagon demonstration in October 1967 and the Columbia action in spring 1968. My own feeling is that this shift did not do much to help the Vietnamese. If the student movement had focused its energy and its activism more directly against the war, it would have been a much more powerful force in cutting down the American military effort. Obviously, anyone rational has to recognize that student insurrections are part of the fallout from the war in Vietnam. But it

---

[1] The trial and execution, in 1953, of Julius and Ethel Rosenberg, two American communists, on charges of conspiracy to commit espionage, provoked widespread protest at home and internationally, among the many who saw in the process a miscarriage of justice, or at least a savagely disproportionate act of retaliation. The case remained controversial for decades. It now appears that Julius was indeed involved in espionage. Ethel's part, if she had any at all, remains unknown.

is not so clear that they would stop if the war stopped. So in this sense they are less effective tactically than unambiguous anti-war actions.

But it is hard to see how the student movement could avoid campus issues. There are real contradictions on the campus which affect the students and which the student movement could not ignore. A number of the insurrections seem to have arisen spontaneously out of the campus situation.

I am not so convinced that people active in the student movement should simply find the most lively issue and work on that. That is a bit unprincipled. They ought to be finding the issues which are the most important and trying to make those issues important to the people whom they are trying to reach. That is different from finding issues which seem to have some life and selecting them because they may be useful issues for building a movement. Now I do not think that is necessarily wrong: building a movement concerned with social change, perhaps revolutionary change, is important. But I think one has to be careful to avoid opportunism and to try always to find principled issues rather than issues which happen to be convenient at the moment. The necessity to end the Vietnam War seems to me so urgent that I would be perfectly willing to be enormously involved in a movement that would end when the war ended, if that movement helped to end the war. I feel that ending the war is the highest priority for any radical or revolutionary movement in America.

It is not simply a question of action limited to universities. For instance, in California there have been actions involving both students and workers. Don't you think this is an important step forward, given that the American working class have not yet played any significant part in the anti-war movement?

If the Vietnamese have to wait until we build a serious political movement against all forms of capitalist repression in the United States, then they are all going to be dead. It is true that active opposition to the war has been middle class or even upper-middle class, but that is a politically very important part of the population. It is difficult to repress, in the sense that there is a high political cost to the repression of these classes and that gives a lever for protest against the war which should be exploited. I have nothing against using the inegalitarian aspects of American society as a weapon against its foreign policy. In any case, we cannot delay on the Vietnam issue in order to build a movement on more long-term issues. Even if these two goals were in conflict, I think we should give priority to the goal of ending the war. But I do not think they are in conflict. Principled opposition to the war will lead directly to principled opposition to imperialism and to the causes of imperialism and hence to the formation of a principled anti-capitalist movement.

You have made many very persuasive and moving indictments of American imperialism in Vietnam. Could you spell out the reasons why the United States went into Vietnam?

I think the United States went in for a lot of reasons and I think they have changed through time. At the moment, I think we are staying in largely because there is a big investment in error and it is very hard for people who have invested an enormous amount of prestige in their commitment to a policy simply to admit defeat. So they are looking for what they choose to call an honourable peace, which does not exist, in their sense. But if we look back further we find a different set of reasons. If you read the State Department propaganda in 1950–51, you will find that their intention then was to give sufficient support to the French to enable them to reconstitute French colonial rule and to eradicate communism there. When the French proved incapable of carrying this out, then the United States simply took over. Dean Acheson made it clear that when China was 'lost' the United States would not tolerate any further disturbance to the integrated world system it was attempting to construct and a revolution in Vietnam was seen as an erosion of that system. Now it is perfectly true, as many people point out, that the United States can survive without Vietnam as a colony, that the United States does not need Vietnamese rubber or anything like that. But I think the very fact that Vietnam is so unimportant in this respect shows how desperately necessary it is felt to be to maintain an integrated world system. They are willing to make this great commitment even to hold a marginal, peripheral piece of their empire.

If one looks into it even more deeply then one discerns other things going on. For example, the United States fought the Second World War, in the Pacific theatre, primarily in order to prevent Japan from constructing its own independent, integrated imperial system which would be closed to America. That was the basic issue which lay behind the Japanese–American war. Well, the United States won. The result is that now it must develop a system in which Japan can function effectively as a junior partner. That means the United States has to grant Japan what it needs as a partner, namely markets and access to raw materials, which for Japan, unlike the United States, are desperate necessities. Now the United States can very well survive without South East Asia. But Japan cannot. So if the United States wants to keep Japan securely embedded within the American system, then it has to pre-serve South East Asia for Japan. Otherwise Japan has other alternatives. It would turn to China or to Siberia, but that would mean the United States had lost the Second World War, in its Pacific phase. Once again a substantial industrial power would be carving itself out an independent space which, taken to its logical conclusion, would be separate and partly sealed off from the American world system.

I think the United States recognized this danger immediately after the

Second World War and accordingly began to reconstitute the imperial relations between Japan and its former colonies. People in the Philippines were upset and taken aback by this. They thought they had helped the United States win the war and they were puzzled to find the United States building up Japan as an industrial power again and ignoring the Philippines. But the reason for that is plain. Japan could not be ignored and the United States wanted it to play its allotted role in the American system, similar to that played by Britain in the Atlantic. The consequence of that is that sources of raw materials and a market for Japanese goods must be maintained in Southeast Asia. The United States does not have to sell motorcycles there for itself but Japan does have to and the United States has to ensure that it can, if the American system there is to remain stable.

Another factor that was very important and is extremely suggestive for the future is that the Vietnam War became an ideological instrument for the strategic theory of the Cold War intelligentsia that moved into power with Kennedy. This was to be the testing ground where they could show how by properly designed counter-insurgency programmes they could control potential revolutionary movements anywhere on the globe. They put an enormous commitment into this. When the technical intelligentsia becomes involved in the design of policy, this is a very different matter from when a corporate elite or an aristocracy becomes involved in policy-making. To put it in a nutshell, when someone like Averell Harriman happens to make a mistake, it does not seem to him he has lost his right to be running the world.[2] His right to be running the world is based on the fact that his grandfather built railroads. But if Walt Rostow or McGeorge Bundy happen to make a mistake, when it turns out they got everything wrong, then they have lost their only claim to be at the centre of power, which was that they had superior knowledge to other people.[3] The consequence of this is that policies designed by this technical intelligentsia have a peculiar persistence. Other people's claim to power need not be diminished by failure in the same way, so they can be somewhat more pragmatic and opportunistic. ·

You do not think that power has been transferred in any substantial way from large capital to the intelligentsia? Would you agree that power still remains where it has always been, with large capital, and that the new prominence of the

---

[2] William Averell Harriman (1891–1986), the son of a railroad baron, served in various domestic and overseas capacities in four US presidential administrations—those of Roosevelt, Truman, Kennedy and Johnson—and was himself a candidate for the Democratic nomination in the 1950s. He also served as governor of New York State.

[3] W. W. Rostow (1916–2003), an economist and political theorist, was a national security adviser in the Kennedy and Johnson adminstrations, and a vigorous support of the US war on Vietnam. McGeorge Bundy (1919–96), a former intelligence officer and Harvard dean, was chief national security adviser to the same administrations and likewise a staunch advocate of the war.

intelligentsia does not mean there is some new mode of production or some new,
qualitatively different stage of capitalism in the United States?

The idea that power has shifted from capital to knowledge is pretty much a
fantasy. But the technical intelligentsia is providing great service to the corporate elite that has been running America throughout this century and I
think they do make their own contribution, a very dangerous contribution.
The intellectual community used to be a kind of critical voice. That was its
main function. Now it is losing that function and accepting the notion that
its role is to carry out piecemeal social engineering.

Don't you think American imperialism is right, within its own terms, to fear
popular uprisings and revolutions wherever they occur, in however small or
distant a country, simply because there is always the threat of contagion?

That is true. There is such a threat, and it is a serious one. The goal of designing an integrated world economy to be dominated by American capital is
the highest priority for the corporate elite that manages the United States.
This is not just a matter of having safe areas for American investment and
markets and control of raw materials, though, of course, these are important. There is also the need to maintain a high level of defence spending,
war spending basically. This has been the main 'Keynesian' mechanism for
maintaining what they call the health of the economy. The United States
was still in the depression in 1939. There were nine million unemployed.
The war ended that. American industrial production quadrupled during the
Second World War. It was done by running a tightly managed economy
with government intervention, largely in arms, but multiplying out to the
rest of the economy. Now this lesson in economics was taught to precisely
the people who could benefit from it, namely the corporate managers who
came to Washington to manage the wartime economy. Arms production is
ideal from their point of view. It keeps the economy running and it does not
conflict with private interests. But of course the taxpayer has to be willing to
foot the bill. Hence the Cold War paranoia which goes with this enormous
arms production. Without this great fear of the Communists or the Third
World or China, there is no particular reason why 50 per cent of a tax dollar
should be spent on a public subsidy to war-based industry. These things all tie
in together.

Could you say something about the campaign you have been involved in against
the participation of your own university, Massachusetts Institute of Technology,
in the United States military programme?

I have simply been following the lead of the students, who have done a
very good job on this. MIT manages two laboratories financed largely by the

Pentagon and NASA to the tune of something like 125 million dollars a year. About 4,000 people are employed there, largely on war-related projects. They are involved in counter-insurgency too, techniques for detecting tunnels and detecting people hidden in dense foliage, everything. Now there are a number of alternatives open to us in a campaign against participation in 'defence' programmes of this kind. We could try to sever the connection between the university and the laboratories where this work is done. This happened recently at Stanford. But the students have opposed this. They have insisted from the beginning that this would not be an acceptable way out. In effect, it would mean only a kind of terminological shift. The work would go on, but under a different name. The same university people would be involved in it, but as consultants maybe instead of as staff. There is no particular point in trying to develop pure universities in a criminal society. I would rather have the laboratories right in the middle of the campus, where their presence could be used to politicize future engineers, for instance, than hidden away somewhere while the campus is perfectly clean and clois-tered. I feel this way about chemical and bacteriological warfare too. I would prefer to have a building in the middle of the campus called Department of Bacteriological Warfare, rather than have it right off the map at Fort Detrick or some place nobody knows of. It could be actually retrograde, in this sense, to try and cut all connections between the university and the Department of Defense.

So this means taking a second alternative. We aim to try and keep control over the laboratories but to try and control also what kind of research is done in them. Of course, this is difficult, because there are limited funds for anything except military research. It brings the problem of establishing a student–worker alliance to the forefront too. As things stand now, the workers in the laboratories—scientists, technicians, unskilled workers—are terrified of the idea that war research might stop. In fact, when we started picketing, the union there, whose members are mostly machinists and so forth, entered a suit to prevent MIT from dropping war research. You can see the logic behind their action. They do not see any alternatives to war research and development within the New England economy.

We have somehow to get people to see that there are other things technol-ogy could be used for, that there is no good reason why the public subsidy they are living on should be used simply for purposes of destruction. We have to keep the issue alive and open. We have to try and reconvert the laboratories. We have to try and build up social and political pressures for a socially useful technology. It means making ideas that sound Utopian at first seem real and possible. It is a big order and we do not expect to do it in a short time.

You seem to reject the liberal idea that there can be limited reforms in American society but, at the same time, you do not seem to see much immediate future for revolutionary action.

We should set up the germs of new institutions where we can. We should try to make people realize what is wrong with this society and give them a conscious vision of the new society. Then we can go on to a programme of action for great masses of people. A democratic revolution would take place when it is supported by the great mass of the people, when they know what they are doing and they know why they are doing it and they know what they want to see come into existence. Maybe not in detail, but at least in some manner. A revolution is something that great masses of people have to understand and be personally committed to.

If there is going to be severe repression of the student movement, as seems more than likely, this brings out the need for better organization and for more intellectual coherence.[4] Do you think the time for relying on ad hoc modes of action and ad hoc slogans is past?

Without a revolutionary theory or a revolutionary consciousness there is not going to be a revolutionary movement. There is not going to be a serious movement without a clear analysis and a theoretical point of view. Naturally the student movement has to be able to defend itself against repression. This has to be broadened out beyond the student movement. The Black Panthers are subjected to intensive repression and we should not allow this to be forgotten.[5]

What do you envisage by revolutionary theory?

There are certain crises of capitalism that cannot be overcome internally. They can be overcome only by the total reconstruction of social relations. All economic and political institutions should be placed under democratic control through direct participation by workers and by those involved because they live in a particular geographical area, for instance, or on the basis of other forms of free association. To take an example, there is at the moment a serious crisis of capitalism with respect to the problem of how to use technological resources to serve human needs rather than the need

---

[4] The Kent State massacre, in which Ohio National Guardsmen opened fire on a peaceful campus demonstration against the invasion of Cambodia, killing four students and wounding another nine, occurred not long after this conversation, in May 1970.

[5] The Black Panther Party (1966–c.76) was a militant, eclectically revolutionary organization initially focused on black communal self-defence against police brutality but evolving rapidly through black nationalism to a more inclusive socialist outlook. Its disintegration was in part a result of inner incoherence but was hastened by official harassment and repression.

to maintain a senseless, irrational and predatory economy. This problem cannot be solved within the framework of capitalist ideology or the capitalist system of production. Certain human needs can only be expressed collectively and that requires an entirely different system. I think issues like the extension of democracy, the satisfaction of human needs, the preservation of the environment, are of the first importance. A revolutionary theory ought to be concerned with developing points of this sort and translating them into something that is immediately meaningful.

Do you not accept Leninism as the basis of the revolutionary theory you would like to see develop? Are you anti-Leninist as well as anti-Stalinist?

It would be a grotesque error to say that Stalin was simply the realization of Leninist principles or anything like that. Lenin himself insisted, quite correctly, that in a backward country like Russia the revolution could not succeed unless there was an international revolution. There are different strands in Lenin's theories. On the one hand, there is *State and Revolution*, which is basically fine, and on the other hand, there is the effective dismantling of the soviets, there is Kronstadt and the suppression of the Workers' Opposition, which was under Lenin's aegis at least. We could go into the history of all this and we could criticize one thing and laud another. But I think there are really two competing tendencies. There is a model which stresses the leadership role of the vanguard party of committed intellectuals, which controls and determines the course of the movement. That is an aspect of the Leninist tradition which laid the groundwork for Stalin. Then, contrasted to this, there is a model which sees the revolutionary movement as based on voluntary mass associations which have control themselves and which are encouraged to exercise it, politicizing themselves in the process. This is a tendency associated more with Rosa Luxemburg and her criticisms of Lenin's concept of the party, though, of course, we should not forget there is also the Lenin of the *April Theses* and of *State and Revolution*.

Do you not think that the Leninist tradition should be held responsible for the Chinese and Vietnamese revolutions if it is going to be held responsible for Stalinism?

Frankly I think the Chinese overestimate their dependence on the Bolshevik model and they underestimate the populist element that exists in Maoism. Without this they might not have had the success they did in involving masses of people in a way which was not characteristic of the Russian revolution.

Lenin stressed the need to involve the masses.

Yes, that is the side of Lenin which shows up in the *April Theses* and *State and Revolution*. But after the Bolsheviks took power, they followed a very different course.

What kind of explanation would you give for the Cold War? Do you accept some version of the convergence theory?

I think there is a kind of convergence in the sphere of the involvement of the technical intelligentsia at the centre of power. There is an old anarchist critique of the role of the intelligentsia in bureaucracies which rings very true. There is also convergence in the evolution of large centralized economic units. But, of course, the Cold War came about without respect to any convergence of this kind. I think the main reason for the Cold War was that the Soviet Union constructed a closed order in Eastern Europe. One can see this by reading statements of the American ruling elite, like the study entitled *The Political Economy of American Foreign Policy* published in the mid-fifties, which identifies the primary threat of Communism as the refusal to continue to complement the industrial economies of the West. Any society which is closed is a threat to the United States. This applies both to the Soviet Union and to pre-war Japan. Of course, the Soviet threat involved socialized production and the Japanese threat did not. But basically they were threats of a very similar sort. They closed off significant areas of the world and made them inaccessible to American capital. The United States had to combat this threat. In one case, by the Pacific phase of the Second World War and, in the other case, by the Cold War.

You do not think it was also because the Soviet Union offered an alternative model of society?

An alternative model of development. If you compare the areas of the Soviet Union which are directly north of Turkey and Iran with the areas directly south of the border, there is a very striking difference in development. But the same was true of pre-war Japan and its New Order. I think the threat of independent development is probably more important than the threat of socialized production. It is a threat to the aim of constructing an international system, dominated by the United States, in which there will be a free flow of capital and goods and raw materials.

But although the American economic penetration of the Soviet Union is still relatively small, there has been a very marked shift in attitude towards a detente. Why is China seen as so much more of a threat than the Soviet Union?

The Soviet Union has already been given up. And it has been a long-standing element of American belief that the China trade is going to be of very great significance for the economic development of the United States. That goes back to the 1780s, back to the time when the west coast of America was settled by merchants interested in the China trade. One of the main reasons why the United States took the Philippines in the late nineteenth century was as a coaling station for the China trade. Of course, there is an element of mythology in this, but in the formation of policy it is what people believe that counts, not what is true.

All the same, that seems a very economistic line of argument. Surely both the Bolshevik and Chinese revolutions were a threat because of force of example, because of the political and ideological repercussions? Japan is a quite different case. The Japanese, like the United States, tried to crush the revolution in China. That is not really true of the Soviet Union.

The Japanese did not set out to crush the Chinese Revolution. For example, there was no Chinese revolution in Manchuria in 1931 or North China in 1937. They set out to dominate China and crushing the Chinese Revolution was a by-product. I think if China happened at the moment to be fascist rather than communist, but also excluded from the present American world system, then it would be perceived as a threat to the United States. But perhaps I have been underestimating the ideological threat. It is true to say that the success of a popular mass revolution, as in China, does give people elsewhere ideas. It teaches people that property is not holy and that we can make a revolution too. If China were fascist, it would not have this ideological impact on other parts of the world, but it would still be perceived as a danger if it were separated from the American world system and engaged on an independent path of development.

We would like to ask you something about your work in linguistics. Do you think there is any connection between your specialized work there and your political views, which you have been talking about?

Scientific ideas and political ideas can converge and, if they converge independently because they have each developed in the same direction, that is fine. But they should not be made to converge at the cost of distortion and suppression, or anything like that.

For instance, in your work in linguistics, you use concepts like 'freedom', 'spontaneity', 'creativity', 'innovation' and so on. Is that connected in any way with your political views? Or is it just accidental?

A little of each. It is accidental in that the way these concepts arise in the study of language and the theses they sustain are appropriate or inappropriate, true or false, quite independently of politics. In that sense, it is independent. And similarly, in my opinion, a Marxist-anarchist perspective is justified quite apart from anything that may happen in linguistics. So that in that sense they are logically independent. But I still feel myself that there is a kind of tenuous connection. I would not want to overstate it but I think it means something to me at least. I think that anyone's political ideas or their ideas of social organization must be rooted ultimately in some concept of human nature and human needs. Now my own feeling is that the fundamental human capacity is the capacity and the need for creative self-expression, for free control of all aspects of one's life and thought. One particularly crucial realization of this capacity is the creative use of language as a free instrument of thought and expression. Now having this view of human nature and human needs, one tries to think about the modes of social organization that would permit the freest and fullest development of the individual, of each individual's potentialities in whatever direction they might take, that would permit him to be fully human in the sense of having the greatest possible scope for his freedom and initiative. Moving along in this direction, one might actually develop a social science in which a concept of social organization is related to a concept of human nature which is empirically well founded and which in some fashion leads even to value judgements about what form society should take, how it should change and how it should be reconstructed. I want to emphasize again that fundamentally the two are logically independent, but one can draw a sort of loose connection. This connection has been made occasionally. Von Humboldt, for example, who interests me particularly, combined a deep interest in human creativity and the creative aspect of language with what were, in the context of his time, libertarian politics.[6]

Another concept which is crucial to your work in linguistics is that of 'rules'. How does that fit in with the stress on freedom?

I think that true creativity means free action within the framework of a system of rules. In art, for instance, if a person just throws cans of paint randomly at a wall, with no rules at all, no structure, that is not artistic creativity, whatever else it may be. It is a commonplace of aesthetic theory that creativity involves action that takes place within a framework of rules, but is not narrowly determined either by the rules or by external stimuli. It is only when you have the combination of freedom and constraint that the question of creativity arises.

---

[6] Wilhelm von Humboldt (1767–1835), government official, diplomat and founder of the Berlin university that bears his name, was an important philologist and contributor to the philosophy of language.

I would like to assume on the basis of fact and hope on the basis of confidence in the human species that there are innate structures of mind. If there are not, if humans are just plastic and random organisms, then they are fit subjects for the shaping of behaviour. If humans only become as they are by random changes, then why not control that randomness by the state authority or the behaviourist technologist or anything else? Naturally I hope that it will turn out that there are intrinsic structures determining human need and the fulfilment of human need.

What is the role of human history? Surely human needs and their fulfilment are historically determined. What kind of scope do you give to historical determinations?

I think we have to be very cautious about this until we have a much broader understanding of the range and extent of possible variations in human behaviour. Things that seem to us great variations in language, for instance, would seem to some super-intelligence as minor modifications. As human beings, as living human beings, we are primarily interested in the differences among ourselves and that is perfectly proper. As a human being, living in the contemporary world, I am very much interested in the difference between English and Japanese because I cannot understand Japanese and it would be useful to be able to. But as a linguist I am interested in the fact that English and Japanese are rather minor modifications of a basic pattern and that other linguistic systems could be imagined which violate that basic pattern, but that they do not in fact anywhere exist. Now it is possible to carry out this study as a linguist because we can move up to a level of abstractness from which we can survey a vast class of possible systems and ask how the existing human linguistic systems fit into this class. And I think we will discover that they fit into a very narrow part of it. A serious study of morals or of social systems would attempt the same thing. It would ask itself what kinds of social system are conceivable. Then it would ask itself what kinds have actually been realized in history and it would ask how these came into existence, given the range of possibilities that exist at some moment of economic and cultural development. Then, having reached that point, the next question is whether the range of social systems that human beings have constructed is broad or narrow, what is its scope, what are its potentialities, are there kinds of social systems human beings could not possibly construct and so on. We have not really begun this kind of investigation. Hence it is only a guess when I say that the range of possible social systems may turn out to be very narrow. Of course, there is an enormous human significance in living in one social system rather than another, in capitalism rather than feudalism, for example. Whereas there is no human significance, other than accidental, in speaking one language rather than another. But that is a different question from asking which kinds of system of social organization are possible for human beings and which kinds are not.

You have spoken about a possible convergence of your work in linguistics with your political ideas. Did your political ideas have any influence in the work you have done in linguistics up till now? Did they suggest hypotheses, for instance?

I do not think so. I worked for quite a few years trying to carry out a behaviourist programme. As a student, I was very much convinced that it would be possible to construct simple inductive principles that would explain how language is acquired. I thought that there should be simple inductive principles which would lead directly from a corpus of data to the organization of that data and that such an organization is what language would, in fact, consist of. But at the same time I was also, on the side, trying to write generative grammars. I assumed that generative grammars were just for fun and my own private hobby. I thought the attempt to build up analytic procedures was the real stuff. It was only much later, a long time later, maybe four years of really hard work, that I finally managed to convince myself that the attempt to build up analytic procedures was nonsense and that generative grammar was the real thing.

How did you get interested in generative grammar?

It had been around a long time. As I understand Humboldt, for instance, he had a concept similar to generative grammar. In any event, whether Humboldt did or did not, one thing at least is clear. If he did have a concept of generative grammar he could not do anything with it, because he did not have the techniques for using it. There was no way to take his insights and turn them into a rich, explanatory theory. That required new notions which eventually grew out of work on the foundations of mathematics. The notion of recursive systems of rules, for example. This work only came to fruition in the 1930s. But by then most people had completely forgotten about Humboldt and his kind of insights. I happened to be very lucky since I began to study the foundations of mathematics, not thinking it had any bearing on linguistics. Of course, it turned out to be just what was needed. I think the ideal situation would have been to have someone in 1940 who was steeped in rationalist and romantic literary and aesthetic theory and also happened to know modern mathematics. Such a person would have seen very quickly what to do. As far as I was concerned, it was pure accident. It just happened I grew up having some knowledge of historical linguistics largely because my father, who was a Hebrew scholar, was working on medieval grammatical texts and the history of the language. In historical linguistics it is taken for granted that there are underlying processes and that you can explain things by looking at how these processes interrelate. Of course, this is usually done in a very atomistic fashion and there is not much theory or system to it, but at least the concept of explanation is there. And then, as I said, I had also done some work in modern mathematics and logic, so I was able to combine these two interests. At first, I thought it was just a hobby. It took years and years before any of it was published. Even after I was convinced myself, I still could not get it published. Very few people saw any value in this work.

Do you now think that your work on generative grammar looks forward to further scientific advances?

I think that among the biological characteristics that determine the nature of the human organism there are some that relate to intellectual development, some that relate to moral development, some that relate to development as a member of human society, some that relate to aesthetic development. I suspect that they are restrictive and that we shall find that all of these constraints can be said to constitute human nature.

To a large extent, they are immutable. That is to say, they are just part of being human the same way that having legs and arms is part of being human.

Are you saying you think there is a generative grammar for social relations?

Not necessarily. That is, I do not think our capacities for having decent social relations, relations that would lead to some new form of society, would necessarily have the same structure as a generative grammar. I simply think that they must be constrained by some set of principles. But, of course, I cannot specify the principles.

You think there is some intrinsic disposition towards order in human beings which would spontaneously emerge if it were not repressed in some way?

I presume so. The only justification for any repressive institution is economic or cultural backwardness. In time, we should move to the gradual elimination of all repressive institutions without limit, as far as I can see. Just looking at the epoch that we are in now, it seems to me that our present level of technology permits enormous possibilities for eliminating repressive institutions. Automation makes it unnecessary for people to carry out the kind of imbecile labour that may have been necessary in the past. It is often said that advanced technology makes it imperative to vest control of institutions in the hands of a small managerial group. That is perfect nonsense. What automation can do first of all is to relieve people of an enormous amount of stupid labour, thus freeing them for other things. Computers also make possible a very rapid information flow. Everybody could be put in possession of vastly more information and more relevant information than they have now. Democratic decisions could be made immediately by everybody concerned. Computers also make simulation possible; you can run simulation experiments, so that you can test decisions without bearing the cost of failure. Of course, that is not how this technology is actually used. It is used for destructive purposes. The percentage of government expenditure on advanced technology has been reduced since the Vietnam war escalated, for the simple reason that you have to supply all the soldiers with uniforms and bullets and shoes and so on. But the end of the war would not divert any money to meeting collective needs or extending democratic practice. It would go back into aerospace and telecommunications, for the Defense Department or the Space Agency. Within a capitalist framework it could hardly be otherwise.

David Harvey was born in Gillingham, in the South-East of England, in 1935, and studied at the University of Cambridge, where he took his doctorate in Geography in 1961. Over the following decades, in a series of university positions ranging from Uppsala to Bristol, Baltimore, Oxford, the London School of Economics and New York City, he has become a crucial critical presence both in his discipline and in the theoretical forums of the Left worldwide. Harvey's interventions have been meta-theoretical in ambition and deeply practical in implication. His first book asserted the intelligible unity of the geographical as an object of knowledge. Since then he has insisted, as a premise of his work, on the irreducible reality of space in an adequately conceived historical materialism and, in doing so, has at the same time refashioned geography as an engaged intellectual force, inescapably answerable to considerations of social justice. This politico-intellectual understanding has led naturally to involvements in local struggles—in Baltimore and Oxford-Cowley, for example—alongside his continuing academic work, as exemplified most recently by his cross-media commentary A Companion to Marx's Capital *and* The Enigma of Capital *(both 2010).*

David Harvey

Reinventing Geography

Since the Second World War, the typical field for Marxist research has been history. Your path was more original. How did you become a geographer?

There's a trivial answer to this, which actually has profundity. When I was a kid, I often wanted to run away from home but every time I tried, I found it very uncomfortable, so I came back. So I decided to run away in my imagination, and there at least the world was a very open place, since I had a stamp collection, which showed all these countries with a British monarch on their stamps, and it seemed to me that they all belonged to us, to *me*. My father worked as a foreman in the shipyards at Chatham, with its very strong naval traditions. We lived in Gillingham. Once every year during the war, we would be taken for tea in the dockyards, on a destroyer; the romance of the high seas and of empire left a strong impression. My earliest ambition was to join the navy. So that even in the very gloomy days of 1946–47, just after the war, there was still an imaginary that encompassed this whole imperial world. Reading about it, drawing maps of it, became a childhood passion. Later, when I was in my teens, I cycled all over north Kent, getting to know a great deal about the geology, agriculture and landscape of our local area. I greatly enjoyed this form of knowledge. So I've always been drawn to geography. At school I was also strongly attracted to literature. When I got into Cambridge, which was still a bit unusual for a boy from my background, I took Geography rather than Literature partly because I had a teacher who had been trained in Cambridge, who made it clear to me that if you studied English there, you didn't so much read literature as deal with F. R. Leavis. I felt I could read literature on my own, and didn't need Leavis to tell me how to do it. So I preferred to follow the track of geography, though of course I never ceased to be interested in history and literature.

Geography was quite a big, well-established school at Cambridge, which gave a basic grounding in the discipline as it was practised in Britain at the time. I went on to do a PhD there, on the historical geography of Kent in the nineteenth century, focusing on the cultivation of hops. My first publication was actually in the house journal of Whitbread, the brewing concern—as a graduate student I earned a tenner for a piece published side by side with an article by John Arlott.

Your first book, Explanation in Geography, *published in 1969, is a very confident intervention, of ambitious scope, in the discipline. But it seems to come out of a very specific positivist setting—a horizon of reference that is exclusively Anglo-Saxon, without any sense of the powerful alternative traditions in geography in France or Germany?*

Explanation in Geography was looking for an answer to what I regarded as a central problem of the discipline. Traditionally, geographical knowledge had been extremely fragmented, leading to a strong emphasis on what was called its 'exceptionalism'. The established doctrine was that the knowledge yielded by geographical enquiry is different from any other kind. You can't generalize about it, you can't be systematic about it. There are no geographical laws; there are no general principles to which you can appeal—all you can do is go off and study, say, the dry zone in Sri Lanka, and spend your life understanding that. I wanted to do battle with this conception of geography by insisting on the need to understand geographical knowledge in some more systematic way. At the time, it seemed to me that the obvious resource here was the philosophical tradition of positivism—which, in the sixties, still had a very strong sense of the unity of science embedded in it, coming from Carnap. That was why I took Hempel or Popper so seriously; I thought there should be some way of using their philosophy of science to support the construction of a more unitary geographical knowledge. This was a moment when, inside the discipline, there was a strong movement to introduce statistical techniques of enquiry, and new quantitative methods. You could say my project was to develop the philosophical side of this quantitative revolution.

What about the external role of the discipline, as these internal changes took hold? Historically, geography seems to have had a much more salient position in the general intellectual culture of France or Germany than in Britain—it's been more closely linked to major public issues. The line of Vidal de la Blache's geography, descending into the Annales School, is clearly concerned with a problematic of national unity; von Thünen's, in Germany, with industrialization; Haushofer's with geopolitical strategies of imperial expansion—there was an Edwardian version of this in Mackinder, but more peripheral. How should postwar British geography be situated?

By the sixties, it was connected here far more than anywhere else to planning—regional planning and urban planning. By that time there was a certain embarrassment about the whole history of empire, and a turning away from the idea that geography could or should have any global role, let alone shape geopolitical strategies. The result was a strongly pragmatic focus, an attempt to reconstruct geographical knowledge as an instrument of administrative planning in Britain. In this sense, the discipline became quite functionalist. To give you an indication of the trend, I think there are hardly any areas where, if you put the word 'urban' in front of research, you would say this is the centre of the field. Urban history is essentially a rather marginal form; urban economics is an equally marginal thing; so, too, is urban politics. Whereas urban geography was really the centre of a lot of things going on in the discipline. Then, too, on the physical side, environmental management is often about the handling of local resources in particular kinds of ways. So that in Britain, the public presence of geography—and I think it was quite strong—operated in these three particular areas; it wasn't projected outwards in any grander intellectual formulation of the sort we might find in Braudel or the French tradition. You need to remember that for many of us who had some political ambitions for the discipline, rational planning was not a bad word in the sixties. It was the time of Harold Wilson's rhetoric about the 'white heat of technology', when the efficiency of regional and urban planning was going to be a lever of social betterment for the whole population.

Yet a striking feature of Explanation *is the absence of any political note in it. It reads as a purely scientific treatise, without any mention of concerns of this kind. One would never guess from it that the author might become a committed radical.*

Well, my politics at that time were closer to a Fabian progressivism, which is why I was very taken with the ideas of planning, efficiency and rationality. I would read economists like Oskar Lange who were thinking along these lines. So in my mind, there was no real conflict between a rational scientific approach to geographical issues, and an efficient application of planning to political issues. But I was so absorbed in writing the book that I didn't notice how much was collapsing around me. I turned in my *magnum opus* to the publishers in May 1968, only to find myself acutely embarrassed by the change of political temperature at large. By then I was thoroughly disillusioned with Harold Wilson's socialism. Just at that moment, I got a job in the US, arriving in Baltimore a year after much of the city had burnt down in the wake of the assassination of Martin Luther King. In the States, the anti-war movement and the civil rights movement were really fired up; and here was I, having written this neutral tome that seemed somehow or other just not to fit. I realized I had to rethink a lot of things I had taken for granted in the sixties.

What took you to the States?

At that time, American universities were expanding their Geography departments. Training in the discipline was much stronger in Britain than in the us, so there was quite an inflow of British geographers to fill the new positions. I had taught in the States on visiting appointments at various times, and when I was offered a job at Johns Hopkins, felt it was an attractive opportunity. The department there was interdisciplinary, combining Geography and Environmental Engineering. The idea was to put together a whole group of people from the social sciences and the natural sciences, to attack issues of environment in a multi-disciplinary way. I was one of the first to come into the new programme. For me, this was a tremendous situation, particularly in the early years. I learnt a great deal about how engineers think, about political processes, about economic problems: I didn't feel constrained by the discipline of Geography.

What was the political atmosphere?

Hopkins is an extremely conservative campus, but it has a long history of harbouring certain maverick figures. For instance, someone who interested me a great deal when I first arrived there—his *Inner Asian Frontiers of China* is a great book—was Owen Lattimore, who had been at Hopkins for many years, before he was targeted by McCarthyism.[1] I spent a lot of time talking to people who were there about what had happened to him, and went to see Lattimore himself. Eventually I tried to get Wittfogel, who had been his accuser, to explain why he had attacked Lattimore so violently.[2] So I was always fascinated by the political history of the university, as well as of the city. It's a small campus, which has always remained very conservative. But, for that reason, even a small number of determined radicals could prove quite effective—at the turn of the seventies, there was quite a significant anti-war movement, as well as civil rights activism around the university.

---

[1] Owen Lattimore (1900–89) was a Central Asia scholar whose engagement with the region, especially Mongolia, was autobiographical and commercial before taking academic form in the late 1920s. He was editor of *Pacific Affairs* in the 1930s, and acted in various specialist advisory capacities for the us government during and after the Second World War. The McCarthyist assault on Lattimore as a Communist and Soviet agent lasted nearly two years, 1950–52, and led to his indictment for perjury. Although the charges were in the end dismissed, the episode ended his involvement in policy matters and effectively undermined his academic career in the usa. Lattimore moved to Britain, where in 1963 he became the first professor of Chinese Studies at the University of Leeds.

[2] Karl August Wittfogel (1896–1988), sinologist and occasional playwright, was a member of the German Communist Party from its foundation and an early member of the Frankfurt Institute for Social Research. He emigrated to the United States in the 1930s and from 1947 was professor of Chinese History at the University of Washington. The Nazi–Soviet Pact triggered his conversion to an increasingly vehement and public anti-communism that reached its greatest intensity in his denunciations of Lattimore and others. His major work is *Oriental Despotism* (1957).

Baltimore itself intrigued me from the start. In fact, it was a terrific place to do empirical work. I quickly became involved in studies of discrimination in housing projects, and ever since the city has formed a backdrop to much of my thinking.

What is the particular profile of Baltimore as an American city?

In many ways, it is emblematic of the processes that have moulded cities under US capitalism, offering a laboratory sample of contemporary urbanism. But, of course, it has its own distinctive character as well. Few North American cities have as simple a power structure as Baltimore. After 1900, big industry largely moved out of the city, leaving control in the hands of a rich elite whose wealth was in real-estate and banking. There are no corporate headquarters in Baltimore today, and the city is often referred to as the biggest plantation in the South, since it is run much like a plantation by a few major financial institutions. Actually, in social structure, the city is half Northern and half Southern. Two-thirds of the population are African American, but there is nowhere near the level of black militancy you find in Philadelphia, New York or Chicago. Race relations are more Southern in pattern. Mayors may be African American, but they are largely dependent on the financial nexus, and are surrounded by white suburbs who don't want anything to do with the city. Culturally, it is one of the great centres of American bad taste. John Waters's movies are classic Baltimore—you can't imagine them anywhere else. Architecturally, whatever the city tries to do it gets a little bit wrong, like an architect who builds a house with miscalculated angles, and then, many years later, people say, 'Isn't that a very interesting structure?' One ends up with a lot of affection for it. At one time, I thought I might write a book called *Baltimore: City of Quirks*.

Your second book, Social Justice and the City, *which came out in 1973, is divided into three sections: Liberal Formulations—Marxist Formulations—Syntheses. Did you write these as a deliberate sequence from the start, to trace an evolution of your own, or did they just emerge* en cours de route?

The sequence was more fortuitous than planned. When I started the book, I would still have called myself a Fabian socialist, but that was a label which didn't make much sense in the US context. Nobody would understand what it meant. In America, I would then have been termed a card-carrying liberal. So I set out along these lines. Then I found they weren't working. So I turned to Marxist formulations to see if they yielded better results. The shift from one approach to the other wasn't premeditated—I stumbled on it.

But you were engaged in a reading group studying Marx's Capital *from 1971 onwards, not long after you got to Baltimore—an experience you have recently*

*described as a decisive moment in your development. Were you the main anima-
tor of this group?*

No, the initiative came from graduate students who wanted to read
Capital—Dick Walker was one of them—and I was the faculty member who
helped organize it. I wasn't a Marxist at the time, and knew very little of
Marx. This was anyway still a period when not much Marxist literature was
available in English. There was Dobb, and Sweezy and Baran, but little else.
Later, you people brought out French and German texts, and the Penguin
Marx Library. The publication of the *Grundrisse* in that series was a step in
our progression. The reading group was a wonderful experience, but I was
in no position to instruct anybody. As a group, we were the blind leading the
blind. That made it all the more rewarding.

At the conclusion of Social Justice and the City, *you explain that you encountered the work of Henri Lefebvre on urbanism after you'd written the rest of the
book, and go on to make some striking observations about it. How far were you
aware of French thinking about space at this stage? Looking back, one would say
there were two distinct lines of thought within French Marxism that would have
been relevant to you: the historical geography of Yves Lacoste and his colleagues
at Herodote, and the contemporary urban theory of Lefebvre, which came out
of the fascination of surrealism with the city as a landscape of the unexpected
in everyday life.*

Actually there was another line in France, which was institutionally more
important than either of these, connected to the Communist Party, whose
most famous representative was Pierre Georges. This group was very powerful in the university system, with a lot of control over appointments. Their
kind of geography was not overtly political at all: it focused essentially on the
terrestrial basis on which human societies are built, and its transformations
as productive forces are mobilized on the land. Lefebvre was not regarded as
a geographer. Georges was a central reference point in the discipline.

*Your response to Lefebvre's ideas strikes quite a distinctive note, one that recurs
in your later work. On the one hand, you warmed to Lefebvre's radicalism,
with a generous appreciation of the critical utopian charge in his writing; on
the other hand, you point to the need for a balancing realism. This two-handed
response becomes a kind of pattern in your work—one thinks of the way you
both imaginatively take up, and empirically limit, the notion of 'flexible accumulation' in* The Condition of Postmodernity, *or your reaction to ecological
apocalyptics in your more recent writing: an unusual combination of passionate engagement and cool level-headedness.*

One of the lessons I learnt in writing *Social Justice and the City* has always remained important for me. I can put it best with a phrase Marx used, when he spoke of the way we can rub different conceptual blocks together to make an intellectual fire. Theoretical innovation so often comes out of the collision between different lines of force. In a friction of this kind, one should never altogether give up one's starting point—ideas will only catch fire if the original elements are not completely absorbed in the new ones. The liberal formulations in *Social Justice and the City* don't entirely disappear, by any means—they remain part of the agenda that follows. When I read Marx, I'm very aware that this is a *critique* of political economy. Marx never suggests that Smith or Ricardo are full of nonsense, he's profoundly respectful of what they had to say. But he's also setting their concepts against others, from Hegel or Fourier, in a transformative process. So this has been a principle of my own work: Lefebvre may have some great ideas, the Regulationists have developed some very interesting notions, which should be respected in their own right, but you don't give up on everything you've got on your side—you try to rub the blocks together and ask: Is there something that can come out of this which is a new form of knowing?

What was the reception of Social Justice *in the discipline? The early seventies were a time of widespread intellectual shift to the Left—did it get a sympathetic hearing?*

In the US there was already a radical movement within geography, built around the journal *Antipode* produced at Clark University in Worcester, Massachusetts—traditionally one of the major schools of geography in the country. Its founders were strongly anti-imperialist, hating the history of geography's entanglement with Western colonialism. The journal spawned strong interventions at national meetings in the United States, and the formation of a group called Socialist Geographers. In Britain, Doreen Massey and others represented a similar sort of movement. So I'd say, at the beginning of the seventies, there was a very widespread kind of movement amongst younger people in Geography, to explore this particular dimension. *Social Justice and the City* was one of the texts which recorded that moment, becoming a reference point as time went on. It was also read outside the discipline, particularly by urban sociologists, and some political scientists. Radical economists, of course, were interested in urban questions, too—they had become central political issues in the States. So the setting was quite favourable for the reception of the book.

The Limits to Capital *appeared some nine years later, in 1982. It is a major work of economic theory—a startling leap from your previous writing. What is the history of this mutation?*

I had some background in neoclassical economics and planning theory, from Cambridge. For any geographer, von Thünen's location theory was a very important point of reference, from the start. Then, of course, in writing *Explanation in Geography* I had steeped myself in positivist discussions of mathematical reason, so that when I came across works by Marxist economists like Morishima or Desai, I had no major difficulties in understanding what was going on. Morishima's work and, naturally, Sweezy's *Theory of Capitalist Development* were very helpful to me. But to be honest, in writing *The Limits to Capital* I stuck with Marx's own texts most of the way. What I realized after *Social Justice and the City* was that I didn't understand Marx, and needed to straighten this out, which I tried to do without too much assistance from elsewhere. My aim was to get to the point where the theory could help me understand urban issues—and that I couldn't do without addressing questions of fixed capital, which no one had written much about at the time. There was the problem of finance capital, fundamental in housing markets, as I knew from Baltimore. If I had just stopped with the first part of the book, it would have been very similar to many other accounts of Marx's theory that were appearing at the time. It was the later part, where I looked at the temporality of fixed-capital formation, and how that relates to money flows and finance capital, and the spatial dimensions of these, that made the book more unusual. That was hard to do. Writing *Limits to Capital* nearly drove me nuts. I had a very difficult time finishing it; also struggling to make it readable—it took me the best part of a decade. The book grounded everything that I've done since. It is my favourite text, but ironically it's probably the one that's least read.

What was the response to it at the time? NLR *certainly paid no attention, but what about other sectors of the Left?*

I can't really recall anyone who would call themselves a Marxist economist taking it seriously. I always found that guild spirit odd, because it is so unlike Marx's own way of proceeding. Of course, there were some circumstantial reasons for the blank reaction. The controversy over Sraffa and Marx's concept of value was still going on, which I think put off many people from any attempt to consider Marx's theories of capitalist development. There were other versions of crisis theory available—Jim O'Connor's or John Weeks's. The ending of the book could be made to seem like a prediction of inter-imperialist wars, which was easy to dismiss. The only real debate about the book occurred when Michael Lebowitz attacked it in *Monthly Review,* and I replied, some time after it appeared. Overall, the book didn't seem to go anywhere.

Well, you were in good company. After all, Marx was so short of responses to Capital *he was reduced to writing a review of it under a pseudonym himself. In retrospect, what is striking is the extent to which your theory of crisis anticipates later work by two Marxists, who also came from outside the ranks of economists: Robert Brenner, from History, and Giovanni Arrighi, from Sociology. In both, space becomes a central category of explanation in a way nowhere to be found in the Marxist tradition, prior to your book. The register is more empirical—detailed tracking of post-war national economies in one case, long-run cycles of global expansion in the other—but the framework, and many of the key conclusions, are basically similar. Your account offers the pure model of this family of explanations, its tripartite analysis of the ways in which capital defers or resolves its tendencies to crisis—the structural fix, the spatial fix and the temporal fix—laid out with unexampled clarity.*

Looking back, you can say it was prophetic in that way. But what I hoped to be producing was a text that could be built on, and I was surprised that it wasn't taken in that spirit, but just lay there, rather flat. Of course, it had some currency among radical geographers, and maybe a few sociologists, but no one really used it as I'd have liked it to be. So today, for example, I might take this account of crisis and rub it against, say, world systems theory—in fact, that's probably what I will try to do in a course next year.

The deeper obstacle to a ready acceptance of what you were doing must lie in the difficulty Marxists have always had in confronting geography as a domain of natural contingency—the arbitrary shifts and accidents of the terrestrial crust, with their differential consequences for material life. The main propositions of historical materialism have a deductive structure independent of any spatial location, which never figures in them. The curious thing is that your theory of crisis in The Limits to Capital, *in one sense, respects this tradition—it develops a beautifully clear deductive structure. But it builds space into the structure as an ineliminable element of it. That was quite new. The geographically undifferentiated categories of* Capital *are put to work on natural-historical terrain—still represented abstractly, of course, in keeping with the demands of a deductive argument. That combination was calculated to throw conventional expectations.*

My own intention was, originally, to bounce some historical enquiries into urbanization off *The Limits to Capital*, but this became too massive a project, and I eventually decanted this stuff into the two volumes of essays that appeared in 1985, *Consciousness and the Urban Experience* and *The Urbanization of Capital*. Some of the material in them predates *Limits* itself. In 1976–77 I spent a year in Paris, with the aim of learning from French Marxist discussions, when I was still struggling with *Limits*—but it didn't work out that way. To tell the truth, I found Parisian intellectuals a bit arrogant, quite unable to handle anyone from North America—I felt a touch of sympathy when Edward Thompson launched his famous attack on Althusser, a couple of years later. On the other hand, Manuel Castells—who was not part of the big-name circus—was very warm and helpful, along with other urban sociologists, so my time was not lost. But what happened, instead, is that I became more and more intrigued by Paris as a city. It was much more fun exploring that than wrestling with reproduction schemes, and out of this fascination came the piece on Sacré Cœur and the Commune, which appeared in 1978. Then I backed into the Paris of the Second Empire, a wonderful subject, which became the topic of the longest essay in the two volumes. My interest was: how far might the sort of theoretical apparatus in *The Limits to Capital* play out in tangible situations?

A notable departure in the Second Empire essay—which could have been published as a short book—is the sudden appearance of so many literary sources, quite absent in your writing up till then. Now they cascade across the pages: Balzac, Dickens, Flaubert, Hardy, Zola, James. Had you been holding back a side of yourself, or was this in a sense a new horizon?

I'd always been reading this literature, but I never thought of using it in my work. Once I started to do so, I discovered how many historical ideas poetry or fiction can set alight. And once I made that turn, everything came flooding out. This had something to do with my position in academia: by then I was fairly secure; I didn't feel I had to stay within any narrow professional channels—not that I'd done that too much anyway. But I certainly felt a liberation in deliberately breaking out of them, not to speak of the pleasure of the texts themselves, after the hard grind of *Limits*.

It looks as if the change also prepared the way for the panoramic style of The Condition of Postmodernity. *Presumably by the mid-eighties your antennae were starting to twitch a bit, as talk of the postmodern took off. But what prompted the idea of a comprehensive book on the subject?*

My first impulse was one of impatience. Suddenly, there was all this talk of postmodernism as a category for understanding the world, displacing or submerging capitalism. So I thought: I've written *The Limits to Capital*; I've done all this research on Second Empire Paris; I know a certain amount about the origins of modernism, and a lot about urbanization, which features strongly in this new dispensation; so why not sit down and produce my own take on it? The result was one of the easiest books I've ever written. It took me about a year to write, flowing out without problems or anxieties. And once I embarked on it, of course, my response became more considered. I had no wish to deny the validity of some idea of postmodernity. On the contrary, I found the notion pointed to many developments to which we should be paying the closest attention. On the other hand, this shouldn't mean surrendering to the hype and exaggeration which was then surrounding it.

The book brings together your interdisciplinary interests in a remarkable way, starting—logically enough—from the urban in its strictest sense, with a discussion of redevelopment in Baltimore that makes two fundamental points against the uncritical celebrations of postmodernism as an 'overcoming' of the blights of architectural modernism. The standard argument of the time—blend of Jane Jacobs and Charles Jencks—went: modernism ruined our cities by its inhuman belief in rational planning, and its relentless monolithism of formal design; postmodernism, by contrast, respects the values of urban spontaneity and chaos, and engenders a liberating diversity of architectural styles. You displace both claims, pointing out that it was not so much devotion to principles of planning that produced so many ugly developments, but the subjection of planners to market imperatives, which have continued to zone cities as rigidly under postmodern as modern conditions; while greater diversity of formal styles has been as much a function of technological innovations, allowing use of new materials and shapes, as any aesthetic emancipation.

Yes, I thought it was important to show the new kinds of serial monotony that the supposed flowering of architectural fantasy could bring, and the naivety of a good many postmodernist staging effects—the simulacra of community you often find them striving for. But I also wanted to make it clear that to understand why these styles had taken such powerful hold, one needed to look at the underlying shifts in the real economy. That brought me to the whole area most famously theorized by the Regulation School in France. What had changed in the system of relations between capital and labour, and capital and capital, since the recession of the early seventies? For example, how far could we now speak of a new regime of 'flexible accumulation', based on temporary labour markets? Was that the material basis of the alterations in urban fabric we could see around us? The Regulationists struck me as quite right to focus on shifts in the wage contract, and reorganizations of the labour process; one could go quite a way with them there—but not to the notion that capitalism itself was somehow being fundamentally transformed. They were suggesting that one historical regime—Fordism—had given way to another—Flexible Accumulation—which had effectively replaced the first. But empirically, there is no evidence of such a wholesale change—'flexible accumulation' may be locally or temporarily predominant here or there, but we can't speak of systemic transformation. Fordism plainly persists over wide areas of industry, although of course it has not remained static either. In Baltimore, where Bethlehem Steel used to employ 30,000 workers, the same quantity of steel is now produced with less than 5,000— so the employment structure in the Fordist sector itself is no longer the same. The extent of this kind of downsizing, and the spread of temporary

contracts in the non-Fordist sector, have created some of the social conditions for the fluidity and insecurity of identities that typify what can be called
postmodernity. But that's only one side of the story. There are many different ways of making a profit—of gaining surplus value: whichever way works,
you are likely to find increasing experiments with it—so there might be a
trend towards flexible accumulation; but there are some key limits to the
process. Imagine what it would mean for social cohesion if everyone was on
temporary labour—what the consequences would be for urban life or civic
security. We can already see the damaging effects of even partial moves in
this direction. A universal transformation would pose acute dilemmas and
dangers for the stability of capitalism as a social order.

That goes for capital–labour; what about capital–capital relations?

What we see there is a dramatic asymmetry in the power of the state. The
nation-state remains the absolutely fundamental regulator of labour. The
idea that it is dwindling or disappearing as a centre of authority in the age of
globalization is a silly notion. In fact, it distracts attention from the fact that
the nation-state is now more dedicated than ever to creating a good business
climate for investment, which means precisely controlling and repressing
labour movements in all kinds of purposively new ways—cutting back the
social wage, fine-tuning migrant flows, and so on. The state is tremendously
active in the domain of capital–labour relations. But when we turn to relations between capitals, the picture is quite different. There the state has
truly lost power to regulate the mechanisms of allocation or competition, as
global financial flows have outrun the reach of any strictly national regulation. One of the main arguments in *The Condition of Postmodernity* is that
the truly novel feature of the capitalism that emerged out of the watershed
of the seventies is not so much an overall flexibility of labour markets as
an unprecedented autonomy of money capital from the circuits of material
production—a hypertrophy of finance, which is the other underlying basis
of postmodern experience and representation. The ubiquity and volatility of
money as the impalpable ground of contemporary existence is a key theme
of the book.

Yes, adapting Céline's title, Vie à Crédit. *Procedurally,* The Condition of
Postmodernity *actually follows Sartre's prescription for a revitalized Marxism
very closely. He defined its task as the necessity to fuse the analysis of objective
structures with the restitution of subjective experience, and representations of it,
in a single totalizing enterprise. That's a pretty good description of what you
were doing. What do you regard as the most important upshot of the book?*

The Condition of Postmodernity is the most successful work I've published—
it won a larger audience than all the others put together. When a book hits

a public nerve like that, different kinds of readers take different things away from it. For myself, the most innovative part of the book is its conclusion— the section where I explore what a postmodern experience means for people in terms of the way they live, and imagine, time and space. It is the theme of 'time–space compression', which I look at in various ways through the last chapters, that is the experimental punchline of the book.

The Condition of Postmodernity *came out in 1989. Two years earlier, you had moved from Baltimore to Oxford. What prompted the return to England?*

I felt I was spinning my wheels a bit in Baltimore at the time, so when I was asked if I would be interested in the Mackinder Chair at Oxford I threw my hat into the ring, for a different experience. I was curious to see what it would be like. I stayed at Oxford for six years, but I kept on teaching at Hopkins right the way through. My career has, in that sense, been rather conservative compared with most academics—I've been intentionally loyal to the places I've been. In Oxford, people kept treating me as if I'd just arrived from Cambridge, which I'd left in 1960—as if the intervening twenty-seven years had just been some waiting room in the colonies, before I came back to my natural roosting place at Oxbridge, which drove me nuts. I do have strong roots in English culture, which I feel very powerfully to this day. When I go back to the Kentish countryside that I cycled around, I still know all its lanes like the back of my hand. So in that sense, I've got a couple of toes firmly stuck in the native mud. These are origins I would never want to deny. But they were ones that also encouraged me to explore other spaces.

What about the university and city themselves?

Professionally, for the first time for many years I found myself in a conventional Geography department, which was very useful for me. It renewed my sense of the discipline, and reminded me what geographers think about how they think. Oxford doesn't change very fast, to put it mildly. Working there had its pleasurable sides, as well as the more negative ones. By and large, I liked the physical environment, but found the social environment—particularly college life—pretty terrible. Of course, you quickly become aware of the worldly advantages afforded by a position at Oxford. From being seen as a kind of maverick intellectual sitting in some weird transatlantic department, I was transformed into a respectable figure, for whom various unexpected doors subsequently opened. I first really discovered class when I went to Cambridge, in the fifties. At Oxford I was reminded of what it still means in Britain. Oxford as a city, of course, is another matter. Throughout my years in Baltimore, I always tried to maintain some relationship to local politics: we bought up an old library, and turned it into a community action centre, took part in campaigns for rent control, and generally tried to spark radical initiatives; it always seemed to me very important to connect my theoretical work with practical activity, in the locality. So when I got to Oxford, the local campaign to defend the Rover plant in Cowley offered a natural extension of this kind of engagement. For personal reasons, I couldn't become quite as active as in Baltimore, but it provided the same kind of connection to a tangible social conflict. It also led to some very interesting political discussions—recorded in the book, *The Factory and the City,* which Teresa Hayter and I produced around it—a fascinating experience. Soon afterwards I read Raymond Williams's novel, *Second Generation,* which is exactly about this, and was astonished by how well he captured so much of the reality at Cowley. So one of the first essays in *Justice, Nature and the Geography of Difference* became a reflection on his fiction.

Isn't there a range of affinities between the two of you? Williams's tone was always calm, but it was uncompromising. His stance was consistently radical, but it was also steadily realistic. His writing ignored disciplinary frontiers, crossing many intellectual boundaries and inventing new kinds of study, without any showiness. In these respects, your own work has a likeness. How would you define your relationship to him?

I never met Williams, though of course I knew of his writing from quite early on. *The Country and the City* was a fundamental text for me in teaching Urban Studies. At Hopkins I always felt an intense admiration for him, in a milieu where so many high-flying French intellectuals were overvalued. Williams never received this kind of academic validation, although what he had to say about language and discourse was just as interesting as any Parisian theorist, and often much more sensible. Of course, when I got to Oxford, I re-engaged with his work much more strongly. The account Williams gives of how he felt on arriving as a student in Cambridge matched almost exactly my own experience there. Then there was this powerful novel, set in Oxford, where I was now working, with its extraordinary interweaving of social and spatial themes. So I did feel a strong connection with him.

There seems to be an alteration of references in Justice, Nature and the Geography of Difference *in other ways, too. Heidegger and Whitehead become much more important than Hempel or Carnap. It is a very wide-ranging collection of texts. What is its main intention?*

It must be the least coherent book I've written. There may even be some virtue in its lack of cohesion, since the effect is to leave things open, for different possibilities. What I really wanted to do was to take some very basic geographical concepts—space, place, time, environment—and show that they are central to any kind of historical-materialist understanding of the world. In other words, that we have to think of a historical-*geographical* materialism, and that we need some conception of dialectics for that. The last three chapters offer examples of what might result. Geographical issues are always present—they have to be—in any materialist approach to history, but they have never been tackled systematically. I wanted to ground the need to do so. I probably didn't succeed, but at least I tried.

One of the strands of the work is a critical engagement with radical ecology, which strikes a characteristic balance. You warn against environmental cata-strophism on the Left. Should we regard this as the latter-day equivalent of economic collapse theories of an older Marxism?

There was quite a good debate about this with John Bellamy Foster in *Monthly Review*, which laid the issues out very plainly on the table.[3] I'm extremely sympathetic to many environmental arguments, but my experi-ence of working in an Engineering department, with its sense for pragmatic solutions, has made me chary of doomsday prophesies—even when these come from scientists themselves, as they sometimes do. I've spent a lot of time trying to persuade engineers that they should take the idea that knowl-edge—including their own technical ingenuity—is still socially constructed. But when I argue with people from the humanities, I find myself having to point out to them that when a sewage system doesn't work, you don't ring up the postmodernists, you call in the engineers—as it happens, my department has been incredibly creative in sewage disposal. So I am on the boundary between the two cultures. The chapter on dialectics in *Justice, Nature and the Geography of Difference* was designed to try to explain to engineers and scientists what this mystery might be about. That's why it is cast more in terms of natural process than philosophical category. If I had been teaching dialectics in a Humanities programme, I would, of course, have had to talk of Hegel; but addressing engineers, it made more sense to refer to Whitehead or Bohm or Lewontin—scientists, familiar with the activities of science. This gives a rather different take on dialectical argumentation, compared to the more familiar, literary-philosophical one.

Another major strand in the book—it's there in the title—is an idea of justice. This is not a concept well received in the Marxist tradition. Historically, it is certainly true that a sense of injustice has been a powerful—if culturally vari-able—lever of social revolt, as Barrington Moore and others have shown. This hasn't seemed to require, however, any articulated theory of rights, or justice. In modern times, there have been many attempts to found these, without much success. Marx, following Bentham, was withering about their philosophical basis. Why do you think these objections should be overridden?

---

[3] See Harvey, 'Marxism, Metaphors and Ecological Politics', *Monthly Review*, vol. 49, no. 11 (April 1998).

Marx reacted against the idea of social justice, because he saw it as an attempt at a purely distributive solution to problems that lay in the mode of production. Redistribution of income within capitalism could only be a palliative—the solution was a transformation of the mode of production. There is a great deal of force in that resistance. But in thinking about it, I was increasingly struck by something else Marx wrote—his famous assertion in the introduction to the *Grundrisse,* that production, exchange, distribution and consumption are all moments of one organic totality, each totalizing the others. It seemed to me that it's very hard to talk about those different moments without implying some notion of justice—if you like, of the distributive effects of a transformation in the mode of production. I have no wish to give up on the idea that the fundamental aim is just this transformation, but if you confine it to that, without paying careful attention to what this would mean in the world of consumption, distribution and exchange, you are missing a political driving force. So I think there's a case for reintroducing the idea of justice, but not at the expense of the fundamental aim of changing the mode of production. There's also, of course, the fact that some of the achievements of social democracy—often called distributive socialism in Scandinavia—are not to be sneered at. They are limited, but real gains. Finally, there is a sound tactical reason for the Left to reclaim ideas of justice and rights, which I touch on in my latest book, *Spaces of Hope.* If there is a central contradiction in the bourgeoisie's own ideology throughout the world today, it lies in its rhetoric of rights. I was very impressed, looking back at the UN Declaration of Rights of 1948, with its Articles 21–24, on the rights of labour. You ask yourself: what kind of world would we be living in today if these had been taken seriously, instead of being flagrantly violated in virtually every capitalist country on the globe? If Marxists give up the idea of rights, they lose the power to put a crowbar into that contradiction.

Wouldn't a traditional Marxist reply: But precisely, the proof of the pudding is in the eating? You can have all these fine lists of social rights, they've been sitting there, solemnly proclaimed for fifty years, but have they made a blind bit of difference? Rights are constitutionally malleable as a notion—anyone can invent them, to their own satisfaction. What they actually represent are interests, and it is the relative power of these interests that determines which—equally artificial—construction of them predominates. After all, what is the most universally acknowledged human right, after the freedom of expression, today? The right to private property. Everyone should have the freedom to benefit from their talents, to transmit the fruits of their labours to the next generation, without interference from others—these are inalienable rights. Why should we imagine rights to health or employment would trump them? In this sense, isn't the discourse of rights, though teeming with contrary platitudes, structurally empty?

No, it's not empty, it's full. But what is it full of? Mainly, those bourgeois notions of rights that Marx was objecting to. My suggestion is that we could fill it with something else, a socialist conception of rights. A political project needs a set of goals to unite around, capable of defeating its opponents, and a dynamic sense of the potential of rights offers this chance—just because the enemy can't vacate this terrain, on which it has always relied so much. If an organization like Amnesty International, which has done great work for political and civil rights, had pursued economic rights with the same persistence, the earth would be a different place today. So I think it's important that the Marxist tradition engage in dialogue in the language of rights, where central political arguments are to be won. Around the world today, social rebellions nearly always spontaneously appeal to some conception of rights.

In the first essay of Spaces of Hope, *'The Difference a Generation Makes', you contrast the situation of a reading group on* Capital *in the early seventies with a comparable one today. Then, you remark, it required a major effort to connect the abstract categories of a theory of the mode of production with the daily realities of the world outside where, as you put it, the concerns of Lenin rather than those of Marx held the stage, as anti-imperialist struggles and revolutionary movements battled across the world. By the nineties, on the other hand, there was little or no revolutionary ferment left, but the headlines of every morning's paper, as corporate acquisitions or stock prices relentlessly dominated the news, read like direct quotations from* Theories of Surplus Value. *Reviewing the contemporary scene at the end of the essay, you criticize the overuse of Gramsci's adage—taken from Romain Rolland—'optimism of the will, pessimism of the intellect', arguing for the validity of a robust optimism of the intellect, too. The conclusion is quite unforced, it comes as entirely natural. But it casts an interesting light on your development. For what it suggests is that the whole Communist experience, unfolding across a third of the earth's land mass, scarcely registered in your line of sight at all—as if you were neither anticommunist, nor pro-communist, but developed your own very energetic and creative Marxism, while bypassing this huge drama altogether. If the collapse of the* USSR, *and the hopes once invested in it, has been the principal background to pessimism of the intellect on the Left, it is logical that you would be rather unaffected. But it still raises the question of how you could mentally avoid such a large object on the horizon.*

Part of the answer is circumstance. I had no background in Soviet geography, and though I was interested in China, I was never involved in anything to do with it. But if that was in a sense fortuitous, there was a temperamental preference as well. Marx was my anchor, and what Marx wrote was a critique of capitalism. The alternative comes out of that critique, and nowhere else. So I was always more interested in trying to apply the critique and see the alternative where I actually was, in Baltimore, or Oxford, or wherever I happened to be. That may be my own form of localism. On the one hand, I develop a general theory, but on the other, I need to feel this rootedness in something going on in my own backyard. Marxism was so often supposed to be mainly about the Soviet Union or China, and I wanted to say it was about capitalism, which is rampant in the USA, and that must have priority for us. So one effect of this was to insulate me a bit from the fallout of the collapse of Communism. But I should also concede that this is a real limitation of my own work. For all my geographical interests, it has remained Eurocentric, focused on metropolitan zones. I have not been exposed much to other parts of the world.

In your most recent writing, you turn a number of times to the theme of evolution, engaging with E. O. Wilson's work in a sympathetic if critical spirit, very unlike most responses to his writing on the Left. His notion of the 'consilience' of the sciences might well appeal to anyone once attracted to Carnap, though you make clear your own reservations. But it is Wilson's emphasis on the genetic dispositions of every species that offers the occasion for a remarkable set of reflexions on human evolution, which you suggest has left the species a 'repertoire' of capacities and powers—competition, adaptation, cooperation, environmental transformation, spatial and temporal ordering—out of which every society articulates a particular combination. Capitalism, you argue, requires all of these—not least its own forms of cooperation—yet gives primacy to a particular mode of competition. But if competition itself could never be eliminated, as an innate propensity of humanity, its relations with the other powers are in no way unalterable. Socialism is thus best conceived as a reconfiguration of the basic human repertoire, in which its constituent elements find another and better balance. This is a striking response to the claims of sociobiology on its own terrain. But a committed champion of the existing system would reply: Yes, but just as in nature the survival of the fittest is the rule whatever the ecological niche, so in society the reason capitalism has won out is its competitive superiority. It is competition that is the absolute centre of the system, lending it an innovative dynamic that no alternative which relativized or demoted the competitive drive into another combination could hope to withstand. You might try to mobilize competition for socialism, but you would want to subordinate it as a principle within a more complex framework, whereas we don't subordinate it—that is our unbeatable strength. What would be your reply to this kind of objection?

My answer is—oh, but you do: you do subordinate competition in all kinds of areas. Actually, the whole history of capitalism is unthinkable without the setting up of a regulatory framework to control, direct and limit competition. Without state power to enforce property and contract law, not to speak of transport and communications, modern markets could not begin to function. Next time you're flying into London or New York, imagine all those pilots suddenly operating on the competitive principle: they all try to hit the ground first, and get the best gate. Would any capitalist relish that idea? Absolutely not. When you look closely at the way a modern economy works, the areas in which competition genuinely rules turn out be quite circumscribed. If you think of all the talk of flexible accumulation, a lot of it revolves around diversification of lines and niche markets. What would the history of capitalism be without diversification? But actually the dynamic behind diversification is a flight from competition—the quest for specialized markets is, much of the time, a way of evading its pressures. In fact, it would be very interesting to write a history of capitalism exploring its utilization of each of the six elements of the basic repertoire I outline, tracing the changing ways it has brought them together, and put them to work, in different epochs. Knee-jerk hostility to Wilson isn't confined to the Left, but it is not productive. Advances in biology are teaching us a great deal about our make-up, including the physical wiring of our minds, and will tell us much more in the future. I don't see how one can be a materialist and not take all this very seriously. So in the case of sociobiology, I go back to my belief in the value of rubbing different conceptual blocks together—putting E. O. Wilson in dialogue with Marx. There are obviously major differences, but also some surprising commonalities—so let's collide the two thinkers against each other. I'm not going to claim I've done it right, but this is a discussion we need. The section of *Spaces of Hope* which starts to talk about this is called 'Conversations on the Plurality of Alternatives', and that's the spirit in which we should approach this. I have questions, not solutions.

What is your view of the present prospect for the system of capital? Limits set out a general theory of its mechanisms of crisis—over-accumulation, tied to the rigidity of blocs of fixed capital, and of its typical solutions—devalorization, credit expansion, spatial reorganization. The Condition of Postmodernity *looked at the way these surfaced in the seventies and eighties. Where are we now? There seem to be two possible readings of the present conjuncture, of opposite sign, allowed by your framework, with a third perhaps just over the horizon. The first would take as its starting point your observation in that book that the devalorization necessary to purge excess capital is most effective when it occurs, not in the classic form of a crash, but rather slowly and gradually—cleansing the system without provoking dangerous turmoil within it. On one view, isn't this what has been imperceptibly happening, through successive waves of downsizing and line-shifting, since the start of the long downturn of the seventies—the kind of cumulative transformation you cited at Bethlehem Steel; finally unleashing a new dynamic in the mid-nineties, with a recovery of profits, stable prices, surge of high-tech investment and increase in productivity growth, giving the system a new lease of life? On another view, equally compatible with your framework, this is not the underlying story. Rather, what we have mainly been seeing is an explosion of the credit system, releasing a tremendous wave of asset inflation—in other words, a runaway growth of fictitious capital—one that is bound to lead to a sharp correction when the stock bubble bursts, returning us to the realities of continued and unresolved over-accumulation. There is also a third alternative, which would give principal weight to the fall of Soviet Communism in Eastern Europe and Russia, and the Open Door to foreign trade and investment in China. These developments pose the question: isn't capitalism in the process of acquiring—in your terms—a gigantic 'spatial fix' with this sudden, huge expansion in its potential field of operations? This would still be in its early phase—as yet the US has a large negative trade balance with China—but aren't we witnessing the construction of a World Trade Organization order that promises to be the equivalent of a Bretton Woods system for the new century, in which for the first time the frontiers of capitalism reach to the ends of the earth? These are three different scenarios, all of which could be grounded in your work. Do you have a provisional judgement of their relative plausibilities?*

I don't think there's any simple choice between these explanations. Both a process of steady, ongoing devalorization—downsizing, reorganizing and outsourcing—and of spatial transformation, along lines traditionally associated with imperialism, are very much part of the real story. But these massive restructurings wouldn't have been possible without the incredible power of fictitious capital today. Every major episode of devalorization or geographical expansion has been imprinted by the role of financial institutions, in what amounts to a quite new dynamic of fictitious capital. Such capital is, of course, no mere figment of the imagination. To the extent that it brings about profitable transformations of the productive apparatus, running through the whole M–C–M' cycle, it ceases to be fictitious and becomes realized. But to do so it always depends on a basis in expectations, which must be socially constructed. People have to believe that wealth—mutual funds, pensions, hedge funds—will continue to increase indefinitely. To secure these expectations is a work of hegemony that falls to the state, and its relays in the media. This is something the two great theorists of the last world crisis understood very well—it is instructive to read Gramsci and Keynes side by side. There may be objective processes that block devalorization, or resist geographical incorporation; but the system is also peculiarly vulnerable to the subjective uncertainties of a runaway growth in fictitious capital. Keynes was haunted by the question: how are the animal spirits of investors to be sustained? A tremendous ideological battle is necessary to maintain confidence in the system, in which the activity of the state—we need only think of the role of the Federal Reserve in the nineties—is all-important. Someone who has written well about this, in a non-economic way, is Slavoj Žižek. So the three explanations are not mutually exclusive: they need to be put together, under the sign of a new drive for hegemony. This is a system that has withstood the shocks from East Asia and Long-Term Capital Management, but each time it was a near-run thing. How long it will last no one can say.

But while the adaptability of capitalism is one of its prime weapons in class struggle, we should not underestimate the vast swathe of opposition it continues to generate. That opposition is fragmented, often highly localized, and endlessly diverse in terms of aims and methods. We have to think of ways to help mobilize and organize this opposition, both actual and latent, so that it becomes a global force and has a global presence. The signs of coming together are there. At the level of theory, we need to find a way to identify commonalities within the differences, and so develop a politics that is genuinely collective in its concerns, yet sensitive to what remains irreducibly distinctive in the world today—particularly geographical distinctions. That would be one of my key hopes.

4

João Pedro Stédile

Asada Akira

Wang Hui

João Pedro Stédile was born in 1953 into a family of small farmers in the Lagoa Vermelha district of Rio Grande do Sul in southern Brazil. He studied economics at the Pontifical University of Rio Grande do Sul and then at the Autonomous National University of Mexico (UNAM). Since that time he has devoted himself to the struggle for agrarian reform in Brazil, both as a writer and as a national leader of the Landless Workers Movement (MST), of which he was a co-founder. His numerous publications include the three volumes of A Questão Agraria no Brasil *(2005) and, with Francisco de Oliveira and José de Genoíno,* Classes Sociais em Mudança e a Luta pelo Socialismo *(2000).*

João Pedro Stédile lives in São Paulo, where he gave this interview to Francisco de Oliveira in 2002.

João Pedro Stédile

Landless Battalions

Which region of Brazil do you come from, and what was your family background and education?

I was born in 1953 in Rio Grande do Sul, and grew up on my parents' farm there until I was about eighteen. There was a community of small farmers of Italian extraction in the region—it had been colonized in the nineteenth century by peasants from those parts of what was then the Austro-Hungarian Empire. My mother's family was originally from the Veneto, and my father's from what is today the Italian Tyrol. My grandfather came to Brazil in 1899. He was a farmer, too. My grandparents were almost certainly illiterate, but my father and mother had three years of primary school. But this was the period of industrialization, in the sixties, and my brothers and sisters already had wider horizons—they wanted to study. One of them became a metalworker. Some of the others went to the city, too.

The greatest influence on me at that stage was the Catholic Church—the Capuchin friars, in particular. In all the colonized regions of Rio Grande do Sul—Colônia, Caxias do Sul, Bento Gonçalves and the surrounding areas—the Church had a very strong presence, and the Capuchins were doing interesting work, preaching against injustice and taking up social issues. I owe my education to my uncle, a Capuchin, who helped me get a place at the Catholic grammar school where they taught the entire curriculum. I loved studying, and in the final year I applied for the advanced course. I was living at the house of an uncle by then, because my father had died. I worked on the land by day and studied by night, walking the ten kilometres to school. I knew I wanted to carry on learning so I moved to Porto Alegre. I worked in various places, still earning my living by day, reading economics by night.

I had a stroke of luck in my second year at Porto Alegre. There was a competition for posts in Rio Grande do Sul's State Agriculture Department. I was from a farming family and I understood agriculture: I decided this was the route I should take. With the Agriculture Department, I'd travel a lot in the interior of the state and my work would still be linked to the farmers' lives. I got the posting, and from there I became involved with the local Sindicato dos Trabalhadores Rurais (Rural Workers Union), especially the grape farmers. My first experience as a social activist was working with the Union's members to calculate the price of grapes. Every year there was a battle with the buyers over this—the big vintners would name a sum and none of the growers could contest it, since they had no idea how to calculate what the harvest was really worth. We went round to the communities, sat down with the farmers and worked out how much it actually cost to produce a kilo of grapes, from trellising the vines to the manual labour of the harvest—since I was reading economics, I was able to help. In the process, the farmers became increasingly conscious, they got together and began to confront the wine producers. This coincided with the multinationals' entry into the market, and we won some important victories—there was a leap in the average price the farmers got for their grapes. At the same time, I'd maintained my links with the Church, and when the Commissão Pastoral da Terra (Pastoral Commission on Land; CPT) was set up in 1975, I met with them to discuss how to organize the farmers.

In 1976, I won a bursary from the Agriculture Department to go and study in Mexico for two years. It was there that I met Francisco Julião, from whom I learned a tremendous amount.[1] I only ever had two questions for him: 'What did you get wrong?' and 'What did you get right?'. It was a great privilege to be at UNAM at the same time as some of the major exiled intellectuals of the Brazilian Left such as Rui Mauro Marini, who gave courses on *Das Kapital*; Teotônio dos Santos himself, in Sociology; Vânia Bambirra, who taught us dependency theory. I concentrated mainly on agrarian questions, but I took a few courses in economics and other disciplines. There were scholars from other Latin American countries who were also in exile in Mexico—Pedro Vuskovic, Allende's Economics minister; Jacques Chonchol, Allende's minister for Agrarian Reform. I was very young, but I learnt a phenomenal amount from them. It was probably the best period of my life.

What were the origins of the Sem Terra Movement?

The MST was the result of the conjunction of three basic factors. First, the economic crisis of the late seventies put an end to the industrialization cycle in Brazil, begun by Kubitschek in 1956. Young people had been leaving the farms for the city, and getting jobs quite easily. Now they had to stay in the countryside and find a living there. The second factor was the work the friars were doing. In the sixties, the Catholic Church had largely

---

[1] Francisco Julião (1915–99): leader of the Farmers' Leagues in the northeast of Brazil, federal deputy for the Brazilian Socialist Party (PSB); exiled after the military coup in 1964.

supported the military dictatorship, but with the growing ferment of liberation theology there was a change of orientation, the emergence of the CPT
and a layer of progressive bishops. Before, the line had been: 'No need to
worry, you'll have your land in heaven.' Now it was: 'Since you've already
got land in heaven, let's struggle for it here as well.' The friars played a
good role in stirring up the farmers and getting them organized. And the
third factor was the growing climate of struggle against the military dictatorship in the late seventies, which automatically transformed even local labour
conflicts into political battles against the government.

It was against this background that land occupations began to spread
throughout the South, the North and the Northeast. None of them were
spontaneous—all were clearly planned and organized by local activists—but
there were no connexions between them. From 1978 onwards, the first
great strikes began to take place in the cities: they served as a good example
of how to lose your fear. In the five years from 1978 to 1983—what you
could call the genesis of the movement—there was an outbreak of large-scale
land occupations, and people really did begin to lose their fear of struggling against the dictatorship. The role of the CPT was of crucial importance
here—the Church was the only body that had what you might call a capil-
lary organization, across the whole country. They soon realized that these
occupations were happening in different areas, and started setting up meetings between the local leaders. I'd already been involved in helping organize
various actions in Rio Grande do Sul, the first one in September 1979. The
CPT contacted me and other comrades and we began to hold national meetings, along the lines Julião and I had discussed. The farmers talked things
over, in their own way: 'How do you do it in the Northeast?', 'How do you
do it in the North?'. Slowly, we realized we were facing the same problems,
and attempting similar solutions. Throughout 1983 and 1984 we held big
debates about how to build an organization that would spread the struggle
for land—and, above all, one that could transform these localized conflicts
into a major battle for agrarian reform. We knew it changed nothing just
to bring a few families together, move onto unused land and think that
was the end. We were well aware from the agrarian struggles of the past
that if farmers don't organize themselves, don't fight for more than just a
piece of land, they'll never reach a wider class consciousness and be able to
grapple with the underlying problems—because land in itself does not free
the farmer from exploitation.

In January 1984 we held an Encontro Nacional in Cascavel, Paraná,
where we analysed all these questions and resolved to set up an organization. The name was of no great importance, but the press already had a
nickname for us. Every time we occupied some land the newspapers would
say, 'There go the Sem Terra again'. Fine, since they called us that, we'd be
the 'Movimento dos Sem Terra'. We were ideologically more inclined to call
ourselves the 'Movement of Workers for Agrarian Reform', because the idea

was to build a social force that would go beyond the struggle just for land itself. But history never depends entirely on people's intentions. We got our reputation as the 'Sem Terra', so the name stuck; the most we did was to invent the abbreviation—MST.

Another important decision we took at the Encontro Nacional was to organize ourselves as an autonomous movement, independent of the political parties. Our analysis of the farmers' movements of Latin America and Brazil taught us that whenever a mass movement was subordinated to a party, it was weakened by the effects of inner-party splits and factional battles. It was not that we didn't value parties, or thought it was wrong to join them. But the movement had to be free from external political direction. It also had to be independent of the Catholic Church. Many of the farmers were strongly influenced by the Church and argued that since it had helped us so much we should form a movement of Christians for agrarian reform. Fortunately, some of the most politically aware comrades were from the Church. They had had previous experience with Ação Católica or in the JOCs, and they themselves warned us against it—the moment a bishop comes to a different decision from the mass organization, the organization is finished. We also decided then on the general tactics we would use. We were convinced that the fight for agrarian reform could only move forward if it were a mass struggle, so we had to try to involve as many people as possible. When we set out on a land occupation, we would try to take everyone along—fathers, mothers, sons, daughters, old people, children, the lot. We listed the ten or twelve objectives our movement would serve—the struggle for agrarian reform, for a different Brazil, for a society without exploiters. That was the initial framework.

So the movement didn't start out from Rio Grande do Sul?

No—that's the usual story, but it's not completely true. It's been characterized like that for various reasons. Firstly, because it was in Rio Grande do Sul, north-east of Porto Alegre, that we built the Encruzilhada Natalino encampment, and the press turned that into a historic event. It was based at the junction of three counties, Sarandi, Ronda Alta and Passo Fundo—hence the name, *encruzilhada* [crossroads]. The president, General Figueiredo, sent the army to destroy the settlement, under the command of Major Curió. It was the dictatorship that politicized our struggle. All we wanted was land, but overnight the encampment was encircled by the Federal police, the army and even the air force, to airlift the farmers to the Mato Grosso—they took over a hundred families, in the end. Curió was such a symbol of the military repression that all those who opposed the dictatorship began to sympathize with us, and Encruzilhada Natalino became a counter-symbol, like the strike at the Scania truck factory, or Lula's imprisonment. There's a commemorative monument there now. The encampment grew into a historic nexus for the Sem Terra—we took over several unproductive *fazendas*—large proper-ties, or ranches—in the area and eventually a new municipality was set up there. It's called Pontão, because 80 per cent of the population are squatters, including the mayor. It's a mini-free territory, the result of agrarian reform.

That was one experience that gave the movement a southern imprint, although, as I said, there were land occupations going on in the Northeast, the North, the Bico do Papagaio, and here in São Paulo, in the Andradina region, between 1979 and 1983—though only a few of these became well known. The other factor that's contributed to the impression of a southern bent to the Sem Terra Movement is that this is where many of our activists have come from—for the simple reason that, south of the Paraná, farmers' children had a better chance of an education: a fundamental requirement if you're going to help to articulate struggles, to get in contact with people, to establish relations with them. Dozens of militants from the South could then be sent to other regions—not because there was an ideology of wanting to teach northerners, but because of the different educational level. We adopted a method others have used before: the Brazilian Army posts officers from the South across the whole country, the Federal Savings Bank transfers its employees—so does the Catholic Church.

Could you describe a typical land occupation?

For two or three months, our activists visit the villages and communities in an area where there are lots of landless farmers, and start work on raising awareness—proselytizing, if you like. They explain to people that they have a right to land, that the constitution has a clause on agrarian reform but that the government doesn't apply it. Next, we ask the farmers if there is a big, underused landholding in the region, because the law is clear: where there is a large unproductive property, the government is obliged to expro-priate it. They get involved in the discussion, and start to become more conscious. Then comes the decision: 'You have a right to land. There are unused properties in the region. There is only one way to force the govern-ment to expropriate them. You think they'll do it if we write them a letter? Asking the mayor is a waste of time, especially if he's a landowner. You could talk to the priest, but if he's not interested, what's the point? We have to organize and take over that land ourselves.'

When that decision is reached, we can bring to bear all the historical expe-rience we've accumulated—which, from a political point of view, is simply what the Sem Terra Movement does: our role is to pass on what we've learnt, as a class. As far as land occupations are concerned, we know our business—not everything, but a lot. Everyone has to go, all the families together. It has to be done during the night to avoid the police. Those who want to join in have to organize themselves into committees of fifteen or twenty people. Then, each committee—there may be twenty or so of them—has to hire a truck, and set up a kitty to buy canvas and stock up on provisions. It takes three or four months to get ready. One day there's a meeting of representatives from each of the fifteen-person committees to decide when the occupation will take place. The decision has to be kept secret. On the night, the hired trucks arrive, well before daybreak, and go round the communities, pick up all they can carry and then set off for the property. The families have one night to take possession of the area and build their shelters, so that early the next morning, when the proprietor realizes what's happened, the encampment is already set up. The committee chooses a family to reconnoitre the place, to find where there are sources of water, where there are trees for shade. There are a lot of factors involved in setting up an open-air encampment. It's better if you're near a road, because then you don't have to carry so much on your back. This sort of logistical experience has a big influence on how an occupation works out. But success really depends on the number of families involved—the more there are, the less favourable the balance of forces for the proprietor and the police; the fewer the families, the easier it is to evict them, and the more limited the political repercussions will be.

By morning, the settlement is established—and the basis for conflict is sprung. It will be covered in the press, and the proprietor will apply to the authorities, asking for the squatters to be evicted. Our lawyers will arrive on the scene, arguing that the property is large and unproductive, and therefore in breach of the constitution. From the Sem Terra point of view, if we win it's because the INCRA makes an inspection of the property and decides to expropriate.[2] If we lose, it's because the proprietor has enough force at his disposal to carry out the eviction. If the police come to evict the squatters, we always try to avoid there being violence. The encampment gets shifted—to the edge of the road, for example—and we go on from there, to occupy another unused property. But the main thing for a group, once it's gathered in an encampment, is to stay united, to keep putting pressure on the government.

The biggest occupation of all was in 1996, on Fazenda Giacometti, in Paraná. The property took up 80,000 hectares—nearly 200,000 acres—of good, fertile land, covering three municipalities. It was an insult to society that that land was lying unused—all the farmers in the region were enraged about it; everybody was. We started work in the region, discussing with the farmers, and decided to set up an encampment by the side of the road where people could gather if they wanted to join the occupation, rather than going to the Fazenda Giacometti straightaway. We kept the encampment there open for a week, and more and more people turned up. When the leaders decided on the date for the occupation, we assumed it would be the traditional method—they'd hire trucks, pile everyone into them and

---

[2] INCRA: Instituto Nacional de Colonização e Reforma Agrária.

drive to the site. But on the night, there were so many families involved that we decided not to use the lorries. We walked the twenty-one kilometres—thirteen miles—all through the night. When we reached the Fazenda the day was breaking, and the police were called out immediately. But there were so many people—ten thousand squatters, with their bundles of belongings on their heads—that all the police could do was to help the procession down the road, and make sure there were no car accidents. The sheer scale of numbers transformed the balance of forces. That was our biggest victory, and since we knew it would be a historic event, we invited Sebastião Salgado to take photographs of the march. It was an epic, the greatest of all the land occupations we've carried out to this day.

What is the structure of the MST—how many are involved? How are decisions taken, at local and national level?

We are a mass social movement, whose principal objective is to gather people for the struggle. How do you join the Sem Terra Movement? There is no membership, no cards, and it's not enough just to declare that one wants to be in the MST. The only way to join is to take part in one of the land occupations, to be active on the ground. That's how we get members. It's very hard to pin down statistically. We wanted to get away from party or union-style bureaucracy—filling in forms, and subscription fees. When your base is poor, illiterate farmers, you have to develop ways of going about things that are as open as possible, drawing people in rather than putting up barriers or bureaucratic hiccups.

To describe the MST's structure: our base is the mass of those who would benefit from agrarian reform—according to the last IBGE census, around four million landless families.[3] This is the layer we're working with. Many of them will come along on some sort of action—protest marches, for example—but not all will dare to occupy land. That's a very radical form of struggle, and you need to have been through several previous stages first. Recently the government tried out a little test on us. They started putting out propaganda saying that it wasn't true that there are so many landless farmers in Brazil, that the MST had invented it. Raul Jungman, Cardoso's minister for Agrarian Development, went on TV to launch a programme calling for the landless to register by post with the INCRA, promising the government would allocate them land. He thought there would be a tiny response, and we'd be demoralized. We took up the challenge. We went to our base and campaigned for postal registration. We said: 'You see this government propaganda saying, whoever wants land should write in for it? Come on, let's reply en masse. Let's organize and do it collectively, instead of on our own'. During 2001, 857,000 families registered, and the

---

[3] IBGE: Instituto Brasileiro de Geografia e Estatística.

government found themselves in a pickle—they couldn't give land to any of them, because that would have meant allocating it to all. It was a simple, effective way of proving the existence of the millions of landless in Brazil.

Many of these people have been mobilized during the eighteen years of the Sem Terra Movement. Some 350,000 families have taken over land. In February 2002, we had 80,000 families camped on roadsides or on unused properties, their problems unresolved—they're in the front line in the battle against the government. There have been about 20,000 activists involved in this—the comrades with the greatest ideological clarity, who've helped to organize the rest. The activists come on courses, they take part in the regional and state-level meetings, where our leading bodies are elected—these consist of between fifteen and twenty-one comrades. Every two years we hold national meetings, where a national commission is elected, with representatives from each state. Every five years we hold a nationwide congress, which is always massive—a moment of real political debate. At the last congress—the fourth at national level—in August 2000, in Brasília, we spent five days in a sports hall with 11,750 delegates. From what I know of farmers' movements, this was the largest farmers' congress in Latin America, and maybe in the world. Though we could be beaten by the Indians and the Chinese. You can get ten thousand people there easily— click your fingers and you get more. But it was certainly the biggest in Latin America.

I also want to stress how much we've learnt from earlier farmers' movements in Brazil and throughout Latin America. It was this that taught us we should organize in collective bodies, that we should have committees to govern political decision-making and the allocation of tasks—that we shouldn't have a president. Even the encampments run themselves and resolve their problems through committees—an encampment doesn't have a president. It's the same at regional, state and national levels—I'm one of twenty-one national directors, but decisions are taken by the whole committee, and tasks divided between us. Some are better known than others, because the press always go for the chatterboxes. But the best known aren't the most vital for the organization. The most important are those who stay quiet but take decisive actions for the movement to grow and spread.

How many Brazilian states do these delegates come from?

Of the twenty-seven states, our movement has a presence in twenty-three. We're strongest where there are most farmers, in the South and Northeast— or, in order of importance: the Northeast and the South. The Southeast is highly urbanized, there aren't many poor people left on the land—they're either rural wage-earners, who dream of going to the big city, or else the *lumpens*, who live on the city outskirts. In the North and West-Central areas there aren't many landless farmers. It's the agricultural frontier—even if there was a big settler movement in these parts, there'd still be a good deal of land available. The most common form of action there is individual initiatives. A tenant moves onto a patch, and for a few years he can delude himself he has land of his own, until someone takes it away from him. In Amazonas, Acre, Roraima and Amapá, the MST doesn't exist, because there is no mass base of farmers. Sometimes sectors of the Catholic Church and the rural unions try to tempt us to work there. The PT runs Acre now, and every time we meet the governor he asks when we're going to come there and organize.[4] The answer is: when you have some farmers. There's no point us going there, putting up banners and opening an office—our problem is not lack of branch offices. If there aren't large numbers who will organize to occupy land, there is not going to be a farmers' movement. That's why we prefer to concentrate our work in regions where there is a real base of land-less farmers—hence the priority of the South and Northeast.

How is the MST financed, and by whom? Does the greater part of your funding come from your own activities, or are there other sources?

In terms of the land occupations themselves, we have a principle: all the costs have to be borne by those who participate. Otherwise things get confused: 'I don't know who' buys the tents, 'I don't know who' pays for the transport; the farmers end up depending on 'I don't know who'. At the first sign of trouble they'd say, 'No, I didn't come here on my own, so-and-so brought me' and they'd leave, because they wouldn't see the struggle as a personal sacrifice. We could carry out much larger actions if we asked for money from outside—but it would have a disastrous ideological effect. Instead, every family taking part in an occupation spends months working, to get materials for shelter, to get food—they know that they'll be surrounded by police, that they'll have no food, that they'll have to hold out for weeks until there are political repercussions, and solidarity begins to bring in resources. On a lot of occupations we've had to reduce the number of families taking part because some were so poor, we would have had to pay for their transport and shelter. We've been faced with this dilemma many times.

Secondly, there is a great deal of solidarity at a local level. Trade unions and churches help us with training courses and funds, which we use to develop the movement. But another of our principles is that everything must be decentralized—we don't have a national treasury, or any centralized state-level ones. Thirdly, when we occupy land, every farmer—if he wants to be in the MST—agrees to give 2 per cent of the encampment's production to the movement. This doesn't go to some far-off authority, but to help the people camped in the region, to organize the movement and train activists. Sometimes a settlement produces very little, and the comrades say: 'We can't

---

[4] PT: Partido Trabalhista.

give you 2 per cent, we're working like dogs just to feed ourselves. But we can release two of our people, and we'll support their families, so that those two can go to train other landless farmers.' This is a very important contribution, although money doesn't enter into it.

Fourthly, when we help set up an encampment we provide for the community's basic needs: housing, electricity, school, teacher training, and so on. But these should be the responsibility of the state, so we try to force the government to make the local authorities pay for these. We get further where the state governments are more progressive; where they are more conservative, it's harder for us. For example, we have agreements with the universities for training seven hundred MST teachers a year. The government bears the cost, but we decide on the curriculum and the orientation. It's the same when we need an agronomist—the state should supply one, it's their responsibility. To those who say 'Ah, the government's paying to train your teachers, you've been co-opted', we reply: 'No, we want to train seven thousand, but they won't give us the money.'

These are our usual sources of funds, although we also get some help from organizations in Europe and the States. Incredible as it seems, there's a group of US businessmen who send us funds every so often, without us even asking. In general the money from Europe goes for training activists. We're building a school—the National Florestan Fernandes School, here on the Via Dutra—as a joint project with the European Union. We wanted it to be near São Paulo, where there's a concentration of well-qualified leftist teachers and intellectuals—it's much easier to get them to come fifty kilometres out of São Paulo than to resettle them in the Normandia encampment in the interior of Pernambuco. It will be a school for training cadres, true to the spirit of Florestan Fernandes.[5] We see no contradiction in going to the EU with a construction project, because the European countries have already stolen so much from Brazil—it's high time some of it was paid back. There are other projects, too—for instance, one with a European human-rights organization, to help us get legal representation.

How would you characterize the MST's social base—not only in terms of class, but also of gender and 'race'? Does it have specific sectors for work with indigenous peoples?

The indigenous peoples are a minority in Brazil and here, unlike in Andean or Aztec America, they were traditionally hunters and gatherers, not farmers as they are in Ecuador, Peru or Mexico, where they work inside the farmers' organizations. Our relations with the indigenous peoples start from the recognition that they are the original inhabitants of Brazil. There is no

---

[5] Florestan Fernandes (1920–95): doyen of radical sociology in Brazil. Via Dutra: motorway connecting São Paulo and Rio de Janeiro.

discussion about that—all the land they claim as theirs is theirs, and they should do with it as they wish.

In terms of ethnic composition, it depends on the situation of the farmers in each state. There are very few blacks in the MST, and very few Sem Terra farmers in the areas where they mainly live—Bahia, Pernambuco, Maranhão. Pedro II's Law 601 of 1850 was designed to prevent freed black slaves from becoming landowners; as soon as they got their formal freedom, they had to migrate to the ports, and work in the docks. Blacks were excluded from the formation of the Brazilian farming classes, and that's had a lasting influence. To this day, the farming layers are composed mainly of *mestizos* in the Northeast, and European immigrants in the South. This is clearly reflected in the composition of the MST.

As far as gender goes, because our form of struggle involves whole families, there's been a break with the traditional model of men-only farmers' movements. This is not to say there's not still a strong macho culture among the men in the countryside—on the contrary. But the way our movement is organized means the women are bound to play a role. In an encampment there are as many women as men—and even more children. In general, the women are very active in the committees set up to solve everyday problems, but they're much less represented at higher levels—which is where the influence of machismo comes in. A male comrade will often object to his partner travelling so much, or going to meetings in the capital. Family life imposes restrictions that impede women's broader participation at state and national level. All the same, even though we haven't adopted a quota system, 40 per cent of the twenty-one comrades on the national executive committee are women—and they got there by contesting elections against men, and not just because we'd saved places for them.

In terms of class, the rural population has been classified in many ways. In our movement, we try to use terminologies that take account of the fact that there are a great many lumpens in the country areas—the numbers living in misery there have risen with the economic crisis. The agrarian proletariat constitutes around a third of the rural population, but their numbers are dropping sharply with mechanization. They're still a strong force in sugar-cane production, in São Paulo and Pernambuco, but in cacao farming the organized workforce has virtually been destroyed. There are a lot of wage workers in cattle rearing, but they're widely scattered, which makes it difficult for them to organize. The same goes for large-scale agribusiness—soya or orange production, for instance: a ranch of 10,000 hectares, or 25,000 acres, with ten tractors, will produce a lot; but there will only be ten employees, who will never be able to provide a solid basis for a union. Then there is the classically defined layer of small farmers, the *campesinato*—those who work with their families on a little bit of land, whether it belongs to them or not. Of this fraction, a third are landless—our base of four million families. They work as share-croppers, or tenants; or they could be farmers' children, who need to earn a wage. Another third—again, around four million families—are small farmer-proprietors, owning up to 50 hectares, about 120 acres. There is also an agrarian petty bourgeoisie, whose properties can vary from 50 hectares in some regions to 500, or 1,200 acres. Over that—the big ranchers and landowners—we'd consider as part of the agrarian bourgeoisie.

According to the Gini index, Brazil has the highest concentration of land ownership in the world. One per cent of the proprietors—around 40,000 of the biggest ranchers, or *latifundiários*—own 46 per cent of the land, some 360 million hectares, in *fazendas* of over 2,000 hectares, more than 5,000 acres each. In general, these are either occupied by livestock or entirely unproductive. Below them, the agrarian bourgeoisie own another 30 million hectares, roughly 75 million acres, on properties of between 500 and 2,000 hectares (1,200 to 5,000 acres); this is the most modernized sector, producing soya, oranges, coffee. The holdings of the small farmers—under 100 hectares, or around 250 acres—produce mainly for subsistence, selling a small surplus at markets.

In which areas has the MST *been involved most actively—Rio Grande, São Paulo, Nordeste, Mato Grosso, Goiás?*

The regions where the social struggle is at its broadest are those where there's the greatest concentration of landless people—in the Northeast and the South. For the press, though—and, sometimes, for Brazilian public opinion—it seems as if most of the confrontations take place in the North or the West-Central region. The reason is that 'Brazilian civilization' has yet to arrive in those parts—in Pará or Rondônia—and the ranchers and landowners exercise a lot more violence: assassinating union leaders, using the police to do their bidding. This ultra-brutality is more entrenched in those regions, but that doesn't mean the struggles there have the same breadth as those in the Northeast and the South.

I wanted to ask you about something not generally raised by the press—the question of fear. Do you or the farmers ever get scared during land occupations?

Collective actions release energy—there's a physical surge of adrenaline, and who knows what else, medical experts say. The occupation itself is a festival. The fear comes with the evictions, especially when the balance of forces is all on their side. If there are fifty or a hundred families facing several hundred shock troops it can be very frightening—they'll lash out at the squatters indiscriminately, women and children too. It's a terrible, fraught situation, with the children screaming and the women getting beaten about. Evictions of small groups of squatters are often tragedies—they impose such a degree of humiliation on the families involved. That's why we always try to stage large-scale actions—they have a much better chance of success. But with the growing social crisis, we're running into difficulties. In many regions, the poverty is so bad and, since the landless movement's gained a reputation, sometimes communities just organize themselves and squat on some land, thinking it'll work. They don't realize the movement has accumulated some vital experience, which it can pass on. The police turn up with their batons and they get evicted in the most brutal way.

What do you consider the greatest successes of the MST?

By the simple fact of existing for eighteen years, a farmers' movement that contests the ruling class in this country can consider itself something of a triumph—it's longer than any previous one has lasted. We've won some economic victories: the lives of the 350,000 families that have occupied land are improving—they may still be poor, but things are getting better. But maybe the greatest success is the dignity the Sem Terra farmers have won for themselves. They can walk with their heads held high, with a sense of self-respect. They know what they're fighting for. They don't let questions go unanswered. That's the greatest victory. No one can take that class-consciousness away.

There have been other actions that have made a big impact in folklore terms, so to speak, like the Giacometti occupation, or the march to Brasília in 1997, when nearly 1,500 comrades covered 1,500 kilometres—1,000 miles—in a few months. That was an epic, too. No mass movement had ever marched such a distance before—the Prestes Column, so important in our history, was on horseback, or in cars.[6] It was a heroic moment when we arrived in Brasília. There were over a hundred thousand people waiting for us there—not just the local people but trade unionists and CUT (Central Única dos Trabalhadores) and Workers Party members who had come from all over the country. The march had a big impact in terms of winning over public opinion. A large part of this was due to Sebastião Salgado and his photographs. The 'Terra' exhibition was a worldwide success, and it gave the Sem Terra Movement a global visibility in the field of the arts, without the need for an ideological discourse. Salgado's images launched us internationally, and for that we're very grateful to him.

When did the MST decide to start organizing in the favelas, as well as in the countryside? What kinds of action are possible in urban areas?

Organizing in the favelas isn't our principal work—there hasn't been a shift of emphasis to the cities. But because the Southeast is highly urbanized, a

---

[6] Luís Carlos Prestes (1898–1990): army captain who led a column of insurgents several thousand miles across Brazil in the late 1920s; later leader of the Brazilian Communist Party (PCB) until his death.

lot of the rural working class has been absorbed into the lumpenproletariat, living on the outskirts—our social base from the country transplanted to the city. We have an obligation to them still, so we have to go to the favelas, to try to organize them. It's for that reason that our work in the cities is mainly in the Southeast—São Paulo, Rio de Janeiro, Minas.

From the realities of organizing there, our activists have come up with a new proposal: what they call 'rurban' settlements—*assentamentos rurbanos*. Instead of grabbing a guy who lives on the outskirts and dropping him into the depths of the countryside, we set up encampments closer to the city, on small lots. These are people who are used to a more urban way of life—as opposed to a farmer from the Northeast, who wants 15 hectares (35 acres). Here in the Southeast that's a vast amount of land. So we get them lots of one hectare, two or three acres, where they can do more labour-intensive sorts of farming, such as fruit growing or chicken rearing, combined with local agro-industrial work for the women and children, so they still have some connection to agriculture. The kids can study computing and work in the administration of a milk or fruit concern, for example. We're discussing this with some of the regional governments, to see if it's viable. In São Paulo, we're working on an experimental settlement project with three hundred families, in partnership with the city Prefecture. There are already 'rurban' settlements like this in other states.

Will this still involve land occupations?

Yes, the struggle will be triggered by occupations, but maybe not in such a dramatic manner. For example, in São Paulo, there was a land occupation on the Anhanguera road out of the city—to a farmer's eyes, there were 10 or 15 hectares, nearly 40 acres, lying totally abandoned—but it's not necessarily the typical unproductive cattle-ranch. There are places close to the city that could be put to better social use, too, and in those sorts of cases there'll be a different focus to the occupations.

Will they follow a similar pattern to those in the country?

The form is similar—occupations have to have a mass character, they have to take place at night, they have to protect the squatters. It's the political work of raising consciousness that's different. Favela people have another sort of culture, with its own habits and vices and pleasures. Working with them is much faster. The farmer is more of a Doubting Thomas, he wants to take it slowly, to try things out. He needs to visit a settlement to see if it works. People on the city outskirts are more in touch with the mass media and the rest of the world, they're quicker to absorb new information and debate things—and also more readily distracted.

What has been the rate and rhythm of growth of the MST—continuous expansion, or sporadic? Has there been any decline in numbers since the early 1980s?

We've grown, but the rhythm has depended on the balance of forces—when the landowners or the government have had the upper hand, our rate of growth has dropped. For the last two years we've made very few gains, despite the fact that we now have a substantial presence as a movement, because the Cardoso government has been drawing us into one fight after another, trying to force us onto the defensive politically. We've resolved to assault their neo-liberal programme, and they're determined to defeat us.

How would you assess the record of Fernando Henrique Cardoso's presidency on the agrarian question, compared with the Sarney (1984–89), Collor (1990–92) and Itamar Franco (1992–94) periods?

The struggle for agrarian reform in Brazil—and the growth of the Sem Terra Movement itself—can't be measured solely in terms of numbers of families settled on land. Our struggle is a social and political one: sometimes we win victories that can't be measured in terms of hectares, and sometime we occupy a lot of land but the cumulative political effect is not so great. It's very complex, but we'd make the following analysis. The Sarney administration in 1984 was faced with the great social ferment that followed the fall of the dictatorship. These were highly favourable times for agrarian struggles. There were lots of land occupations. Brazil's ruling class was in crisis: industry had come to a halt and the old economic model had failed. They didn't know where to go next, which resulted in the elections of 1989. The enemy was weak in this period and we could move forward. The MST was born in 1984, but consolidated during the Sarney years.

Collor's victory in 1989, and the implementation of the first neo-liberal measures, put an end to any hopes for agrarian reform. Collor wanted to crush us. He set the Federal police on us—for two years we had to eat whatever bread the devil kneaded, as we say. Many of our state-level headquarters were raided. There was even an attempt to kidnap me from outside our national office. A comrade from the CUT who looks a lot like me was seized, taken away and tortured. He was only released when they looked at his documents and realized they had the wrong person. The UDR had grown in strength, and there were a lot of assassinations between 1990 and 1992.[7] They were terrible years for us. There was little organic growth, it was more a question of keeping going. Instead of our slogan 'Occupy, Resist, Produce', it was more like 'Get beaten up and hold out'. Fortunately, Globo TV brought Collor down once they realized he was just a lumpen-bourgeois.

---

[7] UDR: União Democrática Ruralista, an organization of ranch owners and agrarian capitalists, modelled on the Ku Klux Klan.

Then came the period of transition, under Itamar Franco. He certainly had no plans for agrarian reform, but he did stop the repression—the boot was lifted, and we began to resurface. The two years under Itamar were a time of restoring our energies. We made few gains, and there were not many new settlements. It was a hybrid government, with no political will and no programme of its own.

The Cardoso administration underestimated the agrarian issue initially, in 1994. Cardoso was being advised by Francisco Graziano da Silva, whose doctoral thesis 'The Tragedy of Land' set out to prove there were neither large landholdings nor landless farmers in Brazil. Cardoso wrote a preface for the book when it was published—it had a strong influence on him. Then came the Rondônia and Carajás massacres and he got a fright—as did the ruling class—at the scale of the social problem they revealed.[8] They were stunned as roaches, as the saying goes. It was a much better period for us in terms of morale—after the Carajás massacre, the government had to give in to the public outcry at the treatment of the Sem Terra. They had no way of repressing us. We had a stronger position in society and that helped us a great deal. There were lots of land occupations between 1996 and 1998, even though the neo-liberal programme Cardoso was implementing didn't seem to offer much hope for land expropriations or agrarian reform.

When Cardoso won his second term in 1998, he put his foot down. The transition to the new economic model had been consolidated. In agriculture, the entry of international capital was put on the fast track, together with what they call the application of the North American model to Brazilian farming, and the internationalization of our food production. The concentration of land and agro-industry in the hands of large-scale capital was speeded up. All agricultural trade is now under the control of the multinationals. The public sector has disappeared—going against the First World's actual practice of developing agriculture through strong state support. Instead, the Cardoso administration has put everything in the hands of the market. The budget of the National Institute for Agrarian Settlement and Reform was three billion reais in 1997; in 2001 it was down to one billion. There is no more technical assistance, no more state stockpiling, no more funding, no more government research; Embrapa has been scrapped.[9] Clearly, there is no room for land expropriation or popular agrarian reform.

In recent years we have been faced with a situation similar to the Collor period, only worse in that the neo-liberal model is widely accepted now. At the same time, the fight of the landless has been transformed into a much wider class question. It's this that has made us recognize that we, too, need to broaden our struggle, as we decided at our last congress in 2000. We'll carry on squatting land, because that's the only way for families to resolve

---

[8] Rural workers were killed by the police in Corumbiara, Rondônia on 9 August 1995 and at Eldorado dos Carajás on 17 April 1996.

[9] Embrapa: Brazilian State Agricultural Research body.

their immediate problems—to have a place where they can work. But if we are to move towards popular agrarian reform we have to confront the neo-liberal programme itself, and that can't be done by land occupations alone. For that reason, the Sem Terra Movement has joined other farmers' organizations to combat the multinationals in milk production and, especially, GM seeds. They are the most extreme expression of the extension of the multinationals' control under the new economic model. In five years' time, all the seeds Brazilian farmers need to plant could be owned by the big corporations. The country's food sovereignty is in jeopardy.

That's our assessment of the Cardoso presidency—a government that has subordinated itself completely to the interests of international capital, and has imposed that surrender on Brazilian agriculture. The Sem Terra have only escaped because over the last eighteen years we've managed to build a social movement with a coherent ideology and a layer of activists. If we had been the usual type of farmers' movement, they would have wiped us out. The avalanche of propaganda against the landless farmers in the media, the economic offensives against us, the attempts to suffocate us, to flatten us along with our settlements—all this has been impressive. For three years not a single newspaper has spoken well of the MST—it's just attack, attack, attack. What's saved us has been the support of the social forces that don't believe their propaganda, and protect us. Otherwise they would have finished us long ago.

What specific measures has the state taken to repress the MST? Have assassinations and arbitrary imprisonments decreased under Cardoso, or gone up?

The number of brutal killings has gone down under Cardoso, partly because Brazilian society has been more vigilant and partly because we've given increasing priority to mass struggles. Under Collor and Sarney, most of the assassinations were of union presidents—it was easier for the ranch owners or the police to pick off a figurehead. Some 1,600 people have been killed in agrarian conflicts since 1984, but only about a hundred of these were Sem Terra members—most of them at Carajás and Rondônia. The point to stress—and I don't say this to boast: on the contrary, we share the grief and solidarity for those comrades from other organizations who were killed—is that our form of mass organization protects our members and activists, our committee structure and collective leadership shelters our leaders, and deters assassinations. This has been an important factor for the drop in the number of killings during Cardoso's second term.

Instead, they've taken up cannier, more disguised forms of repression, linked to the intelligence services. Firstly, Cardoso has reorganized the Federal police, setting up new departments specializing in agrarian conflict in each state, with inspectors who are experts on the movement—they've read more of our literature than most of our activists, since it's their

professional duty; they're Sem Terra PhDs. This is basically a reconstruction of the rural DOPS of the dictatorship years.[10] Their officers keep opening
inquiries on us, so the MST's energies are constantly being wasted on protect-
ing its activists from the Federal police. They listen in on our phone lines and
they've stepped up surveillance on our leadership. The ranch owners are no
longer at liberty just to have us bumped off, but there are men following us
like shadows. Our leaders have to be rock solid in their beliefs, because it's a
terrible drain on their energies.

The second form of repression we're facing is through the judiciary, where
the Social Democratic Party government and the landowners have a lot of
influence. They use the courts as a way to grind us down. Last week I spent a
day in the prison in Mãe do Rio, a small municipality in Pará, where fourteen
of our comrades have been held for thirty-one days, without charge, in a cell
measuring four by six metres, while the judge systematically denies them
the right of habeas corpus. They were in a group of three hundred families,
occupying unused ranch land belonging to Jader Barbalho.[11] It's clear the
local judiciary is under Barbalho's influence, and he's openly told the newspapers that the MST should be taught a lesson: 'They'll see who they've got
mixed up with.' So the fourteen comrades have been held for a month, and
the movement's energies have been spent on getting them freed instead of
going towards the struggle for land.

The third form of repression I've already mentioned: the concerted use
of the media against us, the attempt to stigmatize us among broad layers of
society, and especially among the least politicized sectors of the urban lower-
middle class—the readers of *Veja*, which is very heavily biased against us.[12]
Fortunately, the impoverished working class don't read *Veja*. But the way
the media are systematically ranged against us by the Palácio de Planalto,
in order to conduct a permanent campaign against us, is no less a form of
repression.

What is your opinion of Cardoso as a person, president and statesman?

As a person, I think he was betrayed by his enormous vanity—everyone
who's had a long-term association with him testifies to that. It's led him
to renege on whatever principles he may have had, as an intellectual—or at
least, that his academic reputation suggested. As a president, he's been no
more than a mouthpiece for a ruling class that's given up on national goals,
and united around the programme of becoming the foreman for international capital on Brazilian territory. As a statesman? I've never heard anyone
call him that—he's never had the dignity to represent the Brazilian people.

---

[10] DOPS: Department of Political and Social Order.
[11] A key Cardoso lieutenant in Congress, president of the Senate, forced to resign after
corruption scandals.
[12] *Veja*: the largest circulation news weekly in Brazil.

At most, he represents a bourgeoisie that lives here, but has no national project—so he could never even constitute himself as a statesman in terms of his own class. History will be right to categorize him as the great traitor of the Brazilian people.

Who do you, and the MST, feel closest to internationally, on agrarian questions? How would you compare the MST to the Zapatistas?

Our relations with the Zapatistas are simply those of solidarity. Their struggle is a just one, but its social base and its method are different to ours. Theirs is, at root, a struggle of indigenous peoples for autonomy—and if there's a criticism to be made of their experience, it would be that the slowness of their advance is due to their inability to broaden it into a class struggle, a national one. They have accepted the terms of fighting for a specific ethnic-ity, within a particular territory—whereas ours is a farmers' movement that has been transformed and politicized as a result of the advance of capitalism, of neo-liberalism. If the fight we're carrying on today had been waged in the 1930s—if Brazilian farmers had been able to organize then as well as they can now—it would have just been a movement for agrarian reform, seeking only to meet the needs of its own sector.

On the international plane, the context is far broader, politically. The Sem Terra have made a modest, but proud, contribution to the interna-tional network of farmers' movements, Via Campesina, which has a presence in eighty-seven countries. There have been several international meetings and congresses, the last in 2001 in India. It is very striking that it is only now that farmers are starting to achieve a degree of worldwide coordina-tion, after five hundred years of capitalist development. Workers have had an international day for over a century, and women for not much less, but farmers have only just agreed to mark one—17 April, a source of pride to us: a tribute to Carajás. As long as capitalism meant only industrialization, those who worked on the land limited their struggle to the local level. But as the realities of neo-liberal internationalization have been imposed on us, we've begun to hear stories from farmers in the Philippines, Malaysia, South Africa, Mexico, France, all facing the same problems—and the same exploiters. The Indians are up against Monsanto, just as we are in Brazil, and Mexico, and France. It's the same handful of companies—seven groups, in total, worldwide—that monopolize agricultural trade, and control research and biotechnology, and are tightening their ownership of the planet's seeds. The new phase of capitalism has itself created the conditions for farmers to unite against the neo-liberal model.

In Via Campesina, we're building a platform independent of the particu-lar tendencies of the farmers' movements within each country. One plank on which we agree, at the international level, is that there must be the sort of agrarian reform that would democratize the land—both as a basis for political democracy, and for building an agriculture of another kind. This has major implications. From the time of Zapata in Mexico, or of Julião in Brazil, the inspiration for agrarian reform was the idea that the land belonged to those who worked it. Today we need to go beyond this. It's not enough to argue that if you work the land, you have proprietary rights over it. The Vietnamese and Indian farmers have contributed a lot to our debates on this. They have a different view of agriculture, and of nature—one that we've tried to synthesize in Via Campesina. We want an agrarian practice that transforms farmers into guardians of the land, and a different way of farming, that ensures an ecological equilibrium and also guarantees that land is not seen as private property.

The second plank is the concept of food sovereignty. This brings us into head-on collision with international capital, which wants free markets. We maintain that every people, no matter how small, has the right to produce their own food. Agricultural trade should be subordinated to this greater right. Only the surplus should be traded, and that only bilaterally. We are against the WTO, and against the monopolization of world agricultural trade by the multinational corporations. As José Martí would say: a people that cannot produce their own food are slaves; they don't have the slightest freedom. If a society doesn't produce what it eats, it will always be dependent on someone else.

The third plank we are working on for the Via Campesina programme is the idea that seeds are the property of humankind—agricultural techniques cannot be patented. Biotechnology is a good thing. Scientists can develop things in the laboratory that would take nature millions of years to evolve. But it's only a good thing if these developments are democratized, if everyone has access to them, and if there are proper safeguards for the environment and for human health. This is not the case with GM technology. No scientist is prepared to give an absolute assurance as to what the effects of cloned animals and genetically modified seeds could be, so they should be restricted to experiments in laboratories, in limited areas, and their use shouldn't be extended until we're completely certain. The history of BSE should have taught us this.

Something that's not much known abroad is that, between 1998 and 1999, Cardoso pushed through a patent law granting the right to private ownership of living things. The first draft was circulated to Congress in English, because the American Embassy that had imposed the programme on Brazil didn't even bother to translate it. Locally it was the handiwork of Ney Suassana, the current Minister of National Integration and notorious for toadying to the US. Once the government had bent to their masters and the law was approved, the Institute of Biology here received 2,940 applications for patents, 97 per cent of which were from multinational corporations who wanted property rights over an Amazonian butterfly or some sort of shrub. It sounds absurd. But exactly the same thing is going on in India, Chile, the

Philippines, South Africa—despite the illusion that the ANC would be a progressive government, it's a neo-liberal administration, just like Brazil.

What has been the contribution to the Sem Terra movement of environmentalists and other democratic activists from outside the ranks of the landless?

There are many currents in the environmentalist movement, some very sectarian—sometimes a farmer cuts down a tree on an encampment, and there's a flurry of denunciations—but in general the majority of the groups here have helped us, including Greenpeace, which I find the liveliest. They've taken up the fight against GM technology, and they've been helping us raise people's consciousness on that. We've built a grand coalition on the issue with all the environmental movements in Brazil. There's a division of labour: some of the groups involved work in the juridical sphere, others—such as Greenpeace—on propaganda, and we organize mass actions. Today we occupied a 1,200-hectare—3,000-acre—property in Rio Grande do Sul where all the soya was genetically modified. There were 1,500 young people there and it turned into an educational exercise for them. After an intensive, five-day course on GM plants, they had a practical lesson in destroying a genetically modified soya crop. I think our involvement has also managed to politicize the environmental movements a bit more. Two or three years ago they were still only focusing on animals in danger of extinction, or defending the forest, when here in the Third World, humans are the living beings most at risk.

What is the position of the MST on the use of violence for social ends—including, specifically, agrarian reform?

We have a tradition of ideological pluralism within the movement, in the sense that we never claim to be the followers of any one thinker—we try to treat each one as synthesizing a particular historical experience, and to see how we can make use of them. As far as violence is concerned, we've learnt a lot from two Asians: Ho Chi Minh and Gandhi. Ho was the only one who managed to defeat the USA. He systematically taught the Vietnamese peasants that their strength lay not in what they held in their hands, but in what they carried in their heads. The achievements of the Vietnamese soldier—a farmer, illiterate and poor—came from his being conscious of what he was fighting for, as a soldier and as a man. Everything he could lay hold of, he turned into a weapon. The other main lesson we've learned is to raise people's consciousness, so that they realize it's our vast numbers that constitute our strength. That was what Gandhi taught us—through the Indians' Salt March against the British, for instance. If we ever decided to use the same weapons as our enemies, we would be doomed to defeat.

What is the best help that direct-action groups and NGOs in North America and Europe can give to the MST and sister movements?

The first thing is to bring down your neo-liberal governments. Second, help us to get rid of foreign debt. As long as we're still financially dependent—which is what the plunder of 'debt' represents—it won't be possible to construct economic models that meet the needs of our population. Third, fight—build mass struggles. Don't delude yourself that because you have a higher living standard than us, you can build a better world. It's impossible for you to maintain your current patterns of consumption without exploiting us, so you have to battle to change the type of consumerism that you're caught up in. Fourth, stop importing Brazilian agricultural products that represent nothing but exploitation: wood, mahogany—all that wooden furniture in England made with Amazonian timber. What's the point of campaigning to save the rainforest if your governments and companies carry on boosting the sawmills and timber yards that are exporting its wood to you? Again, stop buying soya to feed your mad cows—let the people here have a chance to organize agricultural production to guarantee our own food needs first. Fifty-six million people in this country go hungry every day.

What is the relationship of the MST to the Brazilian Left in general, and in particular to the Workers Party, the PT?

The MST has historical connexions to the PT—both were born during the same time period. In the countryside there are many activists who helped to form the PT and work for the MST, and vice versa. There's been a natural overlap of giving mutual assistance, while always maintaining a certain autonomy. The majority of our activists, when they opt for a party, generally choose the PT, but there are Sem Terra farmers affiliated to the Partido Socialista Brasileiro, and to Lionel Brizola's Partido Democrático Trabalhista—though not to the PCdoB, because it's adopted the classic line of forming its own farmers' movement, the Movimento de Luta de Terra. Those who came up through the struggle with us but sympathized with the PCdoB automatically preferred to join that.[13] Another reason for the predominance of the PT.

The MST is autonomous from the PT, but at election time we've traditionally supported their candidates, as they're the major Left party. But we feel that the Brazilian Left in general is going through a period of crisis at the moment, presenting difficulties for organic Left accumulation—irrespective of the electoral results of any one set of party initials, or of the diverse currents within the PT. The crisis is a complex one. Firstly, the Left has no

---

[13] Partido Comunista do Brasil : founded in 1961, a Maoist split from the official Communist Party, PCB.

clear project for Brazil—or it falls into the simplification of socialism versus capitalism, without managing to formulate clearly what first steps socialists should take. Secondly, the institutionalization of the parties and currents has distanced them from the mass movements. It seems that the Left has forgotten that the only force that can bring social change is the organized mass of the people, and that people organize themselves through struggle, not through the vote. A vote is an expression of citizenship, not a form of struggle. The Left has to regain the belief that we alone are going to alter the balance of forces, through mass struggles against the bourgeoisie. There is always a preference for negotiations, for accommodating to class pressures.

A third criticism—and this is also a form of self-criticism, because we consider ourselves as part of the Left: we need to recover our predecessors' tradition of grass-roots work, the microscopic business of organizing people—something the Church talks about a great deal. Activists no longer have the patience to conduct meetings with depoliticized people. I don't know how the mass political parties used to do this work historically in England and Europe. Often when we speak of propaganda, it's really only agitation, the sort carried out by the Trotskyists here in Brazil; but they don't raise consciousness, they don't organize—often they simply give up. One constantly hears criticism of this sort of thing: the trade union leadership calls demonstrations for the First of May, which even the union president doesn't attend, let alone the members.

The fourth point is the question of political education. It's very rare for movements of the Left to maintain a consistent education programme for their militants, in the broadest sense. Activists need to read the classics, so they can master the tools necessary for a correct interpretation of reality. The Left here has simply abandoned the classics and even, from a theoretical perspective, the study of Brazilian reality itself. It's lazy when it comes to analysing its own situation, its contradictions, the class struggle, the living conditions of the working class. It falls back on generalizations which it doesn't understand, and is unable to explain. We need to recover the sense of a theoretical training for activism, without resorting to theoreticism. We need to marry theoretical education with political practice. It's pitiful to see where our young people end up, even those affiliated to the PT or the CUT—as if the only thing for young people to do today was hold music festivals or campaign for the legalization of cannabis. The Brazilian Left needs to overcome those challenges in order to reconstitute, in the not-too-distant future, a great mass movement with the consistent, revolutionary aim of an alternative project for our society.

Asada Akira was born in Kobe, Japan, in 1957. He studied at Kyoto University and subsequently taught in its Institute of Economic Research. Asada is a critic and curator, formed in the period after the flagging of the leftist energies of the 1960s and, in contrast with so many of his contemporaries, nevertheless committed to renewed investigation of Japanese and world capitalism today. His first book, published in 1983, was Structure and Power: Beyond Semiotics. *Since then he has published, among other things,* Beyond 'the End of History' *(1999) and* The End of Cinema's Century *(2000). He was co-editor, with Karatani Kōjin, of* Hihyōkūkan (Critical Space) *until its closure in 2002.*

Asada gave this interview in 2000. He is currently head of the Graduate School at the Kyoto University of Art and Design.

Asada Akira

A Left Within the Place of Nothingness

How would you characterize the current situation of the Japanese Left?

We are in a difficult position of political stagnation, even a certain historical impasse. The Japanese Left suffers from two major legacies of its own past: the residual Stalinism of the Japanese Communist Party (JCP), and the simplistic anti-communism of the sixties generation. To understand the first, one needs to look back at the origins of the JCP. The party, founded in 1922, was led in the mid-twenties by Fukumoto Kazuo, an intellectual of considerable theoretical gifts, trained in Germany, where he studied Lukács and was close to Karl Korsch. According to Fukumoto, the principle the party should follow was 'separation–connexion'—it needed first to take its distance from any easy trade unionism by developing a genuine class consciousness, and then to return to build a mass basis in the working class. In 1927 the Comintern cracked down on this 'left extremism'. Bukharin declared that the immediate battle in Japan was against feudalism; and when the JCP, a few years later, again started to speak of the need for a socialist revolution, the Comintern issued a second set of theses, in 1932, reiterating the priority of anti-feudal tasks. In the background was the Koza–Rono debate among Marxist historians. According to the Koza school, the Meiji restoration was only a transition of power within feudalism, and the next upheaval should be a bourgeois revolution. According to the Rono school (including the famous theoretician Uno Kozo), the Meiji restoration was a bourgeois revolution, and the next upheaval should be a socialist revolution. At least on the character of Japanese society in the early twentieth century, the Rono school had a better understanding. But it was unilaterally criticized by the Comintern and excommunicated from the party. In this way, the party lost brilliant intellectuals in those years.[1]

---

[1] For a detailed English-language account, see Germaine Hoston, *The State, Identity and the National Question in China and Japan*, Princeton 1994, pp. 221–72.

The outcome of the interventions from Moscow was to impose a very rigid Stalinism on the JCP, which has remained a stubborn trait of the party to this day. But the peculiar character of the JCP isn't just a product of this inheritance. Equally important was the repression it suffered in the thirties, when its entire leadership was arrested and imprisoned, and after a long public trial received huge jail sentences. The Japanese state went to great lengths to secure public recantations from Leftists, and was generally very successful in 'turning' prominent Marxists into professed converts to the Imperial regime—the phenomenon known as *tenko*. But some of the Communist leaders resisted. Under extreme pressure, they refused to convert, and so had a great moral authority when they were released after the war. We must admire their courage, under extreme militarist oppression. But after the Second World War, their ethical aura became a substitute for political intelligence. Personal courage is one thing; political responsibility is another. The JCP became a gramophone record of moralizing self-righteousness. 'Our brave comrades didn't yield under the worst pressures—that's the proof we are right.' Nothing could be more sterile as an attitude.

Was the intellectual life of the JCP essentially killed off in the thirties?

You couldn't exactly say that. The most important post-war leader of the party, Miyamoto Kenji, was a leading literary critic in his youth, who won a major prize for his analysis of Akutagawa Ryunosuke's novels—relegating Kobayashi Hideo, possibly the nearest Japanese equivalent to a Walter Benjamin, to second position in the competition. This was in the twenties; Kobayashi was outraged by the result. In the thirties Miyamoto was imprisoned in the remote countryside of Hokkaido, where he held out against his jailers unflinchingly. After the war this earned him such moral glory that he was all but deified within the party. By 1958 he was general secretary, and for the next twenty years ruled the JCP with a mailed fist. Official doctrine was still frozen by Stalinist insistence that Japan was not capitalistic enough and that the main enemy was a feudal-imperial system. So after the war the JCP continued to downplay any direct attack on Japanese capitalism. But now it avoided talking about the emperor system too, as it had once done; instead it concentrated its fire on American colonialism and imperialism. The result was that in domestic practice it became more and more moderate, but in theory it remained as dogmatic as ever—indeed, eventually criticizing both the Russian and Chinese parties for changing too much. There was one significant attempt to break this mould, when younger cadres like Ueda Koichiro and his younger brother Fuwa Tetsuzo tried in the late fifties to develop an Italian-style strategy, inspired by Togliatti, of structural reforms within the parliamentary system. Miyamoto crushed this revolt with great violence, and the youngsters were forced to criticize themselves. Fuwa was brought to heel and eventually chosen as heir to Miyamoto, since he had committed himself to continuing Miyamoto's policies, while no doubt inwardly knowing they led nowhere. So the Communist Party became more and more solitary, more and more self-righteous, cast in the petrified image of Miyamoto, with his iron will and heroic past. A sad story.

In the West, student radicalization came in the late sixties, with a counter-cultural ferment sometimes preceding it by a few years. In Japan, the whole movement started a bit earlier?

Yes, the ingredients were much the same, but the mixture arrived sooner. Politically, a powerful critique of the JCP's outlook was available from the late fifties, when Iwata Hiroshi—a pupil of Uno Kozo—published a book called *World Capitalism*. It is almost Wallerstein already. For Iwata, what the Left had to fight was not the remnants of Japanese feudalism, or just American hegemony, but Japanese capitalism as an integral part of the world capitalist system. His theory had a big impact on a *trotskisant* youth, providing it with an intellectual weapon against the JCP's stageism. It was an emphatic assertion of the capitalist modernity of the country. Another kind of criticism of the party came from the opposite direction. Here the key figure was Yoshimoto Takaaki, a poet and literary critic who brought a purified notion of 'the masses' to the fore—not so much in the sense of Luxemburg's critique of Lenin, but rather in a rejection of doctrines imported from Moscow. Instead of such foreign conceptions, the Left should listen to the mass of the Japanese people themselves, starting from their needs and concerns. This line appealed strongly to the romantic strain in the cultural underground at the time, where many young people were reading Feuerbach more than Marx.

The Japanese New Left arose out of the confluence of these different elements. They made a potent concoction, which set off a protest movement well before its counterparts in the other capitalist countries. Already in 1960 the JCP looked outmoded, as the party was outflanked by the Zengakuren—the national student organization, now 'captured by Trotskyists', as the JCP saw it—in huge mass mobilizations against the renewal of the Security Treaty with the US.[2] This was also the period of the last big struggle of labour against capital in Japan, the great miners' strike against Mitsui. By the late sixties a very powerful front of revolutionary youth had built up, which mounted another spectacular battle over the Treaty in 1970. But by then, the movement had become more and more subjectivist and romantic, either pursuing an illusory unity with the masses or seeking a quasi-erotic communality of its own, in a Feuerbachian or Marcusean spirit.

---

[2] See Gavin McCormack, 'The Student Left in Japan', NLR I/65, January–February 1971.

This was a common pattern in Europe and America, too?

Yes, but there was a specific Japanese twist to it. In the West, the radicalization came out of—or gave rise to—issues that later found expression in new
social movements: the Campaign for Nuclear Disarmament in Britain, early
forms of ecological concern, the beginnings of second-wave feminism. In
Japan, although the campaign against the war in Vietnam was very strong,
these elements were all much weaker. The romanticism of the movement
was more martial and male chauvinist. So when its impetus was frustrated, it
turned more quickly and disastrously to internal violence. In 1972 the terrorism of the United Red Army consumed itself, when its adherents killed
each other in a pseudo-military camp on Mount Asama. The shock of that
episode effectively gave the quietus to the Feuerbachian, Luxemburgian
turmoil of the sixties. The following year, the oil crisis brought the very
rapid growth of the previous two decades to a close. It was the end of an
epoch.

*How far did international developments affect the different strands of the
Japanese Left in this period—it was the time of the Sino–Soviet dispute, the
Cultural Revolution in China, the invasion of Czechoslovakia: very big devel-
opments in the external environment?*

This was background music, more than direct influence. When the Sino–
Soviet split occurred, the JCP refused to align itself with the Russians
—Miyamoto purged those loyal to Moscow. But two years later, in
1966, he also broke with the Chinese. Here you could say that the self-
righteousness of Japanese Communism, an insufferable feature within the
country, did include a nationalist reflex that eventually served it well—since,
by the nineties, it could say: we didn't allow ourselves to be told what to
do by the Russians, let alone the Chinese or the Americans, so why should
we be affected by the fall of the USSR or the turn of the PRC to the US? At
the time, of course, the Japanese Communists were, in practice, closer to
the Soviet than the Chinese line, while the student movement was closer to
Maoism. But the Cultural Revolution never had the same degree of appeal
for Japanese youth as it did for French or Italian. We were too close to China
to be unaware of the atrocities committed during the Cultural Revolution,
so Maoist influence remained relatively limited. The Japanese Left remained
essentially divided between a Stalinist-style Communist Party and a heroic-
romantic New Left. For twenty years of very rapid economic progress, from
1950 to 1970, Japan had an extremely active leftist movement, first led by
the JCP, then relayed by the students. But by 1973 everything came to a halt,
as we entered the dismal seventies.

What was the intellectual legacy of this period?

During the sixties, the Communist Party put a lot of effort into criticizing *gauchisme*—the spread of what it saw as Trotskyism. In reaction, the New Left became more and more hostile to the JCP. An obdurate Communist Party and a romantic protest against its authoritarianism left a deep impasse, when the time of upheaval was over. Of course, the JCP continued to be an active force in electoral politics at the local level. Here in Kyoto, for example, they elected the governor down to the end of the seventies. You could compare Kyoto to Bologna, in those days.

In an old city like this, but also in other towns across the country, the party was always effective in organizing small shopkeepers, artisans, doctors or teachers—and willing to form municipal coalitions with the Socialists, who themselves elected governors in Tokyo and Osaka. Naturally, the JCP did not stand on any revolutionary platform, but defended a certain petty-bourgeois egalitarianism. Sometimes this led to curious results. Here in Kyoto, the party opposed affirmative action to help the *buraku*—Japanese outcasts—on the grounds that special measures in favour of them would consolidate, rather than dissolve, the class division on which their oppression was based; whereas the most powerful LDP politician from Kyoto, Nonaka Hiromu—now secretary-general of the LDP, and the brains of the present government—would attack its 'bourgeois arrogance' and champion the special rights of the weak, in order to corner *buraku* votes. By this time, the JCP's national vote was not much more than 5 per cent, but it gained a reputation for honest administration, untainted by corruption, that no other party enjoyed. It still held some influence in the universities, where party economists often held chairs. But over time its intellectual influence became more and more marginal.

Meanwhile, the radicals of the sixties became increasingly anti-communist, and decreasingly anti-capitalist. By the late seventies, we had our equivalent of the *nouveaux philosophes*, talking just like their opposite numbers in France of the death of Marx, the evils of communism, the coming of a new consumer democracy. The rhetoric of the masses, which had played such a large part in their outlook in the sixties, went into political reverse. Since the mass of the Japanese population were no longer poor or discontented, but now declared themselves to be a comfortable middle class, former *gauchistes* argued that, to keep faith with the masses, intellectuals should duplicate this complacent posture. By the eighties, many had become pillars of a new conformism. Today, however, the masses are expressing more frustration than self-satisfaction, as the realities of world politics and world history have closed in on the country again, with the end of the Cold War and the crisis of Japanese capitalism in the nineties. The Japanese public now feels under pressure from America, which insists that Japan must behave in all respects like itself, and from China, Korea and other Asian countries, demanding that Japan apologize properly for its war crimes.

In this new situation, intellectuals from the sixties are lending their voice to nationalist resentments. For example, the critic Katoh Norihiro has recently made a name for himself by attacking the divided mentality of post-war Japanese intellectuals, and their successors who remained on the Left. These people, he maintains, always started 'from the outside', repressing the memory of our dead fathers or grandfathers, while trying to be nice to our Asian neighbours—yet remaining inwardly split. Whereas what we should be doing is 'starting from the inside', by mourning the death of our own ances-tors in the war, before facing or negotiating with the Other in Asia. Katoh does criticize the Yasukuni national shrine, where various war criminals are buried, so this is a relatively benign form of nationalism. But the argument that we should mourn our own war dead before facing others is nonsense. Thousands of Koreans and Taiwanese, as you know, were forcibly recruited into the Imperial Army and killed as Japanese soldiers.

As in the tremendous scene of the funeral of a Taiwanese soldier who fought for the Emperor in New Guinea, in Hou Hsiao-Hsien's film The Puppet-Master?

Exactly: just what Katoh's schema is completely blind to. This generation wants the status of victims. With the US, this can more or less work. 'They are crushing us with their enormous global power'—okay. But with Asians, we were not victims, we were aggressors, and they are not ready to take respon-sibility for that. This talk of 'starting from the inside' is a sort of pre-emptive strike against doing so. It extends to a general hostility to any ideas held to 'come from the outside'. So others—not Katoh himself, but from the same generation—reject feminism, saying this is an import of crazy notions from American Jewish women; or environmentalism; or the more recent peace movements. The thought is: the masses have become mildly nationalist, so we will articulate what they feel. The result is increasing resistance to any ideas that are not home-grown. I had some experience of this myself when I published a book in 1983 on post-structuralism.

So what's your own relation to this generation?

Born in 1957, I entered university in 1975. At Kyoto, there was still a certain student movement, and most of the sixties figures there had not yet turned away from their radical past. I could see the romanticism, the fanaticism and phallocentric militarism that were still part of the campus atmosphere, and I was against them. But by the early eighties, when I published my book *Structure and Power*, the situation had changed completely. Now too many *soixante-huitards* had buried Marx and were basking smugly in what was being hailed as the richest consumer society in the world. They still proclaimed themselves radical, however. My book was the first systematic introduction of certain strands in French philosophical thought, starting with a consideration of Lacan and Althusser, and then moving on to an account of Deleuze and Guattari, whose rather crazy rereading of Marx I enthusiastically set to work in an analysis of contemporary capitalism—especially its patterns of consumption. I wasn't so interested in Deleuze's philosophy as such, the ontology of the virtual; more in the example he and Guattari had given of reading Marx in a much less authoritarian way than the Stalinists did in Japan. My intention was to bring home the need to study Marx afresh, and open a new way of looking at the contradictions of Japanese and world capitalism.

The fate of the book was ironic, however. French philosophy was becoming fashionable just then, and it sold very widely. But it was typically received as an anti-radical manifesto. There's no denying I was quite critical of the legacy of the sixties in so far as it had become—as I saw it—anti-modernist and anti-Marxist. So when I discussed a certain postmodernity, I did not intend to invite any complicity between Japanese pre-modern mentalities and postmodern consumerism, but to point to a possible step up from—beyond—modern capitalism. The book, however, was read in a Baudrillardian key, as a paean to the decentring of the subject, the ubiquity of the simulacrum, and so on. I can't acquit myself of all responsibility for this, since I did touch on Baudrillardian themes, but this strand of the book was extrapolated out of any proportion. The first reaction of the sixties generation was to seize on this, and denounce the book as a manifesto for a demoralized new consumerism. Their second reaction—which you can hear today—is that it was a last remnant of the bad radicalism they had put behind them: a dinosaur of the Marxist heritage, doomed because it was 'imposed from the exterior'.

What explains the wider reception of Structure and Power?

In the course of the eighties, Baudrillard became a popular author in Japan, and his ideas were taken up in some unexpected circles. For example, the owner-manager of the Seibu department store, Tsutsumi Seiji, a versifier himself, adopted an explicitly Baudrillardian marketing strategy for his enterprise, renaming his store *Saisons*, lecturing stockholders on the role of simulacra in his business and cultivating parodic advertising styles. He set a trend at a time when Japanese capitalism was coming out of the depressive seventies, and needed to activate consumption with a certain semiotic *mise en scène*. In this kind of context, there was a predisposition to read an introduction to post-structuralism as a welcome mat for over-consumption. To the extent that I also dealt with contemporary trends in Japanese society, you could say the object of my analysis tended to recuperate it.

Did you feel yourself part of a collective post-sixties generation at the time, or more of an isolate?

Well, I published the book when I was very young, at any rate for a geron-
tocratic country like Japan—I was twenty-six at the time. So I was expected
to represent everything new: new theory, new art, new architecture. That's
obviously impossible, but I survived. On the one hand, I had some ties
to figures from an older—pre-sixties—generation, particularly the critic
Karatani Kōjin and the architect Isozaki Arata. Since the nineties, Karatani
and I have been editing a journal, *Critical Space*, which has tried to make
bilateral connexions between the Japanese and Western critical heritages
from the 1920s to the present, with a programme of reciprocal translations:
an enormous task, on which we've only just started. So I never felt alone
in that sense. On the other hand, my own cohort are coming into view
with a number of significant interventions. For example, when Katoh argued
that the reintegration of the Japanese psyche required mourning for our
dead forebears, Takahashi Tetsuya—a student of Derrida's—criticized him
sharply. So you might say that my generation is now ready to go into battle.
And the younger generation will follow. I don't feel at all isolated within it.

This is not to suggest that the intellectual landscape here is particularly
encouraging. There is a lot to do battle against. For twenty years, from the
mid-seventies to the mid-nineties, the dominant atmosphere in Japan was
one of cynicism. It was the hour of Baudrillard. After the bloodshed of
1972, no one really paid attention to serious political programmes. There
was no feminism, no ecology worth speaking of, nothing to succeed the
ferment of the sixties. But in the nineties this changed. The younger generation are frustrated by the stagnation of the country, and are not allergic
to—at any rate—reformist agendas. But they are also very naive, with little
or no memory of the history of the Left or New Left in Japan. This is
a dangerous innocence, because we are now confronted not just with the
mild kind of pseudo-nationalism advocated by Katoh, but with a much
tougher strain represented, for example, by the comic-strip writer Kobayashi
Yoshinori, who has been hugely successful in winning a mass public.[3] His
slogan is 'gomanism'—a word he has coined from *goman*, meaning 'arrogant'. What Japan needs is a new arrogance, which he at once personifies
and cleverly makes fun of. So he declares that we Japanese had good reasons
to go into Asia, to combat Western colonialism, that the Nanjing massacre
is a myth and so on. This is naked nationalism, but ingeniously configured
as a high-spirited parody of itself—so it's all the more dangerous. Too often,
responses to it on the Left limit themselves to a moralizing reaction, of a kind
widespread among intellectuals after the war, when Max Weber was held up
as the thinker to read—the ethic of responsibility as our guideline. That's
fine, but it's not the same as a political response. The risk is that today, the
younger generation will react to reborn nationalism in the same way, with a

---

[3] See Tessa Morris-Suzuki, 'For and Against NGOS', NLR 2, March–April 2000,
p. 83.

hand-wringing moralism—focusing on responsibility to Others, in the sense of Levinas or Derrida—rather than with a robust alternative politics.

Doesn't that require more accurate discrimination of the Japanese war record, certainly than that current in the West? The standard complaint is that Japan hasn't properly acknowledged its war guilt in the way Germany has done—and there is constant pressure on it to do so. But aren't the two cases quite distinct? Japan waged savage wars of conquest and aggression against Korea and China, with an abundance of atrocities. But its war with the United States, Britain and Holland was another matter—an inter-colonial struggle, in which it was entirely on a par with its enemies. Typical American attitudes, in particular, to the Pacific War are grotesque—it never occurs to those who wax indignant about Pearl Harbour to ask what they were doing in Hawaii in the first place. Once the struggle of imperial powers was unleashed, the US committed incomparably greater war crimes against Japan—the fire-bombing of Tokyo, the nuclear devastations of Hiroshima and Nagasaki—than vice versa. Official apologies should be forthcoming from Washington, if anywhere. The nationalist Right has always played on this duality—covering up the mass slaughters of civilians by Japan in Korea and China with the mass slaughters of civilians by America in Japan. The Left can't dismantle this construction unless it refuses to have any truck with self-serving Western hypocrisies about the war—it has to make its own distinctions.

Yes, but the difficulty is that Japanese consciousness often remains paralysed by the duality. On the one hand, we were cruel aggressors; on the other hand, we were helpless victims. The polarity of Nanjing and Hiroshima—our crimes, and their crimes, against humanity—can lead either to schizophrenic outbursts, or to a sentimentalizing evasion of the complexity of the past. Attitudes to America continue to be deeply ambivalent, because we were, after all, liberated from the militarist regime by defeat, and there was an initial strand within the American occupation, coming from the New Deal, that genuinely tried to democratize Japanese society—though it was rapidly displaced by hard-line restorationism, when the labour movement here proved too insurgent.

On the other hand, no one could forget the deliberate exterminism of the fire-storms over Tokyo and the obliteration of Hiroshima and Nagasaki. But once Japanese conservatives—most of them with an unabashed fascist or colonial past—were put back in power by the US, nationalist feelings were, for obvious reasons, directed by the Right against Asia, not America. Yoshida, the architect of the first post-war order, said the American army was a watchdog, guarding us against socialism, so that we could devote our energies to high-speed economic growth. It is only very recently, partly because of long-term economic success, followed by the current sense of impasse and frustration, that conservatives have emerged willing to

'Say No' to America, as well as China or Russia. Ishihara, the current governor of Tokyo Prefecture, is the first important Japanese politician to be openly anti-American, as well as rabidly anti-Chinese and anti-Korean. This is a new xenophobia: he is potentially a very dangerous figure.

He was a long-time member of the Liberal Democratic Party—does he represent a real departure from the traditions of the party?

There have been successive attempts to create a new 'national' settlement in Japan, through institutional reforms engineered from the Right. This was Nakasone's project in the eighties. He had made his name as defence minister, and presented himself as a strong ruler, the Japanese counterpart to Reagan or Thatcher. In practice, he proved quite skilled at dividing the Socialists from the Communists at the local level, and splitting the trade unions by a series of ostensible privatizations of the railways, telecommunications and so on, that supposedly divided state monopolies into three or four companies, but actually left them in place, while balkanizing the unions. He broke various long-standing taboos against the symbols of militarism, paying his respects to the Yasukuni shrine, and so on. But his bid to push through a revision of the Constitution to allow Japan formal war-making powers was a complete failure. He ended up on the margins of the party.

In the early nineties Ozawa Ichiro, the strongman of the largest LDP faction, again tried to bulldoze the path to a more nationalist (but, like Nakasone's, pro-American) stance, this time linked to schemes for restructuring the electoral system along US lines. But Ozawa's style was too brutish and abrasive for the etiquette of the LDP, and when he walked out of the party he came to grief even more quickly. Finally, Obuchi Keizo—who defeated Ozawa in the struggle for control of the old Tanaka faction—succeeded where the others had failed, setting up a parliamentary commission for revision of the Constitution, and reinstituting the old imperial flag and anthem. Nakasone despised Obuchi, saying he was a walking void—to which Obuchi replied, 'Yes, I am a void, and that's why I arouse no opposition.' He was much more effective than the others in clearing the way for a right-wing revisionism. Nakasone made a lot of noise, but didn't get very far. Obuchi seemed to have no nationalist agenda, but it was under his empty reign that a package of very dangerous bills was passed. Mori Yoshiro, who succeeded Obuchi after his sudden death, is not so clever as his predecessor, but much more nationalistic. In a few years, we could be seeing a major rearmament programme, and Japanese troops once again being sent abroad—naturally, under 'UN auspices'.

The social background of this creeping tide of nationalism is fairly obvious: the strains of a decade of economic stagnation, and the discredit of a corrupt and ineffectual political system, which has been unable to reform itself. The new nationalism is a displaced expression of frustration with all this. Ishihara

promises to propel this dynamic to a further stage. Though he did a spell as
a backbencher in the LDP, he is actually a genuine outsider to the system. By
origin he is a writer, not a politician, who first made his name in the sixties
with a novel considered advanced for the time—a tale of adolescent rebellion, with outspoken sexual scenes (boy's erect penis breaking through paper
partitions, etcetera), which still enjoys esteem. But real fame came with the
biography he wrote of his younger brother, the most popular Japanese actor
of his generation, whose early death made him a legend. Ishihara eventually became bored with the LDP and, when he returned to politics in the
nineties, he did so with all-out attacks on the establishment, as well as on
foreigners. He often doesn't watch what he says, but he speaks a far more
literate and lively language than any other politician in the country, and has
skilfully orchestrated populist as well as nationalist themes, as governor of
Tokyo—for example, not only calling for the closure of American bases, but
imposing taxes on the local banks, a long-standing proposal of the JCP which
he coolly took over. At the level of prefectural politics, he is enormously
popular. He has intellectual support in the younger generation, from critics
like Fukuda Kazuya, and boundless ambition. One can imagine him playing
the role of a Berlusconi in Japan.

*In the event of an intensification of the economic crisis, with the collapse of
major banks and deep recession?*

Exactly. This is the prospect that worries the dovish wing of the LDP most.
The present finance minister Miyazawa represents this tendency. When he
was premier in the early nineties, he saw more clearly than his colleagues the
dangers building up in the banking system, and tried to develop a Keynesian
programme to pull Japan out of the recession, putting public money into
the banks but demanding the resignation of their managers. In the event,
the bureaucrats and bankers thwarted him. Miyazawa also saw the degree to
which the LDP depended on the Socialists to act as an idealistic brake on the
momentum of both capitalism and nationalism in Japan—he called it less a
two-party than a one-and-a-half-party system. Now the brake is so much
weakened, the vehicle is no longer under traditional control. The fear of this
group is that Ishihara could get his hands on the wheel.

What happened to the Socialists?

During the seventies and eighties, they moved steadily to the right—dis-
tancing themselves from the Communists, while losing support in the trade
unions, and stagnating electorally. But at the end of the decade they were
suddenly handed a historic opportunity, when the Takeshita government
was engulfed in a massive corruption scandal and the Showa Emperor
died. In the elections to the Upper House in the fall of 1989, they won a

stunning victory—at a stroke jumping from ten to nearly twenty million votes, well ahead of the LDP. Much of the party's success was due to the fact that it had the first popular leader it had ever produced, who was also the first woman to lead a major political party in Japan—Doi Takako. In a country that had not known any effective feminist movement, she became a sort of symbol—incarnating, quite unconsciously, all that we had missed: a women's movement, a new peace movement, an ecological movement. The LDP panicked, and did everything they could to bring her down. Suicidally, the Socialist bosses—elderly power brokers, threatened by her rise—helped them. Within a couple of years she was ousted as party leader, and the JSP was duly trounced in the general elections of 1992, losing twelve million votes.

But the political crisis—the decline of the 'system of 1955', which stabilized LDP hegemony for thirty-five years—had not gone away. Not only did the economic situation worsen in the early nineties, but the Cold War came to an end. Japan was in a situation very like Italy, where the Cold War had also allowed decades of rule to a faction-ridden Christian Democracy, in which everything was permitted—no matter how corrupt—so long as the Left was excluded from power. In both countries there was a popular revulsion against the system, and a demand that public life be cleaned up. In Japan, Ozawa engineered a split in the ruling party, forming a coalition with forces of 'reform' outside it, under an aristocratic former governor from Kyushu, Hosokawa Morihiro.[4] The Socialists joined the Hosokawa Cabinet, the first non-LDP government in four decades. There was much talk of a fresh start in Japanese politics. But the new government soon proved as conventional as the old, and even more ineffectual. Within a year, the Socialists had changed sides and restored the LDP to power. Miyazawa had caught the cruel truth of the JSP perfectly. The Socialist Party lost all credibility, and has never recovered from this debacle. It was a second suicide. Its voters abandoned it *en masse* for the Communist Party, which is now a larger electoral force.

Could it be said, then, that unlike Christian Democracy in Italy, the LDP has survived the disarray of the early nineties, and is firmly back in the saddle again, once more without any real opposition—that nothing has really changed in Japan over the past ten years?

No, that would be an overstatement. It would be more accurate to say that the system of 1955 has been greatly weakened, but not yet replaced. All attempts to reform the system so far have been fiascos. Ozawa failed; Hosokawa failed; Hatoyama—leader of the current opposition Democratic

---

[4] For this conjuncture, and what followed it, see Karel Van Wolferen, 'Japan in an Age of Uncertainty', NLR I/200, July–August 1993, pp. 15–41.

Party, but son of a famous LDP oligarch—is failing. The LDP has not won, but the reformers always lost. The story of the nineties is that the LDP kept on sinking, but its opponents sank even more. That's true of the Left as a whole, taking the strength of the JSP and JCP together. It's true, however, that in absolute numbers the JCP did rather well—becoming the fourth largest party in the country, with nearly 12 per cent of the vote. Intellectually, it is a bit more open than it was, and since—whatever its limitations—it is the only real opposition in Japan, one has to support it. But there is little to be cheerful about. It was ironic to see the whole organization in suspended animation, waiting for Miyamoto to die. The man who criticized the emperor system became the emperor of the party, whose subjects could not move while they await his interminable death.[5]

Viewed comparatively, one of the most striking features of Japanese capitalism is its management of income distribution. The standard Anglo-Saxon objections to the Japanese model, now relentlessly pressed by the US Treasury, the IMF and media orthodoxy, focus on state regulation, rigged prices, absence of shareholder value. But the same critics are usually forced to admit that, for better or worse, along with these has gone a greater degree of relative social equality. Westerners can sense this very quickly, in the typical lack of dramatic residential contrasts in the big cities: the general absence of slums, ghettoes or zones of luxury that are standard features of metropolitan areas in Europe or the States. Deliberate state policies were certainly necessary to ensure this compression of social differences. What were their origins? Should this abnormal repression of market logic be attributed to the post-war fear of the Left, which was acute in the late forties, or to wartime requirements of national cohesion?

This had already started in the late thirties and forties: one ideological context was the famous debate involving the Kyoto School of philosophy on 'Overcoming Modernity'.[6] The underlying question it posed was: how could Japan compete with the West without simply imitating it? Modernity was American capitalism, Russian Communism, German totalitarianism. The most influential answer was: by adopting a kind of organic corporatism that would separate ownership and control of capital, making management independent of self-interested proprietors, capable of serving the imperial polity in a devoted and selfless spirit. The military regime, determined to mobilize all the nation's resources in the industrialization drive during the war, took a series of measures to block social polarization. So in the early forties, a great deal of legislation was passed to prevent conventional forms of

---

[5] Miyamoto (b. 1908) died in 2007, in his ninety-ninth year.

[6] For English-language accounts of the debate and its post-war sequels, see H. D. Harootunian, 'Visible Discourses/Invisible Ideologies', and Sakai Naoki, 'Modernity and its Critique. The Problem of Universalism and Particularism', in Masao Miyoshi and H. D. Harootunian, eds, *Postmodernism and Japan*, Durham 1989, pp. 63–122.

rent-extraction or profit-taking: tenant-protection laws, housing regulations, food rationing. There were elements in the tradition of Japanese feudalism that favoured this outlook, expressed in the judicial adage of the Tokugawa authorities: 'Side with the weak and crush the strong'. The whole system was designed in such a way that it could function without classic capitalist owners. The American Occupation, by breaking up the old *zaibatsu*, rein-forced this legacy.[7] Once the post-war labour movement had been defeated, this organicist corporatism, sketched out during the war, could come into its own, with further developments like lifetime employment, and function fairly smoothly down to the seventies. Now, of course, it is an obstacle to a rational capitalist purging of the system, despite a decade of crisis: the social interests vested in it are too great for politicians or bureaucrats to attack frontally.

You imply that the ideas of the Kyoto School were of more than arcane signifi-cance in the thirties and forties—that philosophical debates could have national resonance?

Yes, although perhaps one shouldn't overestimate the influence of the Kyoto School itself. Its founder, Nishida Kitaro, in a sense gave theoretical expres-sion to a mentality that was very widespread in Japanese culture. The basic opposition he articulated was between being and nothingness, or a centred structure and a seemingly acentric field. Nishida's key concept was *mu no basho*, or 'the place of nothingness', which he identified historically with the imperial court, envisaged as sort of empty cylinder containing Japan, while actual power was exercised by successive shogunates. Nishida then advocated this notion as the groundless ground for peaceful co-prosperity between nations, between human beings and nature, in the twentieth century. The intellectual roots of the idea lie in Zen thinking, but it could also be described as a kind of negative Hegelianism—instead of a contradiction between two entities, there would be an empty-centred synthesis, within the place of nothingness. The Kyoto School was held in high esteem in the Imperial Navy, which despised the crude totalitarian nationalism of the army, and prided itself on knowing Nishida's arcanum of the empty structure. In the post-war period, a number of prime ministers have claimed allegiance to this tradition, among them Ohira and Nakasone. But perhaps the best example was Takeshita Noboru, who has just died. For the last fifteen years of his life he was the most powerful politician in Japan. Takeshita had certainly read Nishida. He may not have understood much of it, but he incarnated one of its principles: that you have to negate yourself, to become an empty field that can peacefully embrace all opposites. Takeshita was a master in

---

[7] The zaibatsu were the industrial and financial conglomerates that dominated the Japanese economy from the later nineteenth century onwards.

the comportment of humility that is all-powerful. And Obuchi was his best disciple in this regard.

On the other hand, the 'Overcoming Modernity' debate itself—it was organized by the literary journal *Bungakkai* in 1942, soon after the Pacific War had started—involved a varied range of participants. The Kyoto School was represented by Nishitani Keiji, who became the leading exponent of its 'second generation' after the war, when he gave it an increasingly esoteric Zen cast. But there were also the so-called Japanese Romantics, advocates of a 'groundless leap', which had some affinities to Carl Schmitt's decision-ism. Their idea was that you have to make a leap without knowing where you are going; no one knows what to decide, but you have to decide. The famous writer Yasuda Yojuro exemplified this outlook—and today Fukuda, a passionate supporter of Ishihara, tries to fashion himself as a postmodern Yasuda. Then there was a third tendency, intermediate between the other two, represented by the critic Kobayashi Hideo—Miyamoto's rival in the twenties—and his colleagues. They had read Marx, they knew Valéry and the modern Western canon, so they were not unaware of the difficulties of overcoming modernity when the modern itself was not really rooted in Japan. But Kobayashi tried to elude the problem by advocating a flight from the contingency of history into the timeless realms of beauty and art. He never took an unequivocal stand on the political issue.

If the Nishida School offers a striking example of the role of an arcane philosoph-ical doctrine in affairs of state, would it be correct to think of the Uno School in economics as an opposite case after the war—a recondite Marxism with no impact outside the academy?

Not quite. Before the war, Uno was a professional economist working in a statistical research institute as a specialist in agricultural problems. He devel-oped his main ideas in the thirties, but published them only after the war, when he got a chair at Tokyo University. For a long time he dominated the field of Marxist economics, without belonging to the Communist Party. They could never abide a theoretician with an independent mind—so they excluded Fukumoto, a Lukácsian Marxist, and they couldn't accommodate Uno, whose work is essentially a Hegelian systemization of Marxian eco-nomics. Uno's theory is divided into three parts, with very little empirical dimension. The first is a study of 'principle'—that is, pure capitalism; the second is a study of 'stage'—competitive, monopoly, imperialist, etcetera; the third is a study of 'situation'—conjunctures. But there's no real articu-lation between them. Still, though Uno's theory was more academic than it might have been had the Left offered a political home for it, his ideas were not without practical influence. For, ironically, generations of Japanese bureaucrats and managers were taught by professors of Marxian econom-ics at Tokyo University—the obligatory point of entry into the Ministry of

Finance and other key institutions—where they received an education from the Uno School which was very useful to them. Instead of just mathematical apotheosis of market mechanisms by neoclassical economics, they were alerted to the weak links in the capitalist system—its inherent tendencies to instability and crisis. For even if Uno's formalism can sometimes look more Ricardian than Marxian, it is still a theory of the overall structure of production and distribution, not of a homogeneous market which exists nowhere in reality. You can't understand the mentality of Japan's economic bureaucracy, and its lack of inhibition in steering investments and controlling markets, without this intellectual background.

What about the traditions of Japanese liberalism? Are there any successors, for example, to a figure like Maruyama Masao in the field of political theory, who looked back to the example of Fukuzawa Yukichi in Meiji times?[8]

No, after Maruyama there was no comparable figure. Like Uno, he left a school of disciples at Tokyo University, preaching a Weberian Protestant outlook to very small circles. Curiously, there was some revival of Maruyama's ideas in the nineties, because his writings were still relevant to questions of responsibility for war crimes. But Maruyama didn't publish much in his last years, and his legacy has otherwise receded. The most significant Japanese liberal of the post-war period was Ishibashi Tanzan, who was prime minister for a couple of months in 1956–57, then fell ill and resigned. He was an economist by training, and a genuine disciple of Adam Smith. He was also a natural politician, who before the war advocated the independence of Korea and Taiwan on the grounds that colonies were a costly and irrational burden to capitalism. A very interesting figure. You could say he was the last symbol of a middle way in Japan. After Ishibashi there was no politically influential liberal, and after Maruyama no intellectually influential one.

You've mentioned literary critics a number of times. How would you describe the role of such criticism, and literature at large, in Japanese culture?

For a whole historical period, at least down to the end of the seventies, it was the main arena into which public discussion of intellectual or political issues flowed. Other disciplines always remained more confined to the academy (the Kyoto School was an exception—more typical was the narrow neo-Kantian instruction at Tokyo University). Literary criticism, by contrast, was always crucial to the definition of collective meanings in the wider culture. The position enjoyed by Kobayashi, whose career stretched from the twenties to the seventies—he died in 1983—was quite typical. Of course, the role

---

[8] See Ronald Dore, 'Maruyama and Japanese Thought', NLR I/25, May–June 1964, pp. 77–83.

of critics was closely connected to the importance of creative writers. In the generation after Kobayashi we had Yoshimoto and Etoh, the one a more populist, the other a more liberal critic. Etoh, in fact, started out by rejecting everything Kobayashi stood for. He attacked any notion of 'overcoming modernity', arguing that modern subjectivity was precisely what Japan needed. But then he went to the States, where he was treated as more or less a yellow monkey from a defeated country, and unfortunately discovered Erickson's psychology of identity. So when he came back he started talking about national identity, and how Japan could recover it from American distortions—in this regard, you could say Katoh is essentially repeating what Etoh said many years ago. Etoh ended up very conservative. But at the beginning he was close to the writer who became Japan's best-known novelist when he won the Nobel Prize, Oé Kenzaburo, and to Ishihara, in his days as a novelist. For a time the three formed a kind of post-war troika.

In those days, relations between literature and politics were at the centre of intellectual life in Japan. Debates about them reached a peak in 1960, the year of huge turmoil over the Security Treaty with the US. In the aftermath of the demonstrations, however, a seventeen-year-old youth assassinated the chairman of the Socialist Party. Shocked by the killing, Oé wrote two novels in quick succession about the psychosexual genesis of right-wing fanaticism—*Seventeen* and *A Political Boy Dies*—while another writer, Fukazawa Shichiro, published *Furyu Mutan*, a Kafkaesque comedy, which refers to a decapitation of the heir to the throne. The far Right was outraged by both productions, and one of its thugs broke into Fukazawa's house and murdered a maid who was there. Oé, who was himself being harassed anyway, was traumatized by this event. Soon afterwards, he had a disabled son, and went to Hiroshima. From then on, he shifted from political themes to more general issues of individual and collective trauma, and possible salvation. He's a great writer, but the break is quite marked in his work, which has deepened, but narrowed. So far as the consequences are concerned, today we still can't read *A Political Boy Dies* or *Furyumutan*—they remain unavailable, in what amounts to a state of de facto censorship.

The next comparable pairing of critic and writer would be Karatani Kōjin and Nakagami Kenji, who seemed like twins in the eighties. Karatani started out as a rebellious son of Yoshimoto and Etoh. He is a stunning literary critic, with an intellectual range that has made his *Origins of Modern Japanese Literature* the most widely read study of the subject both in Japan and probably abroad. I got to know him in 1980 or 1981, when he came to Kyoto to teach a course on Marx and *Capital*. Nakagami, on the other hand, was a *buraku* novelist who came out as such, depicting the naked structures of power in which Japanese civil society trapped its outcasts;[9] but also the

---

[9] Burakumin; a minority group descended from low-caste Japanese and still vulnerable to discrimination.

interconnected differences between men and women, Japanese and Koreans or Taiwanese. He was a kind of Genet of the accursed glory of the *buraku*. After Oé, it was Nakagami who spotlit really acute political problems in Japan. His fiction is available in French, and should be translated into English. He died at the age of forty-five in 1992, leaving a huge vacuum. Karatani identifed so much with Nakagami that after his death he couldn't find another novelist to write about in the same way, and moved to more general theory.

Better known in the West, of course, is the very different figure of Murakami Haruki, whose works are very popular in the States. Murakami, who started out as a translator of American minimalist fiction, belongs to the sixties generation, but he never refers to anything political directly. Rather he traces subtle changes of sentiments that may be motivated by social turmoil, yet are not reflective on it, in an interiorizing gesture. So after Nakagami's stark contradiction of powers, we have Murakami's highly sophisticated space of subjectivity. Katoh, as you might expect, is a critic very close to Murakami. They both represent a certain return to interiority, after political disillusion.

Abroad, modern Japanese culture is perhaps most often identified with the splendours of Japanese cinema—Mizoguchi, Ozu, Kurosawa—which are much, much better known than its literature. What has happened since this classic era?

The representative figure of the next generation was Oshima, a pure product of the sixties. He was active in the student protests against the Security Treaty in 1960, went into movies, where he was very conscious of the example of Godard and the French *nouvelle vague*, and made political films. His early documentaries, on death by hanging and other subjects, are extraordinary. But over time his output has become more and more marginal, as the industry itself has declined. What you see now, increasingly, is an export product— Oshima playing to the Western gaze, offering images of Japan designed for orientalist expectations. This is already very clear in *Merry Christmas, Mr Lawrence*, where he exploits the exotic stereotype of the Japanese soldier as a modern samurai, complete with repressed homosexuality and suicidal urges. His latest movie *Gohatto*—'Taboo'—involves much the same thematics. For anyone who knows his films of the sixties, the difference is stunning. *Gohatto* is set in the last days of Tokugawa rule, among a guard unit loyal to the Shogunate, on the eve of its overthrow by the Meiji conspirators: a supremely political hour in modern Japanese history. But Oshima discards all of this for a study of homoerotic tensions among the young samurai soldiers, as the appearance of a beautiful boy in their midst brings explosive sexual undercurrents to the surface. The film is in a sense thoroughly reactionary, since after much psychodynamic turmoil, the boy is killed and the homosocial order, with all its misogyny, is restored. Of course, the film will be seen abroad as a great samurai movie, with fantastic scenes of fighting. I was afraid it would be given the grand prize at Cannes, but fortunately even the French cinephiles were not so blind.

This trend actually goes back to Mishima, for whom the original homosexual image was purely Western—Saint Sebastian. Mishima's last performance, his suicide at a Self-Defence Force building, was likewise played out for the Western gaze. He wanted to be remembered as the last samurai who committed suicide, before the eyes of the world. But today this export culture has become much more widespread. Another striking example is Kitano Takeshi, whose films are very popular in Europe just now. He started out as a stand-up comedian on television, and his early movies were very interesting, not unlike Buster Keaton. But after a number of commercial failures, he too opted for satisfaction of the appetites of Western orientalism. So in his recent hit *Hana-bi* we get Mount Fuji, cherry blossoms, fireflies in the snow, the last suicidal voyage of a doomed couple—all these beautiful clichés. So Japanese and so finely done, etcetera: Kitano as our genuine native artist, for the admiration of the West. The phenomenon isn't confined to the cinema, of course. If you look at photography you see the same thing. Who is supposedly the leading Japanese photographer these days? Araki Noboyushi, who started out as a guerrilla against censorship in the seventies and eighties, then won a reputation as a vanguard Japanese artist in Europe and America, and is now reimported to Japan as a representative figure of our contemporary art. He produces images of sadomasochistic anarchy, which he calls 'Ararchy': for example, women in kimonos in bondage. If he were a Westerner, he would have been severely criticized by feminists—and indeed he is, to a certain extent. But as he is Japanese, his sin becomes his charm. There are many more interesting photographers in Japan, but for Manhattan or the *Rive Gauche* Araki is the quintessential Japanese camera.

What are the less exocentric forms?

You could say that rather than anything coming from young *cinéastes*, it is animation directors and games creators who are the real avant-garde in Japan today. This is a huge industry, some of whose products have conquered world markets, but without consciously targeting them. You are dealing with a more endogenous output. Animation remains a subcultural zone, though a gifted individual director like Miyazaki Hayao has generated something like high-cultural works out of it, by transmuting legend—on which this area always feeds—into ideology. You may have seen his powerful ecological fable *Princess Mononoke*, a big success in Japan. Unpredictable inventions, or strange *trouvailles*, bubble up from this commercial underground. The Pokémon craze is a good example. A young guy called Satoshi Tajiri, a conceptual designer, collected insects when he was a kid, and when

Nintendo produced Game Boy, he thought of an exchange system of small monsters. Pokémon has characters, and a narrative, but the important thing is the exchange network that enables the swapping and hybridizing of its bizarre micro-creatures. It is the originality of this scheme—of course, it also taps into the common children's passion for collection—that has caught on. Still, one should not be under any illusions. Most animation and allied forms just recycle archetypal images, usually much more Jungian than Freudian, and all too clichéd stories.

You once offered your own fairy tale, of three kinds of capitalism—elderly in Europe, dominated by transcendental traditions; adult in America, with inner-directed individual responsibility; and infantile in Japan, powered by 'the nearly purely relative competition exhibited by other-oriented children'.[10] So one should take the Pokémon/PlayStation syndrome as another manifestation of Japan's 'infantile capitalism'?

Surely. You could also take as another expression of the same phenomenon the huge popularity of the manga, the Japanese comic book. This has ancient origins in narrative scrolls of the Edo period and earlier. But the modern manga has had a complex history in the post-war period, when it has always been somewhat polyvalent. There were ideological manga fomenting student protest in the sixties, and deviant manga for girls challenging sexual norms in the seventies and eighties. Today you can find ecology or gender criticism in them, just as you can Kobayashi's ultra-nationalism. The form lends itself to subversive parody and burlesque. But, of course, the bulk of production has always been more conventional, instilling all kinds of conformism—baseball manga for boys, romances for girls. The output is enormous, and multilayered: adults read manga in great quantities. The combination is the same you find in the animation or computer games industries: flashes of quirky creativity amid overall regression. Just what you would expect from an infantilized culture.

---

[10] 'Let's call it infantile capitalism. This is a remarkable spectacle and, in many senses, deeply interesting. In the manufacturing sector, for example, we may be able to say that Japanese engineers are cleverly manoeuvred into displaying a childlike passion whereby they are easily obsessed by machines. Further, in such a post-industrial area as advertising, people became carried away by wordplay, parody and all the other childlike games of differentiation ... In fact, children can play "freely" only when there is some kind of protection. They always play within a certain protected area; and this protected area is precisely the core of the Japanese ideological mechanism—however thinly diffused a core. It is not a "hard" ruling structure which is vertically centralized, but "soft" subsumption by a seemingly horizontal, centreless "place" ... Children are running around, each one as fast as possible, at the front lines of the history of capitalism as infantilization proceeds. They are enveloped by a "place" whose age is hardly known—the "place" that is transhistorical in the sense Nishida demonstrated.' Asada Akira, 'Infantile Capitalism and Japan's Postmodernism: a Fairy Tale', in Miyoshi and Harootunian, eds, *Postmodernism and Japan*, pp. 273–8.

*The other area where Japan has registered in a big way internationally is archi-
tecture. What's been the trajectory here?*

Up to the end of the sixties we had a genuine modernist architecture, dominated by Tange Kenzo, who could be described as our Philip Johnson.
But in the seventies one of his students, Isozaki Arata, a contemporary of
Hollein and Eisenman, started to develop all kinds of unbuilt projects which
anticipated what were to become postmodern forms. In 1983 he got his
chance to erect the Tsukuba Centre Building just outside Tokyo, which
set a paradigm for postmodern collage. Lots of commissions, at home and
abroad, followed and Isozaki became the great practitioner and theoretician
of Japanese postmodernism. Since the heyday of the architectural boom of
the eighties, however, there has been a tendency to return to a less critical,
more artisanal approach. Ando Tadao was probably the key architect of the
nineties, with a series of famous minimalist structures. He adopts the stance
of a taciturn craftsman, whose impeccable finish will impress you more than
any construction dreamt up by ambitious theoreticians. Today, with the
bursting of the bubble economy, there are fewer commercial opportunities
for architects, although quite a few mega-projects are still being funded by
the state to pump up the market. Tange, who became a convert to postmodernism like Philip Johnson, has produced some of the worst of these gigantic
schemes. His new City Hall in Tokyo is an act of aesthetic suicide. The
newest wave of architects, on the other hand, pays no attention to theory
or philosophy at all. They look more like techno-barbarians playing with
computer-generated images. In the Western tradition, design was regarded
as inferior to art, whereas in Japan it is our natural way of proceeding. Today
we have every refinement of interior design, of fashion design, of architectural design. What we are short of is original art.

Wang Hui was born in 1959 in the city of Yangzhou, graduating from the Teachers College there before moving to the Chinese Academy of Social Sciences in Beijing in 1985, where he became a research fellow in the Institute of Literature. After the Tiananmen Square massacre of 1989, he was removed to the mountainous countryside of Sha'anxi for a year. On his return to Beijing he published his first book, Revolt Against Despair: Lu Xun and His World, *a bold departure from conventional readings of this central figure in modern Chinese literature. Three years later came a collection of essays on the May Fourth movement (*No Room for Hesitation in a Void*) and then* Self-Selected Essays *(1997) and a collection of his writings on modernization,* Rekindling Frozen Fire *(1999). The four volumes of* The Rise of Modern Chinese Thought *appeared in 2004.*

Widely recognized for his independence of mind and critical spirit, Wang had been a natural choice for the editorship of the literary monthly Dushu *(Reading) when it fell vacant in 1996, and under his direction and that of his colleague Huang Ping the magazine became a key venue for contemporary debates, accommodating all political tendencies. Wang himself was more and more widely perceived as the herald of a 'New Left' in China—a designation he has hesitated to embrace, for the reasons he indicates here, in an interview given in 2000. In the opening years of the new century, fundamental debates over policy took on a vehemence not witnessed since the interwar years, and in July 2007 Wang was dismissed from his editorial post.*

Wang Hui

Fire at the Castle Gate

What is the role of Dushu *in Chinese intellectual life, and how do you conceive your position in it as editor?*

The first issue of *Dushu* was published in April 1979. Its leading article was entitled 'No Forbidden Zone in Reading', and you could say that has been the spirit of the journal from the beginning. This is how we do our editorial job today, and we will never change it in the future. The first editor of *Dushu* came from the Commercial Publishing House in Beijing, historically the most important imprint in modern China. A year later, Fan Yong—a progressive publisher with close links to the intellectual world since the forties—took over. I think he was the most significant figure in the history of the journal, making it a key forum for new ideas and debates in the eighties. From 1979 to 1984, most of these were raised by an older generation of scholars or open-minded official intellectuals, like Li Honglin, Wang Ruoshi and others. It was they, for example, who took up the issue of the relations between Marxism and humanism. Then around 1985 a younger levy of intellectuals took centre stage. Among the most active were the editorial committee of *Culture: China and The World*, a series of translations aiming to introduce classics of modern thought from abroad, most of them produced by the Sanlian Press, which is also the publisher of *Dushu*. The journal ran many reviews of these books, which attracted a lot of attention from university students, graduates and fledgling intellectuals. There was an enthusiastic reception of modern Western philosophy, social theory and economic thought. Nietzsche, Heidegger, Cassirer, Marcuse, Sartre, Freud, not to speak of modernization theory and neoclassical economics were eagerly canvassed in the articles of the time. There was some resistance to all this, since the style in which these notices were written was often criticized as too difficult or obscure. Looking back, one can see that this younger generation was more interested in introducing new theories, without any necessary political bearing, whereas the older generation had a much closer relation to politics. In this phase *Dushu* was not a radical journal—it was relatively detached from the political ferment of the late eighties. But an intellectual space for further discussion was created, which was not without significance in 1989.

That year saw a turning point. Whereas there was a high turnover of editors in other periodicals by late 1989, there was no change at *Dushu*, whose chief editor Shen Changwen carried on till 1996. This was partly just because the journal had played little direct political role in the preceding years. But in the general atmosphere of conservatism and dogmatism after 1989, *Dushu* now stood out as more open-minded. Of course there were pressures on the journal, and after Deng Xiaoping's visit to southern China in 1992, a wave of consumerism and commercialization swept the country. In these conditions, Shen shifted editorial policy towards articles that were easier to read, with less academic discussions, to boost sales. Circulation rose from 50,000 to over 80,000 in five or six years, but while the journal became more popular, it was also criticized for failing to reflect the development of intellectual research in the country. Actually, it was still introducing new themes like orientalism or post-colonialism, and continued to be widely viewed as a symbol of elite culture. But the changes in *Dushu* in the early nineties did mark a new tension between popular culture and high culture in China.

In 1996 I was invited to be a chief editor—joined a year later by my colleague Huang Ping. Since then, our policy has been to keep a readable style for the journal, but to move it away from consumerist preoccupations back to real intellectual discussion, and to expand its range beyond literature and the humanities to the social and natural sciences, including subjects never touched on before like archaeology or historical geography. We have launched a series of major debates on the fate of rural society, ethics, Asia, war and revolution, financial crisis, liberalism, law and democracy, nationalism, feminism. Most of these issues—the current crisis of rural society, for example—were raised for the first time in contemporary China in our pages, and other journals then followed. We carry opinions from right across the political spectrum. I should say that, as chief editor, I publish my own articles in other periodicals, to safeguard the impartiality of the journal. Our roster of contributors has expanded substantially, and many of the newer ones have made their names writing for us. All this has made *Dushu* a focus of lively controversy, and increased its readership to between 100,000 and 120,000.

The internet has exploded as a medium of discussion in China. What changes, for good or for bad, is this bringing to the exchange of ideas, especially among the younger generation?

Yes, this has been a major development. All kinds of different forces are now finding an outlet on the net, and even the Chinese government has stepped in with—not very successful—efforts to regulate it. The internet has brought three significant gains. It creates a space in which direct discussions between mainland and overseas Chinese intellectuals become possible, as a zone beyond the borders of nation-states. Secondly, it allows a lot of directly political issues to be addressed, which the print media in the mainland cannot touch. Thirdly, it spreads information from local levels very quickly across the country, which otherwise would not get national attention. So it offers the possibility of linking local, national and international spaces. But its limitations remain obvious too. The information it purveys is not beyond regulation by various forces. Since much of it is impossible to check, we often have no means of knowing whether something is true or false. The net is also an ideal medium for intervention without responsibility, encouraging personalized attacks and reckless vituperation under cover of anonymity. At the same time, it does not lend itself easily to theoretical discussions, which are still more or less the preserve of print journals in China, though some are now setting up their websites and we can expect more interaction between the two media. Still, the internet has certainly played a role in the intensification of polemical exchanges this year, with new camps springing to life on the most pressing issues of the day.

Looking at the political field, during the eighties the Chinese scene was conventionally divided into two categories—reformers and conservatives, a dichotomy with its own built-in valuations of the two. At some point in the nineties, terms changed, and people started to talk about liberals and then, more recently still, a New Left. What lies behind this development?

Towards the end of the seventies, the terms 'conservatives' and 'reformers' indicated, respectively, holdovers from Mao's last years—also derisively dubbed *fanshipai* or 'whatevers'—and supporters of Deng's policies. At that time, it was figures like Hua Guofeng or Mao's former security chief Wang Dongxing who were the conservatives, while theoreticians like Deng Liqun or Hu Qiaomu belonged to the reforming wing of the party.[1] In the late seventies, Deng Liqun was quite radical: while Hua Guofeng was still chairman of the Chinese Communist Party (CCP), he published some lectures in the Central Party School attacking the conservatives very sharply—even criticizing Mao himself. But after the 'campaign against spiritual pollution' in 1983, the political map changed. Hu Qiaomu published a famous article about socialist humanism, attacking Zhou Yang, Wang Ruoshi, Su Shaozhi and other—generally more open-minded—intellectuals within the party, who had taken up this slogan; and the perception of Deng Liqun changed

---

[1] Hua Guofeng was Mao's short-lived official successor as chairman of the CCP (1976–78). In 1978 Hu Qiaomu—Mao's secretary during the Yan'an period—and Deng Liqun were respectively president and vice president of the Chinese Academy of Social Sciences.

too.[2] Once Hu Yaobang became General Secretary of the CCP, Hu Qiaomu and Deng Liqun were typecast as conservatives. But actually they had earlier been regarded as reformers themselves. All these people belonged to Deng Xiaoping's camp. You can see the same kind of shift in categorizations of Li Peng, whom we considered the arch-conservative in 1989. Known mainly as Chou En-lai's adopted son, he became vice-premier in the mid-eighties. His attitude was quite ambiguous at the time—it was not at all clear whether he was a conservative or a radical reformer. The distinction between the two stances was plain for all to see among the older generation of party leaders, but was much more blurred in this generation.

With the crackdown of 1989, it was ostensibly the conservatives who had taken power. But the label did not so easily lend itself to Deng Xiaoping. After June Fourth he held a series of talks with Yao Yilin, Li Peng and others at which he insisted on a continuation of his reform policies, and picked Jiang Zemin to be his successor, as a politician milder than Li Peng but stronger than Zhao Ziyang.[3] So in the nineties, it became very difficult to give any real content to the categories of reformer or conservative. In one sense, the whole 'reform policy' became more radical than in Zhao Ziyang's time. There were no longer any voices to be heard against it within the power structure. Li Peng himself as premier carried out many drastic reforms, at Deng's prompting.

It was against this background that a change in Chinese political vocabulary started to occur. We can date its beginnings from around 1993. In the spring of 1992 Deng Xiaoping made a trip to Shenzhen in the South, where he gave the signal for an all-out drive for market-led modernization of the PRC economy. The immediate result was a runaway consumer boom—with high inflation—in Shanghai, Guangdong and even Beijing. This outcome of the Southern tour shocked a lot of intellectuals. Most of them had initially welcomed the energetic new burst of reform policies. But when they saw the rampant commercialization of all structures of daily life and culture that followed them, they started to feel a certain disillusion. In the eighties the mainstream outlook of Chinese intellectuals had been—in the phrase of the time—a 'New Enlightenment' very favourable to the Open Door priorities and marketizing thrust of Deng's rule. Two debates now began to alter these parameters. In 1993 the Hong Kong journal *Twenty-First Century* published an article by a young Chinese economist at MIT, Cui Zhiyuan, under the title 'A Second Emancipation'. It argued that if the first intellectual emancipation had been from orthodox Marxism, there should now be a second one, from

---

[2] Zhou Yang—once Mao's chief functionary for Literature—was a victim of the Cultural Revolution; Wang Ruoshi was then deputy chief editor of *The People's Daily*, Su Shaozhi director of the Institute for Marxism–Leninism–Mao Zedong Thought in the Chinese Academy of Social Sciences.

[3] Yao Yilin was director of the State Planning Commission in the late eighties; Zhao Ziyang was general secretary of the CCP from 1987 to 1989.

the rote assumptions of the New Enlightenment. Cui drew on three different strands of thought: critical legal studies in the US, analytical Marxism in the West, and theories of a New Evolution. For Chinese readers, the startling feature of his essay was its calm reference to analytical Marxism—not that anyone much knew what the term meant: it was just the use of the term 'Marxism' itself, long a virtual taboo for many intellectuals. Cui Zhiyuan went on to collaborate with Roberto Unger in a series of articles on the fate of the Russian reforms, as an admonition to would-be reformers in China. At the same time, another young scholar working in the States, Gan Yang, was publishing articles in *Twenty-First Century* on township and village enterprises, as a form of property neither state nor private, but intermediate between the two, as the distinctive Chinese path to modernity. So the first break with the consensus came from overseas students.

However, the following year saw another important debate, this time in *Dushu*, when a number of leading intellectuals attacked the increasing commercialization of life in China as destructive of its 'humanistic spirit'. The topic was launched by scholars from Shanghai, logically enough, since Shanghai is the biggest consumer centre in China and its intellectuals were shocked earlier and more deeply than their counterparts in Beijing by the ruthless wave of commercialization after Deng's Southern tour. Not that these intellectuals were hostile to the market as such. Rather, they lamented that Chinese marketization failed to live up to the standards set in Europe and America. Some tried to trace its deficiencies back to Weber's argument that Protestantism is essential to the true spirit of capitalism. An ideal capitalism should, they felt, be compatible with a humanistic spirit. The underlying attitude was fairly unpolitical—behind it lay the offended dignity of scholars in the humanities. But they were now becoming aware that marketization in China relied on a political system that in their eyes remained unchanged.

Independently—actually a little earlier—the group around the journal *Xueren* ('The Scholars'), with which I was associated, had raised some critical issues, looking back at the June Fourth movement. They found that the intellectuals of the New Enlightenment, who had exercised a great influence on the June Fourth movement, in practice knew very little about Chinese history. Rather than studying Chinese realities, they had simply imported Western ideas into the reform process. That was a big mistake. We thought it was essential to reflect very carefully on modern Chinese history, and started to look at the professional scholarship that had studied it. Most of this was quite traditional, and we went on to propose other methods.

This was the context in which talk started of a 'New Left', more critical of capitalism and more aware of the Yeltsin experience than the New Enlightenment. So far as I know, the first appearance of the term was in a short report in *Beijing Youth Daily*. I didn't use any such phrase myself, simply stressing the need for critical analysis of Chinese realities. Then I saw the report, which spoke of a new Marxism and the ideas of a New Left, in quite a positive tone. Since, however, the editor of *Beijing Youth Daily* was a supporter of the theory that China needed a New Authoritarianism, I suspected the term New Left was just being used as a cudgel to belabour liberals. That is one of the reasons why I have been hesitant to employ it in the Chinese context myself.

Was the term 'liberal' already in widespread usage?

Not yet in its current sense. The government, of course, had waged a campaign against 'bourgeois liberalism' in 1986, not to speak of 1983. But the term was still used much in the way Mao had employed it in Yan'an, to refer to personal misbehaviour and lack of discipline. For its part the New Enlightenment did not take liberalism, understood in a more classical sense, as a model. It tended to appeal to a different kind of socialism. Fang Lizhi, for example, on coming back from a trip to Scandinavia, advocated a Nordic socialism in the tradition of Bernstein for China.[4] The leading philosopher Li Zehou defined himself as a Marxist, not a liberal. Wang Yuanhua, editor of the journal *New Enlightenment,* claimed to be a Marxist. Su Shaozhi published research on Yugoslav, Polish and Hungarian reforms. At the time, the inspiration of this generation was still socialist rather than liberal. The one significant exception was the political scientist Yan Jiaqi, who did look back to the European Enlightenment, the time of the American Constitution and the early phase of the French Revolution, and was concerned with the division of powers in the liberal tradition of government. But in general, from the end of the seventies to the mid-eighties, the New Enlightenment—most of whose leading intellectuals were very close to the government—still spoke of the merits of socialism. It was in the late eighties that the atmosphere changed. By then Hayek's works were more and more widely talked about, though few people had read them. Friedman was received enthusiastically by Zhao Ziyang. The economists advising the government were pressing for large-scale privatizations.

So the current self-identification of most Chinese intellectuals as 'liberals' dates from the nineties? In the eighties, no one could openly say: 'Yes, I am a liberal.' But after 1989, the radicalization of official reform policies created a situation where the term could describe a mixture of support and criticism of the government—approval of marketization, but disapproval of censorship or violation of human rights. The basis of this attitude would be: we are liberal because we believe in liberty, and the precondition of liberty is the dominance of private property in society. Would it be correct to think this became a consensus?

---

[4] Fang Lizhi: astrophysicist who became vice president of the new Science and Technology University in Hefei, and leading liberal critic of the government, in the late eighties; now in exile.

Roughly, yes—but with many shades of opinion. Some of the Shanghai liberals were very uneasy about the commercialization of culture, for example—anxieties that came out in the 'humanistic spirit' debate. Others were worried about growing social inequalities. Actually, the self-definition of Chinese liberals didn't crystallize fully until they discovered an intellectual opponent. The first stirrings of a more critical view of official marketization go back to 1993–94, as I've said. But it wasn't till 1997–98 that the label New Left became widely used, to indicate positions outside the consensus. Liberals adopted the term, relying on the negative identification of the idea of the 'Left' with late Maoism, to imply that these must be a throwback to the Cultural Revolution. Up till then, they had more frequently attacked anyone who criticized the rush to marketization as a 'conservative'—this is how Cui Zhiyuan was initially described, for example. From 1997 onwards, this altered. The standard accusatory term became 'New Left'.

What accounts for the change?

It corresponded to a shift in the cultural atmosphere. As the nineties wore on, more and more voices could be heard criticizing the whole direction Chinese society was taking. Even some economists, a very orthodox community, could be heard doubting whether the country was on the right path—scholars like Yang Fan put forward a lot of data that made uncomfortable reading. In 1997 the Hainan journal *Tianya* published an essay I had written four years earlier—at that time no one wanted to risk printing it—on the failure of successive versions of Chinese 'modernization', which ends with a sharp critique of the kind of capitalist modernity the Reform Era had offered the country. At first there was no open reaction, although I was vehemently taken to task in private, and various unflattering descriptions were circulated about me. The public response was silence, but there was a lot of talk about it. Then *Twenty-First Century* in Hong Kong published two or three articles by mainland intellectuals attacking me. This broke the ice, and several liberals followed up with hostile responses in the PRC press, mainly in Guangzhou. Part of the reason for this reaction was that, after a decade as a contributor, I was by now editor of *Dushu*, and some of its issues had contained material calculated to unsettle conventional wisdom among intellectuals. Circulation went up, though older-generation scholars like Li Shenzi and others, who were friends of mine, would ask me how I could run such articles. But these provoked a lot of discussion, in which a younger generation became very interested. A collection of essays I published in the same year, mainly concerned with problems of Chinese modernity, sold pretty well. At Beijing University, teachers devoted semesters to discussing it with their students. In these new conditions, Gan Yang and Cui Zhiyuan got a real response to their writings in the mainland for the first time. Intellectually, 1997 was a turning point.

A process of political differentiation has continued since?

In 1998 the Asian financial crisis broke out. Naturally, this shook any blind faith in the world market. Suddenly capitalism did not seem such a sure-fire guarantee of stability and prosperity after all. Liberals were put on the defensive. But a much worse blow to them came in 1999, with the NATO bombing of the Chinese Embassy in Belgrade. For many Chinese liberals, who are very pro-Western, it is virtually a reflex to approve any American initiative. So when there was a wave of indignation among ordinary Chinese and spontaneous demonstrations by students, with the government taking up the rear, they suddenly found themselves isolated. The feeling that they had lost credibility with students was especially painful. Some compared the outburst of popular anger to the Boxer riots, as expressions of an irrational xenophobia, while others blamed the New Left for encouraging a primitive nationalism that could only strengthen the government. Very little of this found its way into the media, but a fund of suppressed tensions accumu-lated, which burst into the public domain this year, when the 'New Left' became the target for a violent liberal offensive. Actually, people like myself have always been reluctant to accept this label, pinned on us by our adversar-ies. Partly this is because we have no wish to be associated with the Cultural Revolution, or for that matter what might be called the 'Old Left' of the Reform-era CCP. But it's also because the term New Left is a Western one, with a very distinct set of connotations—generational and political—in Europe and America. Our historical context is Chinese, not Western, and it is doubtful whether a category imported so explicitly from the West could be helpful in today's China. This feeling was strengthened by the Balkan War. So many Western intellectuals describing themselves as on the 'Left' supported the NATO campaign that one couldn't much wish to borrow the word from them. So rather than a New Left in China, I still prefer to speak of critical intellectuals. But the term has probably come to stay.

Historically, the terms Left and Right have tended to buckle and twist into strange shapes in late communist or post-communist societies. In Gorbachev's Russia, which had undergone no Cultural Revolution, the term 'Left' was for a time widely used for Friedmanite reformers who wished to push the country rapidly towards capitalism, as against 'conservatives' attached to the old system. It was not until quite late in the Yeltsin period that this reversal of meaning tilted back into a more familiar classification, when Gaidar and his fellow liberals—who freely described themselves as 'Lefts' at the turn of the nineties—formed a Union of Right Forces to contest Duma elections. It seems that today in China, after a long period in which neither term had any currency, the idea of a—New—Left has resurfaced. What about a Centre or Right? Have these terms been reclaimed too, or are they still empty boxes waiting for the appropri-ate forces to take possession of them?

No one has claimed them so far. But that doesn't mean they fail to correspond to actual positions. A good many of our liberals represent a contemporary Chinese Right. This is especially true of the economists who advocate privatization and marketization without any doubts or limits, without the slightest critical distance. They have taken the idea from Hayek that the market is a spontaneous economic order. In China, they maintain, marketization is the only route to prosperity and democracy—not that they care greatly whether there is a democracy or not, but it is required as a rhetorical add-on. Typically, these people work with the big companies and the government. Someone like Fan Gang, from my generation, would be a representative example. Other liberals, on the other hand, occupy a Centre position. They have discovered marketization in China does not generate a spontaneous economic order—since the market is not free, but determined through and through by political monopolies and official corruption. So they are highly critical of current realities, and call for social justice along with economic growth. On the other hand, at least until recently, they tended to idealize marketization abroad—not just in Europe or America, but in Eastern Europe and Russia as well—as the 'good' path that China has missed. He Qinglian and Qin Hui represented this position. Qin Hui wrote several articles idealizing the Czech and Russian privatization schemes as the distribution of an equal economic starting point to all citizens.[5]

How would the Left's position on these economic and social questions be defined?

There are a number of different perspectives. Cui Zhiyuan, for example, emphasizes the need for institutional and theoretical inventiveness, and calls for a 'republican' combination of distinct principles of political order, and diverse systems of economic property. He has written various articles in the *Journal of Strategy and Management* and other magazines on these themes. His main concern is that a balance should be kept between central and local government, market and planning principles. His basic standpoint does not seem so radical to me. But liberals regard any criticism of the way the central government has ceded so many fiscal and other powers to the provinces—a development that has caused very grave problems—with the greatest alarm. More generally, the characteristic focus of what the liberals call the New Left is the nexus between the market and the state: that is, the relationships between interest groups and power structures, economic forms and political systems. Markets themselves are no novelty in China. Traditional Chinese society had huge regional and interregional markets, with a series of distinctive features that have been analysed by historians of

---

[5] For He Qinglian, see her article 'China's Listing Social Structure', NLR 5, September–October 2000. Qin Hui: agrarian economist at Qinghua University.

the Chinese economy. In the nineteenth century, the process of market formation was for the first time associated with the colonial pressures of world
capitalism. That meant the market had to be organized by the state in a new
way, with the establishment of a customs organization for the regulation
of foreign trade, as a condition of sovereignty. The late twentieth century
saw far greater state intervention to mould and create markets, under the
pressures of globalization.

*But how far does such a focus really differentiate a New Left from a liberal
Centre? Many critical liberals insist no less strongly on the power-political
determination of markets, and the need to correct the social injustices that flow
from it in China.*

The difference is quite deep. Liberals of this sort support marketization of
the economy as the only correct road for China. In their eyes, it is only the
absence of political reform that warps the workings of the market—but if
the constitution were revised to protect the rights of the citizen, then we
would have a reasonably equal society and a satisfactory degree of social
justice. In my view, that is an illusion. Political democracy will not come
from a legally impartial market, secured by constitutional amendments, but
from the strength of social movements against the existing order, and the
interaction between these movements, public discussions and institutional
innovation. This point is central to the genealogy of the critical intellectual
work that is now identified as a New Left. We have certainly learnt a lot from
Western experiences and theories, but we refuse the implication that all the
issues now raised by critical intellectuals come from America or Europe. On
the contrary, they are in continuity with the social mobilizations in China
during the late eighties. In 1989, why did the citizens of Beijing respond so
strongly and actively to the student demonstrations? It was largely because
of the so-called double-track price system and the unequal way in which
wage contracts were introduced. These provided the institutional base for
growing social differentiation, official speculation and large-scale corruption in the late eighties. At that time, the government had twice imposed
adventurist reforms on the price system, generating inflation without any
benefit to ordinary people. Their earnings suffered from the agreements
they were forced to sign by factories, and their jobs were at risk. People felt
the inequality created by the reforms: there was real popular anger in the air.
That is why the citizenry poured onto the streets in support of the students.
The social movement was never simply a demand for political reform, it also
sprang from a need for economic justice and social equality. The democracy
that people wanted was not just a legal framework, it was a comprehensive
social value. It was this great explosion of popular feeling at the end of the
eighties that is the historical background to the work of critical intellectuals
in the nineties.

You can see the gulf between this way of looking at the market and the neo-liberal view of it. For the neo-liberals, the price system of a free market is the signalling mechanism of a spontaneous order of exchange, as opposed to the distortions of central planning. But the failures of Zhao Ziyang showed that the price system is never a spontaneous order. It is always instituted and managed. People felt that, and revolted against it. But after the armed crackdown on the June Fourth movement people lost their chance to protest, and price reform introduced at gunpoint became a success. All-out marketization in China did not originate from spontaneous exchange but from acts of violence—state repression of the social movement. We can see the same logic if we look at the foreign side of the picture. For the market as a system has never been just a domestic question within China. The PRC has always been involved in foreign trade: with the USSR and Eastern Europe in the fifties and early sixties, and even during the Cultural Revolution with the outside world through Hong Kong. But the Open Door policies of Deng Xiaoping demanded a much deeper insertion of China into the world market. How did that happen? A key step in the process was China's invasion of Vietnam in 1978. One reason for this otherwise senseless attack on a small neighbour was the desire for a new relationship with the United States. The invasion was offered as political gift to Washington, and became China's entrance ticket to the world system. Here too violence was the precondition of a new economic order.

The neo-authoritarians of the late eighties and neo-liberals of the late nineties never mention the war against Vietnam; and by the mid-nineties they were often criticizing the June Fourth movement as too radical. They focus on the need for basic political freedoms, and there we can agree. But as soon as one moves from general principles to particular issues, the differences become apparent. They want to separate the political and economic realms, whereas we argue that the problems of each are intertwined—you cannot always distinguish between them, or say which is more decisive. For example, when we argued that it was very important that peasants should become involved in village elections, where official candidates can be defeated, Liu Junning, a young star of our political science, replied 'We don't need that—these elections are totally corrupted; what matters are congressional and judicial reforms.' It is true that there is a lot of corruption in these elections. But the question is whether we still believe in the participation of the masses in political reform.

Have these differences crystallized into articulated programmes yet?

People often ask us: 'But what is your positive alternative?' The truthful answer is that we have no total project of reform to hand, because we don't believe in trying to work out an ideal order in advance of concrete social demands. When social movements do emerge, we should study very closely what sorts of reasons bring ordinary people into them. In 1989, for example, it is clear that socialist values were still alive for many citizens, and informed the ideas of democracy and freedom much more than liberal doctrines. So in that case we have to look back at the history of Chinese society since 1949, which is not exhausted by the dictatorship of the CCP or the failures of central planning, but contained other features as well to which people were attached. In the fifties and sixties, for example, there was a system of cooperative medical insurance in rural areas which meant that local people organized themselves to help each other, setting up funds and providing services. Since the state-run health system is now collapsing, why don't we learn some positive lessons from this? There are still some socialist fragments in China today, which few of us have thought seriously about. Cui Zhiyuan once tried to say something about the Anshan experience, but he confused most of his readers and lost the debate that followed.[6] But I think his basic impulse was right. We should look with an open mind at historical practices of the past, without trying to copy them. An unprejudiced intellectual curiosity is something all Chinese intellectuals need today.

What is your view of China's township and village enterprises (or TVEs)? Various observers—you mentioned Cui Zhiyuan, but this is a view quite widely shared in the West—have argued that these are the really original institutions to emerge in the reform period, as forms of collective but not state ownership that have proved economically very dynamic. Other scholars in China and abroad believe they are already crypto-capitalist companies, typically controlled by corrupt local bosses, often colluding with foreign investors in throwing environmental concerns to the winds in the search for quick profits. How do you assess them?

Historically the TVEs were a real success for a certain period, and their creation was a great achievement. But we should be sceptical of the larger claim made for them, that they represent a Chinese model of development that offers an alternative to the world market system. They owed much of their success to the dual price structures that came into force with the early reforms. On the one hand, the large state enterprises were forced to sell raw materials like iron and steel at low prices. The TVEs, on the other hand, could use these inputs to market goods at higher, uncontrolled prices. Naturally, if they showed any competence, they could prosper; and many proved genuinely able and flexible enterprises. Many also benefited from effective tax exemption. Whereas state enterprises bore a double burden of tax, as late as 1998 only about a third of TVEs paid any taxes at all. With these advantages, it is not surprising that a good number of them posted an impressive

---

[6] Anshan: iron-and-steel complex in Liaoning province, whose shop-floor creativity was hailed in the fifties.

performance. But in recent years, they have entered into a deep crisis. Many have become private firms, others have merged with foreign capital. The ability of village enterprises to absorb labour on the land has declined, leading to greater rural influx into the cities.

How far is the growing social polarization between rich and poor, and the increase in unemployment, a matter of major public debate today?

For several years now there has been a big debate about social polarization among intellectuals, with many articles in journals and books about it. Some younger-generation thinkers have described current trends as a ruthless form of social Darwinism. Liberals of an older generation, scholars like Li Shenzhi and Zi Zhongyun, reply that China has unfortunately not known social Darwinism, but its opposite—socialism as the survival of the unfittest. So this issue is hotly debated in intellectual circles. In general, however, the mass media refuse to touch it. Unemployment is rather different. There have been quite a lot of articles about factory lay-offs in the newspapers, and what arrangements might be made for workers who lose their jobs; but there is very little discussion of the fate of peasants who drift to the city in search of work, and then become a floating population without employment or rights of residence.

Have there been major changes in the position of women in the labour market?

The basic trend is not unlike that in Eastern Europe and Russia in their reform periods—a reversion to an older division of labour, with a loss of employment and independence by women. But the process has not gone so far. Some corporations publicly refuse to take in female graduates from universities, while others are anxious to maintain a gender balance. There is no doubt that women's social position overall is lower than men's in the PRC, even if there are big differences in the size of the gap that exists in the cities and in the countryside. A significant development is the spread of prostitution once again, which has become a major tax resource for local governments, who give no protection to the women whose earnings they exploit. In cities like Guangzhou, you find a large number of young female workers in factories, paid miserable wages, without any form of public oversight.

Moving to the political field proper, would it be true to say that one reason for the still blurred boundaries between different intellectual camps in today's China is that people who disagree sharply about everything else still share at least one aim—they all want greater democracy?

Well, it is true that virtually all intellectuals would like more freedom of expression. It is understandable that intellectuals should care deeply about whether or not they can speak their minds freely. But they should also care about the much larger number of fellow citizens who have lost their jobs or fallen into sickness or poverty, without anyone to look after them. The issue of democracy is so much broader than just the right of intellectuals not to suffer censorship. After the June Fourth movement was suppressed, many concluded that radicalism had undone it, and that there had to be some other way to democracy. The answer would lie in the gradual emergence of civil society from the development of the market economy. For marketization would produce a new middle class that could furnish the sturdy basis for civil associations, without directly antagonizing the state. The resulting civil society would then blossom into a democracy. These ideas were actually first developed by Taiwanese liberals in the eighties. My reaction was: 'But what kind of civil society do you want? What sort of social structure do you have in mind?'

After various debates, some neo-liberals decided that China still lacks the social basis for a civil society, and therefore the priority is to unleash the market to create one. Turning to the right, they made it clear their concern was not democracy as such, but the market at whatever cost. A well-known economist once said: 'Attacks on corruption are an attack on the market—we have to tolerate the one to develop the other'. In the mid-nineties, the group around Liu Junning publicly claimed that true liberalism is a form of conservatism, because of its belief in order. This is a very revealing shift of terms, since in the eighties and early nineties conservatism was always used as a pejorative term to describe anyone who was regarded as insufficiently enthusiastic about the market, or too willing to envisage a positive role for the state—the label was applied to people like Hu Angang or Cui Zhiyuan.[7] Not all liberals, of course, have made such a sharp right turn. There are much more radical figures like Qin Hui, who continue to insist on the importance of social justice and—still more—political democracy. He argues that the Chinese regime basically remains Mao's old socialist state, which we need to replace with a liberal democracy. To some extent I agree with this, because it is true that we need political democracy to solve virtually all other problems. But I don't believe the current state is just a continuation of the old one. The country cannot be described as socialist, and the state itself has changed a lot. Today the state is itself part of the market system. In some ways it functions very well in that capacity—it makes mistakes, of course, but it is now a key factor in the dynamic of marketization. Qin Hui underestimates this.

---

[7] Hu Angang: China's outstanding critic of central-state fiscal weakness and regional polarization.

Turning to the cultural field, how far have questions of modernism and post-modernism been a focus of interest among Chinese intellectuals, and how far do positions on them correspond to points along the political spectrum?

Postmodernism arrived in China when Fredric Jameson gave a course of lectures at Beida (Beijing University) in 1985, which were published as a book a year later under the title of *Cultural Theory and Postmodernism*. That was the beginning. The lectures had a big impact on his students, who included Zhang Yiwu and Zhang Xudong. At the same time another young scholar, Chen Xiaoming, decided to write a book applying postmodern categories and deconstructive techniques to the latest generation of semi-avant-garde writers like Yu Hua and Ge Fei. But these were still very small eddies. Then came June Fourth. Afterwards, most intellectuals fell silent for political reasons. But around 1992–94 Zhang Yiwu and Chen Xiaoming became quite active, contributing articles on postmodernism to journals like *The Literary Review*. They were impressed by the speed of marketiza-tion, and made a deduction from it rather like the theorists of civil society. Consumerism could be a kind of freedom: it would undermine dictator-ship—which, of course, was partially true. After three years of silence, this caused quite a stir.

My generation found it much more difficult to analyse the new consum-erism. They could see it was different from state socialism, and they sensed it was different from the liberalism with which most of them identified. It posed them with a dilemma: if we support market reform, how can we oppose consumerism, however objectionable some of its manifestations? The result was the debate on the 'humanistic spirit'. Hard on its heels came a third discussion. In 1995 *Dushu* started to publish articles by Zhang Kuan, an overseas student, on orientalism. Here was a theme that opened another door to the West, where Saïd had developed his theory, yet also offered a cri-tique of the West, and so would not offend the official ideology. The liberals were vulnerable on this score, since they could be criticized for accepting quasi-orientalist premises in taking their model of democracy from the West. My own view differed from both camps, the liberals and their post-colonial critics. The latter were right that we should acquire a more critical under-standing of the West, whose colonialist legacies have not disappeared, and which could never just be a model for us. On the other hand, a certain kind of insistence on the dangers of orientalism could become a covert pretext for nationalism.

Around the same time, Huntington's article, 'The Clash of Civilizations', provoked a lot of discussion—both *Twenty-First Century* and *Strategy and Management* devoted special issues to it. Liberal intellectuals criticized it very sharply for implying that conflict was inevitable between the West and China. The followers of Saïd argued that the extreme Right in the West was just confirming the Orientalist fixation with China as an alien, hostile land. The former rejected Huntington's arguments as a distortion of the real—better—nature of the West, while the latter denounced them as an all too accurate expression of Western colonialism. In the background of these discussions of Saïd and Huntington was the political context of those years. In Moscow Yeltsin had pounded the Russian Parliament with tank fire, to the applause of the United States. Naturally, ordinary Chinese asked: why is America's reaction so different to its attitude to June Fourth in China? The hypocrisy of US foreign policy was starkly exposed. Then the West manoeuvred to ensure that the Olympic Games of 2000 were not held in China. Many intellectuals disliked the PRC's application to stage the games, but it was popular with ordinary people, who were angered by Western obstruction. This was the atmosphere in which Saïd and Huntington became reference points.

My own view was that, in so far as Orientalism remained a predominantly cultural theory, it couldn't handle a range of problems that were economically and politically pressing in China. It was too soft! In 1995 Li Shenzhi, described as the 'patron of Chinese liberalism' by the *New York Times*, published perhaps the first article in the PRC on globalization, which he essentially welcomed.[8] In an indirect response I wrote a short piece in *Dushu*, assessing Samir Amin's works—I had heard him talk in Denmark the year before—as a variant of dependency theory, from which we could learn something in China, without accepting his idea of 'delinking' from the world economy, which Mao had in a sense attempted. The article was very sharply criticized by Li Shenzhi, who said: 'That article is so left-wing! How could you talk in that way?' What I was talking about was the power of the world system, as another way of formulating 'globalization', and the need for democracy on a world scale to counter it.

What about theoretical discussions in the later nineties? Zhang Xudong has taken up the theme of postmodernism in a major essay, which develops at least two central arguments.[9] Postmodernism, he maintains, is a theory and practice of what is hybrid and heterogeneous, and as such well suited to the mixed forms and realities of China's economy and society. Where modernity was always conceived as a universal process, moving towards a single end-state, postmodernity does away with this teleology, opening up a horizon of different possible futures. To this intellectual liberation, freeing the Chinese mind from preordained norms and goals, there corresponds a popular emancipation in the postmodern culture of mass consumption—which can be seen as an ambiguous form of democratization: the entrance of ordinary people's desires into the space of culture, through the market. What is your view of this argument?

---

[8] Li Shenzi: vice president of the Chinese Academy of Social Sciences at the time of his death in 2003.

[9] Xudong Zhang, 'Postmodernism and Post-socialist Society: Cultural Politics in China after the "New Era"', NLR I/237, September–October 1999.

There is an interval between the original introduction of postmodern themes by Zhang Yiwu and Chen Xiaoming—and Zhang Xudong's rewriting of these. His intervention is in part a response to debates over modernity that have divided some liberal from critical intellectuals. Whatever the differences between Gan Yang, Zhang Xudong and myself, we share a sceptical attitude to the codified idea of modernity itself. Chinese liberals, on the other hand, tend to accept standard definitions of the Enlightenment uncritically, and take it for granted that modernity is our only possible goal. They refuse any reflection on it. Modernity—naturally, as it has emerged in the West—is simply assumed to be a model for China without frictions or self-contradictions, even as compared with Habermas, who remains attached to the project of modernity, but tries to see the tensions and incompletions in it. My own position has always been that Chinese modernity was itself a self-critical project. If you look at the writings of Zhang Taiyan or Lu Xun, who were deeply committed to the modern movement, you find at the same time the resources for a critique of it. Against this background, I can understand why Zhang Xudong wanted to draw a firm line between liberal and critical views of modernity, and to uphold what he sees as the more open-minded standpoint of a postmodernity beyond it.

What is less easy for me to follow is why he should think that the market in China would be a force for democratization, or a check to the homogenizing pressures of the world system. The first part of this argument paradoxically becomes close to that of the liberals he criticizes. The second part seems self-contradictory to me. If one is critical of the world system, the American-dominated global market order, how can one avoid criticism of the Chinese market? Not only is the Chinese market locked into the world market—just as the Chinese state is integrated into the international system, as you can see from its role in the Security Council—but in so far as it is different, it is not necessarily better than the Western markets with which it is now interconnected. In some ways it is even worse. The Chinese state, of course, differs from Western states in a much more significant way, and Zhang Xudong is right to emphasize this. But we also need to see the extent to which the old system rested on monopoly structures that have since changed their form, without losing their role in allowing China to compete as a trading power within the world system.

In this argument about the significance of ideas of postmodernity for China, there is more than an echo of the famous Japanese debate, held in Kyoto in the forties, on 'Overcoming Modernity'. The basic terms of the discussion are the same, for both sets of thinkers. Are we forced either to accept Western modernity or to retreat into Eastern tradition, as the only two possible choices? Or can we invent a future that escapes the terms of this dilemma, by creating something at once more rooted in local tradition and more powerfully modern than the modernity imposed on us from outside? This way of looking at the problem poses the question of contemporary uses of tradition very sharply. China has the longest continuous intellectual history of any society in the world. What is the range of attitudes to it in the PRC today—irrelevant? negative? positive? selective?—and how do they relate to the spectrum of political viewpoints?

Mao's revolution made much more of a clean sweep of traditional culture than anything that ever happened in Japan. So today, knowledge of pre-revolutionary Chinese culture remains comparatively thin among intellectuals—something the overseas diaspora has accentuated. The basic attitude of the liberals to the Chinese past is pretty negative. Their inspiration comes overwhelmingly from the West. This is also true of most of the intellectuals of the New Left, who have done very little research into pre-modern periods. The reference points may differ—the American Constitution or early French Revolution for one camp; American postmodernism or French deconstruction for the other—but the underlying outlook is quite similar. But there are scholars seriously engaged in these questions. It was to explore them in a new spirit that the journal *Xueren*, which I mentioned earlier, was formed. Most of those associated with it were working in the humanities—especially history, philosophy and literature. Many of them became professional historians, concentrated on their field and unwilling to draw wider conclusions from it. Their scholarship is good, even if their methodology may sometimes be old-fashioned: they do hard work on the documents and come up with important results. But of our previous group, there are now perhaps only four or five who are still trying to rethink the modern history of China in a spirit that connects it to contemporary problems.

Would it be right to think there is a particular problem in the appropriation of cultural tradition in China, stemming from the way in which classical Chinese has become a semi-dead language, creating a barrier somewhat like—if less radical than—the switch from Ottoman script to modern Turkish?

That is true. For the newer generations, it is a major obstacle. The very talented levy of young Chinese scholars now working in the States, for example, is largely cut off from the resources of the classical tradition. Most of them were trained in English departments in the PRC, and have little command of classical Chinese. But there is another problem, related to PRC culture itself. I often ask myself why we have no radical historiography of the British sort. Research into working-class or even peasant history is still very limited. The official Marxism of the PRC did talk about modes of production, classes, capitalism and so on, and had some achievements to its credit. But it was so mechanical as a framework that nowadays very few scholars pay much attention to it. So the younger generation is divorced even from a quite recent tradition of writing about the past. The result has been a swing away from social to intellectual history, which is where the best work has been done for some time now.

How would you situate your own work in this context, especially The Rise of Modern Chinese Thought? *What is most distinctive about it?*

I have great respect for the kind of scholarship represented by Yu Yingshin and others, which could be described as a philosophical study of intellectual history, of neo-Confucian inspiration; as I do for the sort of social history practised by American historians like Ben Elman.[10] But my focus differs from either. What I have tried to do is look at the connexions between intellectual history and social history, over quite a long stretch of Chinese history—that is, the way ideas emerged and altered within a fabric of social practices and institutional changes. Without this double focus, taking the ideas and their settings equally seriously, there is the risk of a slide towards a mere account of 'cultural production'. When I first started working on the project, I was interested mainly in thinkers of the late Qing period. I quickly realized their conceptions of knowledge, for example, were always intimately related to their occupational practices and to their understandings of the social structure and political order. So when they talk about cognitive issues, they always refer to politics, to ethics, and to their self-identity too. I also found that when they discussed political alternatives—notions of kinship as perhaps an equivalent of civil society in the West, or feudalism, or a new authoritarianism—they always used terms from long-standing intellectual traditions in China to develop or reinforce their current arguments. So I was forced to move back in time to trace the origins and transformations of these terms. In doing so, it became clear that the standard notion that modern times in China started in the Late Qing—only from that period does everything begin to change—is an illusion. A lot of things started much earlier. Tracing them back to Ming or Song times is also a way of criticizing the claims capitalism makes for itself, as if it were the absolute origin of everything new, responsible for inventing the market, social mobility, intellectual curiosity or whatever. That is what explains the first volume, *Essence and Substance*, which is devoted to what might be called ideas of Reason, whereas the principal concern of the second volume is with ideas of Science.

The interweaving of past and present in the thought of even the most radical figures of the late Qing period is striking. Take Zhang Taiyan, for example. He was a first-class classical scholar, who was influenced by Fichte and Nietzsche, although he had difficulty reading them, and at the same time was deeply involved in Buddhism and Taoism. Around 1900 he was the editor of a revolutionary journal, *Min Bao*, the most important

---

[10] See Yu Yingsh, ed., *Intellectual History in Late Imperial China*, Princeton, NJ 1984; Benjamin Elman, *From Philosophy to Philology*, Cambridge, MA 1984; and *Classicism, Politics and Kinship*, Berkeley, CA and Oxford 1990.

periodical produced by the Tongmenghui. In it, he published a lot of articles about Buddhism. For a younger generation, this was baffling. What has
Buddhism got to do with the revolution? But for Zhang Taiyan, Buddhism
was a source for the revolution, and at the time an expression of the revolution
—indeed of modern history itself. This was the typical pattern. Yan Fu bor-
rowed from Comte's positivism, and combined it with neo-Confucianism.[11]
The choice of sources always had some political or economic implication at
the time. So in studying these thinkers, I always tried to find what constituted
their basic framework of knowledge—which would include their views of
nature, the political structure, the family and their own identity.

The title of the second volume, *The Making of Chinese Modernity*, speaks
for itself. My focus is on the origins of the Chinese reflections on modernity.
If we look at Zhang Taiyan, Liang Qichao, Lu Xun or Yan Fu, we discover,
in their world of thought and their relations to the surrounding reality, self-
ironical, self-contradictory, self-paradoxical attitudes towards modernity.
The sources they drew on were Western and Chinese, and—we should not
forget—Japanese too. In the introduction, I suggest that we have to return
to that point, the beginning of the modern, if we are to understand our problems today; and that when we do so, it becomes clear how much of what we
think we know about the state, the individual, the market of that time—or
ours—is a myth. The Chinese intellectuals of the period were facing very
complex issues, which they tried to resolve in all kinds of unexpected ways.
Lu Xun's attitudes, for example, seem quite paradoxical. He criticized many
Chinese traditions savagely; yet he was also an excellent classical scholar,
who did fine work on texts from the remote past. He hated reaction, but
he was curiously sceptical about progress itself. He became a writer of the
Left, but he was always quite critical of the Left. Why? What was the intellectual and political background of these ambivalences? In 1907 Zhang Taiyan
became the first person of significance to speak of a Republic of China, and
drew a map of the boundaries of the future post-revolutionary state. Yet he
also criticized the nationalist project very sharply, even while he was attacking the colonial powers. If his answers were never coherent, the questions
he left are in a sense still with us. The questions this generation posed were
much more complicated than those that preoccupy contemporary Chinese
intellectuals. Why could they do that? It was possible only because they were
not pure intellectuals, or scholars isolated in the academy. They were social
activists. They sensed problems very acutely—different dangers, different
potentials, different frameworks—even when they couldn't articulate them
so well. Because their work was often improvised and rough, it is virtually
ignored by our intellectuals today, who are accustomed only to academic
theories. But it is full of implications for us.

---

[11] Yan Fu (1854–1921): translator, writer and reformer, champion of evolutionary
theory.

The project as you describe it sounds—if one wanted a Western analogy—as if it had something in common with Raymond Williams's Culture and Society, *as an exploration of the historically changing meaning of a set of key terms. Of course,* Culture and Society *is a history of ideas in a fairly pure sense—it doesn't say much about social practices or institutions, save at the end, when it suddenly shifts to the labour movement. That conclusion, however, made it an intellectual history with a strong contemporary charge. How do you envisage your project ending?*

The third volume will focus on rebellion and revolution. In China we have no strong tradition of scholarly research on either. What we have is much good research on the literati or scholar-gentry. There are some studies by historians like Qian Mu, highly conservative in their attitude towards the present, but capable of interesting work on the past. But there is much less of a canon in the area I want to enter now. The themes of rebellion and revolution remain more delicate topics for scholars.

Would it be wrong to think that the Chinese intellectual scene in the nineties was, despite a more restrictive political context, actually livelier and more diversified than in the eighties? Could it in some measure be compared—in vigour of discussion, overlapping of positions, absence of rigid labels or definitions—to, say, stretches of the twenties?

Perhaps there is a touch of the later twenties. In the mid-twenties, after May Fourth and before the Northern Expedition, there was a process of differentiation among intellectuals, as some anarchists turned to the Right and others to the Left, some joined the KMT, others became organizers for the CCP. But there is a big difference. The debates of that time were much more directly political—not so theoretical—because there were powerful social movements, social and national, in the background: in 1923, and on a much bigger scale in 1925, and so on. The issue was no longer the meaning of modernity, or how to relate to tradition. These were new political languages. A closer parallel might be with the years just after the establishment of the KMT regime in Nanjing, when a lot of radical overseas students, who had become Marxists in Japan, came back to China and launched various literary movements and cultural watchwords, like the need for a 'Revolutionary Literature', even criticizing Lu Xun and Mao Dun as elitists.[12] Then two years later, in 1930, there was a big debate about the nature of Chinese society, that Arif Dirlik has studied.[13] You could compare that to the questions that confront us today, when people are trying to figure out what is going on in Chinese society now. Is it a socialist country with a capitalist

---

[12] Mao Dun (1896–1981): leading left novelist of the thirties and forties.
[13] Arif Dirlik, *Revolution and History: Origins of Marxist Historiography in China*, Berkeley, CA 1978.

market, or a capitalist country? What's the nature of the state? What is the logic of globalization? What will happen to us? The different groups have to work out their own theoretical or political strategy.

One of the themes of your history of modern Chinese thought is the changing organization of knowledge—how it was structured or segmented in different periods. Comparing the period of your second volume with the situation today, what were the disciplines that have dominated the intellectual field?

In the late Qing period, sociology occupied the highest position in the hierarchy of knowledge. Its theorists generally refused to use the term *shehui* (society), preferring *qun* (community or group) instead. But they were sure that sociology was the science of sciences—that is, it arranged the order of the different kinds of knowledge. The kind of order it produced served the state, but in a state-building rather than merely conserving sense: it was linked to various projects of social reform from above. When we move to the May Fourth movement, however, we see that the main figures wanted to discard any form of social science, and just base themselves on the natural sciences—which would yield a new map of the cosmos, within which social problems could be practically resolved, and whose mastery might offer a kind of moral grace. Individual thinkers could have more complicated positions—Lu Xun never subscribed to this scientism, Liang Qichao gave more importance to literature, and so on.[14] But it is striking that for such a central figure as Hu Shih, even literature itself was modelled on scientific practice—he called a volume of his poems *A Collection of Experiments*.[15] Later, this produced a vigorous debate between two schools, dubbed 'Mr Science' and 'Mr Metaphysics', or vitalist philosophy, out of which ethics, aesthetics and literature separated out as independent fields, remapping the whole taxonomy of knowledge. Overseas students who had been disciples of Irving Babbitt's 'new humanism' in America played an important role in this shift. In each episode, you can see how the dominant 'discipline' in a given period is really more than that—its status is closer to a world view. It was just this function that Marxism came to fulfil in the later twenties, even for many natural scientists.

Today, of course, the dominant discipline in China is neoclassical economics. This is a development of the nineties. In the eighties, most of the leading economists like Wu Jinlian were still people who had been trained in the planned economy. They had learnt something from the West, but they were completely at home in the structure of the Communist state, and were quite capable in adapting and reforming it, once the Open Door policy was proclaimed. There were much more radical economists—figures like

---

[14] Liang Qichao (1873–1929): key theorist of late Qing reform era.

[15] Hu Shih (1891–1962): the leading liberal thinker of the May Fourth generation.

Li Yining, bent on importing pure free-market doctrines into China—but they were not yet of great use to the state, and had little influence. But after 1990, Hayekian ideas gained real ascendancy. Today economics—understood in its most rigidly liberal acceptation—has acquired the force of an ethics in China. Laissez-faire axioms form a code of conduct, as rules of the commodity which no agent may violate. So currently economics is not just a technical discipline, any more than its predecessors: it too is an imperative world view. Of course, no hegemony ever absorbs the whole cultural field. Political science or law are basically tributary to economics, as strongholds of the Right. By contrast, critical intellectuals today mostly work in the humanities, although there are also quite a few radicals in the natural sciences.

In the eighties, the West was viewed in a naively enthusiastic way by many Chinese intellectuals. Typical of that time was the television series River Elegy, *a hymn to Zhao Ziyang's policies, counterposing the disastrous inland traditions of Chinese autocracy to the dazzling azure of the open sea, symbol of foreign trade and Western freedom. This vision was widely shared at the time. In the nineties, the role of the West didn't always appear in such a flattering light, and Chinese opinion has itself become more diversified. The terms of discussion have also shifted, as 'globalization' has become the current watchword—in theory, a more encompassing category than simply the West. Entry into the World Trade Organization (WTO), as a practical priority for the CCP, has put the issue of relations between China as a nation-state and the institutions of the world market directly on the political agenda. How far have the pressures and probabilities of globalization been debated within the country, and what would be the main lines of division arising from it?*

Issues of globalization were first raised at a conference around 1994, by a number of intellectuals who later described themselves as liberals. One argued that if China did not reform swiftly, it would fail to enter the main trend of globalization. Another spoke of the Enlightenment prospect of a perpetual peace coming true. At about the same time, *Strategy and Management* published a critical article on globalization by Samir Amin. So the debate about it really dates from that year. At the time, I argued globalization as such was a misleading abstraction, since the advent of high-tech information systems and other innovations cannot obscure the fact that it is not a new phenomenon but simply the latest phase of a long history, which could be defined as the whole process of the development of capitalism from the colonial and imperialist epochs onwards. In other words, globalization is not a neutral concept for a natural process. You have to identify the dominant force in its spread round the world.

These early discussions were not very conceptualized, and it was clear that, whatever the differences of opinion between them, feelings about the issue were quite ambivalent on both Right and Left. For there was a general sense that there would be many dangers and risks for China in accepting globalization, but how could we avoid it? Even critics of WTO entry like Cui Zhiyuan and Gan Yang don't say, 'China must never join the WTO.' Their position would be: 'For the moment China should wait. There are a lot of changes we need first.' Most people on the Left believe that the government has been in too much of a hurry to enter the WTO, that a more measured approach would have been more sensible. Liberals on the Right, of course are eager to get the PRC into the WTO as soon as possible. This is a prime minister who has lost confidence in the ability of the government to resolve the problems of state-owned enterprises, and hopes that competition from foreign capital will take over as the driving force of economic reform. But at the same time, everyone is very aware that the reason why China could avoid the East Asian crisis of 1998 is because it was shielded from financial-market contagion by the strength of the national state. This is something even the enthusiasts for globalization are bound to recall.

The NATO bombing of China's embassy in Belgrade forcibly brought home another reality. The world market, it made plain, is not just an economic space of competition: undergirding it is a powerful set of political and military structures. These make it very difficult to argue that the nation-state, whatever changes it may or may not have undergone, has collapsed. Behind the screens of NATO, the IMF or the WTO, American globalism functions as another version of nationalism. After the embassy was destroyed, there was an indirect debate between Zhu Xueqin, the Shanghai scholar who is perhaps China's leading liberal spokesman, and myself about the Balkan war and popular reaction to it. Zhu Xueqin maintained that nationalism was the most dangerous force in modern Chinese history. We should enter the world system at top speed, because globalism was much, much better than nationalism. I replied that it was an illusion to think they could be counterposed so simply. Nationalism as a historical force is not just a subjective sentiment that drew people into the streets, but also a set of social relations on which states essential for the operation of the world market themselves rest. That kind of nationalism is a parallel structure of global capitalism, not its opposite, and we should certainly criticize it.

At the same time, we need to be able to distinguish between different kinds of nationalism. While national states were passive or silent about NATO's action in Yugoslavia, Chinese people poured into the streets and even threw a few bricks. That was positive. A spontaneous protest of this kind is a social movement that has a democratic potential. It can also be used by the government for official purposes, as the Boxers were—Zhu Xueqin was not wrong in warning of this danger. Any social movement contains different possibilities within it: our job is to analyse their range and support those that move in a democratic direction. For there is a logic here. This kind of nationalism is a movement of resistance against imperialism. But if we look at the intellectuals of the early part of the century, we see that when people like Zhang Taiyan or Lu Xun talked about nationalism, they paid attention to the other nations that imperialism had also oppressed: Greece, India, Poland, African countries. They tried to combine nationalism with cosmopolitanism. This tradition contained what I've called a self-negating, or self-transcending logic: embracing modernity as a national project generated a counter-logic that made them also critical of nationalism. They knew that even if they could transform China from an empire into a nation-state, nationalist goals could not be easily achieved within a national framework.

The same kind of dialectic is evident in the revolutionary tradition in China. After the late twenties, the Communist movement changed direction and increasingly set itself the goal of national liberation. Mao said that the national conflict with Japan had become the main social contradiction within China itself. But the revolution could not be compressed into just a nationalist project. Its self-negating logic drove it beyond that limit, to the early forms of internationalism you find in the Bandung Conference or Chou En-lai's visit to Yugoslavia. At that stage the CCP tried to help bring Third World countries together in a common struggle for national independence and international equality. Those days are long past. But we should be thinking of these different legacies today, when we reflect on contemporary protests against globalization, in China or elsewhere. They do represent expressions of local protest against outside forces, but their democratic potential will only be truly realized if they can link up with similar protests in other countries, to become a factor for democracy on a global scale. In the world system, as capital moves across borders everywhere, social conflicts should in principle no longer be so easily confined within national structures. But we lack any conceptualization of such struggles, potential or actual. Internationalism is an old-fashioned term, weighed down by too many connotations dating from the nineteenth or early twentieth centuries. We need to rethink its meanings, or invent new ones, for our contemporary context.

How did liberals—still the great majority of Chinese intellectuals—react to the Balkan War? Presumably the outburst of popular feeling was a discomfiting phenomenon for them, since it was directed against the very Western powers to which many looked with boundless admiration—it must have seemed like an attack on what is in some ways their ideal. But equally it must have been difficult for them to defend the NATO bombing?

The war was a big crisis for them. Whereas we supported the popular movement against the bombing, they opposed it. Their dislike of the demonstrations was not based just on their sympathy—which in the circumstances could not be openly expressed—for the West, or their alarm at the way the government used them, but also on their long-term attitude to the Chinese masses. Most liberals view ordinary Chinese benevolently so long as they are helping to develop the market as consumers. For them the danger of popular nationalism is that the masses may become not only too critical of the West, but also too mobilized as citizens—veering away from the passive role of consumers to the more active one of militants. They are fearful of popular participation, always remembering its negative examples, and rarely seeing the positive potential of social movements as a condition of democracy. Since civil rights themselves are historically anchored within the structure of the nation-state, the typical narrative of Western liberalism directly connects nationalism and democracy. But Chinese liberals never face these connections. They only believe in the Open Door and the global system. All China needs to do is to enter the 'mainstream'—this is the term they use—and then everything will be okay. For them, integration into the world system is the only pass to democracy. This disbelief in the democratic potential of social movements is why more and more of the younger generation are turning away from them. If you log onto the internet now, you find a lot of criticisms of them. In that sense they have become quite isolated, even while they continue to represent the mainstream in intellectual circles—though even there, an increasing number of people have become less neutral, as between the Left and the Right. Fewer now define themselves simply as liberals.

Has the current Chinese government really made so much use of popular nationalist sentiment? From the outside, it often gives the impression of a regime obsessed by the power of America, but not pitted against it. If you look at what they do in the UN, *or even in the wake of the bombing, they usually take care not to thwart the will of the* US, *but to comply unobtrusively with it. This doesn't seem to be just bowing to superior force. Isn't there also a deeper lack of confidence in the regime? Many of its highest officials appear convinced that the route America has taken is the way to go: they have no wish to resist it, since they privately think there's no alternative. So although spontaneous nationalist protests might break out from time to time in China, the government would quickly put a stop to them, as it did in 1999?*

It is true that the attitude of the government to any social movement of this kind is to use it, as a modest lever, in its constant bargaining with the West. Protests can be handy as a pressure on the Americans, even while they are compromising every minute with them. Telling the students to withdraw, they could say: 'Yes, you are right to protest on this occasion. We have firmly condemned the bombing. But enough is enough. You will serve our country best by getting back to your studies, and helping our nation progress in your work. That will be better for our goals.' This is another version of the logic of the nation: a critique of spontaneous nationalism for the purposes of state nationalism. Could there be the same kind of conflict over Taiwan?

The Chinese government can scarcely avoid the issue, given the interventionist displays of American military power in the Strait. It has no choice in the matter, given national sentiment on the mainland. Ordinary people can be heard saying, 'Why don't we just go in and take the island?' This isn't a majority attitude, but it is something the government bears in mind. The potential is there for a sharp power struggle at the top over Taiwan. In the event of a factional conflict in the regime, we can be absolutely sure each side will try to use this issue against the other—already we can see signs of various forces waiting for the opportunity to attack their opponents. It is a general rule of contemporary Chinese history that social upheavals from below are triggered by struggles for power above, as rival leaders appeal openly—or secretly—for support from the masses. As the old Chinese saying puts it: 'Fire at the castle gate means trouble for fish in the moat.'

5
Giovanni Arrighi

Giovanni Arrighi was born in 1937 in Milan, into a manufacturing family, and studied economics there, at Bocconi University. His first university appointment was in southern Africa, in the University College of Rhodesia and Nyasaland, in present-day Zimbabwe. Active in the resistance to the white settlers' unilateral declaration of independence in 1965, he was detained and then deported. He spent the next three years in Dar es Salaam (in present-day Tanzania), where he continued his work on the political economy of southern Africa and in particular the dynamics of proletarianization in the region, working as a part of a brilliant group including Samir Amin, André Gunder Frank, Walter Rodney, John Saul and Immanuel Wallerstein.

At the end of the sixties, Arrighi returned to Italy, to the University of Trento. There he redirected his interest in proletarian class formation to the Mezzogiorno, and helped to create the Gruppo Gramsci, an important component in the formation of autonomism as a current in the militant workers' movement. A decade later, Arrighi made a further intercontinental move, this time to join Wallerstein at the State University of New York at Binghamton, the emerging centre of world-systems theory. It was here that his biggest project was launched. The Long Twentieth Century, *the first in a sequence of three works on the origins and systemic transformations of capitalism, appeared in 1994. Then, shortly after leaving Binghamton for Johns Hopkins University, he and his companion Beverly Silver published* Chaos and Governance in the Modern World System *(1999).* Adam Smith in Beijing: Lineages of the Twenty-first Century *followed in 2007. Arrighi gave this interview to David Harvey in late 2008, some six months before his death in June 2009.*

Giovanni Arrighi

The Winding Paths of Capital

Could you tell us about your family background and your education?

I was born in Milan in 1937. On my mother's side, my family background was bourgeois. My grandfather, the son of Swiss immigrants to Italy, had risen from the ranks of the labour aristocracy to establish his own factories in the early twentieth century, manufacturing textile machinery and, later, heating and air-conditioning equipment. My father was the son of a railway worker, born in Tuscany. He came to Milan and got a job in my maternal grandfather's factory—in other words, he ended up marrying the boss's daughter. There were tensions, which eventually resulted in my father setting up his own business, in competition with his father-in-law. Both shared anti-fascist sentiments, however, and that greatly influenced my early childhood, dominated as it was by the war: the Nazi occupation of Northern Italy after Rome's surrender in 1943, the Resistance and the arrival of the Allied troops.

My father died suddenly in a car accident, when I was eighteen. I decided to keep his company going, against my grandfather's advice, and entered the Università Bocconi to study economics, hoping it would help me understand how to run the firm. The Economics Department was a neoclassical stronghold, untouched by Keynesianism of any kind, and no help at all with my father's business. I finally realized I would have to close it down. I then spent two years on the shop floor of one of my grandfather's firms, collecting data on the organization of the production process. The study convinced me that the elegant general-equilibrium models of neoclassical economics were irrelevant to an understanding of the production and distribution of incomes. This became the basis of my dissertation. Then I was appointed as *assistente volontario*, or unpaid teaching assistant to my professor—in those days, the first rung on the ladder in Italian universities. To earn my living I got a job with Unilever, as a trainee manager.

How did it come about that you went to Africa in 1963, to work in the University College of Rhodesia and Nyasaland?

Why I went there was pretty straightforward. I learnt that British universities were actually paying people to teach and do research—unlike the position in Italy, where you had to serve for four or five years as an *assistente volontario* before there was any hope of a paid job. In the early 1960s the British were setting up universities throughout their former colonial empire, as colleges of British ones. The UCRN was a college of the University of London. I had put in for two positions, one in Rhodesia and one in Singapore. They called me for an interview in London and, because the UCRN was interested, they offered me the job as lecturer in Economics. So I went.

It was a true intellectual rebirth. The mathematically modelled neoclassical tradition I'd been trained in had nothing to say about the processes I was observing in Rhodesia, or the realities of African life. At UCRN I worked alongside social anthropologists, particularly Clyde Mitchell, who was already doing work on network analysis, and Jaap Van Velsen, who was introducing situational analysis, later reconceptualized as extended case-study analysis. I went to their seminars regularly and was greatly influenced by the two of them. Gradually, I abandoned abstract modelling for the concrete, empirically and historically grounded theory of social anthropology. I began my long march from neoclassical economics to comparative-historical sociology.

This was the context for your 1966 essay, 'The Political Economy of Rhodesia', which analysed the forms of capitalist class development there, and their specific contradictions—explaining the dynamics that led to the victory of the settlers' Rhodesian Front Party in 1962, and to their Unilateral Declaration of Independence in 1965. What was the initial impulse behind the essay, and what is its importance for you, looking back?

'The Political Economy of Rhodesia' was written at the incitement of Van Velsen, who was relentlessly critical of my use of mathematical models. I had done a review of Colin Leys's book, *European Politics in Southern Rhodesia*, and Van Velsen suggested I develop it into a longer article. Here, and in 'Labour Supplies in Historical Perspective', I analysed the ways in which the full proletarianization of the Rhodesian peasantry created contradictions for capital accumulation—in fact, ended up producing more problems than advantages for the capitalist sector.[1] As long as proletarianization was partial,

---

[1] See respectively: Arrighi, 'The Political Economy of Rhodesia', NLR I/39, September–October 1966; Leys, *European Politics in Southern Rhodesia*, Oxford 1959; Arrighi, 'Labour Supplies in Historical Perspective: A Study of the Proletarianization of the African Peasantry in Rhodesia', collected in Arrighi and John Saul, *Essays on the Political Economy of Africa*, New York 1973.

it created conditions in which the African peasants subsidized capital accumulation, because they produced part of their own subsistence; but the more proletarianized the peasantry became, the more these mechanisms began to break down. Fully proletarianized labour could be exploited only if it was paid a full living wage. Thus, instead of making it easier to exploit labour, proletarianization was actually making it more difficult, and often required the regime to become more repressive. Martin Legassick and Harold Wolpe, for example, maintained that South African Apartheid was primarily due to the fact that the regime had to become more repressive of the African labour force because it was fully proletarianized, and could no longer subsidize capital accumulation as it had done in the past.

The whole southern region of Africa—stretching from South Africa and Botswana through the former Rhodesias, Mozambique, Malawi, which was then Nyasaland, up to Kenya, as the north-east outpost—was characterized by mineral wealth, settler agriculture and extreme dispossession of the peasantry. It is very different from the rest of Africa, including the north. West African economies were essentially peasant-based. But the southern region—what Samir Amin called 'the Africa of the labour reserves'—was in many ways a paradigm of extreme peasant dispossession, and thus proletarianization. Several of us were pointing out that this process of extreme dispossession was contradictory. Initially it created the conditions for the peasantry to subsidize capitalist agriculture, mining, manufacturing and so on. But increasingly it created difficulties in exploiting, mobilizing, controlling the proletariat that was being created. The work that we were doing then—my 'Labour Supplies in Historical Perspective', and related works by Legassick and Wolpe—established what came to be known as the Southern Africa Paradigm on the limits of proletarianization and dispossession.

Contrary to those who still identify capitalist development with proletarianization *tout court*—Robert Brenner, for example—the Southern Africa experience showed that proletarianization, in and by itself, does not favour capitalist development—all kinds of other circumstances are required. For Rhodesia, I identified three stages of proletarianization, only one of which was favourable to capitalist accumulation. In the first stage, the peasants responded to rural capitalist development by supplying agricultural products, and would only supply labour in return for high wages. The whole area thus came to be characterized by a shortage of labour, because whenever capitalist agriculture or mining began developing, it created a demand for local produce which the African peasants were very quick to supply; they could participate in the money economy through the sale of produce rather than the sale of labour. One aim of state support for settler agriculture was to create competition for the African peasants, so that they would be forced to supply labour rather than products. This led to a long drawn-out process that went from partial proletarianization to full proletarianization; but, as already mentioned, it was also a contradictory process. The problem with the simple 'proletarianization as capitalist development' model is that it ignores not just the realities of southern Africa's settler capitalism but also many other cases, such as the United States itself, which was characterized by a totally different pattern—a combination of slavery, genocide of the native population and the immigration of surplus labour from Europe.

You were one of nine lecturers at UCRN *arrested for political activities during the Smith government's July 1966 clampdown.*[2]

Yes, we were jailed for a week, and then deported.

You went to Dar es Salaam, which sounded then like a paradise of intellectual interactions, in many ways. Can you tell us about that period, and the collaborative work you did there with John Saul?

It was a very exciting time, both intellectually and politically. When I got to Dar es Salaam in 1966, Tanzania had only been independent for a few years. Nyerere was advocating what he considered to be a form of African socialism. He managed to stay equidistant from both sides during the Sino–Soviet split, and maintained very good relations with the Scandinavians. Dar es Salaam became the outpost of all the exiled national liberation movements of Southern Africa—from the Portuguese colonies, Rhodesia and South Africa. I spent three years at the University there, and met all kinds of people: activists from the Black Power movement in the US, as well as scholars and intellectuals like Immanuel Wallerstein, David Apter, Walter Rodney, Roger Murray, Sol Picciotto, Catherine Hoskins, Jim Mellon, who later was one of the founders of the Weathermen, Luisa Passerini, who was doing research on Frelimo, and many others; including, of course, John Saul.

At Dar es Salaam, working with John, I shifted my research interests from labour supplies to the issue of national liberation movements and the new regimes that were emerging out of decolonization. We were both sceptical about the capacity of these regimes to emancipate themselves from what was just starting to be called neocolonialism, and actually deliver on their promises of economic development. But there was also a difference between us, which I think has persisted until today, in that I was far less upset by this than John was. For me, these movements were national liberation movements; they were not in any way socialist movements, even when they embraced the rhetoric of socialism. They were populist regimes, and therefore I didn't expect much beyond national liberation, which we both saw as very important in itself. But whether there were possibilities for political developments beyond this is something that John and I still quarrel about to this day,

---

[2] Ian Smith (1919–2007), prime minister of the British colony of Southern Rhodesia (now Zimbabwe) from 1964 until 1979 and architect of white settler minority rule in a breakaway state from 1965 onwards.

good-humouredly, whenever we meet. But the essays we wrote together were the critique that we agreed upon.

When you came back to Europe, you found a very different world to the one you'd left six years before?

Yes. I came back to Italy in 1969, and I was immediately plunged into two situations. One was at the University of Trento, where I had been offered a lectureship. Trento was the main centre of student militancy, and the only university in Italy that gave doctorates in Sociology at the time. My appointment was sponsored by the organizing committee of the university, which consisted of the Christian Democrat Nino Andreatta, the liberal socialist Norberto Bobbio, and Francesco Alberoni; it was part of an attempt to tame the student movement through hiring a radical. In the first seminar I gave, I only had four or five students; but in the fall semester, after my book on Africa came out in the summer of 1969, I had almost a thousand students trying to get into the classroom.[3] My course became the big event of Trento. It even split Lotta Continua: the Boato faction wanted students to come to the class, to hear a radical critique of development theories, whereas the Rostagno faction was trying to disrupt the lectures by throwing stones at the classroom from the courtyard.

The second situation was in Turin, via Luisa Passerini, who was a prominent propagator of the Situationists' writings, and therefore had a big influence on many of the cadres of Lotta Continua who were picking up on Situationism. I was commuting from Trento to Turin, via Milan—from the centre of the student movement to the centre of the workers' movement. I felt attracted and at the same time bothered by some aspects of this movement—particularly its rejection of 'politics'. At some of the assemblies, very militant workers would stand up and say, 'Enough of politics! Politics is dragging us in the wrong direction. We need unity.' For me, it was quite a shock, coming from Africa, to discover that the Communist unions were considered reactionary and repressive by the workers in struggle—and there was an important element of truth in this. The reaction against the PCI unions became a reaction against all trade unions. Groups like Potere Operaio and Lotta Continua established themselves as alternatives, both to the unions and to the mass parties. With Romano Madera, who was then a student, but also a political cadre and a Gramscian—a rarity in the extra-parliamentary Left—we began to develop the idea of finding a Gramscian strategy to relate to the movement.

That's where the idea of *autonomia*—of the intellectual autonomy of the working class—first emerged. The creation of this concept is now generally attributed to Antonio Negri. But in fact it originated in the interpretation

---

[3] Arrighi, *Sviluppo economico e sovrastrutture in Africa*, Torino 1969.

of Gramsci that we developed in the early 1970s, in the Gruppo Gramsci co-founded by Madera, Passerini and myself. We saw our main contribution to the movement not as providing a substitute for the unions, or for the parties, but as students and intellectuals who were involved in helping the workers' vanguards to develop their own autonomy—*autonomia operaia*—through an understanding of the broader processes, both national and global, in which their struggles were taking place. In Gramscian terms, this was conceived as the formation of organic intellectuals of the working class in struggle. To this end we formed the Colletivi Politici Operai (CPOS), which became known as the Area dell'Autonomia. As these collectives developed their own autonomous practice, the Gruppo Gramsci would cease to have a function and could disband. When it actually was disbanded in the fall of 1973, Negri came into the picture, and took the CPOS and the Area dell'Autonomia in an adventurous direction that was far from what was originally intended.

Were there any common lessons that you took from the African national liberation struggles and Italian working-class struggles?

The two experiences had in common the fact that, in both, I had very good relations with the broader movements. They wanted to know on what basis I was participating in their struggle. My position was: 'I'm not going to tell you what to do, because you know your situation much better than I ever will. But I am better placed to understand the wider context in which it develops. So our exchange has to be based on the fact that you tell me what your situation is, and I tell you how it relates to the wider context which you cannot see, or can see only partially, from where you operate.' That was always the basis of excellent relations, both with the liberation movements in Southern Africa and with the Italian workers.

The articles on the capitalist crisis originated in an exchange of this kind, in 1972.[4] The workers were being told, 'Now there is an economic crisis, we have to keep quiet. If we carry on struggling, the factory jobs will go elsewhere.' So the workers posed the question to us: 'Are we in a crisis? And if so, what are its implications? Should we just stay quiet now, because of this?' The articles that comprised 'Towards a Theory of Capitalist Crisis' were written within this particular problematic, framed by the workers themselves, who were saying: 'Tell us about the world out there and what we have to expect.' The starting point of the articles was, 'Look, crises occur whether you struggle or not—they're not a function of workers' militancy, or of "mistakes" in economic management, but fundamental to the operations of capitalist accumulation itself.' That was the initial orientation. It was

---

[4] See, in English, Arrighi, 'Towards a Theory of Capitalist Crisis', NLR I/111, September–October 1978; first published in *Rassegna Comunista*, Nos 2, 3, 4 and 7, Milan 1972–73.

written at the very beginning of the crisis; before the existence of a crisis was widely recognized. It became important as a framework that I've used, over the years, to monitor what is happening. From that point of view, it has worked pretty well.

We'll come back to the theory of capitalist crises, but I wanted first to ask you about your work in Calabria. In 1973, just as the movement was finally starting to subside, you took up the offer of a teaching position at Cosenza?

One of the attractions of going to Calabria, for me, was to continue in a new location my research on labour supplies. I had already seen in Rhodesia how, when the Africans were fully proletarianized—or, more precisely, when they became conscious that they were now fully proletarianized—this led to struggles to get a living wage in the urban areas. In other words, the fiction that 'We are single males, our families continue to live peasant lives in the countryside', cannot hold once they actually have to live in the cities. I had pointed this out in 'Labour Supplies in Historical Perspective'. It came into clearer focus in Italy, because there was this puzzle: migrants from the South were brought into the northern industrial regions as scabs, in the 1950s and early 1960s. But from the 1960s, and especially the late 1960s, they were transformed into class-struggle vanguards, which is a typical experience of migrants. When I set up a research working group in Calabria, I got them to read the social anthropologists on Africa, particularly on migration, and then we did an analysis of the labour supply from Calabria. The questions were: what was creating the conditions for this migration? And what were its limits—given that, at a certain point, instead of creating a docile labour force that could be used to undermine the bargaining power of the northern working class, the migrants themselves became the militant vanguard?

Two things emerged from the research. First, capitalist development does not necessarily rely on full proletarianization. On the one hand, long-distance labour migration was occurring from places where no dispossession was taking place; where there were even possibilities for the migrants to buy land from the landlords. This was related to the local system of primogeniture, whereby only the eldest son inherited the land. Traditionally, younger sons ended up joining the Church or the army, until large-scale, long-distance migrations provided an increasingly important alternative way to earn the money necessary to buy land back home and set up their own farms. On the other hand, in the really poor areas, where labour was fully proletarianized, they usually could not afford to migrate at all. The only way in which they could do so was, for example, when the Brazilians abolished slavery in 1888 and needed a substitute cheap labour force. They recruited workers from these deeply impoverished areas of Southern Italy, paid their fares and resettled them in Brazil, to replace the emancipated slaves. These are very different patterns of migration. But generally speaking, it is not the very poor who migrate; it is necessary to have some means and connections in order to do so.

The second finding from the Calabrian research had similarities with the results from the research on Africa. Here, too, the migrants' disposition towards engaging in working-class struggles in the places to which they had moved depended on whether the conditions there were considered as permanently determining their life chances. It's not enough to say that the situation in the out-migrating areas determines what salaries and conditions the migrants will work for. One has to say at what point the migrants perceive themselves as deriving the bulk of their subsistence from wage employment—it's a switch that can be detected and monitored. But the main point to emerge was a different kind of critique of the idea of proletarianization as the typical process of capitalist development.

The initial write-up of this research was stolen from a car in Rome, so the final write-up took place in the United States, many years after you moved to Binghamton in 1979, where world-systems analysis was being developed. Was this the first time you explicitly situated your position on the relationship between proletarianization and capitalist development vis-à-vis those of Wallerstein and Brenner?

Yes, although I was not sufficiently explicit about this, even though I mentioned both Wallerstein and Brenner in passing; but the whole piece is, in fact, a critique of both of them.[5] Wallerstein holds the theory that relations of production are determined by their position in a core–periphery structure. According to him, in the periphery, you tend to have relations of production that are coercive; you don't have full proletarianization, which is a situation that you find in the core. Brenner has, in some respects, the opposite view, but in other ways it is very similar: that relations of production determine position in the core–periphery structure. In both, you have one particular relationship between position in the core–periphery and relations of production. The Calabrian research showed that this is not the case. There, within the same peripheral location, we found three different paths developing simultaneously, and mutually reinforcing each other. Moreover, the three paths strongly resembled developments that had, historically, characterized different core locations. One is very similar to Lenin's 'Junker' route—*latifundia* with full proletarianization; another to Lenin's 'American' route, of small and medium farms, embedded in the market. Lenin doesn't have the third one, which we called the Swiss route: long-distance migration, and then investment and retention of property back home. In Switzerland, there is no dispossession of the peasantry but rather a tradition of migration

---

[5] See Arrighi and Fortunata Piselli, 'Capitalist Development in Hostile Environments: Feuds, Class Struggles and Migrations in a Peripheral Region of Southern Italy', *Review* (Fernand Braudel Center) vol. x, no. 4, 1987.

that led to the consolidation of small farming. The interesting thing about Calabria is that all three routes, which elsewhere are associated with a position in the core, are found here in the periphery—which is a critique both of Brenner's single process of proletarianization, and of Wallerstein's tracing of relations of production to position.

Your Geometry of Imperialism *appeared in 1978, before you went to the US. Rereading it, I was struck by the mathematical metaphor—the geometry— which you use to construct the understanding of Hobson's theory of imperialism, and which performs a very useful function. But inside it, there's an interesting geographical question: when you bring Hobson and capitalism together, the notion of hegemony suddenly emerges, as a geometry-to-geography shift in what you're doing. What was the initial spur to writing* The Geometry, *and what is its importance for you?*

I was disturbed, at the time, by the terminological confusions that were swirling around the term 'imperialism'. My aim was to dissipate some of the confusion by creating a topological space in which the different concepts, which were often all confusingly referred to as 'imperialism', could be distinguished from one another. But as an exercise on imperialism, yes, it also functioned as a transition to the concept of hegemony for me. I spelled this out explicitly in the Postscript to the 1983 second edition of *The Geometry of Imperialism*, where I argued that the Gramscian concept of hegemony could be more useful than 'imperialism' in analysing contemporary dynamics of the inter-state system. From this point of view, what I—and others—did was simply to reapply Gramsci's notion of hegemony to inter-state relations, where it had originally been before Gramsci applied it to an analysis of class relations within a national political jurisdiction. In doing so, of course, Gramsci enriched the concept in many ways that had not been graspable before. Our re-exportation of it to the international sphere benefited enormously from this enrichment.

A central influence in the conception of The Long Twentieth Century, *published in 1994, is Braudel. After absorbing it, do you have any significant criticisms of him?*

The criticism is fairly easy. Braudel is an incredibly rich source of information about markets and capitalism, but he has no theoretical framework. Or more accurately, as Charles Tilly pointed out, he is so eclectic that he has innumerable partial theories, the sum of which is no theory. You can't simply rely on Braudel; you have to approach him with a clear idea of what you are looking for, and what you are extracting from him. One thing that I focused on, which differentiates Braudel from Wallerstein and all other world-systems analysts—not to speak of more traditional economic historians, Marxist or otherwise—is the idea that the system of national states, as it emerged in the sixteenth and seventeenth centuries, was preceded by a system of city states; and that one has to look for the origins of capitalism there, in the city states. This is the distinguishing feature of the West, or Europe, compared to other parts of the world. But you easily get lost if you just follow Braudel, because he takes you in so many different directions. For example, I had to extract this point and combine it with what I was learning from William McNeill's *Pursuit of Power*, which also argues, from a different perspective, that a system of city states preceded and prepared the emergence of a system of territorial states.

Another idea, to which you provide much greater theoretical depth, but which nevertheless comes from Braudel, is the notion that financial expansion announces the autumn of a particular hegemonic system, and precedes a shift to a new hegemon. This would seem a central insight of The Long Twentieth Century?

Yes. The idea was that the leading capitalist organizations of a particular epoch would also be the leaders of the financial expansion, which always occurs when the material expansion of productive forces reaches its limits. The logic of this process—though again, Braudel doesn't provide it—is that when competition intensifies, investment in the material economy becomes increasingly risky, and therefore the liquidity preference of accumulators is accentuated, which, in turn, creates the supply conditions of the financial expansion. The next question, of course, is how the demand conditions for financial expansions are created. On this, I relied on Weber's idea that inter-state competition for mobile capital constitutes the world-historical specificity of the modern era. This competition, I argued, creates the demand conditions for the financial expansion. Braudel's idea of 'autumn' —as the concluding phase of a process of leadership in accumulation, which goes from material to financial, and eventually to displacement by another leader—is crucial. But so is Marx's idea that the autumn of a particular state, experiencing financial expansion, is also the springtime for another location: surpluses that accumulate in Venice go to Holland; those that accumulate in Holland then go to Britain; and those that accumulate in Britain go to the United States. Marx thus enables us to complement what we have in Braudel: autumn becomes a spring elsewhere, producing a series of inter-connected developments.

The Long Twentieth Century *traces these successive cycles of capitalist expansion and hegemonic power from the Renaissance to the present. In your narrative, phases of material expansion of capital eventually peter out under the pressure of overcompetition, giving way to phases of financial expansion, whose exhaustion then precipitates a time of inter-state chaos which is resolved by the emergence of a new hegemonic power, capable of restoring global order and restarting the cycle of material expansion once again, supported by a new social bloc. Such hegemons have been in turn Genoa, the Netherlands, Britain and the United States. How far do you regard their punctual appearance, each putting an end to a preceding time of troubles, as a set of contingencies?*

Good and difficult question! There is always an element of contingency. At the same time, the reason why these transitions take so long, and go through periods of turbulence and chaos, is that the agencies themselves, as they later emerge to organize the system, go through a learning process. This is clear if we look at the most recent case, that of the United States. By the late nineteenth century, the United States already had some characteristics that made it a possible successor to Britain as the hegemonic leader. But it took more than half a century, two world wars and a catastrophic depression before the United States actually developed both the structures and the ideas that, after the Second World War, enabled it to become truly hegemonic. Was the development of the United States as a potential hegemon in the nineteenth century strictly a contingency, or is there something else? I don't know. Clearly, there was a contingent geographical aspect—North America had a different spatial configuration than Europe, which enabled the formation of a state that could not be created in Europe itself, except on the eastern flank, where Russia was also expanding territorially. But there was also a systemic element: Britain created an international credit system that, after a certain point, favoured the formation of the United States in particular ways.

Certainly, if there had been no United States, with its particular historical-geographical configuration in the late nineteenth century, history would have been very different. Who would have become hegemonic? We can only conjecture. But there *was* the United States, which was building, in many ways, on the tradition of Holland and Britain. Genoa was a bit different: I never say that it was hegemonic; it was closer to the type of transnational financial organization that occurs in diasporas, including the contemporary Chinese diaspora. But it was not hegemonic in the Gramscian sense that Holland, Britain and the United States were. Geography matters a lot; but even though these are three spatially very different hegemons, each built on organizational characteristics learned from the previous one. There is considerable borrowing by Britain from the Netherlands, and by the United States from Britain; these are an interlinked set of states—there is a kind of snowball effect. So, yes, there is contingency; but there are also systemic links.

The Long Twentieth Century *doesn't cover the fate of the labour movement. Did you omit it because you regarded it, by then, as of lesser importance, or because the architecture of the book—its subtitle is* Money, Power and the Origins of Our Times—*was already so far-reaching and complex that you felt to include labour would overload it?*

More the latter. *The Long Twentieth Century* was originally supposed to be co-authored with Beverly Silver—whom I first met in Binghamton—and was to be in three parts. One was the hegemonies, which now actually forms the book's first chapter. The second part was supposed to be capital—the organization of capital, the business enterprise; basically, competition. The third part was supposed to be labour—labour and capital relations, and labour movements. But the discovery of financialization as a recurrent pattern of historical capitalism upset the whole project. It forced me to go back in time, which I never wanted to do, because the book *was* really supposed to be about the 'long twentieth century', meaning from the 1870s Great Depression through to the present. When I discovered the financialization paradigm I was thrown completely off balance, and *The Long Twentieth Century* became basically a book about the role of finance capital in the historical development of capitalism, from the fourteenth century. So Beverly took over the work on labour, in her *Forces of Labour*, which came out in 2003.[6]

Co-authored by the two of you in 1999, Chaos and Governance *seems to respect the kind of structure you'd initially planned for* The Long Twentieth Century*?*

Yes, in *Chaos and Governance* there are chapters on geopolitics, business enterprise, social conflict, and so on.[7] So the original project was never abandoned. But it certainly was not adhered to in *The Long Twentieth Century*, because I could not focus on the cyclical recurrence of financial expansions and material expansions and, at the same time, deal with labour. Once you shift the focus in defining capitalism to an alternation of material and financial expansions, it becomes very difficult to bring labour back in. Not only is there too much to cover, but there is also considerable variation over time and space in the relationship between capital and labour. For one thing, as we point out in *Chaos and Governance*, there is a speeding up of social history. When you compare transitions from one regime of accumulation to another, you realize that in the transition from Dutch to British hegemony in the eighteenth century, social conflict comes in late, relative to financial expansions and wars. In the transition from British to US hegemony in the early twentieth century, the explosion of social conflict was more or less simultaneous with the take-off of the financial expansion and wars. In the current transition—to an unknown destination—the explosion of social conflict in the late 1960s and early 1970s preceded the financial expansion, and took place without wars among the major powers.

---

[6] Beverly J. Silver, *Forces of Labour: Workers' Movements and Globalization Since 1870*, Cambridge 2003.

[7] Arrighi and Silver, *Chaos and Governance in the Modern World System*, Minneapolis 1999.

In other words, if you take the first half of the twentieth century, the biggest workers' struggles occurred on the eve of the world wars, and in their aftermath. This was the basis of Lenin's theory of revolution: that inter-capitalist rivalries turning into wars would create favourable conditions for revolution, which is something that can be observed empirically up to the Second World War. In a sense one could argue that, in the present transition, the speeding up of social conflict has prevented capitalist states from waging wars on one another. So, to return to your question, in *The Long Twentieth Century* I chose to focus on elaborating fully the argument about financial expansions, systemic cycles of capital accumulation and world hegemonies; but in *Chaos and Governance* we returned to the issue of the interrelations between social conflict, financial expansions and hegemonic transitions.

In his discussion of primitive accumulation, Marx writes about the national debt, the credit system, the bankocracy—in a way, the integration between finance and state that occurred during primitive accumulation—as being absolutely critical to the way in which a capitalist system evolves. But the analysis in Capital *refuses to deal with the credit system until you get to* Volume Three, *because Marx doesn't want to deal with interest, even though the credit system keeps on coming up as crucial to the centralization of capital, to the organization of fixed capital, and so on. This raises the question of how class struggle actually works around the finance–state nexus, which plays the vital role that you're pointing to. There seems to be a gap in Marx's analysis: on the one hand, saying the important dynamic is that between capital and labour; on the other hand, labour doesn't seem to be crucial to the processes that you're talking about—transferences of hegemony, jumping of scales. It's understandable that* The Long Twentieth Century *had a hard time integrating labour into that story, because in a sense the capital–labour relation is not central to that aspect of the capitalist dynamic. Would you agree with that?*

Yes, I agree, with one qualification: the phenomenon I mentioned of the speeding up of social history. The worker struggles of the 1960s and early 1970s, for example, were a major factor in the financialization of the late 1970s and 1980s, and the ways in which it evolved. The relationship between workers' and subaltern struggles and financialization is something that changes over time, and has recently developed characteristics that it didn't have before. But if you are trying to explain the recurrence of financial expansions, you cannot focus too much on labour, because then you will be talking only about the latest cycle; you are bound to make the mistake of taking labour as the cause of financial expansions, when earlier ones took off without the intervention of workers' or subaltern struggles.

Still on the question of labour, then, could we track back to your 1990 essay on the remaking of the world labour movement, 'Marxist Century, American

Century'.[8] You argued there that Marx's account of the working class in the Manifesto *is deeply contradictory, since it stresses at once the increasing collective power of labour, as capitalist development proceeds, and its increasing immiseration, corresponding in effect to an active industrial army and a reserve army. Marx, you pointed out, thought that both tendencies would be united in the same human mass; but you went on to argue that, in the early twentieth century, they in fact became spatially polarized. In Scandinavia and the Anglosphere, the first prevailed, in Russia and further east the second— Bernstein capturing the situation of the former, Lenin of the latter—leading to the split between reformist and revolutionary wings of the labour movement. In Central Europe—Germany, Austria, Italy—on the other hand, you argued that there was a more fluctuating balance between active and reserve, leading to Kautsky's equivocations, unable to choose between reform or revolution, contributing to the victory of fascism. At the end of the essay you suggested that a recomposition of the labour movement might be coming about—misery reappearing in the West, with the return of widespread unemployment; and collective power of workers, with the rise of Solidarity, in the East, perhaps reuniting what space and history had divided. What is your view of such a prospect today?*

Well, the first thing is that, along with this optimistic scenario from the point of view of uniting the conditions of the working class globally, there was a more pessimistic consideration in the essay, pointing to something that I've always considered a very serious flaw in Marx and Engels's *Manifesto*. There is a logical leap that does not really hold up, intellectually or historically—the idea that, for capital, those things that we would today call gender, ethnicity, nationality, do not matter. That the only thing that matters for capital is the possibility of exploitation; and therefore the most exploitable status group within the working class is the one they will employ, without any discrimination on the basis of race, gender, ethnicity. That's certainly true. However, it doesn't follow that the various status groups within the working class will just accept this. In fact, it is precisely at the point when proletarianization becomes generalized, and workers are subjected to this disposition of capital, that they will mobilize whatever status difference they can identify or construct to win a privileged treatment from the capitalists. They will mobilize along gender lines, national lines, ethnicity or whatever, to obtain a privileged treatment from capital.

'Marxist Century, American Century' is therefore not as optimistic as it might have seemed, because it pointed to this internal working-class tendency to accentuate status differences, to protect themselves from the disposition of capital to treat labour as an undifferentiated mass that would be employed

---

[8] Arrighi, 'Marxist Century, American Century: The Making and Remaking of the World Labour Movement', NLR I/179, January–February 1990.

only to the extent that it enabled capital to reap profits. So the article ended on an optimistic note, that there is a tendency towards levelling; but at the same time one should expect workers to fight to protect themselves through status-group formation or consolidation against this very tendency.

Does this mean that the differentiation between the active army and the industrial reserve army also tends to be status-divided—racialized, if you will?

It depends. If you look at the process globally—where the reserve army is not just the unemployed, but also the disguisedly unemployed and the excluded—then definitely there is a status division between the two. Nationality has been used by segments of the working class, of the active army, to differentiate themselves from the global reserve army. At a national level, this is less clear. If you take the United States or Europe, it's much less apparent that there is actually a status difference between the active and reserve army. But with immigrants currently coming from countries that are much poorer, anti-immigration sentiments which are a manifestation of this tendency to create status distinctions within the working class have grown. So it's a very complicated picture, particularly if you look at transnational migration flows, and at the situation where the reserve army is primarily concentrated in the global South rather than the North.

In your 1991 article, 'World Income Inequalities and the Future of Socialism', you showed the extraordinary stability of the regional wealth hierarchy in the twentieth century—the extent to which the gap in per capita income between the core North/West and the semi-peripheral and peripheral South/East of the world had remained unchanged, or actually deepened, after half a century of developmentalism.[9] Communism, you pointed out, had failed to close this gap in Russia, Eastern Europe and China, though it had done no worse in this respect than capitalism in Latin America, South-East Asia or Africa, and in other respects—a more egalitarian distribution of income within society, and greater independence of the state from the North/Western core—it had done significantly better. A couple of decades later, China has obviously broken the pattern you were describing then. How far did this come—or not come—as a surprise to you?

First of all, we should not exaggerate the extent to which China has broken the pattern. The level of per capita income in China was so low—and still is low, compared to the wealthy countries—that even major advances need to be qualified. China has doubled its position relative to the rich world, but still that only means going from 2 per cent of the average per capita income

---

[9] Arrighi, 'World Income Inequalities and the Future of Socialism', NLR I/189, September–October 1991.

of the wealthy countries to 4 per cent. It is true that China has been decisive in producing a reduction in world income inequalities *between* countries. If you take China out, the South's position has worsened since the 1980s; if you keep it in, then the South has improved somewhat, due almost exclusively to China's advance. But of course, there has been a big growth in inequality inside China, which thus has also contributed to the world-scale increase in inequalities *within* countries in recent decades. Taking the two measures together—inequality between and within countries—statistically China has brought about a reduction in total global inequality. We should not exaggerate this—the world pattern is still one of huge gaps, which are being reduced in small ways. However, it's important because it changes relationships of power between countries. If it continues, it may even change the global distribution of income from one that is still very polarized to a more normal, Pareto-type distribution.

Was I surprised at this? To some extent, yes. In fact, that's why I shifted my interest over the last fifteen years to studying East Asia, because I realized that, although East Asia—except for Japan, clearly—was part of the South, it had some peculiarities that enabled it to generate a kind of development that did not quite fit within that pattern of stable inequality among regions. At the same time, no one ever claimed—I certainly did not—that stability in the global distribution of income also meant immobility of particular countries or regions. A fairly stable structure of inequalities can persist, with some countries going up and others down. And this, to some extent, is what has been happening. From the 1980s and 1990s, in particular, the more important development has been the bifurcation of a highly dynamic and upwardly mobile East Asia and a stagnant and downwardly mobile Africa, and particularly Southern Africa—'the Africa of the labour reserves', again. This bifurcation is the thing that interests me most: why Southern Africa and East Asia have moved in such opposite directions. It's a very important phenomenon to try to understand, because to do so would also modify our understanding of the underpinnings of successful capitalist development, and the extent to which it relies or not on dispossession—the complete proletarianization of the peasantry—as happened in Southern Africa, or on the very partial proletarianization that has taken place in East Asia. So the divergence of these two regions brings up a big theoretical question, which once again challenges Brenner's identification of capitalist development with the full proletarianization of the labour force.

Chaos and Governance argued early on, in 1999, that American hegemony would decline principally through the rise of East Asia, and above all of China. At the same time it raised the prospect that this would also be the region where labour might in the future pose the sharpest challenge to capital, worldwide. It has sometimes been suggested that there's a tension between these perspectives— the rise of China as a rival power centre to the United States, and mounting unrest among the labouring classes in China. How do you see the relationship between the two?

The relationship is very close, because, first of all, contrary to what many people think, the Chinese peasants and workers have a millennial tradition of unrest that has no parallel anywhere else in the world. In fact, many of the dynastic transitions were driven by rebellions, strikes and demonstrations—not just of workers and peasants, but also shopkeepers. This is a tradition that continues down to the present. When Hu Jintao told Bush, a few years ago, 'Don't worry about China trying to challenge US dominance; we have too many preoccupations at home', he was pointing to one of the chief characteristics of Chinese history: how to counter the combination of internal rebellions by the subordinate classes and external invasions by so-called barbarians—from the Steppes, up to the nineteenth century, and then, since the Opium Wars, from the sea. These have always been the overwhelming concerns of Chinese governments, and they set narrow limits on China's role in international relations. The late eighteenth- and nineteenth-century imperial Chinese state was basically a kind of pre-modern welfare state. These characteristics were reproduced throughout its subsequent evolution. During the 1990s, Jiang Zemin let the capitalist genie out of the bottle. Current attempts to put it back again have to be set in the context of this much longer tradition. If rebellions of the Chinese subordinate classes materialize in a new form of welfare state, then that will influence the pattern of international relations over the next twenty, thirty years. But the balance of forces between the classes in China is still up for grabs at the moment.

Is there a contradiction between being a major centre of social unrest and being a rising power? Not necessarily—the United States in the 1930s was in the vanguard of worker struggles, at the same time that it was emerging as hegemonic. The fact that these struggles were successful, in the midst of the Great Depression, was a significant factor in making the US socially hegemonic for the working classes as well. This was certainly the case in Italy, where the American experience became the model for some of the Catholic trade unions.

Recent statements from China suggest a great deal of worry about the levels of unemployment that may result from a global recession, with an array of measures to counteract it. But does this also entail the continuation of the development model in ways that may, in the end, challenge the rest of global capitalism?

The question is whether the measures that Chinese rulers take, in response to the subordinate groups' struggles, can work in other places where the same conditions do not exist. The issue of whether China can become a model for other states—particularly other big Southern states, like India—is dependent on a lot of historical and geographical specificities that may not be reproducible elsewhere. The Chinese know this, and they do not actually set themselves up as a model to be imitated. So what happens in China will be crucial in terms of the relationship between the People's Republic itself and the rest of the world, but not in terms of setting up a model for others to follow. Nevertheless there is an interpenetration of struggles there—of worker and peasant struggles against exploitation, but also of struggles against environmental problems and ecological destruction—that you don't find to the same extent elsewhere. These struggles are escalating at the moment, and it will be important to see how the leadership responds. I think that the change in leadership to Hu Jintao and Wen Jiabao is related to nervousness, at the least, about abandoning a long-standing welfare tradition. So, we'll have to monitor the situation and watch for possible outcomes.

To return to the question of capitalist crises. Your 1972 essay, 'Towards a Theory of Capitalist Crisis', turns on a comparison between the long downturn of 1873–1896 and the prediction, which proved completely accurate, of another such crisis, which historically started in 1973. You've returned to this parallel several times since, pointing out the similarities but also the important differences between the two. But you've written less about the crisis of 1929 onwards. Do you regard the Great Depression as continuing to be of less relevance?

Well, not of less relevance, because in fact it is the most serious crisis that historical capitalism has experienced; certainly, it was a decisive turning point. But it also educated the powers that be in terms of what they should do so as not to repeat that experience. There are a variety of recognized and less recognized instruments for preventing that type of breakdown from happening again. Even now, though the collapse in the stock exchange is being compared to the 1930s, I think—I may be wrong—that both the monetary authorities and the governments of the states that actually matter in this are going to do all they can to avoid the collapse in the financial markets having similar social effects to the 1930s. They just cannot afford it, politically. And so they will muddle through, do anything they have to. Even Bush—and before him Reagan—for all their free-market ideology, relied on an extreme kind of Keynesian deficit spending. Their ideology is one thing, what they actually do is another, because they are responding to political situations which they cannot allow to deteriorate too much. The financial aspects may be similar to the 1930s, but there is a greater awareness and tighter constraints on the political authorities not to let these processes affect the so-called real economy to the same extent that they did in the 1930s. I'm not saying that the Great Depression is less relevant, but I'm not convinced that it is going to be repeated in the near future. The situation of the world economy is radically different. In the 1930s it was highly segmented, and that may have been a factor in producing the conditions for those break-downs. Now it's far more integrated.

In 'Towards a Theory of Capitalist Crisis' you describe a deep structural conflict within capitalism, in which you differentiate between crises that are caused by too high a rate of exploitation, which lead to a realization crisis because of insufficient effective demand, and those caused by too low a rate of exploitation, which cuts into demand for means of production. Now, do you still hold to this general distinction, and if so would you say that we are now in an underlying realization crisis, masked by expanding personal indebtedness and financialization, due to the wage repressions that have characterized capitalism over the last thirty years?

Yes. I think that over the last thirty years there has been a change in the nature of the crisis. Up to the early 1980s, the crisis was typically one of falling rate of profits due to intensifying competition among capitalist agencies, and due to circumstances in which labour was much better equipped to protect itself than in the previous depressions—both in the late nineteenth century and in the 1930s. So that was the situation through the 1970s. The Reagan–Thatcher monetary counter revolution was actually aimed at undermining this power, this capacity of the working classes to protect themselves—it was not the only objective, but it was one of the main objectives. I think that you quote some adviser of Thatcher, saying that what they did was …

… to create an industrial reserve army; exactly …

… what Marx says they should do! That changed the nature of the crisis. In the 1980s and 1990s, and now, in the 2000s, we are indeed facing an underlying overproduction crisis, with all its typical characteristics. Incomes have been redistributed in favour of groups and classes that have high liquidity and speculative dispositions; so incomes don't go back into circulation in the form of effective demand, but they go into speculation, creating bubbles that burst regularly. So, yes, the crisis has been transformed from one of falling rate of profit, due to intensified competition among capitals, to one of overproduction due to a systemic shortage of effective demand, created by the tendencies of capitalist development.

A recent report of the National Intelligence Council predicted the end of US global dominance by 2025, and the emergence of a more fragmented, multipolar, and potentially conflictual world. Do you think that capitalism as a world system requires, as a condition of possibility, a single hegemonic power? Is the absence of one necessarily equivalent to unstable systemic chaos—is a balance of power between roughly comparable major states impossible?

No, I wouldn't say that it's impossible. A lot depends on whether the incumbent hegemonic power accepts accommodation or not. The chaos of recent years has been due to the response of the Bush administration to 9/11, which has in some respects been a case of great-power suicide. What the declining power does is very important, because it has the ability to create chaos. The whole 'Project for a New American Century' was a refusal to accept decline. That has been a catastrophe. There has been the military debacle in Iraq and the related financial strain on the US position in the world economy, transforming the United States from a creditor nation into the biggest debtor nation in world history. As a defeat, Iraq is worse than Vietnam, because in Indo-China there was a long tradition of guerrilla warfare: they had a leader of the calibre of Ho Chi Minh; they had already defeated the French. The tragedy for the Americans in Iraq is that, even in the best possible circumstances, they have a hard time winning the war, and now they are just trying to get out with some face-saving device. Their resistance to accommodation has led, first, to an acceleration of their decline, and second, to a lot of suffering and chaos. Iraq is a disaster. The size of the displaced population there is far bigger than in Darfur.

It is not clear what Obama actually wants to do. If he thinks that he can reverse the decline, he's going to have some very nasty surprises. What he can do is to manage the decline intelligently—in other words, change the policy from: 'We are not accommodating. We want another century', to one of de facto managing decline, devising policies that accommodate the change in power relationships. I don't know whether he's going to do so because he's very ambiguous; whether because in politics you cannot say certain things, or because he doesn't know what to do, or because he just is ambiguous—I don't know. But the change from Bush to Obama does open up the possibility of managing and accommodating the decline of the United States in a non-catastrophic way. Bush has had the opposite effect: the credibility of the American military has been further undermined, the financial position has become even more disastrous. So now the task facing Obama, I think, is managing decline intelligently. That's what he can do. But his idea of escalating US intervention in Afghanistan is worrying, to say the least.

Over the years, while always basing your work on Marx's conception of capital accumulation, you've never hesitated to express a number of leading criticisms of Marx—his underestimation of power struggles between states, his indifference to space, the contradictions in his account of the working class, among others. For a long time you've also been fascinated by Adam Smith, who plays a central role in your latest work, Adam Smith in Beijing. *What would be your comparable reservations about him?*

The comparable reservations about Smith are the same as Marx's reservations about him. Marx took a lot from Smith—the tendency of the rate of profit to fall under the impact of inter-capitalist competition, for example, is a Smithian idea. *Capital* is a critique of political economy: Marx was criticizing Smith for missing what was going on in the hidden abodes of production, as he put it—inter-capitalist competition might drive down the rate of profit, but it was countered by the tendency and ability of capitalists to shift the relationships of power with the working class in their favour. From this point of view, Marx's critique of Smith's political economy was making a crucial point. However, one also has to look at the historical evidence, because Marx's was a theoretical construct, with assumptions that may not correspond to the historical reality of particular periods or places. We cannot infer empirical realities from a theoretical construct. The validity of his critique of Smith has to be assessed on the basis of the historical record; that applies to Smith as much as it applies to Marx, or anybody else.

One of Marx's conclusions in Capital, *particularly* Volume One, *is that adoption of a Smithian free-market system will lead to increases in class inequality. To what degree does the introduction of a Smithian regime in Beijing carry the risk of even greater class inequalities in China?*

My argument in the theoretical chapter on Smith, in *Adam Smith in Beijing*, is that there is no notion in his work of self-regulating markets as in the neo-liberal creed. The invisible hand is that of the state, which should rule in a decentralized way, with minimal bureaucratic interference. Substantively, the action of the government in Smith is pro-labour, not pro-capital. He is quite explicit that he is not in favour of making workers compete to reduce wages, but of making capitalists compete, to reduce profits to a minimum acceptable reward for their risks. Current conceptions turn him completely upside down. But it's unclear where China is headed today. In the Jiang Zemin era, in the 1990s, it was certainly headed in the direction of making workers compete for the benefit of capital and profit; there is no question about that. Now there is a reversal, one which as I've said takes into account not only the tradition of the revolution and the Mao period, but also of the welfare aspects of late-imperial China under the Qing in the eighteenth and early nineteenth centuries. I'm not putting bets on any particular outcome in China, but we must have an open mind in terms of seeing where it's going.

In Adam Smith in Beijing, *you also draw on Sugihara Kaoru's work in contrasting an 'industrious revolution', based on intensive labour and husbanding of nature, in early modern East Asia, and an 'industrial revolution', based on mechanization and predation of natural resources, and speak of the hope that there could be a convergence of the two for humanity in the future. How would you estimate the balance between them in East Asia today?*

Very precarious. I am not as optimistic as Sugihara in thinking that the East Asian tradition of 'industrious revolution' is so well entrenched that it may, if not become dominant again, at least play an important role in whatever hybrid formation is going to emerge. These concepts are more important for monitoring what's happening than saying, East Asia is going this way, or the United States is going the other way. We need to see what they actually do. There is evidence that the Chinese authorities are worried about the environment, as well as about social unrest—but then they do things that are plain stupid. Maybe there is a plan in the works, but I don't see much awareness of the ecological disasters of car civilizations. The idea of copying the United States from this point of view was already crazy in Europe—it's even crazier in China. And I've always told the Chinese that in the 1990s and 2000s, they went to look at the wrong city. If they want to see how to be wealthy without being ecologically destructive, they should go to Amsterdam rather than Los Angeles. In Amsterdam, everybody goes around on bicycles; there are thousands of bikes parked at the station overnight, because people come in by train, pick up their bicycles in the morning and leave them there again in the evening. Whereas in China, while there were no cars at all the first time I was there in 1970—only a few buses in a sea of bicycles—now, more and more, the bicycles have been crowded out. From that point of view it's a very mixed picture, very worrying and contradictory. The ideology of modernization is discredited elsewhere but so far is living on, rather naively, in China.

But the implication of Adam Smith in Beijing *seems to be that we might need something of an industrious revolution in the West, and that therefore this is a category that's not specific to China, but can actually be much broader?*

Yes. But Sugihara's basic point is that the typical development of the industrial revolution, the substitution of machinery and energy for labour, not only has ecological limits, as we know, but it has economic limits as well. In fact, Marxists often forget that Marx's idea of the increasingly organic composition of capital, driving down the rate of profit, has to do substantively with the fact that the use of more machines and energy intensifies competition among capitalists in such a way that it becomes less profitable, besides being ecologically destructive. Sugihara's point is that the separation of management and labour, the growing dominance of management over labour, and the fact that labour is deprived of its skills, including those of self-management, which is typical of the industrial revolution, has limits. In the industrious revolution there is a mobilization of all the household's resources, which develops, or at least preserves, managerial skills among the labourers. Eventually the advantages of these self-management skills become more important than the advantages derived from the separation of conception and execution that was typical of the industrial revolution. I think he has a point, in the sense that this is pretty crucial to understanding the present Chinese rise; that having preserved these self-management skills through serious limitations on the processes of proletarianization in a substantive sense, China now can have an organization of the labour process that is more reliant on the self-management skills of labour than elsewhere. This is probably one of the main sources of the competitive advantage of China, under the new circumstances.

Which would take us back to the politics of the Gramsci Group, in terms of the labour process and autonomia?

Yes and no. They are two different forms of autonomy. What we are talking about now is managerial autonomy, whereas the other was autonomy in struggle, in the workers' antagonism towards capital. There, the idea of autonomy was: how do we formulate our programme in such a way that we unite workers in the struggle against capital, rather than divide labour and create the conditions for capital to re-establish its authority on the workers in the workplace? The present situation is ambiguous. Many look at Chinese self-management skills and see them as a way of subordinating labour to capital—in other words, capital saves on managerial costs. One has to put these self-management skills in context—where, when, and for what purpose. It is not that easy to classify it in one way or another.

You ended 'World Income Inequalities' in 1991 by arguing that, after the collapse of the Soviet Union, deepening and widening conflicts over scarce resources within the South—the Iraq–Iran War or the Gulf War can be taken as emblematic—were forcing the West to create embryonic structures of world government to regulate these: the G7 as an executive committee of the global bourgeoisie, the International Monetary Fund and World Bank as its Ministry of Finance, the Security Council as its Ministry of Defence. These structures, you suggested, might fifteen years hence be taken over by non-conservative forces. In Adam Smith in Beijing *you speak rather of a world-market society as a potentially hopeful future, in which no power is any longer a hegemon. What is the relationship between the two, and your conceptions of them?*

First, I didn't actually say that the structures of world government emerged because of the conflicts within the South. Most of them were Bretton Woods organizations, set up by the United States after the Second World War as mechanisms that were necessary to avoid the pitfalls of self-regulating markets in the global economy, and as instruments of governance. So, from the start of the post-war era there were embryonic structures of world government in place. What happened in the 1980s was an increasing turbulence and instability, of which these conflicts in the South were an aspect, and therefore these institutions were brought in to manage the world economy in a different way than before. Could they be taken over by non-conservative forces? My attitude to these institutions was always ambivalent, because in many ways they reflect a balance of power among the states of the North and the South—within the North, between North and South, and so on. There was nothing in principle that ruled out the possibility that these institutions could actually be put to work to regulate the global economy in ways that might promote a more equal distribution of incomes world-wide. However, what happened is exactly the opposite. In the 1980s, the IMF and the World Bank became the instruments of the neo-liberal counter-revolution, and therefore promoted a more unequal distribution of income. But even then, as I've said, what happened in the end was not so much a more unequal distribution between North and South, but a big bifurcation within the South itself, with East Asia doing very well and Southern Africa doing very badly, and other regions somewhere in the middle.

How does that relate to the world-market society concept that I discuss in *Adam Smith in Beijing*? It is now clear that a world state, even of the most embryonic, confederal type, would be very difficult to bring about. It is not a serious possibility in the near future. There is going to be a world-market society, in the sense that countries will be relating to one another through market mechanisms which are not at all self-regulating, but are regulated. This was also true of the system developed by the United States, which was a highly regulated process whereby the elimination of tariffs, quotas and restrictions on labour mobility was always negotiated by states—most importantly by the United States and Europe, and then between these and the others. The question now is what regulation is going to be introduced to prevent a 1930s-style breakdown of the market. So the relationship between the two concepts is that the organization of the world economy will be primarily market based, but with an important participation of states in the regulation of this economy.

In The Long Twentieth Century, *you sketched three possible outcomes of the systemic chaos into which the long wave of financialization that started in the early 1970s was leading: a world empire controlled by the United States, a world-market society in which no states dominated others, or a new world war that would destroy humanity. In all three eventualities, capitalism, as it has historically developed, would have disappeared. In* Adam Smith in Beijing, *you conclude that, with the failures of the Bush administration, the first can now be ruled out, leaving just the last two. But isn't there, logically at least, one other possibility within your own framework—that China could emerge over time as a new hegemon, replacing the United States, without altering the struc-tures of capitalism and territorialism as you describe them? Do you exclude this possibility?*

I don't exclude that possibility, but let's begin by putting the record straight about what I actually say. The first of the three scenarios that I envisaged at the end of *The Long Twentieth Century* was a world empire controlled not only by the United States, but by the United States in cooperation with its European allies. I never thought that the US would be so reckless as to try to go it alone for a New American Century—that was just too crazy a project to contemplate; and, of course, it backfired immediately. In fact, there is a strong current within the US foreign-policy establishment that wants to patch up the relationship with Europe, which was strained by the unilateralism of the Bush administration. That's still a possibility, although it's now less likely than it used to be. The second point is that the world-market society and the greater weight of China in the global economy are not mutually exclusive. If you look at the way in which China has behaved towards its neighbours historically, there has always been a relationship based more on trade and economic exchanges than on military power; this is still the case. People often misunderstand this: they think I am depicting the Chinese as being softer or better than the West; it's nothing to do with that. It has to do with the problems of governance of a country like China, which we've discussed. China has a tradition of rebellions that no other territory of similar size and density of population has faced. Its rulers are also highly conscious of the possibility of new invaders from the sea—in other words, the US. As I point out in Chapter 10 of *Adam Smith in Beijing*, there are various American plans for how to deal with China, none of which is exactly reassuring for Beijing. Apart from the Kissinger plan, which is one of cooptation, the others envisage either a new Cold War directed against China or getting China involved in wars with its neighbours, while the US plays the role of 'happy third'. If China does emerge, as I think it will, as a new centre of the global economy, its role will be radically different from that of previous hegemons. Not just because of cultural contrasts, rooted as these are in historical–geographical differences; but precisely because the different history and geography of the East Asian region will have an impact on the new structures of the global economy. If China is going to be hegemonic, it's going to be hegemonic in very different ways to the others. For one thing, military power will be far less important than cultural and economic power—particularly economic power. They have to play the economic card far more than the US ever did, or the British, or the Dutch.

Do you foresee greater unity within East Asia? There is talk, for example, of a sort of Asian IMF facility, unification of currency—do you see China as the centre of an East Asian hegemon, rather than a solo player? And if so, how does that fit with the rising nationalisms in South Korea, Japan and China?

What is most interesting about East Asia is how, in the end, the economy is determinant of states' dispositions and policies towards one another, in spite of their nationalisms. The nationalisms are very well entrenched, but they are related to a historical fact often forgotten in the West: that Korea, China, Japan, Thailand, Cambodia, all of these were national states long before there was a single nation-state in Europe. They all have histories of nationalist reactions to one another, in a framework that was predominantly economic. Occasionally there were wars, and the attitude of the Vietnamese towards China, or the Koreans towards Japan, is deeply rooted in the memory of these wars. At the same time, the economy seems to rule. It was striking that the nationalist resurgence in Japan, under the Koizumi government, was suddenly checked when it became clear that Japanese business was interested in doing business with China. In China, too, there was a big wave of anti-Japanese demonstrations, but then they stopped. The general picture in East Asia is that there are deep nationalist dispositions, but at the same time they tend to be superseded by economic interests.

The current crisis of the world financial system looks like the most spectacular vindication of your long-standing theoretical predictions that anyone could imagine. Are there any aspects of the crisis that have surprised you?

My prediction was very simple. The recurrent tendency towards financialization was, as Braudel put it, a sign of the autumn of a particular material expansion, centring on a particular state. In *The Long Twentieth Century*, I called the onset of financialization the signal crisis of a regime of accumulation, and pointed out that over time—usually it was around half a century—the terminal crisis would follow. For previous hegemons, it was possible to identify both the signal crisis and then the terminal crisis. For the United States, I ventured the hypothesis that the 1970s was the signal crisis; the terminal crisis had not yet come—but it would. How would it come? The basic hypothesis is that all these financial expansions were fundamentally unsustainable, because they were drawing into speculation more capital than could actually be managed—in other words, there was a tendency for these financial expansions to develop bubbles of various kinds. I foresaw that this financial expansion would eventually lead to a terminal crisis, because bubbles are as unsustainable today as they have been in the past. But I did not foresee the details of the bubbles: the dot-com boom, or the housing bubble.

Also, I was ambiguous about where we were in the early 1990s, when I wrote *The Long Twentieth Century*. I thought that in some ways the *belle époque* of the United States was already over, whereas it was actually only beginning. Reagan prepared it by provoking a major recession, which then created the conditions for the subsequent financial expansion; but it was Clinton who actually oversaw the *belle époque*, which then ended with the financial collapse of the 2000s, especially of the Nasdaq. With the bursting of the housing bubble, what we are observing now is, quite clearly, the terminal crisis of us financial centrality and hegemony.

What marks your work off from almost everyone else in your field is your appreciation for the flexibility, adaptability and fluidity of capitalist development, within the framework of the inter-state system. Yet in the longue durée, *such as the 500-, 150- and 50-year framework you adopted for the collective examination of East Asia's position in the inter-state system, patterns emerge that are astonishingly clear, almost stark in their determinacy and simplicity.[10] How would you characterize the relationship between contingency and necessity in your thinking?*

There are two different questions here: one concerns an appreciation of the flexibility of capitalist development and the other is the recurrence of patterns, and the extent to which these are determined by contingency or necessity. On the first, the adaptability of capitalism: this is partly related to my personal experience in business, as a young man. Initially I tried to run my father's business, which was relatively small; then I did a dissertation on my grandfather's business, which was bigger—a medium-sized company. Then I quarrelled with my grandfather and went into Unilever, which in terms of employees was the second-largest multinational at the time. So I had the luck—from the point of view of analysing the capitalist business enterprise—of going into successively larger firms, which helped me understand that you cannot talk about capitalist enterprises in general, because the differences between my father's business, my grandfather's business and Unilever were incredible. For example, my father spent all his time going to visit customers in the textile districts, and studying the technical problems that they had with their machines. Then he would go back to the factory and discuss the problems with his engineer; they would customize the machine for the client. When I tried to run this business, I was totally lost; the whole thing was based on skills and knowledge that were part of my father's practice and experience. I could go around and see the customers, but I couldn't solve their problems—I couldn't even really understand them. So it was hopeless. In fact, in my youth, when I used to say to my father, 'If the Communists come, you are going to be in trouble', he said, 'No, I'm not going to be in trouble, I'll continue to do what I'm doing. They need people who do this.'

When I closed my father's business, and went into my grandfather's, it was already more of a Fordist organization. They were not studying the customers' problems, they were producing standardized machines; either the customers wanted them or they didn't. Their engineers were designing

---

[10] Arrighi, Takeshi Hamashita and Mark Selden, eds, *The Resurgence of East Asia: 500, 150 and 50 Year Perspectives*, London 2003.

machines on the basis of what they thought there would be a market for, and telling the customers: this is what we have. It was embryonic mass production, with embryonic assembly lines. When I went to Unilever, I barely saw the production side. There were many different factories—one was making margarine, another soap, another perfumes. There were dozens of different products, but the main site of activity was neither the marketing organization nor the place of production, but finance and advertising. So, that taught me that it's very hard to identify one specific form as 'typically' capitalist. Later, studying Braudel, I saw that this idea of the eminently adaptable nature of capitalism was something that you could observe historically.

One of the major problems on the Left, but also on the Right, is to think that there is only one kind of capitalism that reproduces itself historically; whereas capitalism has transformed itself substantively—particularly on a global basis—in unexpected ways. For several centuries capitalism relied on slavery, and seemed so embedded in slavery from all points of view that it could not survive without it; whereas slavery was abolished, and capitalism not only survived but prospered more than ever, now developing on the basis of colonialism and imperialism. At this point it seemed that colonialism and imperialism were essential to capitalism's operation—but again, after the Second World War, capitalism managed to discard them, and to survive and prosper. World-historically, capitalism has been continually transforming itself, and this is one of its main characteristics; it would be very short-sighted to try to pin down what capitalism is without looking at these crucial transformations. What remains constant through all these adaptations, and defines the essence of capitalism, is best captured by Marx's formula of capital M–C–M', to which I refer repeatedly in identifying the alternation of material and financial expansions. Looking at present-day China, one can say, maybe it's capitalism, maybe not—I think it's still an open question. But assuming that it is capitalism, it's not the same as that of previous periods; it's thoroughly transformed. The issue is to identify its specificities, how it differs from previous capitalisms, whether we call it capitalism or something else.

And the second part of the question—the emergence of such distinct, longue-durée *patterns in your work, and the transformations of scale?*

One point is that there is a very clear geographical dimension to the recurrent cycles of material and financial expansion, but you can see this aspect only if you do not stay focused on one particular country—because then you see a totally different process. This is what most historians have been doing—they focus on a particular country, and trace developments there. Whereas in Braudel, the idea is precisely that the accumulation of capital jumps; and if you don't jump with it, if you don't follow it from place to place, you don't see it. If you stay focused on England, or on France, you miss what matters most in the development of capitalism world-historically. You have to move with it to understand that the process of capitalist development *is* essentially this process of jumping from one condition, where what you've termed the 'spatial fix' has become too constraining, and competition is intensifying, to another one, where a new spatial fix of greater scale and scope enables the system to experience another period of material expansion. And then of course, at a certain point the cycle repeats itself.

When I was first formulating this, inferring the patterns from Braudel and Marx, I had not yet fully appreciated your concept of spatial fix, in the double sense of the word—fixity of invested capital, and a fix *for* the previous contradictions of capitalist accumulation. There is a built-in necessity to these patterns that derives from the process of accumulation, which mobilizes money and other resources on an increasing scale, which in turn creates problems of intensifying competition and over-accumulation of various kinds. The process of capitalist accumulation of capital—as opposed to non-capitalist accumulation of capital—has this snowball effect, which intensifies competition and drives down the rate of profit. Those who are best positioned to find a new spatial fix do so, each time in a larger 'container'. From city states, which accumulated a huge amount of capital in tiny containers, to seventeenth-century Holland, which was more than a city state, but less than a national state, then to eighteenth- and nineteenth-century Britain, with its world-encompassing empire, and then to the twentieth-century, continent-sized United States.

Now the process cannot continue in the same way, because there is no new, larger container that can displace the United States. There are large national—in fact, civilizational—states, like China and India, which are not bigger than the United States in terms of space, but have four or five times its population. So now we are switching to a new pattern: instead of going from one container to another, spatially larger, one, we are going from a container with a low population density to containers with high population densities. Moreover, previously it was a switch from wealthy to wealthy, in terms of countries. Now we are going from very wealthy to what are still basically poor countries—China's per capita income is still one-twentieth that of the United States. In one sense, you can say, 'Okay, now hegemony, if that's what is happening, is shifting from the rich to the poor.' But at the same time, these countries have huge internal differences and inequalities. It's all very mixed. These are contradictory tendencies, and we need to develop additional conceptual tools to understand them.

You end Adam Smith in Beijing *with the hope of a commonwealth of civilizations living on equal terms with each other, in a shared respect for the earth and its natural resources. Would you use the term 'socialism' to describe this vision, or do you regard it as outdated?*

Well, I would have no objections to it being called socialism, except that, unfortunately, socialism has been too much identified with state control of the economy. I never thought that was a good idea. I come from a country where the state is despised and in many ways distrusted. The identification of socialism with the state creates big problems. So, if this world system was going to be called socialist, it would need to be redefined in terms of a mutual respect between humans and a collective respect for nature. But this may have to be organized through state-regulated market exchanges, so as to empower labour and disempower capital in Smithian fashion, rather than through state ownership and control of the means of production. The problem with the term 'socialism' is that it's been abused in many different ways, and therefore also discredited. If you ask me what would be a better term, I've no idea—I think we should look for one. You are very good at finding new expressions, so you should come up with some suggestions. Yes, you have to work on a substitute for the term 'socialist' that disentangles it from the historical identification with the state, and brings it closer to the idea of greater equality and mutual respect. So, I'll leave that task to you.

Acknowledgements

The following were interviewed by members of *New Left Review*'s editorial committee as it stood at the time of the event. (Issues of NLR are identified here by number and year. The roman numeral *I*, before the arabic issue number, e.g. I/66, marks the journal's first series, which ran from 1960 until the end of 1999. Issues in the new series are identified by the arabic number only.) Georg Lukács, I/68 (1971); Hedda Korsch, I/76 (1972); Jiří Pelikan, I/71 (1972); K. Damodaran, I/93 (1975); Ernest Mandel, I/213 (1995); Lucio Colletti, I/86 (1974); Luciana Castellina, I/151 (1985); Adolfo Gilly, 64 (2010); Jean-Paul Sartre, I/58 (1969); Noam Chomsky, I/57 (1969); David Harvey, 23 (2000); Asada Akira, 5 (2000); Wang Hui, 6 (2000). The interviewers, varying in number and composition from one occasion to another, were: Tariq Ali, Perry Anderson, Robin Blackburn, Alexander Cockburn, Ronald Fraser, Fred Halliday, Quintin Hoare, Gareth Stedman Jones, Peter Wollen, Tony Wood.

Dorothy Thompson was interviewed by Sheila Rowbotham, I/200 (1993); João Pedro Stédile was interviewed by Francisco de Oliveira, 15 (2002); Giovanni Arrighi was interviewed by David Harvey, 56 (2009).

Most of the interviews have been lightly re-edited for this republication, chiefly in an effort to ease minor anachronisms, where this could be done without risk of misleading readers today. That with Pelikan has been abbreviated in its last part; that with Castellina has been rearranged and abbreviated in its last part. The text of the interview with Adolfo Gilly includes additional material supplied by Gilly after the original had gone to press.

The Chronology follows the example of Raymond Williams's *Culture and Society* (1958) in its dating of individual lives.

Index